MARTHA WASHINGTON

First Lady of Liberty

Helen Bryan

John Wiley & Sons, Inc.

Copyright © 2002 by Helen Bryan. All rights reserved

Published by John Wiley & Sons, Inc., New York
Published simultaneously in Canada

This publication is designed to provide accurate and authoritative information in regard to the subject matter covered. It is sold with the understanding that the pub-lisher is not engaged in rendering professional services. If professional advice or other expert assistance is required, the services of a competent professional person should be sought.

ISBN 0-471-15892-5

Printed in the United States of America

10 9 8 7 6 5 4 3 2 1

*This book is gratefully dedicated
To the memory of my father, Bates William Bryan
To my mother, Helen Anderson Bryan
To my dear husband, Roger Low
And to Cassell and Niels Bryan-Low
With love always*

Contents

Illustrations

Preface

Like every American child I learned about George Washington at school, but knew nothing about his wife, except that her name was Martha. It was not until many years later that I began to wonder why history had paid so little attention to Martha Washington. In an age when political wives can expect an onslaught of media interest in every aspect of their lives, from their academic records to their hemlines, their professional qualifications to their cookie recipes, their views on child raising to their views on global debt, the wife of the most famous American remains a curiously obscure figure. To the extent she is known at all today, Martha is a bland domestic icon, more a reflection of the Victorian values of a later age than of her own robust colonial era. Then I stumbled across an anecdote that suggested that during her lifetime, Martha was regarded as an extremely important figure in her own right and essential to the success of her better known husband. A story has survived of an aged Revolutionary War veteran who once accosted George Washington, saying, "You think people take every grist from you as the pure grain. *What would you have been if you hadn't married the Widow Custis?*"

I decided to find out more about this "Widow Custis," and soon desultory curiosity became research for this book as one intriguing piece of information led to another. Martha proved to be a difficult subject to research, because she left little correspondence and no diaries, and because before her death she burned nearly all the letters she and George Washington had written to each other over forty years of married life. The collection of her surviving correspondence in *Worthy Partner, the Papers of Martha Washington*, edited by the late Joseph E. Fields has, of course, been a vital resource, but even so, some of Martha's surviving correspondence is not what it seems. Many of her later letters included in the collection were not actually written by her but by George Washington or his secretary. Martha rewrote some in her own handwriting, and some she simply signed. Occasionally letters to her friends and political contacts during the war were drafted in the expectation they would be intercepted by the British, who would then be misled by the contents. Some letters written on her behalf during Washington's presidential terms contain high-flown sentiments Martha herself would never have written. Martha was a deeply practical woman whose own letters were written to exchange news and give advice. She was far too busy to philosophise, yet her supposed philosophy, such as saccharine statements like, "I care only for what comes from the heart" are often quoted as evidence of her personality. What this means, of course, is that the popular perception of Martha, based on such quotes, is probably wrong.

Since part of her surviving correspondence must be read subject to these reservations, this has meant relying on a variety of other sources of information to construct a realistic picture of Martha and her life. There is information about her ancestors, her parents, her siblings, her slaves, her husbands, her children, and her grandchildren, as well as her homes, the lifestyle of women in eighteenth-century Tidewater Virginia, and the economics of tobacco. There are also letters from friends, family memoirs, firsthand accounts by people who visited Mount Vernon or met her in the winter camps during the Revolutionary War, and family tradition. There are family wills with far-reaching consequences that would have intrigued a Wilkie Collins or a Charles Dickens. And, I soon discovered, there are some glaring omissions in the family memoirs, what Sherlock Holmes might have regarded suspiciously as the "dog that didn't bark," and what I began to call "the veil of silence" that descended when the family wanted to conceal something. In several cases this "veil of silence" descended over the matter of children born to slaves and fathered by men in Martha's family, but it was also used to obscure the malevolence of her first father-in-law, her daughter's epilepsy, the profligacy of her son, and the odd nature of her eldest granddaughter.

Against the background of the circumstances that governed her life, Martha began to emerge as a character. Some aspects of her personality, such as her attitudes toward children and clothing, are easily comprehensible to modern readers, and it is fair to say she was a charming woman, and universally well liked. It is extraordinary that, save for her first husband's father, no one had a bad word to say about her. But her story is far from all sweetness and light. It requires a greater leap of imagination today to grasp the moral principle that preferred "duty over inclination," which regulated the lives of Martha and women of her generation, and the sense of validation, if not happiness, that was duty's main reward. Set against these sympathetic traits were Martha's attitudes toward slavery, and the fact that she was an unabashed slave owner. The end result is a complex picture of a woman who was very much a product of an earlier period in American history, and who simply cannot be understood in terms of twentieth-century attitudes.

Making sense of many disparate sources and small pieces of information was a lengthy exercise. I am indebted to a great many people for their assistance in piecing together the different elements of Martha's story, because this book truly could not have been written without them. There has been a generous pooling of information from all the sources I contacted, and I hope this biography adds to the exciting process of historical discovery we share.

First, I owe a great debt of thanks to the Mount Vernon Ladies' Association of the Union, who have been immensely supportive of the project. In particular I need to thank Mount Vernon historian Mary V. Thompson, not only for providing me with material I would never have found on my own, but for putting me on the track of some of the most elusive aspects of Martha's life, such as the existence of her half sister Ann Dandridge. A rigorous scholar, Mary spent much time tracking down small details from Mount Vernon records to verify theories I "tested" on her when I came to a seemingly unbridgeable gap in the narrative. We have had many fascinating and illuminating discussions, and happily, in the process Mary has also become a friend. I am also grateful to Curator Dawn Bonner and to Director James Rees for all their help in providing many of the illustrations. Finally, I would like to pay tribute to the many excellent guides who usher visitors through Mount Vernon and who are a fund of information on the Washingtons' lives there.

It was thanks to Mary Thompson that I made contact with another writer and academic, Polly Longsworth, who had written an excellent piece "Martha, Belle of New Kent" on Martha's life as a young woman for the *Colonial Williamsburg* magazine. Polly generously shared her research with me and took an interest in the project. We compared our impressions of the area around the Pamunkey River and debated theories about John Custis IV, the complications of his will, and the possible fate of Mulatto Jack, his child by a slave, who may have died an untimely death.

Curator Brian Clark Green of the Virginia Historical Society was most helpful, discussing with me at some length the history of White House Plantation, the changes to the house over the years and why the drawing of White House included in the book is likely to show the house as it was in Martha's day when she arrived there as Daniel Parke Custis's bride.

I am grateful to Curator Holly Bailey at Washington and Lee University, my father's alma mater, for her assistance in providing copies of the Wollaston portraits of Martha, her first husband Daniel Parke Custis, and their two children Patcy and Jacky, as well as her father-in-law, John Custis IV.

Craig Tuminaro, Director at Woodlawn Plantation, Nelly Custis Lewis's married home, went to considerable trouble unearthing the James Sharples portrait of Nelly I had set my heart on using. He is also a repository of fascinating information about the Lewis family, and clearly enjoys the challenge of bringing history to life. His enthusiasm is catching, and his knowledge of the family and his insights helped me form a clearer view of Martha's relationship with her granddaughter Nelly.

Colleen Curry, Curator at the Custis Lee Mansion, unearthed the rare daguerreotype of Martha's great-granddaughter Maria Carter Custis Syphax and painstakingly reproduced it. Arts Resources in New York was particularly helpful in providing an image of Edward Savage's painting *The Washington Family*, and I am likewise grateful to the Arents Collection for permission to use the engraving of *A Tobacco Plantation* and to the American Antiquarian Society for tracking down and supplying an image of a 1769 "Broadside announcing the sale of slaves."

I am also indebted to the staff at the British Library, who were consistently good-humored and helpful, as were the staff at the Virginia Historical Society and at the New York Historical Society. I am indebted to the latter in particular for seeking out articles and books they thought might be of particular use to me, and for kindly unearthing and photocopying a long rare document just before closing time, hours after I should have made the request. I would also like to mention an interesting staff member there, who told me the first presidential mansion occupied by the Washingtons was now a spot marked by a plaque under the Brooklyn Bridge.

A lovely lady who was a guide at Sully Plantation, near Dulles Airport, deserves a special mention, because she showed me where to begin Martha's story. After an informative tour of Sully, the home of Richard Bland Lee, during which we had admired fine china, pretty bed hangings, paintings, and handsome furniture, just by the door on the way out she showed me a basket of small folded papers. When school groups came to tour the house, she said, each departing child would be given one of the slips of paper. The slips of paper were slave passes, without which a slave could not leave the plantation. The guide sighed, "You know, there was so much elegance, but underneath there was always this raw colonial core," neatly summing up the two defining elements of the society that produced Martha and her two husbands.

I would like to thank my father-in-law, Dr. Niels Low, former professor of pediatric neurology at Columbia Presbyterian Hospital, who was an invaluable source of information on medical matters beyond my ken, from tuberculosis to sickle cell anemia to epilepsy.

Thanks are due to my agent, Bob Silverstein of Quicksilver Books Literary Agents, who was enthusiastic and encouraging about this biography from the start. I have also been extremely fortunate in having Hana Lane as my editor. Her knowledge of, and interest in, eighteenth-century America, combined with her considered advice and painstaking editing, have transformed my unwieldy manuscript into a finished book.

I am indebted to Michael Thompson, assistant to Hana Lane, who was always available with advice and assistance on a range of practical matters connected with the book. I would also like to thank Lia Pelosi for the work she put in as managing editor and Alexa Selph for her painstaking copy-editing.

Above all I am grateful for the help and support of my family. My Virginia-born mother sent information about colonial costumes, pointed out a little-known portrait of Martha painted just before her death, and tracked down recipes attributed to Martha in a variety of old Virginia cookbooks. For the past four years my husband, Roger, has sought out relevant articles and books he thought I might find useful, provided every possible comfort to make the long days I spent writing easier, and above all, has given me time and space to write undisturbed in the spot I like best, at a window overlooking the garden. His encouragement never faltered, though my energy occasionally did, and I could not have written the book without him. When I became too immersed in past lives and other times, he and our son and daughter were always on hand to remind me of the joys of the present. This book is for them—Roger, Niels, Cassell, and my mother—my first, best, and dearest readers.

Printed for & Sold by BOWLES and CARVER, Nº 69 in Sᵗ Pauls Church Yard.

A TOBACCO PLANTATION

Introduction

Writing about the woman who married George Washington is a daunting task for three reasons. First, mainstream historians prefer to focus on men's achievements, allocating women minor roles somewhere on the margins of events, if they feature at all. The enormous body of writing on George Washington testifies to his enduring fascination for historians, from his role as commander in chief of the Continental army during the American Revolution, his political career as president, his diaries, speeches, political feuds, and in private life, his boyhood, his beloved estate at Mount Vernon, his views on slavery and religion, and his innovative approach to farming. Almost no aspect of George Washington's life has escaped minute scrutiny and analysis, save for the woman to whom he was married for forty years.

Mrs. Elizabeth Ellet, a nineteenth-century female historian and by definition a rare breed, was unusual in her attempt to challenge the traditional view that history was the sum of male achievements. In the introduction to her *Women of the American Revolution,* first published in 1848, she wrote,

> The actions of men stand out in permanent relief, and are a safe guide in forming a judgement of them; a woman's sphere, on the other hand, is secluded, and in very few instances does her personal history, even though she may fill a conspicuous position, afford sufficient incident to throw a strong light upon her character.[1]

Continuing with a statement that is particularly apt in Martha Washington's case, Mrs. Ellet wrote:

> The heroism of Revolutionary women has passed from remembrance, with the generation who witnessed it; or is seen only by faint and occasional glimpses. . . . To render a measure of justice, inadequate as it must be, to a few of the American matrons, whose names deserve to live in remembrance and to exhibit something of the domestic side of the Revolutionary picture is the object of this book.

No other eighteenth-century American woman moved in so conspicuous a sphere as Martha, and few led a life more packed with "sufficient incident." Yet over 150 years after Mrs. Ellet's valiant effort to draw attention
to women's contributions to the Revolution, the wife of its foremost figure
languishes in obscurity.

This was not always the case. A contemporary anecdote confirms that
Martha commanded respect in her own right during her lifetime, and suggests an awkward truth later historians have preferred to ignore—that without Martha and her fortune, George might never have risen to social,
military, and political prominence. Toward the end of his life, George Washington, war hero, retired president, and object of universal fame and ven-
eration, was negotiating to purchase a plot of land in the new capital city, to
be named in his honor. The seller, an aged veteran of the Revolution, was
reluctant to part with the plot, even to so distinguished a purchaser. Washington persisted until the veteran's patience snapped: "You think people take
every grist that comes from you as the pure grain. *What would you have
been if you hadn't married the Widow Custis!*"[2]

It was not just money that Martha brought to the marriage. A wife in colonial Virginia had an important role as her husband's active partner. In an agricultural society like Virginia, most wives, whether married to small holders or
planters with thousands of acres, shouldered responsibility for homes, and for
the health and well-being of many people, from her own husband and children, to a wider "family" within the ambit of her care, which often included
slaves, indentured servants, and orphaned or infirm relatives. Martha began
her marriage to George on just such a basis, as George's active, indispensable
partner, at Mount Vernon, and the same relationship extended to her later
role at army headquarters and in the presidential mansion in their later lives.
By necessity rather than design, Martha and George Washington became the
"power couple" of their age, and the dynamics of their personal relationship
had far-reaching public and private consequences that are little known today.

It is a relationship historians have never probed very deeply, possibly
thanks to the second obstacle in writing about Martha Washington, namely that
the existing material about her life draws heavily on the work of nineteenth-
century "lady biographers" or the recollections of the two grandchildren she
and George Washington fostered and raised. While these are clearly valuable sources of information, they only tell a small part of her story. All were
written after her death with the object of highlighting Martha's suitability as
the consort of America's greatest hero. To this end, they clothed Martha in
the Victorian virtues of the nineteenth century, when in reality Martha's
strengths, graces, and shortcomings were derived from an earlier and rawer
period in American history. She was essentially colonial.

Martha was, of course, occupied with matters common to women everywhere of every age, such as courtship, marriage, childbearing, the raising
and care of families, and all their attendant concerns. But the circumstances

that defined and governed a woman's life in colonial Virginia in the seventeenth and eighteenth centuries were different from those that shaped women's lives elsewhere in the American colonies during this period. Following Martha's death in 1802, American society was evolving from its colonial phase and entering what we regard as the Victorian era. In a process akin to covering the legs of furniture with frilly skirts to avoid embarrassing associations with "limbs," nineteenth-century Victorian assessments of Martha stifle the real woman under a convenient stereotype and gloss over any awkward aspects of her life, replacing the flesh and blood woman with a bland nonentity in a mobcap, a paragon of American feminine virtues: motherly, domestic, dignified, discreet, religious, patriotic and none too well educated—the Victorian ideal of womanhood, in fact. Forced to live in the public eye for the last twenty-seven years of her life, Martha once famously described herself as a "state prisoner." She has, in a sense, remained a state prisoner in death. Both Martha and George Washington, once conveniently dead, were resurrected to serve a posthumous political purpose as a model First Couple, embodying the values of the new republic amidst the political uncertainties that beset America in the years before the Civil War.

The third major problem confronting anyone researching Martha is that before her death, she burned all but a few pieces of correspondence between herself and George. Martha left no diaries, and only a small part of her social, family, and business correspondence survives today in scattered locations. Of that correspondence, many of her letters surviving from her husband's two terms as president were drafted on her behalf by George's secretaries, mainly the Harvard educated Tobias Lear, who composed letters for her using terms and phrases Martha would never have used herself.

The result was letters with her signature, or even copied in her own handwriting, containing statements such as "I only care for what comes from the heart," or "I have also learnt from experience that the greater part of our happiness or misary [*sic*] depends upon our dispositions and not upon our circumstances; we carry the seeds of the one, or the other about with us, in our minds, wherever we go." These are frequently quoted passages, but it is highly unlikely that Martha composed them. They are pure Tobias Lear, and simply not the kind of pontification it would have occurred to Martha to write. Such manufactured sentiments are what we call today "spin doctoring." To put those quoted above in their proper context, they were written in Martha's quasi-official capacity as wife of the president to a female friend and acquaintance with important political connections at a time when Martha was finding her new role a straitjacket and loathing life in New York. In contrast, her private correspondence with her niece in Virginia candidly reveals the extent of her dissatisfaction with life in the presidential mansion in New York, but since such views would have been politically damaging, it was thought necessary to manage her official correspondence.

To understand what Martha was really like requires a twofold approach: first, to look at the wider social, economic, and political framework in which she lived, and second, to read between the lines to note what has been omitted in the official accounts of her life. The results are startling.

Martha was part of a hybrid generation, the product of a society in a ferment of transition, a raw, thrusting New World environment whose Old World allegiances and cultural ties had been eroded by the pragmatic considerations of the New. She cannot be viewed in isolation from the early colonial environment in which she lived, nor from the wider political developments of the eighteenth century that had a direct impact on her later life. Her generation had come a long way, culturally, socially, and economically since the first English settlers had set foot in the New World and struggled for survival there. The experiences of these earliest Virginians had spawned a society driven by its own imperatives, which would turn the accepted political order of the old, European world, with its monarchs and their divine rights, on its head. An English popular song of the period reflected the mood of stunned bewilderment the Revolution left in its wake:

If buttercups buzzed
After the bee
And boats went on land
And horses on sea
If ponies road men and if grass ate the cows
And cats could be chased into holes by a mouse
Then all the world would be
Upside down

Martha was not a passive participant in the process. In middle age she was obliged to adapt to and assume a leading role in developments that would have been shocking to Virginians at the time of her birth and were only marginally less shocking forty years later. While Martha's life unfolds amidst the political and social turmoil of the era, it also provides insight into the private lives of people she knew—her extended family and friends, her neighbors and slaves, and the wives of George's fellow generals and politicians, revealing the significant, though little-known, roles that she and other women, American and British, played in the Revolution.

To tell Martha's story accurately it is essential to know something of the world of colonial Virginia that produced her. If Martha's life reflected a wider political and social transition, the progressive changes in her circumstances can be marked by the changes in her name and status, each of which furnishes a different image of Martha and her changing world. As a girl, Martha Dandridge was "John Dandridge's daughter." As a young matron, she was the socially prominent Mrs. Daniel Parke Custis. For a short time she was the temptingly rich, independent Widow Custis, before becoming Mrs. George Washington. Most affectionately, she was known to George's troops by what was a curious title under the circumstances, the English-sounding "Lady Washington."

Born in the largest and richest English colony, Virginia, she was "British" by birth, and living in an environment that defined itself by a variety of cultural reference points to all that was "English." At the same time Martha grew up in a world decidedly unlike England, where survival depended upon a resourcefulness and determination peculiarly colonial in nature, and from a young age she absorbed its lessons.

Virginia colony had had a turbulent evolution since the first settlers arrived from England, a century and a half earlier, seeking riches in the North American continent to rival those that England's enemy, Catholic Spain, had found further south, such as gold and silver in South America and sugar, rum, and spices in the Caribbean. These earlier expeditions had been singularly ill-fated, thanks to the incompetence of their leaders and poor planning. The first expedition was so inadequately supplied that when its members found themselves floundering hopelessly lost off the coast of Labrador. Facing a lingering death by starvation, they turned to murder and cannibalism before being rescued by a French vessel. A later expedition to found a "Cittie of Raleigh" in Chesapeake Bay resulted in the mysterious disappearance of all the inhabitants of the first English colony on Roanoke Island, leaving behind the haunting story of Virginia Dare, the first English baby born in the New World.

The world Martha knew traced its beginnings to England in 1606, when King James I succeeded to the English throne and Captain John Smith, a twenty-five-year-old soldier of fortune prepared to brave the lurid terrors of the New World in search of wealth, drew up a scheme with some like-minded adventurers for a new expedition to Virginia colony as a commercial venture, and managed to obtain the King's support. James I gave specific instructions that seemed appropriate at the time to regulate a commercial undertaking, but that would have unimaginable consequences.

There was to be a simple plan for administration of the colony, by means of a council appointed by the king in London. There would be a subordinate council in the colony chosen more widely from the settled population. The latter body would have the capacity to sit as a court and try civil cases. There was a right to trial by jury in criminal cases arising in the colony.

In hindsight, the striking aspect of this arrangement was that, reduced to its essentials, it bypassed Parliament altogether. A purely administrative arrangement conceived to regulate life and disputes among a limited number of people involved in a business undertaking across the Atlantic, it nevertheless amounted to government by royal whim, a practice out of favor in England since the Magna Carta. It was this approach that would later shape

English attitudes toward the colony, and that a few years later, when the colony's status was amended by Royal Charter, laid the groundwork for a rebellion that would turn Martha's world and the American colonies upside down 170 years later.

At the outset, no one could have foreseen how the numbers of settlers would swell and the colony evolve from a straightforward commercial venture into a social, political, and economic entity of its own five thousand miles from London, nor that the inhabitants of this distant outpost would grow restive at being denied what they regarded as their constitutional rights as Englishmen. At their most basic, these were the right to representation in Parliament and, the first rule of the unwritten English constitution, "no taxation without representation." But when Captain Smith's expedition set out, that was all in the future, an invisible storm cloud on a distant horizon.

An all-male band of about a hundred would-be settlers was organized, attracted by the promise of adventure and quick wealth. In December 1606, there may well have been Dandridges, who were a prosperous London family, among the crowds who cheered as prayers were said and church bells pealed as the *Susan Constant,* the *Discovery,* and the *Godspeed* slipped down the Thames and out to sea. The route from England went southwest across the Atlantic to the Caribbean, where ships turned north to sail up the coast. The expedition's goal was again Roanoke Island, but at the end of April 1607 a storm forced the ships further north to Chesapeake Bay.

The shipbound settlers' optimism at their first view of the lush and flowery wilderness of the Chesapeake was swiftly quashed when, in a foretaste of troubles to come, an advance landing party was promptly driven back to their ships by a party of Indians who unleashed a volley of arrows from their hiding place on shore. The discouraged settlers sailed south again, finally alighting on a low, flat peninsula that they named Jamestown, in honor of the King.

The settlement nearly failed at the outset when instant riches failed to materialize, relationships among the settlers deteriorated, and tensions mounted with a local tribe, the Powhatans, who repeatedly attacked the settlement. In the summer, the marshy coast of Virginia was a sickly place, a breeding ground for mosquitoes, malaria, and other deadly fevers to which the Englishmen had no resistance. In July, five months after Smith's expedition arrived, a malaria epidemic nearly wiped out the settlement. Settlers perished wretchedly from fever and famine in their steaming cabins, with none well enough to nurse fellow sufferers. By September over half the colonists had died and the miserable remainder were weak, bickering, dispirited and facing starvation. To distract everyone, Captain Smith proposed an expedition in the direction of the mountains to the west, today known as the "Blue Ridge." It was popularly believed the Pacific Ocean bisected the continent there. It would prove to be a fortuitous expedition, but not for the reasons Smith imagined.

In Smith's time, much of what had been termed Virginia was an area of about eight thousand square miles ruled over by the Emperor Powhatan and occupied by the Powhatans, a confederation incorporating some thirty different tribes of Algonquin Indians and thousands of people, a substantial number of whom were warriors. The Powhatans attacked the expedition and Smith was taken prisoner and escorted by his captors to the Emperor's headquarters where the York River forked into two branches.

It was this very spot, where Smith was taken, that gave its name to the Pamunkey River. "Pamunkey" derives from an Indian term "Ullamusak at Pamunkee," which referred to the triangular peninsula separating the two main branches of the York River. Smith later recorded in his *Generall Historie of Virginia New England and the Summer Isles* that this was where the Powhatans had their "great home filled with images of their kings and devils, and the tombs of their predecessors."[3]

According to Smith's account of the events that followed, he was on the point of having his head crushed between two heavy stones when Powhatan's favorite daughter, Pocahontas, rescued him. Pocahontas was probably about twelve years old at the time. According to Smith, she rushed forward and laid her own head on his before the stone could drop. As a result Smith's life was spared, and he spent some weeks with Powhatan, possibly carving toys for Pocahontas, before returning to Jamestown.

Smith was a charismatic figure, and his ability to exert leadership in the troubled settlement to which he returned was a crucial factor in its survival. Equally important was Smith's newfound ability to negotiate with the Indians for food, usually with the help of Pocahontas. Without Smith and Pocahontas, starvation, Indian attack, or inertia would probably have killed off the remainder of the colonists, and Jamestown would have vanished as completely as the earlier settlement at Roanoke.

Jamestown continued to flirt with one catastrophe after another. The wooden buildings put up by the colonists burned down, and large swaths of the colony were continually being rebuilt due to fire. Indian attacks, famine, and disease continued to kill settlers. In 1609, James I declared Virginia a Crown Colony and amended its charter. James replaced the colony's governing council in London with a royal governor in the colony. The terms of the royal charter under which the English Crown held and governed Virginia remained in place until the Revolution.

In 1609, John Smith was injured in a gunpowder explosion and returned to England. The colony of five hundred was struck by a terrible famine. With Smith's departure the colony could no longer rely on Pocahontas, who had disappeared from the colony, probably marrying an Indian brave in 1610. Back in England in 1624, Smith wrote an account of "The Starving Time" based on reports that filtered back to him. According to Smith, the colonists who were already under attack from the Indians were first reduced to eat-

ing the skins of horses, then having killed and buried an Indian, dug him up
again to eat him:

> nay so great was our famine, that a Salvage we slew, and buried, the poorer
> sort tooke him up againe and eat him, and so did divers one another boyled
> and stewed with roots and herbs; and one among the rest did kill his wife, pow-
> dered [salted] her, and had eaten part of her before it was knowne, for which
> he was executed as hee well deserved; now whether she was better roasted,
> boyled or carnoado'd [grilled], I know not, but of such a dish of powdered wife
> I never heard of. This was that time, which still to this day we called the starv-
> ing time; it were too vile to say and scarce to be believed what we endured.[4]

The grim stories of life in English Virginia had an impact in Europe. In Spain
three convicts sentenced to death were offered a choice between hanging
and exile to America. Only two chose exile. The third preferred to hang.

In 1614 Pocahontas converted to Christianity, took the name "Rebecca,"
and married John Rolfe, one of the settlers. The marriage stabilized relationships between the whites and the Indians for the time being, which in
turn allowed John Rolfe to become a pivotal figure in the history of the
colony by introducing a profitable new crop, tobacco.

The tobacco indigenous to Virginia was of an inferior type for export,
but before his marriage, the enterprising Rolfe had imported an improved
and more aromatic variety from Trinidad as an experiment. In 1612 he
exported his first crop of this new strain of tobacco. By 1619, Virginia had
exported ten tons of it, and despite an unhealthy climate and hostile Native
Americans, Jamestown found itself in the midst of a boom. The New World,
with its unlimited land available for tobacco crops, was turning out to be El
Dorado after all. Exports grew and profits soared, bringing sudden pros-
perity to the raw new settlement, akin to that experienced by gold mining
towns in western movies. It provided all the trappings of English "civiliza-
tion" money could buy, but tobacco also triggered a whole new chain of
developments with unimaginable consequences, both in Martha's time and
to the present day.

Tobacco proved to be a kind of Coca-Cola of its time—semimedicinal,
pleasurable, and affordable. The supply from the colony could not keep pace
with the runaway demand for it in England and Europe, but there was an
unforeseen downside. Tobacco was a ticking agricultural and political time
bomb for the colony. Agriculturally, it is a labor-intensive crop that wears
out the land. This meant more and more land had to be put into tobacco
production to maintain it as a profitable enterprise. The political effects were
twofold: first, it concentrated the largest patents of land in the hands of a
few of the wealthiest and most ruthless settlers, and second, tobacco generated an insatiable demand for labor to grow it. England responded in two

ways: first with legislation that regulated trade in the new commodity by making it illegal for the colonies to carry on their lucrative trade except through English channels—ships, insurance, agents, and so on—and second, with its enthusiastic and highly profitable participation in a spin-off of tobacco, the African slave trade.

Acquiring land was a matter of expelling the Indians, which was gradually accomplished through superior numbers of whites with guns, despite feeble attempts by England to protect native rights. Labor proved more problematic. The settlers first impressed Native Americans into slavery, but it was not a success. The Native Americans made poor slaves, either absconding to the wilderness or dying. Indentured labor imported—or more often press-ganged—from among the destitute and criminal element in Europe was introduced, but that also proved insufficient. Conditions in the colony were ripe for an institution already well established in the Caribbean by the Dutch, French, and Spanish settlers there—the importation of black slaves from Africa.

The first Africans arrived in the colony under relatively innocuous circumstances. In 1619 a Dutch vessel arrived in Jamestown with twenty black indentured servants or "contracted labor." This meant a person bound him- or herself to a fixed period of servitude in exchange for the cost of passage. The period of indenture was normally seven years, unless the indentured person was released early or had the period of indenture extended as punishment. Anyone "indentured" was legally bound by terms almost indistinguishable from those of slavery. The master had almost total power over the individual and controlled the conditions of his or her labor. Brutality to extract labor was the order of the day. However, it was a contractual arrangement that also required the purchaser to provide room and board for the duration of the indenture. When the term of indenture ended, the person was released from the contract, in theory supplied with a few basic implements and a small sum of money, and allowed to own property and participate in political affairs. While indentured servants were often looked down upon socially as the dregs of society, drunkards and criminals, there was no racial connotation attached to indentured servitude.

The same Dutch ship also carried ninety English women. Until they arrived there had been no English women in the colony. The contracts of the indentured Africans had been bought for food supplied to the ship. An English company supplied the women, and any man wishing to marry one of the women had to pay her passage. The legal status of these two groups, the African indentured servants and the English women, was not distinguishable on racial or legal grounds in 1621 or for many years afterwards. But this would change with the rapid institutionalization of a source of forced labor that was based on race.

Recognizing a profit opportunity, a royal company in England was soon set up to cash in on the slave trade from the Caribbean and Africa. The legal status of nonwhite forced laborers underwent a swift transformation in the space of a few years. Gradually slavery was institutionalized in Virginia by legislation, and as the number of slaves grew, ever-stricter measures, such as severe whipping, branding, or maiming, were adopted to control them, enforce discipline in the fields and to punish runaways. By 1680 slavery had fully developed as a system, codified in law and characterized by the brutality necessary to make it function.

Slavery became synonymous with black (African) or brown (Indian) skin, and slaves themselves were reduced to the legal status of livestock. They could not marry or own property. Children of a female slave were the property of the owner, as children took their mother's status. Even if a white man fathered a child, the child of a female slave was legally a slave also.

To the white enslavers, slaves were an investment and a means of production. Slaves had to be fed, housed, and clothed at minimum expense, and the maximum labor extracted to justify the investment in them, but the system had sabotage, inefficiency, and resistance built into it. Slaves retaliated by the limited means within their power—working slowly, breaking equipment, mistreating animals, claiming illness, causing accidents, setting fires, and occasionally attempting to poison their owners and their families. They also ran away whenever possible, often to enclaves of Native Americans who had armed themselves and taken refuge in the wilderness. But if captured, runaways were subject to brutal punishments ranging from whippings to amputation of part of a foot, to an iron "cage" soldered on to the runaway's head; in some instances a slave was forced to wear a bridle with a bit between the teeth. Barbaric as these punishments sound, they were used to control slaves on an everyday basis.

One of the most disturbing aspects is that such measures were not isolated incidents or sadistic aberrations in the colony. Vivid historical evidence from two contemporary sources, both concerning some of the most prominent Virginians of the period, confirms that slavery brought out the worst in slave owners. The first source is the secret diary of William Byrd II of Westover Plantation, who recorded a litany of vicious punishments routinely meted out to his slaves for the simple purpose of keeping his house and plantation in good running order.[5] The second is the account of Philip Fithian, a tutor to the wealthy Carter family at Nomini Hall Plantation. In his diary, he recorded his struggle to reconcile the charming and kind Carters and their gracious life at Nomini Hall with what he saw of the workings of the slave system that made it possible.

George Washington, whom modern-day historians often hold up as an example of that contradiction in terms "enlightened slave owning," nevertheless wrote of the brutality of overseers in general and his own in particular, and of the "unfortunate" consequences of too much whipping. He was also a

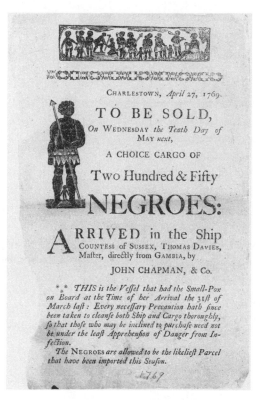

"Broadside Announcing the Sale of Slaves 1769." Courtesy of the American Antiquarian Society.

stickler for detail and a hard taskmaster. No one seems to have examined his methods of ensuring efficiency at Mount Vernon too closely, nor has anyone considered just how it was possible for Martha to run her homes so efficiently.

It is ironic that Martha and the people she knew who would play a leading role ostensibly in a struggle for "liberty" were themselves beneficiaries of genocide and slavery, and equally ironic that within a few years the dispossessed descendants of those Native Americans driven west would harass and annihilate white settlements on Virginia's western frontier, taunting a sparsely manned, ill-equipped, and reluctant Virginia militia and nearly killing its commander, a young provincial colonel named George Washington.

By the time the capital of the colony moved from Jamestown to Williamsburg at the end of the seventeenth century, Virginia had eclipsed the glorified trading post envisaged by James I. In place of the crude wooden dwellings of Jamestown, Williamsburg had become the social and political hub of the colony. It was a town of about two hundred houses, a handsome palace for the royal governor, and streets elegantly designed to intertwine the initials of the English monarchs, William and Mary. It had a raw new university, also named after the king and queen. The students it attracted, sons of the newly rich planters, were a notoriously rowdy and undisciplined lot, so much so that at Bruton Parish Church, where they were required to attend services, there was a special pew into which they had to be locked to contain their mayhem.

The colony was now firmly dependent on an entrenched combination of agriculture, English markets, and slaves. Gradually slavery introduced an uneasy element into the colony as it dawned on a society made up of far-flung plantations that increasing slave imports swelled an already large dis-affected labor force with every incentive to rise in a bloody revolt. The planters began to fear they would be murdered in their beds.

Consequently in 1691 a law was passed in Virginia prohibiting masters from freeing a slave unless the freed slave was transported out of the colony.[6] By 1715, a quarter of Virginia's inhabitants were slaves, a store of gunpowder was kept in Williamsburg for distribution if the long-feared slave rebellion came to pass, and some members of the colony had begun to lobby England to restrict the numbers of slaves being imported into Virginia. Greed, how-ever, prevailed on both sides of the Atlantic. The planters needed workers, and the slave trade was immensely profitable both for the American colonies and in England.

The first fissures between the New World and the mother country developed as vast empires of land were amassed and consolidated by the end of the seventeenth century, giving rise to a new aristocracy. At the pin-nacle of Virginia society were a small number of powerful families, among whom were the Fairfaxes, the Carters, and the Randolphs—the last of whom traced their ancestry from Pocahontas—and the Lees, the Parkes, and the Custises. Among these families was a sprinkling of English "gentlemen" who had aristocratic connections, sometimes black sheep of a grand family packed off to make their fortunes in Virginia, illegitimate sons of titled par-ents, and a fair number of people who had suffered financial reverses by supporting the Royalists in the English Civil War. Some had no pretensions, only ambition. What was significant about them all was the fact they were able to measure their wealth in vast tracts of land and hundreds of slaves.

These self-made colonial grandees shipped their tobacco to England for sale, built country mansions in the English style, hunted foxes, drank tea, attended balls, and married their offspring to each other to consolidate their wealth even further, just as if they were English aristocrats. A few even sent their sons to be educated in England.

Men from this echelon of society dominated the Virginia Assembly, composed of the governor, appointed members of the Governor's Council, and the elected members of the House of Burgesses. The assembly met twice a year in Williamsburg. These sessions were known as "Publik Times," and the sitting of the assembly was an occasion for the planters to gather in town to enjoy balls, dinners, plays, and concerts, and to flaunt their new clothes and carriages ordered at vast expense from England.

With the king and Parliament five thousand miles away, these powerful planters saw themselves as the equivalent of England's hereditary landed peers and dominated the colony, often dictating to the royal governor. In their own eyes, and indeed in the eyes of the rest of the American colonies, they became aristocrats by virtue of their wealth and influence. The English establishment dismissed such upstart social pretensions, but was only too pleased to capitalize on the lucrative trade generated by Virginia.

The planters imported nearly everything wanted or needed from England. There was little domestic production in Virginia. The colonists not only ordered their clothes and carriages from England, they ordered everything, from farm equipment to saddles, from musical instruments to books, furniture, glass, paint, medicines, spices, and toys. The grander families even imported British architects to design their new houses. They kept carriages, danced minuets, played cards, and observed Court Mourning and other ceremonies. People were baptized, married, and buried according to the liturgy of the Church of England. Those who could not afford an English education sent their sons, who had been educated—more or less—at home to the new university at Williamsburg. As closely as possible, they emulated life in the English shires.

For the majority of the colony's inhabitants, however, life was harder. There were few schools and no hospitals. From the rough newly built churches in cleared wilderness, parish councils and vestrymen administered what amounted to the only poor relief, which usually involved selling debtors and their families—usually separately—into indentured servitude for a fixed period to prevent their becoming a charge of the parish. Illiteracy and drunkenness were rife, and few women could read or write.

Though Martha Washington is often thought of as a woman typical of her time, as the daughter and wife of planters of substance, in reality she was in a minority. Planters' wives were far outnumbered by women who were indentured servants, slaves, or the wives of small farmers. Indentured servants who completed their term of servitude were by law supposed to receive "freedom dues," a kind of stake to get them on their feet. This was a tract of land—generally about fifty acres—a hoe, a small sum of money, and sometimes a suit of clothes. Women who either married former indentured servants or had been indentured servants themselves found this stake rarely allowed for more than a meager subsistence and a hard life. Slaves also survived on the barest essentials in terms of food, shelter, and clothing, enduring brutal working conditions and a precarious existence, reduced to the legal status of nonhuman chattels. For the vast majority of women it was a life of hard work, at home or in the fields.

Because she married a famous man, Martha's life is better documented than that of most of her female contemporaries in the colony. Though she was relatively privileged, aspects of her life tell us much about concerns shared by other women in colonial Virginia—the domestic skills necessary to maintain a household, the types of food available, recipes, courtship, marriage, raising children, the treatment of illness, care of the extended family, women's rights to property, the ways women coped with bereavement, and who married whom, the role of religion, and the social and political significance of clothing in the colony.

Socially, Martha, both her husbands, and most of her Virginia friends saw themselves either as part of, or aspiring to, the colonial upper crust. As in England, this class was defined by their relationship to the Crown, so their political allegiance was firmly Royalist. At the same time, after generations in the colony, they were firmly rooted in the economic and practical realities of a society dependent on agriculture. Martha's generation was a new breed produced by this dichotomy between the Old World and the New, the English and the American, the contrast between country life on the plantation and the cosmopolitan aspirations of Williamsburg with its public times, attractively laid-out streets, gardens, balls, plays, university, craftsmen, and shops, all of which represented a triumph of English colonization combined with tobacco affluence. In the cultivated wilderness outside Williamsburg, however, life took on a rougher cast.

Summarizing the peculiar characteristics of the society into which Martha was born, George Washington's biographer Rupert Hughes captures its colonial core: "They formed a strange community, these old Virginians with their stately mansions rising here and there in a wilderness yet unconquered, with their arms and their tithes and their carriages, their slaves and their aristocracy set in a jungle of pioneering crudities; with their dances, intrigues, love affairs and bad spelling."[7]

CHAPTER 1

Twenty-Five Miles as the Crow Flies from Williamsburg

Martha Dandridge Custis Washington, destined to become the best-known American woman of the eighteenth century, was born in provincial obscurity. Until she reached the age of fifteen, there is little documentation of Martha Dandridge's life. A family Bible kept by Martha's younger sister, Elizabeth Dandridge Henley, records that she was the first child of John and Frances Dandridge, born between midnight and 1 o'clock on June 2, 1731, in the upstairs "east room" at Chestnut Grove Plantation, her father's newly built house on the banks of the Pamunkey River in New Kent County, Virginia, about twenty-five miles inland, as the crow flies, from Williamsburg.

What is known about Martha's childhood is meager, aside from the brief notation in the Bible. This leaves the circumstances of her early life to be deduced from what is generally known of her childhood home, her ancestors, her immediate family, their neighbors, and the church she attended, her connections in Tidewater society, and her later behavior.

As a child born in the Tidewater in the eighteenth century, the immediately noteworthy thing about her birth was that Martha and her mother both survived it. In 1731 the odds of both mother and baby surviving were not good. No official statistics exist, but it is estimated that a quarter of all children died before their first birthday and half of all marriages ended in the death of one of the partners before the end of seven years, usually the wife, thanks to complications associated with pregnancy and childbirth. The Angel of Death was a silent guest at weddings and hovered in birthing rooms, leaving the Tidewater full of fractured families that were constantly reforming, as widowers

15

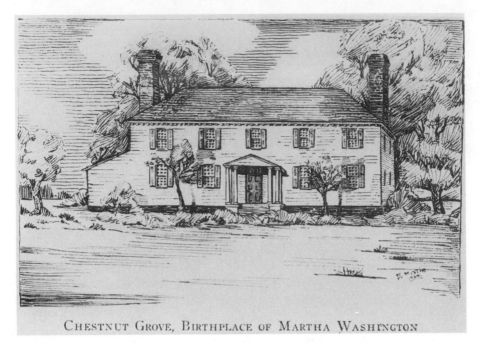

CHESTNUT GROVE, BIRTHPLACE OF MARTHA WASHINGTON

"Chestnut Grove, Birthplace of Martha Dandridge." Courtesy of the Virginia Historical Society.

married second and third wives, widows remarried new husbands, and the children of one marriage were absorbed into a new extended family group.

Even if the mother and child survived the birth, there were plenty of other hazards waiting to carry them off afterward—from childbed infections to fevers, food that spoiled quickly in the heat, "biliousness" (probably jaundice), "colics," and worms and other intestinal parasites; failing that, malaria, yellow fever, typhus, tuberculosis and smallpox were endemic and usually fatal. Frances and her new daughter were fortunate. Both survived, and though Martha was a popular girl's name in both her parents' families, Martha was said to have been specially named after her cousin, Captain William Dandridge's ten-year-old daughter, Martha Dandridge of Elsing Green, in King William County on the northern bank of the Pamunkey.

The house where Martha was born was built around 1730. Unlike many other houses in the neighborhood, which burned down one or more times and were rebuilt on the original foundations, the Chestnut Grove house in which Martha grew up survived in its original state until it too burned down nearly two hundred years later. In November 1926 a fire made to warm the house while fall cleaning was in progress grew out of control. Details of the house come from old photographs and a sketch.

The sketch shows a two-story frame building with a hipped roof and a chimney at either end. The house also had a basement, which ran the length of the house and must have been used for storage. The inside of the house was plain, and the railing and staircase at the time the photographs were made were typical of those found in other houses built in the early eighteenth century. The house was paneled in pine and, if it had not been substantially altered since Martha grew up there, must have had a pleasant "piney" smell inside.

Further details of the house appear in an advertisement from 1768. That year, nearly twenty years after Martha had married and left her childhood home, and her widowed mother had moved to live with her second daughter, Martha's younger brother Bartholomew Dandridge put Chestnut Grove up for sale. Bartholomew's advertisement for Chestnut Grove reads:

> To be sold
>
> A tract of land on Pamunkey River in New-Kent County, about 4 miles below the Court-House containing 500 acres. On it is a dwelling house, with three rooms and a passage-way on each floor, and all the necessary out-houses, with a good orchard. The terms may be known of Bartholomew Dandridge.
> Virginia Gazette, December 24th 1768, No. 85

In the eighteenth century New Kent County was sparsely dotted with plantations similar to Chestnut Grove. Though large tracts of land had been cleared of trees and scrub for crops, much of the area was forested wilderness in Martha's time just as it was at the time of Pocahontas' girlhood five generations earlier. With the exception of Williamsburg, Virginia was an agricultural society. Separated by fields and forests, beyond a plume of smoke rising from a distant chimney, New Kent planters could not see each other's homes.

The term *plantation* conjures up the image of a vast white mansion with columns, like Tara in *Gone with the Wind,* but when Martha Dandridge was growing up, the plantations of eighteenth-century Virginia, Carolina, and Maryland had more in common with a working English manor farm of the sixteenth and seventeenth centuries than with Tara. The "Taras" of the plantation world were of a later period, built mostly in Victorian times. They also are more likely to be found further south and west, in Georgia, Alabama, and Mississippi. In the 1700s *plantation* was a blanket term for almost any sizable landholding that could be described as "larger than a farm" and usually indicated there was a house. Locating Martha's home in the social hierarchy in terms of land owned, Chestnut Grove plantation had five hundred acres, while the richest man in the area, John Custis, owned seventeen thousand acres spread across several counties. In northern Virginia, Baron Fairfax owned five million acres.

Although some houses belonging to the wealthiest families and large-scale planters, like the Custises' Six Chimney House in Williamsburg, the Carters' Shirley and Nomini Hall, and the Masons' Gunston Hall, were large and handsome brick homes, to modern eyes many other "plantation houses" of Tidewater Virginia resemble rambling shacks. The plantation dwelling house was only one part of what was a functioning, self-contained unit of agricultural production, and architectural grandeur was not the first priority. The main house was surrounded by outbuildings devoted to practical tasks. Due to the risk of fire the kitchen was usually a separate building. There would also be a tobacco-drying house, a washhouse, a smokehouse, a still room for making beer and cordials, a springhouse, a poultry yard, a pigpen, a barn, a stable, slave quarters, a kitchen garden, an herb garden, a privy, an orchard, and sometimes a building used as a "schoolhouse."

Chestnut Grove was the home of an up-and-coming man. By the standards of colonial Virginia, a new house of six good rooms was a large one, probably not luxurious but certainly very comfortable for a large family. All colonial houses were necessarily furnished with an eye to function, but unless a planter was very wealthy, there were usually few purely ornamental objects like paintings, fine china, silverware, or books. There would be beds, cradles, tables and chairs, and household items such as candlesticks, warming pans, cooking pots, serviceable cutlery and crockery, pewter mugs and pitchers, and sewing boxes. Everyday clothing hung on pegs, with the best clothes ordered from England packed away in trunks, with lavender to keep out moths. There would be guns, a spinning wheel, baskets, a Bible, a few books, probably including a book of sermons and schoolbooks for the children, a few simple toys, and bedding. Medicines and any precious food items, like spices, tea, coffee, and sugar, were kept under lock and key. Typically the parents of the family occupied one bedroom, together with any babies or very young children. The daughters would share one bedroom and sons another. That meant there was a spare room for guests.

An interesting indication of John Dandridge's wealth, or at least a surplus of disposable income beyond the norm, is that there is said to have been a portrait of Martha painted as a child. And one of her nieces, her brother Bartholomew's daughter, was said to have looked very much like a portrait of John Dandridge. However, if portraits of Martha and her father still exist, their whereabouts are unknown today. Any such portraits at Chestnut Grove were likely to have been painted by an itinerant artist and probably in a "naïf" style, but having a portrait painted at all was a status symbol. It was a particularly extravagant status symbol to have a child's portrait taken.

The size of Chestnut Grove suggests John Dandridge expected to have many guests and was socially part of what might be called the "visiting classes." Virginia planters lived in the constant expectation and hope of company, and they usually got it. There were few inns beyond Williamsburg, and it was a society that had turned easy hospitality into an art. Friends, acquaintances, or even respectable-looking strangers—as well as their entire families and accompanying slaves and horses—could always be assured of a warm welcome, with an invitation to stay for a meal, the night or even days. It was tantamount to running a hotel seven days a week, but guests were a source of entertainment and news, and anyone passing by in the Tidewater, with the intricate family networks of kith and kin that had evolved with the colony, was likely as not to be related to the host or hostess.

The custom—even in the grandest homes—was to put all the female guests in one room and all the gentlemen in another, but any overspill would have to have been accommodated somehow, and there may well have been a bed, or something to serve as a bed, in every room. When the beds were full, pallets were made up on the floor. Martha grew up in a hospitable if crowded atmosphere, sharing a bedroom with her younger sisters and ready to make company welcome at a moment's notice.

Aside from the Bible recording her birth, one of the few documents to mention Martha's girlhood is a letter written by a grandson of Martha's childhood friend and neighbor, a member of the Chamberlayne family, testifying to the fact Martha attended school with his grandmother and went "up country" at the age of about twelve or thirteen.[1]

This slender documentation is supported by surviving family tradition and, more important, by Martha's own recollections, incorporated into another source, the memoirs of her grandson George Washington Parke Custis. This grandson, called "Mr. Tub" or more generally "Wash" for short, and his sister Nelly were raised from infancy by Martha and George Washington. Although his florid memoirs, *Recollections and Private Memoirs of Washington*, were written in the first half of the nineteenth century, and thus somewhat removed from earlier events, he must have relied on his grandmother's reminiscences of her early days.

Children loved Martha, and Wash was no exception. He was devoted to his grandmother and spent much of his young life at her knee. But the timing of Wash's biographical sketch of Martha and her family is important to consider in judging its accuracy. By the time he was writing his *Memoir* about his step-grandfather George Washington in the half century following Martha's death, he had a double purpose. It was written primarily as a paean to the virtues of George Washington, who after his death came to represent the embodiment of the American ideal and all that was good and noble in the Revolution. As the American republic continued its turbulent evolution to resolve its opposing Federalist/Democrat political orientation, which by the nineteenth century had begun to focus on the issue of slavery, the country needed a unifying hero. Wash's priority in writing about Martha was not so much to record what he knew about Martha and her relations, and Wash's own antecedents, as to ensure that his grandmother's public image complemented that of George.

There was, in fact, much that had gone on beneath the surface of Martha's life that did not fit the image Wash wanted to convey. There were things the family did not want publicly known, or that Wash felt it would be prudent to ignore for a variety of reasons. Thus while Wash's accounts reflect what Martha actually told him, there are enough significant omissions, both in Wash's record and in many other documents about Martha and her family, to amount to what Sherlock Holmes regarded suspiciously as the "dog who didn't bark" and that point to skeletons in the family closet.

About Martha's ancestors, Wash was brief, writing only that "Martha Dandridge was descended from an ancient family, which first migrated to the colony of Virginia, in the person of the Reverend Rowland Jones, a clergyman of Wales." In 1674, while Virginia's capital was still at Jamestown, the Oxford-educated Reverend Rowland Jones had immigrated to Virginia and been appointed the first vicar of Bruton Parish Church, a new church in an isolated wilderness inland from Jamestown that became the site of Williamsburg. Reverend Jones had married twice and fathered several children to whom he left land and silver. Rowland's son Orlando Jones became a lawyer in Williamsburg and a burgess, as well as owning some land, and married Martha Macon, whose Macon grandfather, probably a French Huguenot, had been a secretary and Indian interpreter to the governor, Sir William Berkeley. They had a daughter named Frances Orlando Jones and a son, Lane Jones. Thus Frances Jones, who would become Martha's mother, had roots as "urban" as was possible for the time and place, and she was connected to the respectable "professional classes," the clergy and the law of Williamsburg. This was slightly unusual in that most settlers to the colony had been attracted by the prospects of land ownership rather than professional opportunities and, once there, reckoned their standing in how much land they had been able to acquire and put into production.

A glaring omission in Wash's account of Martha's antecedents was any mention of Martha's father and Wash's great-grandfather John Dandridge, in spite of the fact that there seems to have been more known about the Dandridge side of the family than about the Joneses. The Dandridges had prosperous relations in England. Martha's uncle, William Dandridge, John's elder brother, had grown wealthy and prominent in the colony, and it was his daughter after whom Martha was named. In Virginia both brothers used a family coat of arms, that of the Dandridge family of Malvern in England.

John Dandridge was a more modest colonial success story than his elder brother. He was born in London in 1700, eleven years younger than William, one of thirteen children of a prosperous father who was a master painter-stainer and a member of that guild. Seven children survived infancy and had to be provided for, so in 1715, fifteen-year-old John accompanied his elder brother, twenty-six-year-old William Dandridge, to Virginia. They took one of their younger nephews with them, William Langbourne, the son of their sister Mary. William Dandridge was already an officer in the British navy, where he eventually rose to the rank of captain. In an age when there was a huge influx of contracted or indentured laborers swelling the ranks of immigrants to Virginia, it is significant that John was not among them. This suggests his family had been sufficiently wealthy to pay his passage, and it may be that young John had been given some capital by his father before setting off to the New World. Indeed, John landed on his feet remarkably quickly.

The brothers promptly demonstrated an entrepreneurial spirit. Captain William Dandridge set up as a merchant in King William County and by 1727 had been appointed a member of the Governor's Council and a colonel of a local militia, while retaining his rank in the British navy. Captain Dandridge married twice, and his second wife brought him over a thousand acres of land. He built a handsome brick house, Elsing Green, in King William County on the north bank of the Pamunkey River. By the time he died in 1743, he was definitely "somebody" in Virginia, and nothing attests to his status more eloquently than that he was able to build in brick.

Bricks were time-consuming and expensive to make, and superior brick for building was often ordered from England, itself a costly process that involved a long wait before the bricks were delivered. It then required a skilled bricklayer to build with them. The social and economic nuances of building in bricks linger still in the small towns and rural areas of the South. Anyone asking directions is likely to find that a brick house, if available, is used as a reference point: "Go down the road two miles until you come to a brick house. Turn left half a mile after that" or "You'll know you're almost there when you see a brick house up the hill."

John also rose in the colony. He did not marry land as so many men did, but within seven years of his arrival he could afford to buy it. He bought riverfront land on the Elizabeth River and more land in Hanover County in 1722; in 1730 he acquired five hundred acres from the larger Burnell estate on the south bank of the Pamunkey in New Kent County.

New Kent must have felt isolated to someone like John, who was used to the bustle of London. Even today in New Kent County a sense of wilderness prevails. Off the highway, which runs between Richmond and Historic Williamsburg, it has an oddly remote and primitive feeling. Nature has never really relinquished the upper hand. The trees grow thick and very tall, dominating small churches, new homes, and the tiny New Kent courthouse. Today's sprawling industrial estates, mostly odoriferous pulp and paper plants that replaced the sprawling plantations of two hundred years ago, are soon lost from sight in the flat landscape amidst the trees. Summers are suffocatingly hot and humid, and mosquitoes still breed in the brackish rivers and marshy ditches to torment local inhabitants.

By 1722, when John Dandridge acquired his land, Native American tribes who had inhabited the region had been driven west, exterminated, or enslaved. The land in that region was cheap, available, and fertile, and the climate inland was healthier than the marshes of Jamestown on the coast. Chestnut Grove in New Kent County had the great advantage of being situated on the river. This provided an important link to Williamsburg by boat in an age when roads were poor and often impassable.

Unlike his brother William, John's resources did not extend to building his new home in brick. Wood, on the other hand, was readily available. Trees had to be felled and sawed into boards and seasoned, but it was quicker and cheaper than building in brick. It was also more flammable, hence the need for outbuildings where heat from a large fire was needed to carry out domestic tasks like cooking or boiling laundry. These wood houses could and did burn down easily, and were often a target for arson or "accidental fires" by disaffected slaves who seized any opportunity for revenge on their masters. Many a slave suspected of setting fire to his master's house or barn was executed, and throughout the American colonies slave owners were continually on the alert against the possibility of slaves taking revenge in arson attacks or by other means. A visitor to the colony noted: "There are long the [James] river the ruins of many houses which I was told had been accidentally burned by the Negroes, whose carelessness is productive of infinite mischief." The same visitor noted there was often a ladder fixed to the roof of houses still standing to allow the family to escape, seeing it as "evidence of an extraordinary fear or extraordinary danger."

John Dandridge may have been able to build such a substantial house because he found employment. At some point after his arrival in the colony in 1715, John became friends with the clerk of the court of New Kent County, John Thornton. The clerk of the court was an important civil post and carried a salary. In a short time John Dandridge was appointed Thornton's deputy clerk.

The appointment was profitable in two ways, because the friendship with Thornton was the means to a wife as well as a job. Twenty-year-old Frances Jones was the unmarried niece of Thornton's wife, Anna Maria Jones Thornton. On July 22, 1730, John Dandridge and Frances were married. John Thornton died that same year, and John Dandridge succeeded to the post of county clerk, based at New Kent Court House, a convenient four miles from Chestnut Grove. John Dandridge also became a colonel in the New Kent Militia, the local armed force that the colonies were obliged to maintain by the Crown. Just eleven months after their wedding, Frances bore their first child, Martha.

Born during the hot months in the Tidewater, which lasted from April until the end of October, Martha's first impressions were of the distinctive sounds and smells of the plantation drifting in on the hot summer air—the sounds of people and barnyard animals, the slave quarters, the poultry yard, and the smells of manure, the privy, tobacco drying, food cooking, laundry boiling, beer fermenting, hay drying, and silage curing at the end of the summer for winter animal feed. Strongest of all must have been the tang of wood smoke from domestic fires and the smokehouse. There would have been bees in the orchard and the kitchen garden, and hordes of flies attracted by the farm animals. Indoors the air would have been filled with the sounds of footsteps on the uncarpeted wooden floors, the noises of domestic animals—cattle and chickens and dogs and horses—and children, both slave and white. And surely, since coercion drove the slave system, Martha grew up accustomed to the sound of the whip, used for the purpose of what was euphemistically called "slave correction," and the cries of the slaves themselves.

Martha lived in an environment where nervous white planters on their widely separated plantations enforced discipline among the slaves with a heavy hand. Discontent simmered among the slaves, and real or rumored rebellions erupted frequently. The year before Martha's birth a slave conspiracy had been discovered in nearby Norfolk and Princess Anne Counties. In cases of real or even suspected rebellions, the suspected perpetrators were executed brutally in order to discourage other slaves, and owners and overseers would redouble their guard to quell further signs of insurrection or insolence, laziness, or dissatisfaction. Almost any response from a slave qualified as a sign of trouble.

Martha's birth was followed by the birth of three brothers: John in 1733, William in 1734, and Bartholomew in 1737; and then by four sisters: Anna Maria in 1739, Frances in 1744, Elizabeth in 1749, and Mary in 1756. It was markedly unusual for the time and place that Martha passed her childhood and adolescence in a family that had not suffered the loss of a parent or a sibling.

However, near the house is a small family graveyard where Martha's younger brother William, who drowned in the Pamunkey in 1776, is said to be buried, but this would have been after Bartholomew Dandridge sold Chestnut Grove. There are also said to be a number of other children buried there, but since there are no markers on the children's graves, and the Dandridge family Bible records the birth and death of only eight children born to John and Frances Dandridge, it is possible that later owners of the house buried children there. The Henley Bible records that three of Frances's children died before she left the property: John died at age sixteen, Frances at age thirteen, and Mary at age seven.

It was common practice for a planter to include everyone resident at the plantation—whites, slaves, and indentured servants—in the term "family," and the Chestnut Grove "family" included slaves as well as indentured servants. John Dandridge owned slaves to work his land, but there is no record of how many. There is also no record of his treatment of those slaves, but it cannot be supposed he was any better or worse than his fellow planters. He must have attended slave auctions or purchased slaves from his neighbors and, like them, been concerned primarily with extracting the necessary maximum of labor for the minimum cost.

The Dandridge "family" at Chestnut Grove also included at least one member whose existence was never recorded in later accounts of the first First Lady's life, including those by Wash Custis, his sister Nelly, or by any official accounts. Martha Dandridge had a half sister Ann Dandridge (as distinguished from her younger sister Anna Maria Dandridge). The evidence of Ann's existence is contained in an obscure document that appeared many years after her death, a report to Congress in 1870 on the "schools of the colored population" in Washington, D.C. Specifically, the report mentioned a school run by Louisa Parke Costin and went on to say she was the daughter of Ann Dandridge Costin's son William Costin.

The report traced the relationship to Martha in the following way:

> Louisa Parke Costin's school was established in her father's house on Capitol Hill on A Street south, under the shadow of the Capitol. This Costin family came from Mount Vernon immediately after the death of Martha Washington in 1802. The father, William Costin, who died suddenly in his bed, May 31, 1842, was for twenty four years a messenger for the Bank of Washington. . . . John Quincy Adams . . . alluded to the deceased in these words "The late William Costin, though he was not white, was as much respected as any man in the District, and the large concourse of citizens that attended his remains to the grave, as well white as black, was an evidence of the manner in which he was estimated by the citizens of Washington."
>
> William Costin's mother, Ann Dandridge, was the daughter of a half-breed (Indian and colored), her grandfather being a Cherokee chief, and her reputed father was the father of Martha Dandridge, afterwards Mrs. Custis, who in 1759 was married to General Washington. These daughters, Ann and Martha, grew up together on the ancestral plantations. William Costin's reputed father was white . . . but the mother, after his birth, married one of the Mount Vernon slaves by the name of Costin, and the son took the name of William Costin. . . . His mother [Ann] being of Indian descent, made him under the laws of Virginia, a free man. . . . This is the account which William Costin and his wife and his mother, Ann Dandridge, always gave of their ancestry, and they were persons of great precision in all matters of family history, as well as of the most marked scrupulousness in their statements.[2]

Virginia was teeming with mixed-race children, a fact that graphically raises the issue of nonconsensual sexual relations between white planters and African American or Native American slave women. The records of births, deaths, and christenings at St. Peter's Parish Church in New Kent County, which was attended by the Dandridges and surrounding families, records the births and deaths of many mulatto slave children. The fact that some of these were recorded as being baptized suggests either an unlikely excess of piety on the part of the planter in having a slave child baptized (slaves were excluded from the Christian sacrament of "marriage" lest they pollute it) or more likely as acknowledgment of paternity by the planter. A child took its status as "slave" or "free" from its mother. A planter who had a child with a slave woman had a new slave. Martha's uncle Lane Jones, Frances's brother, had had at least one slave child, "Elizabeth," baptized at the local church.[3] The Dandridges and neighboring planters' children grew up in a world where mixed-race half siblings and cousins were commonplace.

Ann, however, was an unusual case of a mixed-race child who enjoyed free status, and it is odd there is no record of her birth in the St. Peter's Parish records. However, there is no record of Martha's birth in the parish records either. It is likely that some of the parish records either perished over time or were destroyed during the Civil War. Two factors suggest that Ann must have been considerably younger than Martha: first, her son William was born in 1780, meaning Ann must have been a small child when Martha married, and second, she outlived Martha.

History does not record the views of Frances Jones Dandridge or plantation wives in general on the subject of their husbands' mulatto offspring, but later accounts of escaped slaves record forced sexual relations with female slaves as part and parcel of the slave system. It is impossible to say to what extent a slave woman might have entered into a relationship with her own master or other white man voluntarily, though white men were a slave woman's only source of protection, and some slave women may have done so in the hopes their children would receive better treatment and possibly some education, or that their father might be reluctant to sell his own blood away from his plantation.

It is also impossible today to second-guess how someone like Frances Dandridge might have coped with the situation. On the one hand it was common, almost the norm; slaves were chattels, and many white women may have taken the view that their husbands' relationships with slave women were nothing to be concerned about. Women did not leave their husbands on this account. In fact, they rarely left even husbands who were drunk or abusive. On very large plantations planters sometimes kept a second family fathered with a slave at a discreet distance, but family tradition has it that Ann and Martha were "raised together." If Ann's mother was technically "free," Ann was too, despite her interracial heritage. How this free little half sister Ann Dandridge, with dark skin, fitted into the scheme of things at Chestnut Grove is not known, but Ann's existence highlights two patterns of behavior that were common.

The first is the absence of written records, and the second the pact of silence on the topic of interracial half brothers and half sisters, or "brothers and sisters of colour," that seems to have been observed within the "family," and indeed by anyone connected with the family in such circumstances. In a similar situation, Thomas Jefferson's two daughters were silent about their father's long-standing affair with his slave Sally Hemming and the children Sally bore him, though the relationship was conducted under their very noses at Monticello. In a further little-known twist, Sally Hemming herself was a mulatto half sister of Jefferson's deceased wife, and technically aunt to Patsy and Polly Jefferson. Yet somehow no hint of this tangle of interracial family relationships has surfaced in any of the many papers of Thomas Jefferson or in his correspondence with family and friends. The likelihood that there is no written Dandridge, Custis, or Washington record of Ann Dandridge is another example of the kind of family matter Wash did not wish to expose in his memoir.

Surprisingly, considering that the slave system depended on slaves being viewed as a species of animal, behind this veil of silence a planter, and even his family, sometimes acknowledged responsibility for children born from relationships with slaves. Such relationships were almost always between a white man and a black woman, and very rarely between a white woman and a black man.

In fact, by the time Martha was born, it had long been an offense for a white indentured servant to bear a mulatto child. The mulatto child would be "free," and the last thing the colony wanted was a horde of free mulatto children nursing a grievance that their fathers were not free. Nevertheless, white indentured servant women often were thrown together with male African slaves, with whom they formed relationships and bore children, and this carried draconian penalties. The mother's period of indenture would be extended and "sold" with the profit going to the parish. The child was automatically bound into indentured servitude until the age of thirty-one. As a result, though some of the many mulatto children born in the colony had a white mother and a black father, there were far more mulatto children born to white fathers and black or mixed-race mothers.

However the presence of Ann Dandridge may have complicated the situation at Chestnut Grove, she was born after Martha had left childhood behind. Family life at Chestnut Grove provided Martha with a stable and secure environment during her early years when her family was intact. With his salaried position as clerk to the court, John Dandridge did not have to rely entirely on tobacco production to support his family, which provided an unusual degree of financial security for his family. In addition to the distinction of being appointed colonel of the New Kent Militia, he held office as a vestryman at St. Peter's Church and blended into the easygoing life of men in the neighborhood, who enjoyed racing, cockfights, hunting, guns, and whiskey.

There is some evidence John had another son, and thus Martha another brother, or more probably half brother, named Ralph. There is no mention of Ralph in the Henley Bible or in any other document connected with Martha and her family, save one. John and William Dandridge had an elder brother named Francis who lived in London and with whom they kept in contact. Francis Dandridge was well-off, as evidenced by the will he left at his death in 1763. By that time John Dandridge was dead, and among other bequests, there was one to "Mrs. Frances Dandridge, widow of my late brother John Dandridge, £600 in 4% Bank Stock" and "To Ralph, son of my late brother John, £100."[4] It was a significantly large bequest to a woman Francis Dandridge had never met, and £100 was a very large sum to leave his nephew Ralph. It was of a magnitude to set up a young man in life. Had Ralph been John and Frances Dandridge's son, his existence would surely have been in the Henley Bible. The inescapable conclusion is that if Ralph was John's son, his mother was not Frances. Nor was she a slave, because a slave woman's child was also a slave and could not own property or possess such a large sum of money.

As the eldest of nine, or possibly ten, children, Martha's maternal instincts must have formed at an early age as a result of helping care for her younger brothers and sisters. She was always particularly fond of her sister Anna Maria Dandridge, seven years her junior, who was named after Anna Maria Thornton. Martha's pet name for Anna Maria was "Nancy." Judging by Martha's later behavior within her own and George's extended families, relationships within the Dandridge family were affectionate. Although Martha had a formidable temper when roused, throughout her life she was famously good-natured and what the eighteenth century called "amiable."

In later life, Martha took a rigorous approach to the education and upbringing of her favorite granddaughter Nelly Custis, Wash's sister, which emphasized academic subjects, as well as art, music, and domestic training. Her attitudes toward Nelly's upbringing probably reflect her own experiences. Frances allowed her daughters to waste little time as children. Assuming a mother lived long enough, her daughters' education was her responsibility, and there was a good deal of ground to cover in the space of a few years to prepare girls for the early marriages that were common in the colony.

One of Martha's nineteenth-century lady biographers, Margaret C. Conkling, in her *Memoirs of the Mother and Wife of Washington*, published in 1850, wrote approvingly that Martha "possessed only such artificial [i.e., academic] accomplishments as the system of domestic instruction, then the sole means of female education in her native land enabled her to acquire" and that in Martha the absence of formal education was supplanted with the happier endowments of "self respect, good sense, gentleness of temper."[5]

Revealing as this is about the nineteenth century's idea of Martha as "the little woman," the not overly academic "angel in the house," it is wrong. While it is true that few Virginia girls had the kind of education that made them bookish, as did Martha's later friends and contemporaries like Abigail Adams, Mercy Otis Warren, and Eliza Powell, who were raised in New England or Philadelphia, Martha and the other Dandridge children had an education that was good for its time and place. Given her forebears, it is unlikely Frances Jones Dandridge was illiterate, as the majority of women in the colony were, or that she would have neglected her daughters' formal education.

Rural Virginia, however, had few schools. As Martha's grandson noted, "The education of females in the early days of the colonial settlements, was almost exclusively of a domestic character, and by instructors who were entertained in the principal families, that were too few, and too 'far between' to admit of the establishment of public schools."[6] The very wealthiest planters, like the Carters at Nomini Hall, often hired a resident tutor for their children. Lesser planters like the Dandridges probably hired an itinerant tutor because a woman like Martha's mother would have been far too busy to teach her children full-time. Many plantations had a room set aside as a schoolroom in one of the outbuildings, such as the stable, or in some cases a one-room schoolhouse was an outbuilding where children from neighboring plantations shared lessons. These lessons were often taught by an itinerant schoolmaster. The Dandridge children certainly attended a "school" and may have been taught by an itinerant tutor, an indentured servant named Thomas Leonard. In addition to formal lessons, Thomas Leonard may have taught Martha to dance, the most important social accomplishment for any young lady. Dancing was extremely popular in the colony.

To modern eyes, the grammar, spelling, and lack of punctuation in Martha's surviving correspondence give the impression that her formal education was limited and poor. In fact, the correspondence simply reflects forms of spelling and grammar that were common in England and later in Virginia in the sixteenth and early seventeenth centuries. By today's standards, most Virginians, educated as Martha and her siblings had been, had atrocious spelling and dubious grammar by today's standards.

Martha learned some music as well—most planters' daughters did, as it was regarded as a genteel English accomplishment. The playing of most girls, however, revealed shortcomings in the level of colonial musical instruction available. Philip Fithian, the Princeton-educated tutor at Nomini Hall, noted in his diary that while nearly all the girls he met seemed to play an instrument, they rarely played well. They were, he said, given to "thumping."[7] Martha had a genuine lifelong love of music, but there is no record that she played an instrument. However, when raising Nelly many years later, Martha saw to it that Nelly was provided with a fine harpsichord and a good music teacher. Nelly herself was required to practice up to four hours a day under Martha's gimlet eye. Nelly's brother later wrote that Nelly would "play and cry, and play and cry," but the result was that Nelly played beautifully all her life.

Martha attended school lessons with her friend, the daughter of a nearby family named Chamberlayne at Poplar Grove Plantation. Richard Pye Cook, a descendant of the Chamberlayne family living at Chestnut Grove in 1887, gave the following reply to an inquiring correspondent:

> "you want to know something about the birth place of Miss Martha Dandridge. My grandmother and Miss Dandridge were visitors and school mates went to school together 4 or 5 years Miss D. left this place Chestnut Grove (where she was born) between 12 and 13 years old and went up the country Dandridges and Gen Chamberlayne's families were very intimate and visited regularly. . . . I now own the birth place of Mrs. Martha Washington. She was born in the East room of the Chestnut Grove house."[8]

Martha's trip "up the country," which may have marked the end of her formal schooling, probably coincided with the death in 1743 of her uncle, Captain William Dandridge, at Elsing Green in Prince William County. She may have been dispatched by Frances to comfort and help William's widow, Unity Dandridge, at a time when Frances was unable to go herself, or to be company for her cousin, William's daughter Martha, after whom she was named and who was ten years her senior.

In addition to her school lessons, like all colonial girls Martha was not brought up to idleness and must have had a share in the household work from an early age. The frequently pregnant Frances probably had her hands full. Though some household tasks may have been performed by slaves, only the grandest families could afford slaves to do housework exclusively. Despite their treatment, slaves were an expensive investment for planters, and more productive economically in the field than in the home. On a five-hundred-acre farm like Chestnut Grove, John Dandridge probably could afford only a few slaves, and those, both men and women, would have been employed in the fields under the direction of an overseer.

Frances knew her daughters' futures depended on more than books. Girls tended to marry very young in the colony. Martha's cousin married a fourteen-year-old daughter of Governor Spottswood, for example. Marrying at twenty, Frances was older than the norm. Like any right-thinking colonial mother, Frances understood the need to train her daughters to take their place at the head of their own establishment when they married. An essential part of Martha's childhood training was in domestic skills.

A plantation mistress managed the domestic side of a self-contained unit of production. She oversaw the health, welfare, food, drink, clothing, and religious instruction of everyone on it. The feeding, clothing, and nursing of her own family and the slaves were her responsibility, as were the poultry yard, the smokehouse, the springhouse, the laundry, and the kitchen garden. Wool had to be greased to make it flexible, then carded and spun, and flax turned into thread; the slaves' summer and winter clothing had to be cut out and stitched and made; food had to be preserved, beer brewed, and cordials and home remedies distilled and prepared. Judging by Martha's lifelong reputation for the excellence of her domestic skills, from exquisite needlework to the plain sewing of soldiers' shirts, from the making of quilts and the smoking of hams to the smooth running of her household, she learned well.

In modern times housewifely skills are often dismissed as trivial, engaged in only by women of limited intellect, ability, or opportunity, but it was very different in Martha's day. If a planter was to succeed in the colony, he needed a wife as a helpmeet and partner as much as he needed land, capital, and slaves. Men outnumbered women in Virginia, and wives were much in demand. Even in the grandest families, where a bride might come with a generous dowry of money, land, and slaves, a plantation wife was an active partner as well as a breeder of children.

In addition to the sewing lessons little girls had from an early age, Martha must have spent many a long day in the bustle of the kitchen learning, among other things, how to make "marmalets" when the fruit was ripe. Because there was no canning, fruit was cooked with sugar and sometimes aromatic flavorings, such as bitter almonds and ambergris, to make a stiff, lumpy jam with medicinal and restorative properties. The sugar and flavorings for making the marmalets had to be imported from England, the West Indies, or Spain, and because of the cost of these ingredients, it would have been important not only to make the marmalets properly so that nothing was wasted, but also to store them so they did not spoil. These marmalets, intended as a "restorative," had a medicinal function and were not lavished on bread but doled out carefully in times of illness.

In addition to keeping her family fed, Frances and other plantation wives were expected, as a matter of course, to be ready for company, invited or not, and in whatever numbers. Many an English traveler was surprised by the warmth of his welcome into the home of strangers. This prospect would be daunting to most modern women, even with access to a freezer, a microwave, a self-cleaning oven, and a deli around the corner that delivers. A woman in Frances's day must have been a miracle of organization in order to cope and cope gracefully.

One interesting aspect of Martha's upbringing in colonial Virginia is that at an early age Martha absorbed lessons about the message conveyed by clothing and appearance. Both sent vitally important signals in the colony. She must have developed her lifelong fondness for pretty clothes as a child, with Frances's encouragement, but she clearly absorbed other, more subtle, lessons about clothes and how they influenced perceptions of the wearer.

It was more a clothes consciousness as distinct from the present-day term "fashion consciousness," but it was a finely developed sensitivity for reasons peculiar to the colony. In later life, this instinctive knack for wearing the right thing would have political repercussions she could never have dreamed of as a girl.

In the colony, women and men alike adored dressing up for social occasions. New England's Puritan restraint and Quaker plainness were alien concepts in the southern colonies. Clothes were one of the few frivolous distractions on the plantation. A wife was expected to be an entertaining companion at the many social gatherings, and she had to look her best. At home on their plantations both masters and mistresses went about their many tasks in a state of dishabille that bordered on the slovenly. To compensate, the planters and their wives dressed to the teeth for social occasions. To outsiders, planters and their families often appeared ridiculously overdressed. But more than just fun, clothes were an important badge of distinction in the colony and spoke volumes about the social and economic status of the wearer. Headgear in the form of ladies' caps and men's hats was essential, as was powder for the hair. A lack of headgear marked the bareheaded immediately as social outcasts, and indentured servants arriving without it were often fitted out with headgear as a charity to make them respectable enough to hire.

The reason clothing conveyed the message it did was that the fine apparel worn on social occasions by both men and women had to be ordered at vast trouble and expense from England, and its cost was calculated in pounds of tobacco. Southern ladies on their far-flung plantations could not visit shops in towns as their New England sisters did. Ladies sent to England for their gowns, fans, dancing slippers, stockings, gloves, and bonnets, specifying hopefully that the items ordered would be "of the latest fashion."

But dressing well from a distance was a challenge. By the time the order crossed the Atlantic, been filled in England and shipped back to the colony, nearly a year would have elapsed, and anything could have happened. There must have been much anxious opening of parcels in Virginia, assuming the order had not gone astray, the ship not taken by pirates or French privateers, or the goods not damaged by seawater. The colonists could never be sure they would get what they had ordered or wanted. Despite sending measurements and specific requests for items to be "of the best quality," orders from the colonists were often carelessly filled with shabby merchandise of an inferior standard known as "colonial."

To the planters' chagrin, orders for items of clothing and shoes were also filled with complete disregard for the planters' specifications as to size. The vast amounts of finery dispatched to the colonies was, for the English merchants who supplied it, a license to print money. There must have been many a pair of feet crammed into shoes a size too small or dancing slippers padded out with stuffing, stomachs sucked in to accommodate waistcoats smaller than those ordered, or a new gown that might have fit a dwarf or an elephant, but not the woman for whom it was intended. The alterations that must often have been necessary provided a powerful incentive for young girls to learn sewing. A slave who was a good seamstress was almost certain to have an easier life.

Another element of Martha's lessons in domestic skill would have been slave management. Ann Dandridge notwithstanding, it would be a mistake to suppose there was any cozy aspect to the Dandridges' relationship with their slaves, or that they were different from other planters in this respect. It is unlikely Martha was brought up to view slaves as anything other than the chattels they were by law.

In the world Martha knew, they lived in the slave quarters and were roused at sunup to work until sundown. Since they were an expensive investment, they had to be worked as hard as possible while being maintained at the least possible expense. Their food was doled out in subsistence rations, mostly cornmeal occasionally supplemented by a little fat meat or fish, and they wore garments made of cheap material known as "slave cloth." Their history, tribal affiliations, native culture, language, and names disappeared in the waters of the Middle Passage, and in the colony they were bestowed with new names as if they had been horses or dogs. There was no reason Martha would have seen them as anything other than a subhuman working presence.

Martha would have been brought up aware that slaves were a deeply hostile workforce who normally only performed under coercion, and she would have known that throughout the colony planters lived in fear of the consequences if the strictest control was not maintained. In the Caribbean bloody slave revolts erupted continuously. In Virginia the threat permeated society, with good reason. Slaves sabotaged the system by the limited means in their power, shamming illness, stealing, working as slowly as possible, breaking household and agricultural equipment, mistreating livestock, committing arson, and in extreme cases self-mutilation and suicide. They ran away whenever possible, sometimes attempting to poison planters or their families. In Thomas Jefferson's childhood at least one female slave was burned at the stake on the order of the local sheriff for witchcraft. Slaves were an inefficient source of labor requiring an extraordinary degree of violence to extract any work.

As mentioned briefly in the introduction, the litany of abuse of slaves belonging to William Byrd II of Westover Plantation and his wife Lucy, recorded by Byrd himself in his diary in 1709, and the details of slave treatment at delightful Nomini Hall recorded by a horrified Philip Fithian sixty years later provide a disturbing insight into what went on behind the scenes and actually sustained life on the plantation. These accounts were not isolated incidents and reflected common practices observed, or carried out, by men regarded as exceptionally well educated and cultivated gentlemen of the period. They beg the question of what Martha might have seen or absorbed as necessary in the way of "slave management."

Byrd, who lived in the first half of the eighteenth century not far from Williamsburg, was one of Virginia's wealthiest planters and an uncle by marriage of Martha's first husband. Well-educated in England, Byrd customarily began his day early, reading in Greek, Hebrew, or Latin, ate sparingly, and said his prayers morning and night. He was a self-taught medical practitioner and widely regarded as "the ornament of his age." He described in passing the casual cruelty of the routine discipline of household slaves at Westover: his wife Lucy Byrd beating a young slave named Jenny with a hot iron, having a female slave whipped for serving undercooked bacon, fitting a slave suspected of malingering with an iron bit in his mouth, forcing a young boy named Eugene to drink "a pint of piss" for wetting his bed, and beating "little Jenny" for concealing it. On other occasions Eugene was whipped for doing nothing, Moll "whipped for a hundred faults," and Jenny whipped for running away. A female slave had a bit put in her mouth for running away. Hot-tempered Mrs. Byrd branded Jenny with a hot iron. Moll was whipped for "failing to make the shoats fat." Byrd had a slave whipped for falling asleep and admitted there had been an incident where he "beat little Jenny too much," though that did not prevent his beating her again ten days later. What, the stunned reader wonders, might Byrd have regarded as "too much"?[9]

Things were no better at Nomini Hall, where tutor Philip Fithian lived in 1770 as one of the family. He was uneasy at learning that in contrast to the luxury enjoyed at the main house, the slaves were issued only a peck of corn and a pound of meat each week. He was appalled by the way management of the slaves was delegated to overseers, a group of men universally acknowledged to be brutal, and often alcoholic, and the methods they used to keep the Carter slaves in line were described in full sadistic detail by a horrified Fithian. What Fithian described was standard practice, the kind of thing Martha and her contemporaries took in their stride:

> At breakfast Mr. Carter entertained us with an account of what he himself saw the other Day, which is a strong Representation of the cruelty and distress which many among the negros suffer in Virginia! Mr. Carter dined at Squire Lee's some weeks ago; at the same place that day, dined also Mr. George Turberville & his wife—As Mr. Carter rode up he observed Mr. Turberville's Coach-Man sitting on the Chariot-Box, the Horses off—after he had made his compliments in the House, He had Occasion soon after to go to the Door, when he saw the Coach man still sitting, and on examination found that he was there fast chained. The Fellow is inclined to run away, and this is the method

which this Tyrant makes use of to keep him when abroad; and so soon as he goes home he is delivered into the pitiless hands of a bloody Overseer.[10]

Fithian had spent some time around the overseers, long enough to make the following observations on their methods of workforce motivation:

> And Mr. Carter is allow'd by all, & from what I have seen of others I make no Doubt at all but he is, by far the most humane to his slaves of any in these parts! Good God! Are these Christians?—When I am on the subject I will relate further, what I heard Mr. George Lee's Overseer, one Morgan, say the other day that he himself had done to Negroes, and found it useful; he said that whipping of any kind does them no good, for they will laugh at your greatest Severity; But he told us he had invented two things, and by several experiments had proved their success.—
>
>   For Sulleness, Obstinacy, or Idleness, says he, Take a Negro, strip him, tie him to a post; take a sharp Curry-Comb and curry him severely until he is well scrap'd; and call a Boy with some dry hay and make the Boy rub him down for several Minutes, then salt him and unlose him. He will attend to his business . . . afterwards.
>
>   But savage cruelty does not exceed His next diabolical Invention. To get a secret from a Negro, says he, take the following Method- Lay upon your floor a large thick plank, having a peg about eighteen inches long, of hard wood and very sharp, on the upper end, fixed fast in the plank- then strip the Negro, tie the cord to a staple in the ceiling, so as that his foot may just rest on the sharpened Peg, then turn him briskly round, and you would laugh . . . at the Dexterity of the Negro while he was relieving his Feet the sharpen'd Peg![11]

Fithian also recorded that a family in the Carters' neighborhood came within a hairbreadth of being murdered in their beds by their slaves.

Many slaves escaped. The *Virginia Gazette,* published in Williamsburg, carried many ads for runaways offering rewards for those captured "dead or alive." Apprehended runaways were taken to the sheriff, who usually administered a severe whipping before returning the slave to his or her owner. Slaves were often branded and runaways often had part of a foot amputated. It is impossible to believe that Martha was unaware of current practices, nor that she would not have been taught to regard them as necessary even if she personally viewed them as regrettable.

On first consideration the issue of slave management seems at odds with the final component in Martha's education, religion. All her life Martha was devoutly religious, probably thanks to Frances and her connection with Bruton Parish Church. Like many women of the time, Martha found religion a way to hang on to sanity in times of unbearable grief, given the frequent deaths from smallpox, fevers, tuberculosis, and childbirth. As an adult

Martha was punctilious about attending church each Sunday as well about her private devotions. She had a lifelong habit of retiring to her room for an hour after breakfast to read her Bible and pray. In her later years her granddaughter Nelly also used to read Bible verses, pray, and sing a hymn with Martha before bed.

Religious or moral instruction also laid the foundation for another aspect of women's lives, one that often proved to be their greatest support in a difficult life. Girls like Martha and her sisters, growing up in a comfortable but not wealthy family in the colonial Tidewater, were arguably even more limited in their options than girls elsewhere. In England or the northern colonies it was possible to work, even if only in the capacity of maid, governess, or schoolteacher. In Virginia there were few schools, and there were slaves or indentured servants. The Dandridge girls, like their neighbors, were unlikely ever to travel beyond Williamsburg, let alone out of the colony, and geography was another factor that narrowed their options to marriage and motherhood. Marriage was an inflexible institution, and motherhood was hedged with bereavement over the likely death of children or of the mother herself. A mother could not guarantee her daughters would be happy but she could provide them with another prop—a clear concept of their duty to God and within the family. A woman might be unhappy in her marriage, experience economic disasters, lose children, endure the loss of her husband and experience ill health and personal suffering herself, but provided a woman did her duty, no matter what happened she could feel "validated."

It is a concept that was very much of its time and place, an almost foreign one in the present age, when women have options and an ability to exercise them to pursue their own happiness and satisfaction. But it was a fundamental and important one for Martha, who lived her own life in strict adherence to this eighteenth-century concept of duty she learned as a girl. Revealingly, she inculcated the same principle in her granddaughter Nelly. Martha and Nelly were both to draw heavily on this sense of "validation" of doing their duty in times of difficulty.

The Church of England was the established church of Virginia, although in the colony it seems to have thrived in its Low Church form—no incense, plainsong or lavishly appointed altars. Unlike churches in the northern colonies, where Quakers and dissenters made their influence felt, the Anglican church in Virginia was not given to introspection on individual matters of conscience or subverting the status quo. The northern colonies would prove a breeding ground for antislavery sentiments, drawing on diverse religious and ethical traditions, such as the Quakers and other dissenting sects. The church in Virginia was conservative, its vestrymen were prominent slave owners, and its bread was buttered firmly on the side of slavery.

In St. Peter's Church, where the Dandridges attended services, Martha would have heard the proclamation required by law to be read aloud from

Virginia pulpits on a Sunday in March and a Sunday in September. The congregation was reminded that in view of the ever-present threat from disaffected and vengeful slaves, it was unlawful for Negroes to be armed, to depart from the master's property without a pass, or to assemble in large numbers at feasts or funerals. No strange Negro was to be allowed to stay on a plantation beyond four hours without checking his pass. Freedmen must go armed to church and assemblies to prevent an attack by slaves. Any slaves caught without a pass after dark off the master's property were to be dismembered.[12]

The established clergy, besides lending ecclesiastical support to the institution of slavery, were often odd personages themselves. Writing about the clergyman Jonathan Boucher, who would tutor Martha's teenage son many years later, Worthington Chauncey Ford had this to say:

> 'It must be admitted that Boucher was, in ability, much above the ordinary divine to be found in Virginia at that time. Many very peculiar characters were exported to lead the souls of the American colonists into the paths of righteousness. . . . Like the merchandise sent to America, many of the clergymen might have been called "colonials" meaning a quality of article not good enough for use at home, but quite good enough for use in a colony thousands of miles away, and where the curing of tobacco was of equal importance to the curing of souls.'[13]

It is a passage that casts Martha's great-grandfather Reverend Rowland Jones in a new light.

Martha's first acquaintance with the clergy involved one of the oddest specimens of the colonial clergy. From 1727 to 1767 the vicar of St. Peter's was the Reverend David Mossom. The man who instructed Martha in her catechism had such a notoriously volatile temper it is a wonder that Martha maintained her devoutly Christian outlook. Once during a service Reverend Mossom became involved in a heated argument with the church clerk, whom he finally threatened from the pulpit to thrash. The unruffled clerk responded coolly by announcing the next hymn "With restless and ungovern'd rage / Why do the heathen storm? / Why in such rash attempts engage. / As they can ne'er perform?"[14]

A later bishop felt Reverend Mossom's behavior was eccentric enough to call for some explanation—that Reverend Mossom had been "married four times and much harassed by his last wife . . . which may account for and somewhat excuse a little peevishness."

St. Peter's Church was built of brick and attended by most of the planters in the neighborhood, though usually only the women and children actually attended the service indoors. Most men saw religious practice as women's business, though the position of vestryman was an important office.

Church services provided the men with an opportunity to meet and socialize, and the men generally hung about outside, swapping stories about crops and horses.

Between learning to run a house, sew, cook, look after pigs and chickens, read, write, dance, welcome company, help with the younger children, and memorize her catechism, family tradition tells us that Martha was very fond of riding. Riding would have been a necessary skill, as many places would have been more easily reached on horseback than in a horse-drawn vehicle. An anecdote whose source it is impossible to trace describes how a mischievous Martha once scandalized her mother and aunt by riding her horse onto the porch of Elsing Green and threatening to ride on into the house.

But such youthful pranks aside, by the time Martha was fifteen, Frances had done her best. Martha's childhood and its lessons were over. She was a woman, and it was time for her to be married.

CHAPTER 2

"John Dandridge's Daughter"

Frances's main concern in life now was to see Martha settled. According to family tradition, Martha was taken to Williamsburg to make her debut at fifteen. This suggests something about the Dandridges' social connections, their aspirations, the fact they could afford the clothes, and simply their desire to show their eldest daughter a good time and put her in the way of a good husband. Martha's late uncle Captain William Dandridge was their grandest family connection, though Frances's Williamsburg associations had been prominent too, but because Martha did not stand to inherit land or money, it is difficult to see what justified launching Martha with more fanfare than most other girls into the marriage market. It was not essential for a girl to have a debut to get married. Given the shortage of young women in the colony, any girl could expect to find a husband without making a formal "debut."

Debut, as the term is understood today, is a grander term than it was in Martha's day. The formalities of her debut probably involved attending a ball at the governor's palace in Williamsburg, not the lavish private party the term conjures up today. What is significant about the event is that if John Dandridge was in a financial position to afford enough finery for his daughter to hold her own at the governor's palace, it sent a signal about his own standing. If Martha was fifteen at the time, the ball she attended would have coincided either with the autumn session of "publick times" in 1746, or in the spring session of 1747, months before her sixteenth birthday in June. If Martha was presented in the autumn season of 1746, she attended one of the most splendid occasions of the social year, the royal Birth Night Ball held at the governor's palace on October 31 to commemorate the birthday of the English king, George II.

The palace was modest by European standards, but it was the grandest building in the colony. It was a focus of civic pride, and symbolized the dignity of the King's vice regal appointee. Situated at the end of a long avenue called Palace Street, the palace was a five-bay Georgian mansion behind imposing wrought-iron gates. It was surrounded by a naturalistic park, which stretched north with fine gardens, orchards, walks, and even a canal. In addition to the annual Birth Night Ball, the palace was the scene of many other balls and formal dinners, which constituted the apogee of the colony's social life.

By comparison with life in New Kent, a ball at the palace was a fabulously exciting prospect. Though Martha had probably been to Williamsburg to visit her mother's relations on previous occasions, her status had changed. If she was grown-up enough to go to the ball, it marked a distinct and sudden transition to adulthood. But like most teenage girls attending their first ball or grown-up party, she must have alternated between giddy excitement, the frisson of her new status as a marriageable woman, and nervous anxiety about whether anyone would dance with her, and whether she would remember her manners and her dance steps. The question of what she was to wear must have consumed Frances and Martha considerably, in the ordering and in hoping the clothes would arrive on time, would be what they had ordered, and would fit.

At the palace Martha would have entered the main hall, which displayed the royal coat of arms, and danced in a ballroom with the larger-than-life portraits of King George and Queen Caroline. On that occasion and most others, everyone present would have drunk the loyal toast, "God Save the King." In preparation for appearing in such grand surroundings, back at Chestnut Grove Martha would have practiced her curtsy and her dance steps, while Frances, in order to have Martha's clothes in time, must have dictated a list of clothing and accessories for John to order from London many months earlier, when Martha was only fourteen. Like all the younger sisters of a teenager, little Anna Maria Dandridge must have watched wide-eyed the exciting fuss over Martha's clothes, overheard many lectures on appropriate deportment for young ladies about to meet the governor, and wondered when her turn would come.

The social whirl of Williamsburg, into which Martha now entered, consisted of balls and parties, plays, concerts, card parties, dinners, fox hunts, croquet, and picnics—almost anything anyone could dream up in a society where people had to invent their own amusements and did so with a will. Each morning the hairdresser made the rounds of Williamsburg to dress and powder ladies' hair, and there would be the careful unpacking and dressing up in the fine clothes from England. Compared to country social life on the Pamunkey it was madly glamorous, but in Williamsburg Martha must have met many of the country neighbors she had known since childhood in

New Kent. Most knew each other, many were related by marriage or other ties of kinship, and the easy hospitality of the region guaranteed Martha would have seen many of them as visitors at Chestnut Grove. It is unlikely she found herself in a sea of complete strangers, and Frances, who was familiar with Williamsburg and its ways, must have made sure Martha did not appear a bumpkin in polite town society, or most crucially, in front of the governor.

In town the Dandridges stayed at one of the many inns that flourished during "publick times." It is said some verses in Martha's honor were published in the town. If so, they have not survived to the present day, but the local newspaper, the *Virginia Gazette*, often interspersed its six-month-old English news and notices offering rewards for the return of runaway slaves and indentured servants with verses composed by love-struck young men to a "Fidelia" or some similar classical name. Allusions to a particular girl were rather oblique, but girls must have put their heads together and giggled as they tried to work out who had written what about whom. Since men substantially outnumbered women in the colony, any girl who did not have two heads and a vile temper to boot was sure to qualify as a "belle" and be paid plenty of attention.

Family tradition, says, unsurprisingly, that Martha was "the most attractive belle at the court of Williamsburg"[1] At fifteen, Martha was pretty rather than beautiful, with brown hair and hazel eyes. She was short, less than five feet tall, with a tendency to plumpness, characteristics common to the women in her family. As Wash put it in his flowery style: "Of the early life of Miss Dandridge, we are only able to record, that the young lady excelled in personal charms, which, with pleasing manners, and a general amiability of demeanour, caused her to be distinguished amid the fair ones who usually assembled at the court of Williamsburg, then held by the royal governors of Virginia."[2]

Family license aside, as a girl Martha probably gained her reputation for popularity in Williamsburg for the same reasons she was popular later in life. She was not a beauty, a flirt, or a sharp wit, but she was an attractive, good-natured, and vivacious girl who talked easily to people and liked music and dancing. All her life people were drawn to her by her sweet disposition and her self-possessed charm.

It turned out to be enough for one suitor, if not for his father. Martha must have made a good impression in her grown-up finery, because she was soon being courted by one of her neighbors, her godfather[3] and a man she had known all her life, Daniel Parke Custis, who was twenty-one years her senior and the richest bachelor in Virginia. Daniel was definitely a catch, and he and Martha were mutually attracted to each other. Their courtship was the stuff of a Tidewater fairy tale—the wooing of a pretty and deserving girl by a rich and handsome older man—but as in all fairy tales true love met an obstacle. Daniel's father, John Custis IV, did not approve of his son's choice. His violent opposition to the match stands out as one of the few instances in which anyone ever stood against Martha, and this was noteworthy, because for all his eccentricities, Daniel's father was an exceptionally clever, shrewd, and well-educated man. A difficult courtship followed in the face of his opposition, one that would have reduced a lesser girl to despair. But young as she was, Martha showed unexpected mettle for a teenager facing the wrath of one of the most influential and formidable men in the colony.

The Custises were one of the oldest families in Virginia. Though English, they had kept a well-known inn in Holland before immigrating to Virginia around 1640. Through hard work and prudent marriages they had amassed money, land and slaves, and a tobacco-growing empire to become one of the wealthiest and most powerful families in the Tidewater. But by the time Daniel Parke Custis came courting Martha Dandridge, the family had taken an odd turn.

In 1678, shortly after the Reverend Rowland Jones arrived to take up his pastoral duties at Bruton Parish Church, John Custis IV, a great-grandson of the first Virginia Custis, was born. John Custis IV's grandfather had left money earmarked for his grandson to be educated in England, which conferred a mark of great distinction in the colony. He also left him extensive property at a family estate named "Arlington" on the eastern shore (not to be confused with the later estate of Arlington that would be built by Martha's son near Mount Vernon in northern Virginia). By the time Daniel was courting Martha in the late 1740s, Colonel John Custis IV had acquired the reputation of being one of the most notoriously eccentric and difficult individuals in the colony. Daniel was terrified of his father, so much so that he was afraid at first to broach the subject of marrying Martha at all. The obstacles to the marriage had a long history, a chronicle of tempestuous family relationships and tangled fortunes that said much about the kinds of individuals who could flourish unchecked in the colony.

Daniel was the remarkably normal end product of several generations of what was, even by the robust standards of the colony, a rampantly dysfunctional family, though a very rich one. The turbulent relationships experienced by Daniel left him longing for nothing so much as a normal life, an aspiration complicated by the fact that he was heir to a fortune whose size was equaled only by the complex provisions of a will that rendered that fortune potentially precarious. Martha, with her amiable nature, her experience of stable family life at Chestnut Grove, and no fortune to speak of or to complicate matters further, must have looked like a refreshingly straightforward proposition, a calm port amidst the storms of the Custis family history.

Following his years of education in England, John Custis IV returned to Virginia and married Frances Parke, heiress to another great Virginia fortune. It was a miserably unhappy marriage. Frances had no knowledge or expectation of marital felicity and even as a girl was temperamental enough to discourage men who might otherwise have been attracted by her status as an heiress. By an unhappy coincidence, she was the daughter of the one person in the colony as rich as, but odder than, John Custis. This was the notorious Daniel Parke. At a young age Daniel Parke had scandalized Williamsburg with his bizarre and extreme behavior, on one occasion wreaking havoc during a church service:

> With a view to recommend himself to the Governor's favour, young Parke undertook a crusade against all friends of the College [i.e., William and Mary]. He abused and challenged to mortal combat Francis Nicholson, who was then, though Governor of Maryland, a member of the Board of Visitors and Governors of the Institution: and at length to vent his ill humour against Dr. Blair [a distinguished clergyman in Williamsburg] personally, whose gown protected him from challenges, he set up a claim to the pew in church where Mrs. Blair sat, and one Sunday with great fury and violence pulled her out of it in the presence of the minister and congregation, who were greatly scandalized at his violent and profane action.[4]

At seventeen Daniel Parke had married Jane Ludwell, but the marriage proved unhappy. Daniel Parke soon went abroad, abandoning his young wife, Jane, and two small daughters, Lucy and Frances. In England he attached himself to the Duke of Marlborough as an aide-de-camp and accompanied him at the battle of Blenheim. Daniel Parke was given the honor of carrying the news of the British victory back to Queen Anne, who at his request awarded him, in place of the customary £500 reward for such news, her own portrait in miniature. It came set in a locket circled with diamonds and accompanied by a further gift of a thousand guineas from the gratified queen.

Daniel Parke returned briefly to Virginia to visit his wife and daughters. On this occasion he was accompanied by his mistress, oddly referred to as "Cousin Brown" and their infant, Julius Caesar Parke. Soon Daniel decamped again, taking "Cousin Brown" with him but leaving Julius Caesar for his long-suffering wife Jane to bring up, though eventually Julius Caesar Parke was sent back to England.[5]

Daniel's daughters grew up at Queens Creek Plantation near Williamsburg, and on the same day in May 1706 that Frances married John Custis IV of Arlington, her sister Lucy married William Byrd II of Westover Plantation. The two grooms were both recently returned from being educated in England, where they had most likely been friends as fellow colonials. Both brides brought the promise of fortune, wealthy and influential family connections, and memories of an unhappy domestic life to their respective marriages.

John and Frances Parke Custis lived at Arlington. At first John had been an ardent lover when courting Frances. He wrote her love letters calling her his "Fidelia." On marriage, John's affection rapidly cooled. He had been warned by others before the marriage that Frances's temper was "little calculated to allow happiness," and he soon realized how accurate the warning had been. John and Frances became a famously unhappy couple in the colony. One contemporary anecdote records an outing in the family carriage, driven by John. John drove abruptly off the road and into Chesapeake Bay. The horses were practically swimming when Frances finally asked,

"Where are you going, Mr. Custis?"
"Straight to hell, Madam."
"Drive on, Mr. Custis, any life would be better than this."[6]

Realizing she was not frightened, John pulled up and the couple did not drown, but save for occasional interludes of marital peace, things got worse. Eventually relations between the couple deteriorated to the point that in 1714 a lengthy legal document was drawn up, which itself reflects the embattled state of their daily lives. In it Frances undertook to return John's money, plate, and other things she had taken from him, and promised to take nothing else and call him no more "vile names or use bad language" to him. For his part, John agreed not to abuse Frances and to give her half the profits from his estate to maintain her household. Both agreed, somewhat unconvincingly, to live "lovingly together and behave themselves as a good husband and wife ought to do."

Despite their differences, the Custises had four children. Two died in infancy, but a daughter, Fanny, and a son, Daniel, survived. In 1715, a year after their agreement to live together amicably, Frances died of smallpox when Daniel was four. Her sister Lucy Byrd would also die of smallpox a few years later in London. John Custis inherited his wife's property on Queens Creek, as well as her Parke inheritance from her father. Oddly, given their tempestuous marriage, John had Frances's portrait painted posthumously, ten years after her death, and lived mainly at her old home at Queens Creek.

Frances had lived long enough to pass on to her husband a tangled mess of an inheritance from her father. In 1709 Daniel Parke had reappeared in the Leeward Islands, where he had somehow inveigled an appointment as governor. In 1710 he was murdered in Antigua, being almost torn apart at the hands of a mob incensed by years of corrupt administration in general, and by Daniel Parke's having personally corrupted a number of their women in particular.

His will proved to be a legal minefield. The Parke inheritance was huge, but its confused provisions would drive John Custis and his heirs, including Daniel, Martha, and eventually George Washington, to distraction.

One of its more straightforward provisions was that no future heirs could ever inherit any part of the Parke fortune unless they bore the name of Parke. This accounts for the "Parke" that crops up confusingly in the names of so many people associated with Martha for the next three generations: for example, her husband, Daniel *Parke* Custis; her children John *Parke* Custis and Martha *Parke* Custis; grandchildren Eliza *Parke* Custis Law, and Nelly *Parke* Custis Lewis; and Nelly's daughter *Parke* Lewis.[7]

But it was another, ambiguous, provision, that led to immense complications over the Parke fortune and property and everyone connected with it. Daniel Parke left his extensive property in England and Virginia to his daughter Frances Parke Custis. In the eighteenth century a married woman's property automatically by law became the property of her husband, so Frances's inheritance from her father legally became the immediate property of John Custis. This mingled the Custis and Parke fortunes and, under normal circumstances, would simply have had the effect of making John Custis a richer man, subject to the just claims against the estate.

Both then and now, legally any person who is owed money by a deceased person has first claim for that preexisting debt against the dead person's estate. Some of the bequests in Daniel Parke's will were relatively straightforward, namely that his daughter Frances inherited his property in Virginia and Hampshire, England, but out of this property, the will required Frances to make a number of payments. Frances was to give her sister, Lucy, his only other legitimate child, the sum of £1,000, Julius Caesar Parke £50 annually, and the same to each of Julius Caesar's sisters and their children.

However, a problem arose with the wording of the customary clause about payment of Daniel Parke's just debts out of the estate assets. There was a provision requiring his "daughter Frances Custis pay out of my estate in Virginia and Hampshire all my legal debts and bequests." The fatal word "all" in relation to "legal debts and bequests" hung the sword of Damocles aloft over the Parke fortune and all would-be heirs to it, for the next three generations.

Daniel Parke had sowed wild oats far and wide, and a number of illegitimate offspring in England and Barbados soon made claims against his estate. He had also accumulated vast debts and yet another illegitimate family in the Leeward Islands. While an illegitimate daughter in the Leeward Islands named Lucy Chester inherited his property there, that property seems to have been heavily burdened with debts. It was unclear whether the term of the will requiring that Frances pay "all my legal debts and bequests," meant that the estate inherited by Frances in Virginia and England was responsible for the debts against the Leeward Islands property, so the husband and heirs of Lucy Chester took the matter to court. To complicate matters further, from England there came word of another man bearing the name of Parke and claiming to be Daniel's son and entitled to inherit as well. Given the life Daniel had led, anything was possible.

On the strength of the word "all," the vast Parke/Custis estate became mired in a Byzantine labyrinth of claims and counterclaims that would occupy lawyers on two continents for the next seventy years. This massive tangle of lawsuits was known collectively as "the Dunbar Suit," and when Frances Custis died in 1715, John Custis inherited the mess automatically with the rest of her estate. It plagued him for the rest of his life, and he worried incessantly about the financial drain of the lawyers' fees involved, both in the colony and in England.

He had cause to be worried about it, because if it was eventually determined that all claims everywhere had to be paid out of Frances Parke Custis's inheritance, the claims far exceeded the Parke/Custis assets. Wealthy as he was, John Custis lived with the knowledge that financial ruin was a distinct possibility. If the foreign claims were valid, they stood to wipe out the entire Parke inheritance and sweep the Custis fortune along with it. While there may have been a legal process available that could have extricated the Parke assets from those of the Custis assets for the purposes of satisfying any claims, this would have been a costly, complex, and time-consuming legal process in itself. The Parke/Custis fortune, while vast, was precarious so long as the Dunbar Suit litigation continued.

The Dunbar Suit dragged wearily on unresolved until finally the claimants either died or ran out of steam at about the time of the Revolution. However, it was very much a live issue when Daniel Parke Custis was courting Martha Dandridge and may have contributed to John Custis's concern that Martha was not a wealthy enough bride. The one way of "insuring" his son against ruin if the Dunbar Suit succeeded was to find a bride wealthy enough to have a substantial sum of her father's money "settled" on her at marriage. Although a married woman had no legal rights to her own property, which became her husband's on marriage, any money "settled" on her was a kind of trust fund, set up so that she, and not her husband, was legally entitled to the income. It was the only means of ensuring that a woman and her children would be provided for if her husband lost everything of his own. Of course, if a woman wished to share the income from this settlement with her husband, it was a matter for her to decide.

After his wife's unlamented death in 1714, John Custis refused to marry again, possibly because he had had enough of marriage. He diverted himself by building a handsome brick house in Williamsburg, called "Six Chimney House," and threw his energies into the garden he designed and cultivated there. This garden soon became the passion and pride of his life and the focus for all his intellectual abilities and creative and scientific interests. By the end of his life and despite his personal peculiarities, John Custis had become an accomplished horticulturist and botanist of note, experimenting with many varieties of plants and importing specimens from abroad. On them he lavished most of his time, interest, and attention, taking elaborate precautions to protect them in times of drought and noting carefully what conditions caused them to thrive or fail. He corresponded with two prominent horticulturalists in England, including distinguished London botanist Peter Collinson, comparing notes on new and unusual varieties and exchanging seeds and cuttings and interesting fossils. He cosseted his exotic seedlings and agonized if they died.

He remained a member of the council and alternated his time between Six Chimney House in Williamsburg and the property he had inherited from Frances at Queens Creek Plantation, her childhood home. He was in some ways devoted to his children Fanny and Daniel, once writing to a friend that they were all his happiness in the world and that he had not remarried for their sakes. But while he professed a desire to see them make grand dynastic marriages, in practice he did his best to prevent them from marrying at all.

As the elder, Fanny was the first to encounter her father's opposition in this respect. John Custis feared his daughter was an easy mark for fortune hunters, and subsequent events bore out his suspicions. Fanny was first courted by a ship's captain. The suitor then began to badger John Custis about the land and money he proposed to settle on Fanny. Custis suspected he was attracted only by the prospect of his daughter's fortune and declared that if she married him she would be cut off without a penny. The suitor disappeared.

The second man who sought Fanny's hand thought better of it two days before the wedding, when John Custis, again scenting a fortune hunter, reneged on the promise of Fanny's dowry. Fanny eventually married twice, in the teeth of her father's opposition, and was disinherited. There is little further known about Fanny, save that she died in 1744. But her unhappy example convinced her younger brother that their father would not hesitate to disinherit him as well if Daniel married without his approval.

At some stage Daniel had courted a "Miss Betty," a pursuit that came to nothing. Later there was talk of his marrying his cousin Evelyn Byrd, a few years older than he, the daughter of his aunt Lucy Byrd and William Byrd at Westover. That match foundered, either because Evelyn was in love with someone else or because John Custis could not agree on reasonable terms for a marriage settlement with his brother-in-law. Like her mother Lucy, Evelyn died of smallpox. William Byrd remarried, and attempts were made to arrange a match between Daniel and sixteen-year-old Annie Byrd, a daughter by Byrd's second wife. There is an entry in William Byrd's diary that on July 21, 1741, Daniel Parke Custis was at Westover: "Mr. Custis stayed and came with a design to make love to Annie."

After extensive negotiations between William Byrd and John Custis over the marriage settlement, that match again came to nothing. In November 1742 Maria Byrd, William's sister, wrote regretfully to Daniel:

My Dear Mr. Custis,

   I am heartily concerned that we could not bring your Father to agree to any Terms that were reasonable; for without a compliment I should (as you very well know) have preferred you, to any other match in the colony . . .

There could have been few more prestigious matches in the colony for Daniel than a daughter of William Byrd. The Byrds were not only as prominent, and nearly as wealthy, as the Custises, they had grander connections back in England. If all these factors could not induce John Custis to agree to the terms of a marriage settlement with his brother-in-law, with whom he had an extremely amicable relationship, what hope was there with another girl?

   Following the fiasco with Anne Byrd, a consoling letter from Daniel's close friend John Blair hints at Daniel's state of mind: "And my Dear Friend I will not yet despair to see you blest in a sweet Companion for life with all the Endearments that attend the State when most happy. But patience yet awhile."

   Five years later, in 1747, Daniel was thirty-seven, rather long in the tooth for a bachelor in a colony where everyone who had the means tended to marry young. He still longed to marry and have his own family but despaired of ever being allowed to do so. He lived a lonely single existence, managing the Custis plantation at White House in New Kent and occasionally making the journey into Williamsburg. John Custis alternated between the home at Queens Creek and Williamsburg. John Custis was not exactly mellowing with age, and his health had begun to fail, which shortened his temper even further. There was an extraordinary outburst in the spring of 1747, when Daniel informed his father that the slaves at White House needed shoes. John Custis flew into a rage and expressed it in a peculiar way.

   John Custis had a favorite child by a slave referred to only as "young Alice," a little boy also named John but called Jack, and also known as Mulatto Jack. Because his mother was a slave, Mulatto Jack inherited her slave status. John Custis was extremely fond of this child, and in that society had few ways in which to show it. One was to acknowledge paternity by having the child baptized. Also, light-skinned mulatto slaves were often used as house servants, which provided some scope for favorable treatment, such as better accommodation, food, clothing, and privileged status as a personal servant. This happened at Monticello, where guests of Thomas Jefferson reported being startled to look up and see a mulatto slave with Jefferson's features serving at the table. John Custis went a step further.

   Irritated out of all proportion either by Daniel or the request for shoes, John Custis made the unusual gesture of freeing Mulatto Jack, by a deed of manumission, though by law, between 1723–1782, a slave could be freed in

"Col. John Custis IV," by an unknown American artist. Courtesy of Washington and Lee University.

Virginia only by special acts of the governor and the council for "meritori-ous service." Jack was probably too young to qualify as having performed meritorious service, and there was no evidence of the requisite special act. As a result the deed of manumission was probably invalid.

A month later John Custis made Mulatto Jack a gift of a tract of land near Queens Creek, which had once belonged to Frances, as well as mak-ing him a gift of his own mother, "young Alice," and four other slaves. He may have also drawn up a will leaving everything to Jack. Daniel must have protested furiously about this use of his late mother's property, and friends may have remonstrated, because the will leaving everything to Jack was rescinded and the deed to the tract of land was withdrawn.

Still, the incident must have shaken him. If a request for shoes for his father's slaves provoked such an extreme reaction, Daniel was at a loss as to how to bring up the subject of Martha. So, he procrastinated, with unfor-tunate results.

John Custis was enraged when he eventually heard rumors—probably by 1748—that Daniel was courting Martha Dandridge without his consent.

By this time John Custis's behavior had become increasingly odd. In addition to his tantrum when Daniel requested shoes for the slaves at White House, he had also begun giving away possessions on a whim, on one occasion giving away fifteen young slaves between the ages of two and twenty, on other occasions parting with sizable tracts of land.

The news that Daniel was courting Martha Dandridge triggered all of John Custis's latent suspicions about fortune hunters. Either despite the fact that he had known John Dandridge as a neighbor and fellow vestryman in New Kent for years, or because of it, John Custis did not like John Dandridge, and he now extended this dislike to Martha. The Dandridges' main fault seems to have been that they were neither grand enough nor rich enough for their daughter to marry his only son. To anyone looking at the match as a dispassionate outsider, Martha's main attraction for Daniel must have been her very normality, her good nature, and the fact that marriage to her would offer a haven of domestic comfort to a man whose own parents had ended up communicating through their slaves and their lawyers. The couple had also known each other since Martha was a baby, and while it was undoubtedly an advantageous match for Martha, it seems to have been a love match on both sides. This was not a consideration that swayed John Custis.

John Custis was not a man to keep his feelings to himself, and he went out of his way to broadcast them in Williamsburg. He made public and uncomplimentary remarks about Martha and her father, which must soon have been repeated all over town. He gave away many valuable possessions to an innkeeper's wife named Mrs. Moody, who may have also been his mistress. These included a vast quantity of crested Custis silver, a dozen black walnut chairs, a dozen pewter plates, silver buttons and rings, a roan horse and chair harness, a silver tankard, and gold shoe buckles inscribed "In Memory of John Custis." When she protested that perhaps he ought to give these items to Daniel, Custis called her an old fool and said that if she would not take them he would throw them in the streets of Williamsburg rather than let "John Dandridge's daughter" have them. So the Moodys displayed the silver prominently, and the message would not have been lost on anyone in Williamsburg. It must have been humiliating for Martha and her whole family.

As a final insult, John Custis let it be known publicly that if Daniel married Martha against his wishes, he would be disinherited. With poor Fanny's example before him, Daniel had every reason to believe this threat. This was bad enough, but John Custis added a sting in the tail by threatening to leave everything he had to Mulatto Jack.

By the late 1740s freeing a slave was regarded as a dangerously antisocial act in a colony where over a quarter of the inhabitants were slaves. Unless strictly controlled, slaves in their hostile numbers represented a serious threat. The first serious slave conspiracy was recorded in Virginia in 1663, a concerted effort by slaves and disaffected white servants. In 1712 there had been a slave revolt in New York, in which nine whites had been killed. Eighteen slaves were executed in the most brutal ways possible—burned alive, broken on the wheel, or otherwise tortured to death. In 1730 a slave conspiracy came to light in Norfolk and Princess Anne Counties in Virginia, and in 1739 eighty slaves in Stono, South Carolina, took up arms and attempted to flee to Florida to join the Spanish, who were at war with England. They were overtaken by armed whites, and in the ensuing battle forty-four blacks and twenty-one whites were killed. In 1741 New York experienced a wave of suspicious fires that were attributed to a slave conspiracy. These failed revolts always ended in large numbers of slaves being burned at the stake and hanged.

In this uneasy atmosphere Virginia, with a far higher ratio of slaves to white inhabitants, was a racial tinderbox. In New Kent County, the slaves made up half, and possibly more than half, of the population.[8] If they were a threat, their sheer numbers made them a significant one. The wealth of the colony in general and the tobacco planters (who made up the council and the house of burgesses) depended on maintaining the slave system that, within the space of a few generations, had become firmly enshrined in, and regulated by, law. An irregular manumission was not a precedent Virginia slave owners would have wished to encourage, but even so, Jack's "manumission" might have been tolerated as another of John Custis's oddities, provided it had been kept quiet. Instead, typically, John Custis had to throw it in everyone's face. What would have alarmed everyone was the prospect that a former slave might inherit property or wealth. Runaways were certain to gravitate to a freed slave who owned property, and in addition to furnishing a haven for disaffected slaves, putting wealth in his hands might enable him to obtain weapons and thus arm the runaways.

Feeling powerless to change his father's mind, in the spring of 1749 Daniel turned to his friends John Blair and Thomas Lee. They wanted to help, but their motives would have been mixed. Like practically everyone else, they would have viewed manumission and empowerment of slaves as dangerous. The best solution would be to help Daniel get his father's approval to marry Martha. Blair and Lee believed things had gotten off to a bad start with John Custis hearing rumors about the engagement rather than hearing it from Daniel himself. They advised Daniel that it was better late than never to approach his father directly on the subject, and they promised to support him.

It could hardly have reassured Martha that her fiancé was still too terrified of his father to mention the subject of their marriage, and that despite his friends' advice, Daniel continued to vacillate. It must have looked hopeless for a time. His friends suggested the alternative of marrying first and obtaining his father's consent later. Daniel was afraid to risk it. Blair arranged to spend the night at John Custis's house and tried to talk him round, with no success. Shortly afterwards, another friend, attorney James Power, had more success at playing Cupid. He too arranged to stay the night at Custis's mansion, and by exercising his persuasive powers as a lawyer and a well-judged gift to Mulatto Jack of a horse, saddle, and bridle (all of which were actually the property of Power's own small son) in Daniel's name, in the course of an evening he managed to effect a complete change in John Custis's mind. Astonished at his own success, Powers wrote the good news to Daniel at once:

> Dear Sir:
>
> This comes at last to bring you the news that I believe will be the most agreeable to you of any you have ever heard—that you may not be long in suspense I shall tell you at once—I am empowered by your father to let you know that he heartily and willingly consents to your marriage with Miss Dandridge that he has so good a character of her, that he had rather you should have her than any lady in Virginia nay, if possible, he is as much enamored with her character as you are with her person, and this is owing to a prudent speech of her own. Hurry down immediately for fear he should change the strong inclination he has to your marrying directly. I stayed with him all night, and presented Jack with my Jack's horse, bridle and Saddle in your name, which was taken as a singular favor. I shall say no more as I expect too see you soon tomorrow, but conclude what I really am,
>
> Your most obliged and affectionate humble servant
J. Power[9]

Having expressed himself robustly on his views of Martha's unworthiness, logic suggests it would have taken a fairly extraordinary "prudent speech" on Martha's part to impress John Custis. It would be interesting to know what the "prudent speech" of Martha's was that had such an effect. Though we can never know for sure, from what is known of his one great passion at the time, the only thing likely to have swayed him in Martha's favor may have had something to do with gardening. Martha was a gardener herself, and it may be that Martha's prudent speech was simply a sound piece of gardening advice. It is equally possible that John Power passed on a piece of gardening advice and attributed it to Martha. Whatever it was that persuaded him to agree, later developments suggest John Custis regretted his change of heart.

Opinions vary as to whether Martha and Daniel struck while the iron was hot and married immediately in May 1749 or waited a year, until May 1750. In May of 1749, Frances Jones was heavily pregnant with her seventh child and may have been unable to deal with a wedding. Soon after giving consent to the marriage, John Custis's health began to fail. He resigned his seat on the Governor's Council in August 1749. On November 14 he made his final will and died on November 22. In addition to Frances's condition, his worsening health may have caused the happy couple to postpone the wedding. During this period the Dandridge family was also mourning the death of Martha's teenage brother John, who died in July 1749.

The Custis-Lee family Bible records that the wedding took place on Tuesday May 15, 1750, with the service performed by the Reverend Chichely Gordon Thacker according to the marriage service of the Church of England. Wash's account of the affair disagreed about the date and dealt in veiled terms with John Custis's opposition to the match: "Miss Dandridge was married to Colonel Daniel Parke Custis, of the White House, county of New Kent. This was a match of affection. The father of the bridegroom, The Honorable John Custis, of Arlington, a kings counsellor, had matrimonial views of a more ambitious character for his only son and heir; and was desirous of a connection with the Byrd family, of Westover, Colonel Byrd being, at that time, almost a count palatine of Virginia."[10]

Though it was not specifically recorded that Martha and Daniel were married at Chestnut Grove, it is probable the wedding was there and not in St. Peter's Church. In England weddings had to take place in a church, but in the colony weddings normally took place at the bride's home, for several reasons. Churches in the colony were few and far between, and it was the custom for guests to gather at the bride's home to celebrate. It was on the one hand a simple matter of convenience, in that it spared guests likely to have traveled from far away a second journey. Given that the guests would have seen a wedding as a chance to air their imported finery on the occasion, and roads were likely to be dusty or knee-deep in mud, it made sense for everyone to gather in one place and stay there for the festivities. A plantation wedding could go on for days. There was also a subtle cachet attached to the fact that the bride had a home from which to be married. This nuance lingers today in the South, where a "home wedding" remains something of a social coup.

As Wash continued, "The counsellor having at length given his consent to the marriage of his son with Miss Dandridge, they were married. They settled at the White House, on the banks of the Pamunkey River, where Colonel Custis became an eminently successful planter."

The tone is that of a Tidewater fairy tale, with a curmudgeonly parent giving way in the face of love. Daniel could at last look forward to life with his "sweet Companion" without being disinherited. Martha had married for love and made a brilliant match. She remained close to her family. All their friends and relations must have felt the couple was starting out with every advantage, both of affection and of worldly goods. Surely with John Custis gone, there could be little to mar the future prospects of Martha and Daniel.

CHAPTER 3

The Young Matron and Her Family

Martha's new home was older than Chestnut Grove, a few miles further west and several bends of the river further inland along the Pamunkey. It was built by a local family, the Lightfoots, around 1700. John Custis acquired it around 1735. It was built of wood with brick foundations and was probably a larger house than Chestnut Grove when Martha came to it as a bride. Between 1700 and its ultimate destruction by fire in the nineteenth century, the house suffered fire damage and was rebuilt and added to on several occasions. A sketch of White House as it is believed to have looked when Martha and Daniel lived there shows a frame house that resembles Chestnut Grove in many respects. Like Chestnut Grove, it was built to serve a functional purpose as the focus of the plantation, and not to impress.

Since 1735 White House had been Daniel's bachelor's quarters when he acted as his father's plantation manager, and it had not had a mistress for years. An inventory of the furnishings of White House carried out seven years after the marriage suggests that when Martha arrived as a bride it still had the distinct air of a bachelor's quarters.

Even allowing for the fact that some of the items listed in the inventory of 1758 must have been acquired after the marriage, Martha arrived to find her new home crammed with a haphazard accumulation of household goods and functional items. The inventory listed beds, tables, tea chests, candlesticks, fire tongs, warming pans, easy chairs, bedsteads, and dressing mirrors, together with old cups, earthenware, an assortment of men's hats, sugar boxes, smoothing irons, bedding, plate baskets, razor cases, firearms, and kitchen utensils and equipment, plus huge bolts of cloth and some paper. There were surprisingly few objects of value. There was a modest assortment of silver: two tankards, six candlesticks, tea things, and some spoons and serving dishes. There were also "41 table cloaths."[1]

"White House Plantation home of Martha Dandridge Custis and Daniel Parke Custis." Courtesy of the Virginia Historical Society.

It is unlikely the house and its contents were a picture of colonial elegance. Instead, they bring to mind the kind of modern-day garage used for storing the accumulated "odds and ends" a family cannot bring themselves to get rid of—unread magazines, half-empty paint cans, broken furniture, and Granny's collection of jelly glasses. In Martha's day, when functional items usually came from England and were considered precious, people were reluctant to dispose of them even if worn or broken.

However, the couple also had the use of the handsome Six Chimney House in Williamsburg with the ornamental garden, which had been John Custis's passion, but it seems they did not use it often, preferring the clutter of White House. The Williamsburg house contained many of the finer objects amassed by the Custis family over the generations: handsome furniture, paintings, and John Custis's collection of hand-blown wineglasses, though most of the crested Custis silver remained with the Moodys.

The life at White House was comfortable but not idle. Martha assumed the role of plantation mistress for which her mother had trained her. Even though she was married to one of the richest men in the Tidewater, Martha was a busy woman. Food preparation consumed a large part of her time. A valuable tool in her domestic armory was a handwritten cookbook she inherited on her marriage. The book must have been one of her treasured possessions, because she later gave it to her favorite granddaughter Nelly Custis when Nelly married in 1799. The cookbook has since been republished under the slightly misleading title *Martha Washington's Booke of Cookery and Booke of Sweetmeats.*[2] In fact the cookbook had belonged to Martha's late mother-in-law, Frances Parke Custis and had probably been written in England.

The recipes are very much in the English tradition of housewifery of the preceding 150 years. The spelling, grammar, and ways of preparing food reflect a style of cooking traceable to Tudor times. Some drew on more ancient traditions and superstitions, like the grisly recipe for a restorative called "Red Cock Water," which begins with plucking a live red cockerel, beating it nearly to death, and cutting it up while it is still breathing. Altogether it is a revealing document, both about domestic life and the English traditions of cookery and housekeeping that the early settlers brought over and adapted to life in the colonies.

Other recipes have a familiar ring today: meat hashes, roasts, custards, cakes, pastry, meat and fish pies, spiced gingerbread, pancakes, and fritters. Some are exotic: almond butter, syrup of violets, elder and rose vinegar, mint cakes, pickled broomebuds or a method to "to keep neats [beef] tongues and dry them," while some would make a modern reader faintly queasy, such as recipes for stewed sparrow, baking mutton in blood, or "a Calues [calf's] head Pio." In addition to methods of food preparation, including possets, broths, pickles, marmalets, and dried fruit, it contains recipes for a variety of things for which a housewife or plantation mistress was responsible: cordials, restoratives, medicines, powders, ointments, perfumes, tooth-cleaning powder, herb and flower oils, hair pomatum, and an appealing recipe "to make sweet water to perfume cloaths in the foulding after they are washed."

The editor of a 1940 edition of this cookbook clearly appreciated the kinds of cooking skills Martha and other girls would have needed to learn in order to cook or smoke food to preserve it, living as they did in a place where the plentiful supply of meat and fish meant a diet was based on meat—from domestic beef, pork, and chicken to wild turkey, ducks, deer, other game, river fish, and shellfish from the coast. There were many people to feed, and no way to know from one day to the next how many unexpected guests might arrive, and there was no refrigeration in a climate that was hot seven months of the year. Icehouses were a later development, and though the Tidewater is cold in winter, it did not have the kind of hard freeze that would have produced huge slabs of ice. Instead there was often a "dry well," precisely what it sounds like, deep and cool and dry, for storing milk, butter, cream, and cheese, or, if there was a spring, a shaded springhouse. Fresh meat and fish spoil easily and could make everyone violently ill, incapacitate the workforce, and possibly kill. Unless hams, bacon, and other cured meats were thoroughly smoked, salted, dried, and protected from flies, they would become infested with maggots. Under the circumstances, food preparation and preservation were both an art and a science.

The editor, Marie Kimball, wrote:

> The cooking was carried on under conditions that would seem to us to present insurmountable difficulties. Stoves of course were unknown, and everything—stewing, boiling, broiling and baking—was accomplished in the huge fireplace. In it were the hangers to which the pots and kettles were hung by the pothooks and roasting spit. Near at hand were the countless implements employed by the cook of the period: pot racks, spit racks, a Dutch oven. . . .
>
> Cumbersome and difficult as the cooking method of Martha Washington's day seem to us, they presented no difficulties to the housewife of the period . . . she knew however, many things that have been lost to us. She knew that fire was not just fire and heat not just heat. She knew what flavor would be imparted by the smoke of hickory, pine, sassafras, red or white oak, and even the humble corn cob. She knew which woods would produce a quick fire and which a lazy one.[3]

Although her daily routine and home at White House were similar to her mother's at Chestnut Grove, the fact that Martha had married "up" was marked by the fact the White House "family" for whom she was now responsible included house slaves to assist her—waiters, a cook, a seamstress, and housemaids. Her duties now included overseeing production of many raw ingredients for household consumption in the kitchen and herb garden, poultry yard, and dairy. It took the work of many hands to produce what had to be grown and harvested (fruits, vegetables, grain, herbs); raised (sheep, cows, pigs, chickens); caught (fish and shell fish); shot (game); or imported at great expense calculated in pounds of tobacco (sugar, spices, currants, citrus fruits, and alcohol such as rum or brandy), before their often complex preparation could begin.

It staggers the modern mind to think of the hours of labor represented by a simple meal of cold ham, bread, butter, and pickles, the kind of thing that sounds easy to get on the table at the drop of a hat for unexpected company: a pig reared and slaughtered; ham salted and smoked hard as a board to discourage pests, then soaked to rehydrate it, scrubbed again to remove excess salt, simmered to soften, baked for hours, and then cooled before slicing; the bread dough mixed, the slow rising, baking, glazing and cooling; cows milked, cream skimmed, butter churned, salted, shaped into pats and kept cool; cucumbers grown, picked, and washed, the pickle crocks scrubbed, the brine prepared, the salting, storing in the cellar or springhouse against spoilage.

Since many methods of smoking, drying, or preserving food meant using salt or precious sugar and spices, Martha doled out what was necessary and oversaw its use. She also had to make use of whatever was plentiful in any given season. Pigs could be butchered for curing as ham and bacon only when the weather turned cold. In the spring game is too lean after the winter and is at its best after a summer's worth of fattening. Fish were available year-round. Martha had to make sure basics like cornmeal, the staple of the slaves' diet, and flour were kept dry and protected from pests, root vegetables stored properly, fruits and vegetables dried, and sugar used with an eye to economy.

Food stores, especially expensive commodities like tea, coffee, sugar, spices, and citrus fruits, were kept under lock and key. Slaves often stole to supplement their meager rations. A plantation mistress kept a careful note of what food would be served to family and guests and as well as doling out weekly food allowances to the slaves on her own plantation. Commonly this was a peck of cornmeal, called "Indian meal," per adult slave and less for children, with a measure of salt and some lard or fat. Sometimes slaves were given, or allowed to grow, vegetables and given a little salt meat. Slaves might also supplement their diets by trapping game or catching fish. Household slaves were probably given some table scraps, at least, but hungry slaves were adept at filching from the kitchen.

If the wider White House "family," including slaves and indentured servants, enjoyed relatively few of the dishes in Martha's cookbook, they were liberally dosed with its medicines. The housewife with her pharmacopoeia of herbal medicines and remedies was the first port of call in a medical emergency for most inhabitants on the plantation, save for slaves on outlying plantations who might be treated by an overseer. Doctors were few and far between in the colony, often untrained, and usually no better at treating ailments. They were a port of last resort and prone to bleed everyone for everything. Slaves and servants had an economic value, and the plantation mistress had to do her best to keep them capable of work. Claiming illness was one of the weapons in a slave's limited armory of resistance. Plantation owners often bemoaned the fact that their slaves were prone to malingering as a way to avoid work.

White House probably produced some cloth, and Martha would have been responsible for overseeing the operation. It was common at most plantations to spin wool and flax into thread and make enough cloth for some of the slaves' clothing. Making cloth was a laborious process, whether from flax or wool. Wool, for example, had to be greased and combed to make it flexible enough to spin into yarn. Once the cloth was made, there was the job of cutting and sewing it into the slaves' clothing. Slaves were usually issued the most basic items—a shift for women and pants and a shirt for men. Once or twice a year the mistress would supervise the cutting out of all the slaves' clothes and their being sewn into garments.

Slaves were usually issued a set of winter clothes each year. If they were lucky, they had shoes as well, either bought cheaply in bulk by the planter or sometimes made by a resident slave shoemaker. Both clothing and shoes for slaves were of a rough variety, and labeled "slave shoes" or "slave cloth." Occasionally there were "slave blankets." A house slave might be given a worn-out item of clothing belonging to the planter's family. House slaves often received additional clothing to enable them to make a better appearance in the house.

When not otherwise occupied with activities related to food, the kitchen garden, and other household tasks, Martha spent a good deal of her time sewing or teaching her slaves to sew. Martha was known all her life for her exquisite needlework. She must have must have done much of the sewing, both plain and fancy, at White House, stitching quilts and bedding and attending to some of the mending and darning. She also supervised the laundry, a time-consuming chore, which in those days involved much boiling and bleaching and homemade soap. Martha would have overseen the making of both soap and candles.

If having slaves in the house spared Martha having to do many tasks herself, it was her responsibility to see that the slaves performed their allotted tasks, and she performed an active managerial role in making sure they did their work properly. Since slaves were understandably inclined to work as little as possible and given to claiming illness, her reputation for domestic efficiency begs the question of exactly what means the young bride employed to establish her authority in a house where the slaves had not had a mistress for years. Martha's households famously ran like clockwork.

Though White House was not grand, Daniel and Martha maintained a lavishly sociable lifestyle that called for plenty of new clothes. Daniel was a generous husband and placed extensive orders for clothing, shoes, gloves, and dressmaking materials for Martha: linen, calico, brocades and "tabby," a kind of silk, allowing Martha to indulge her taste for pretty outfits to wear to events that made up social life in the country—balls, fish fries, christenings, weddings, dinners, and horse races.

Daniel also ordered for Martha what was for the time a rare and extravagant gift. It was a watch, made to Daniel's order in London, and the charm of the concept must have reflected the happiness he found in his marriage. Contained in a gold case, the watch face was a circle of white enamel edged and backed in gold. Over each number on the face was a letter of Martha's name, so the twelve hours of the day and night spelled M.A.R.T.H.A.C.U.S.T.I.S.

Happily married to a wealthy, steady older man and ensconced in her new home, Martha appeared to be one of the most fortunate young women in the colony. Behind the scenes however, there were a few clouds on the horizon. Some involved perennial problems that beset most planters in Virginia, and others involved wills. Both put Daniel under pressure.

First of all Daniel had to deal with the usual problems attending estate management on a much larger scale than previously. As a planter's daughter Martha was familiar with these and could understand and sympathize with her husband's difficulties. He had been managing the business side of White House plantation for his father for years but had now inherited plantations in other parts of New Kent, King William, King and Queen, York, and Northampton Counties, a total of more than 17,000 acres where he grew and exported grain and tobacco. Daniel had over two hundred slaves in the fields, who were kept hard at work and productive by overseers, prevented from running away, and advertised for and recovered if they somehow managed to abscond. Daniel also had to oversee his overseers, who were often drunkards and at worst sadistic bullies who controlled the slaves by terror. A planter wanted efficiency, but if a slave died it was a lost investment, and overseers had to be watched closely to prevent them from killing slaves in the exercise of their duties.

Like all planters Daniel shipped his crops to London for sale. Vast though the Custis estate was, he and other planters of his generation were beginning to experience the drawbacks of colonial dependence on trade with the mother country, and they could not afford to be complacent. By English law, the colonists were forbidden to trade directly with a third country or to ship produce on non-English ships, so that in order to sell tobacco, grain, or other commodities produced in Virginia, planters like Daniel had to conduct all their business through England, and someone in the English chain of agents, shippers and merchants took a cut at every stage.

Planters paid for the shipping and insurance of their crops to England, where import duty was charged on entry. In England firms of "factors" on retainer for the planter received and undertook to sell the crops, and these factors took a percentage of the sale price. If the goods, such as tobacco, were reexported to another country, the shipping, handling, and insurance costs of reexport were also paid for by the planters. The factors were often the owners of the ships and the insurers, so they were paid several times over.

The factors also acted as the planters' bank in England. Once they had sold the crops, they applied the money to previous outstanding debts on the planters' accounts and held the balance on account to offset the costs of goods, commodities, and luxuries the planters ordered from England. The factors were responsible for seeing that the orders were filled, and since there was little domestic production in the colonies, or intercolony trade, the planters' orders to their factors were lengthy, ranging from carriages and bridles to farm equipment, medicines, laundry bluing, fine clothing, toys, sweets, and musical instruments. The factors also lent money against the expected return on the next year's crops, by filling orders and charging them, at interest, against the planters' accounts.

There was always risk that the planters' produce would never reach England or that the orders placed in England would never make it back to the colonies, due to the constant risk of shipwreck, pirates, or privateers. Finally, the English goods shipped back to the colonies were not subject to any form of quality control, and the system allowed unscrupulous merchants to pawn off their most inferior merchandise on the Virginia planters.

The system was skewed uncontrollably and very profitably in the favor of the English factors and merchants because everyone knew the colonial planters had no alternative. Fraud was rife, and the colonists complained to no avail. In order to maintain a standard of living as well as to replace farm equipment, invest in expansion, and service past debts, planters had to increase production. Even then they could easily fall into debt, borrowing against the next year's crops, which sometimes failed due to bad weather or poor growing conditions.

Given that their most profitable crop was tobacco, this was a double bind. The colony's fortunes in the seventeenth century, like those of the Parkes and the Custises, had been built on tobacco, but tobacco gradually wears out the land. By the eighteenth century the profit margins were diminishing. From London factors wrote complaining of the low quality of produce that fetched lower and lower prices, while the price, if not the quality, of English goods ordered by the planters rose.

The kinds of worries that were the usual planter's lot were compounded by the fact that following his father's death, Daniel was now burdened with two accursed wills. The primary worry was the Dunbar Suit, which Daniel had inherited. His Virginia lawyers James Power and John Mercer continued to represent the Custis interests in Virginia, but he also had to retain lawyers in England to deal with the English aspects of the case. While legal fees mounted on two continents, Daniel's lawyers took a pessimistic view of the final outcome, but Daniel had little option but to contest the claims made by the various descendants of Daniel Parke, because the entire Custis property stood to be wiped out to satisfy foreign debts if the Dunbar Suit succeeded. The lawyers anticipated the case would run for a long time.

The combined effect of these pressures, after years of trying to stay on the right side of his overbearing father, took its toll on Daniel's health. Following John Custis's death in 1749, Daniel was appointed to his father's seat on the Governor's Council. It was an honor and an influential office, but Daniel declined it on health grounds.

The pressure on Daniel mounted. By the spring of 1751 nineteen-year-old Martha was pregnant, and since Daniel was the last of the Custises, the prospect of an heir was a welcome one. However, the happy prospect raised issues about preserving the estate and the Custis property for the next generation. Given the short life expectancy in the colony, the matter of preserving family assets to pass on to the next generation was an important one.

A planter never knew when he or his wife might die, but there was a grim consolation in knowing his children or other heirs would benefit. Eighteen months after John Custis's death and on the threshold of starting a family of her own, Martha continued to feel the lingering malevolence of her late father-in-law.

The Moodys remained a source of irritation. They retained valuable property given to them by Daniel's father, including the family silver, furniture, and jewelry. With the birth of their first child imminent, in 1751 Daniel brought an action in the Williamsburg court to recover the property, but it backfired. The Moodys' evidence about the circumstances under which John Custis had given them the various items of valuable property simply opened old wounds. The Moodys protested that the items had been gifts and, moreover in their defense, publicized what John Custis had said about Martha at the time he made them:

> That he had rather the Defendt. (the Moodys) should have them than any Dandridge's Daughter or any Dandridge that ever wore a head he said he had not been at Work all his Life time for Dandridges daughter alluding as this Deft. understood to be a Daughter of Mr. John Dandridge of New Kent County to whom the complainant as this Deft. heard about that Time was making his addresses by way of Courtship for which Match this Deft. had at several Times heard the sd: John Custis express a very great Dislike imagining as the Defent. had understood that the sd: Mr. Dandridge's Daughter was much inferior to his Son the Complaint. in point of fortune.[4]

The Moodys were bad enough, but John Custis's will was another source of trouble in the early part of Martha's marriage, almost as if he had reached out a cold and malevolent hand from the grave. The timing of the will is as curious as its ultimate consequences.

John Custis had given his consent to the marriage of Daniel and Martha in April 1749 and, by the end of the summer of 1749, was in declining health. In November 1749 he made his final will and died a week later, at the end of that month. Though it is known the couple married in May, it has never been determined whether they were married in 1749 or 1750. Either way, John Custis's will was designed to cause maximum distress and have an impact on the marriage.

If Daniel and Martha were married in May of 1749, the terms of a will made six months *after* the wedding suggest that a closer acquaintance with his daughter-in-law had not reconciled him to the match and that he regretted giving his approval for it. However, if Martha and Daniel were married in 1749, the complications arising from the will would not have impinged on their married life until nearly a year after the wedding, when the will was probated in April 1750. On the other hand, if Martha and Daniel did not marry until May 1750, they would have begun married life under a cloud as soon as the dust settled from the wedding.

There were two provisions, which could have been dictated only by malice toward Daniel and Martha. They were not accidental, or the result of careless drafting. No one had a better appreciation for the consequences of poorly or imprecisely drafted wills than John Custis had acquired in his experience of the Dunbar Suit, and if he had forgotten, there were plenty of people to remind him. He counted prominent Williamsburg lawyers among his close friends and also had contacts with lawyers in England. The inescapable conclusion is that John Custis used his will as a means of revenge on the son who defied him and the daughter-in-law he disliked to the last.

The will specified that Daniel would be cut off with only one shilling if he failed to comply fully with the first odd provision. John Custis had been quite specific about what was to be done with his remains. Even in death John Custis wanted to keep his distance from his wife, Frances, who had died of smallpox in 1714 and been buried at Queens Creek in the family graveyard there. Her tombstone contained no reference to her husband and was simply inscribed:

> Here lies the Body of
> Frances Custis, daughter of Daniel Parke Esq:
> Who Departed this Life March the 14th 1714/5 in the 29th Year
> Of Her Age

John specified he wanted his "real dead body"—begging the question what he thought the alternatives might have been—to be buried beside his grandfather at Arlington plantation on the Eastern Shore, beneath a tombstone ordered from England. The tombstone was to cost £100, be made of the best white marble, and be carved with the Custis arms and the following inscription:

> Under this Marble Stone lyes the Body
> of the Honourable John Custis Esq.,
> of the City of Williamsburg
> And Parish of Bruton,
> Formerly of Hungars Parish On The
> Eastern Shore
> Of Virginia, and County of Northampton
> Aged 71 Years and Yet Lived But Seven Years
> Which was the Space of Time He Kept
> A Bachelors Home at Arlington
> On the Eastern Shore of Virginia
> This Inscription Put on His Tomb Was By
> His Own Positive Orders[5]

The will went on to say that if the tombstone should be lost in transit his executor—Daniel—should order another. The peevish inscription was clearly intended to upset Daniel by flinging a final insult at his mother Frances, suggesting life had ceased upon marrying her. Frances herself was obviously past caring, and her daughter Fanny, her sister Lucy, and her mother were dead. That left only her son Daniel as the person likely to be affected by the sentiments expressed on the monument.

While Daniel inherited most of his father's estate, among the other bequests he was obliged to carry out were a gift of Mulatto Jack's portrait and £20 annually to Anne Moody, which must have made Daniel gnash his teeth, £200 to Thomas Lee, and £100 to John Blair. Five guineas were left to Mrs. Blair to buy a mourning ring, a common bequest. Another friend, John Cavendish, was to keep the house and land where he had been John Custis's tenant.

The worst provision however, concerned Daniel's half brother, Mulatto Jack. Jack's—probably invalid—manumission was confirmed in the will and he was liberally provided for:

> And whereas by my deed of manumission . . . I have freed and set at liberty my negro boy christened John, otherwise called Jack. . . . My will and desire is that as soon as possible after my decease my executor build on the said land . . . situated near the head of Queen's creek . . . for the use of the said John otherwise called Jack, a handsome, strong, convenient dwelling house according to the dimensions I shall direct, and a plan thereof drawn by my said friend John Blair Esq., and that it be completely finished within side and without, and when the house is completely finished it is my will that the same be furnished with one dozen high Russia leather chairs, one dozen low Russia chairs, a Russia leather couch, good and strong, three good feather beds, bedsteads and furniture and two good black walnut tables. I desire that the houses, fencing and other appurtenances belonging to the said plantation be kept in good repair and so delivered to the said John . . . when he shall arrive to the age of twenty years. I also give to him when he shall arrive to that age a good riding horse and two young able working horses . . . It is my will and desire that my said Negro boy John . . . live with my son until he be twenty years of age, and that he be handsomely maintained out of the profits of my estate given him.

As noted earlier, Jack had already been "given" his mother, Alice, and four of his uncles.

From the perspective of the twenty-first century John Custis's attempt to free Jack and leave him property looks like a commendable effort to do the right thing. But to Daniel, Martha, and everyone they knew, it was an alarmingly illegal, provocative, and dangerous act. It raised a host of conflicting considerations, legal and otherwise. Planters would have regarded this as a deeply dangerous and undesirable precedent—had it been legal. In a society whose worst nightmare was the long-dreaded slave rebellion, freeing a slave and providing him with an estate and a means of financing the purchase of weapons created the opportunity for runaway slaves to arm themselves and plot an uprising.

Just how large a threat freed slaves, with grievances to settle, posed can be measured by the legislation designed to eliminate their presence in the colony. By 1691 the assembly was passing increasingly harsh measures to control slaves, and a slave could be whipped, mutilated, or even killed with impunity for any perceived infringement of discipline, but the arch crime was running away. In cases of runaway slaves, planters and the authorities were positively encouraged to punish offenders with a brutality that would discourage other slaves from absconding. The measures gave the white population carte blanche to treat slaves any way they saw fit—if slaves died in the process there were no legal sanctions for their murder.

The laws had simultaneously tightened restrictions on the right of masters to free their slaves. The last thing the colony wanted was a restless, landless, disaffected, and deeply hostile body of former slaves roaming the countryside out of control, settling scores. As it was, there was already a problem with escaped slaves who stole livestock, set fires, and joined forces with the few remaining enclaves of Native Americans holed up in the most inaccessible swamps and backwoods.

By 1691 the law limited an owner's right to manumit any of his human property, as sometimes happened in the case of an exceptionally favored slave. After 1691, a slave could be freed only on grounds of "exceptional service" and even then only with the Assembly's approval. Worries about the growing number of mulatto children born to black mothers, and hence a growing number of mulatto slaves, had the effect of causing the slave laws to be extended specifically to the mulatto children of female slaves.

Act XIV of 1691, passed by the Virginia Assembly, hints at the prevailing anxiety on the subject of freed slaves. Significantly, it provided that any slave or mulatto who had somehow slipped through the tightening net on manumission and been freed had to be transported out of the colony. As a planter and substantial slave owner, John Custis shared white planters' concerns about keeping their slaves under control. As a member of the Governor's Council since 1729, he must have been familiar with the law enforcing that control. When John Custis executed a deed of manumission for Jack in 1747, it seems inconceivable that he was unaware of the legal restrictions on freeing a mulatto slave, and in the unlikely event he was, his lawyer friends in Williamsburg could have advised him of both the wording and intention of the following law:

And forasmuch as great inconvenience may happen to this country by the setting of negroes and mulattos free, by their entertaining negro slaves from their masters service, or receiving stolen goods, or being grown old bringing a charge upon the country, for prevention thereof, be it enacted . . . that no negro or mulatto be after the end of this present session of assembly set free by any person or persons whatsoever, unless such person or persons, their heirs, executors or administrators pay for the transportation of such negro or negroes out of the countrey [*sic*] within six months after such setting them free, upon penalty of paying of tenn [*sic*] pounds sterling to the Church wardens of the parish where such person shall dwell, with which money or so much as shall be necessary, the said Church wardens are to cause the said negro or mulatto to be transported out of the countrey, and the remainder of the said money to imploy [*sic*] to the use of the poor of the parish.[6]

Under these circumstances the bequest to Jack, so well-meaning to modern eyes, was fraught with social problems and legal contradictions for Daniel and, significantly, risk for Jack himself. It was legally impossible to implement the terms of the will. As a slave, Jack could not legally own property, but even if he were no longer a slave, thanks to the deed of manumission executed by John Custis, he could not live on the property left to him.

Although Jack's age at the time is unknown, he was described as the son of a "young" slave named Alice and was under the age of twenty. It is highly unlikely that he qualified for manumission on the only legal grounds available at the time, those of having performed "meritorious service." Even if he had performed "meritorious service," his freedom would have required the governor's and the Assembly's consent. And even if that consent had been forthcoming, freed slaves by law had to leave the colony within six months. That makes a mockery of the gift of a house to be built on Queens Creek, near the Parke property Daniel now owned at what had been Daniel's mother's childhood home. And if Jack's manumission was invalid, he remained a slave, and a chattel himself in the eyes of the law, legally incapable of owning either land or other slaves.

The will put Daniel, his father's sole executor, in an awkward if not impossible situation, because an executor has a strict duty at law to carry out the wishes of a testator. While it was technically possible to contest the will and have it amended by the court, it would mean yet another legal battle, involving complex and abstruse legal principles about executorship that could drag out indefinitely and cost yet more money. Daniel and Martha must have spent many sleepless nights at White House agonizing about how to resolve the problem. Since the will was a public document, its provisions could not be kept secret, and Daniel must have discussed it at length with John Blair and James Power. Meanwhile, there was a great deal of money at stake, and it could only have been prudent for Daniel and Martha to comply with the will for the time being. If so, Jack must have lived with them at White House. No one knows how Daniel and Martha felt about Jack. Daniel himself seems to have been a gentle soul, known to be a fond husband to Martha, a doting father to his children, and kind to his white tenants, and he may have been fond of his young half brother. However, John Custis had left a portrait of Jack to Mrs. Moody, and not to Daniel, on the grounds no one else was likely to look after it, suggesting he knew Daniel and Martha would not want it.

Treating Jack kindly as a mulatto half brother in the same house where the status quo was preserved was one thing. As with Martha's half sister Ann Dandridge, sisters and brothers "of color" were occasionally raised within a planter's house with a peculiar status somewhere between slave and family member, though in Ann's case, there had not been any issue of her slave status. Behind the customary veil of silence, everyone knew and tolerated the situation but avoided any mention of it. Daniel and Martha could probably have managed a similar discreet situation vis-à-vis Jack, giving him special treatment, easy tasks, good food, better clothing, and even some education—so long as Jack's legal status as a slave was unchanged.

But the problem of Jack had ramifications beyond White House, because for Daniel to live with Jack on equal terms as brothers—and Martha with Jack as a brother-in-law—was a dangerously radical situation vis-à-vis the other slaves. The arrangement may have amused them or possibly provoked them to greater insolence. This would have held Daniel and Martha up to ridicule and generally undermined discipline—very dangerous and a bad example to all the slaves in the colony.

Then in September 1751 the insoluble problem was neatly resolved. Jack died. John Blair's diary entry on September 19, 1751, records: "abt 1 or 2 in ye morng. Col Custis favourite Boy Jack died in abt 21 hours illness being taken ill a little before day the 18th wth a Pain in the back of his Neck for which he was blooded."

It was a most convenient death. It solved a multitude of problems—in fact it was the only way of solving the problems Daniel faced. But like all too-neat solutions, it inevitably raises questions about how it came to pass.

On the one hand there is no proof that anything untoward happened to Jack. In the colony, children both black and white died all the time from a variety of causes. From what is known about both Daniel and Martha, neither sounds like the murdering kind. Quite the reverse in fact. On the other hand, it is unavoidable to note that "motive, means, and opportunity," the classic preconditions of crime, existed. The motive was clear. As to the means and opportunity, Daniel and Martha were products of a society where planters could and did kill slaves without fear of reprisal under the law. Martha was pregnant. No one knew what the outcome of the Dunbar Suit would be, and now there was a new mess with John Custis's will. According to the latter will, Jack should have been living with Daniel and Martha at White House, where neither means nor opportunity would have presented any difficulties. Finally, even if Daniel and Martha had been overjoyed at the prospect of Jack living with them until he was old enough to receive his considerable inheritance, few whites in the colony would have shared their view. Certainly not the lawyers in the colony, aware of both the necessity and the impossibility of implementing the will.

So was Jack murdered?

Ivor Noel Hume, a distinguished archaeologist and historian at Williamsburg, commented trenchantly as follows:

> As quickly as Jack was rid of his pain in the neck, Daniel and Martha were relieved of theirs. So convenient a death should have been enough to make any coroner suspicious and to send even the most dim-witted detective reaching for his quizzing glass, but under the circumstances it is hardly likely that Daniel Parke Custis's peers had anything but unquestioning compassion for the nice young couple who, by the Grace of God, had been relieved of an intolerable burden. There is in fact, a convincing medical explanation for Jack's sudden death. His neck pain may have been a symptom of meningitis, and if the boy was also suffering from sickle-cell anemia, bleeding could easily have killed him.[7]

However, of these two suggested possibilities for cause of death, sickle-cell anemia may be ruled out, because it requires that both parents carry the sickle-cell gene. The sickle-cell gene is usually found in people of African or Mediterranean extraction—hot countries where malaria thrives—and makes carriers immune to malaria because people with the defective sickle blood cell do not attract the malaria-carrying mosquito. Mulatto Jack's mother Alice was a slave, of African extraction, and could have carried and passed the sickle-cell trait to her son but John Custis was of English stock and probably incapable of doing so. Under the circumstances it is virtually impossible that Mulatto Jack would have suffered from sickle cell anemia. That leaves the possibility of meningitis or some other unspecified disease that may have been connected to the neck pain, or that he was killed—intentionally or accidentally by too much bleeding; by overenthusiastic dosing with purges, another popular remedy of the day; or by poison.

In a further twist, the will provided that if Jack died before coming into his inheritance, Daniel was Jack's heir.

It is difficult to reconcile the image of Daniel the vestryman, the godfather, the doting husband and father, with that of a murderer or someone who may have acquiesced to the murder of Jack by well-meaning friends. It is even harder to see sweet-natured and religious Martha in the role of murderess or murderer's accomplice. It is somewhat less difficult to imag-

ine some of the couple's friends responding to a "who will rid me of this turbulent half brother" cri de coeur or simply taking the matter out of the couple's hands as a kindness, just as Daniel's friends helpfully intervened when
Daniel's desire to marry Martha looked doomed. Alternatively, overseers
were not a squeamish lot.

There is also the issue of timing, shortly before the birth of Martha and
Daniel's first child, when Daniel as a doting husband may have wanted to
spare Martha stress, which adds to uncomfortable doubts about what could
have happened. What was certain was that if there was a murderer, he or
she would be protected by a colonial "omerta" as forceful as that of the mafia
today. The other certainty was that Daniel and Martha and their children
could only benefit from Jack's death. Everyone—except for Jack's mother,
relatives, and the other slaves—must have breathed a sigh of relief.

Two months after Jack died, the all-important Custis son and heir was
born in November 1751 at White House. He was named Daniel after his
father, followed by the necessary *Parke* in order to qualify to inherit his share
of the Parke fortune. For the next few years the family expanded, and the
way Martha and Daniel's first child Daniel Parke Custis II and their subsequent children were named reflects the practice of naming children after
relatives, both living and dead, which was typical of the time and place. It
is important to understand how common this was, because Martha spent
her life surrounded by people bearing similar or the same names. Names
were important because they signified family connections. A pedigree could
be read in a signature. The naming customs current in Martha's day were
not only typical of colonial Virginia but survive in many parts of the American South today.

In April 1753 Martha had a second child, a daughter named Frances
Parke Custis, presumably named after Daniel's mother and sister as well as
after Martha's mother, Frances. In 1754 a second son was born, John Parke
Custis, who inherited the name *John* from both his grandfathers and possibly Martha's younger brother, who had died in the summer of 1749. This
child was always known as "Jacky."

The Dunbar Suit remained a problem. In 1754, nearly thirty years after
it began, John Mercer, growing desperate about the money he personally
had spent on the conduct of the Dunbar case, asked Daniel for a loan of
£1,000, an immense sum of money. Mercer seems to have been retained on
a kind of contingency-fee basis by John Custis in the Dunbar Suit, but by
1754 he was seriously in debt as a result of the length of time the case had
dragged on and the costs he had incurred, which had yet to be reimbursed
by the Custises. Daniel did not pay him.

A year later, in 1756, a fourth child was born, a daughter, Martha Parke
Custis. To distinguish her from her mother, this child was always called
"Patcy," or as Martha once wrote, "my little Patt." Family tradition suggests

it was an extremely difficult birth. That same year Martha's nineteen-year-old sister Anna Maria married a wealthy widower, Burwell Bassett, thirty years her senior, and moved to the Bassett home, Eltham Plantation in New Kent, several miles along the Pamunkey to the east. Martha had been too encumbered by her pregnancy to attend her sister's wedding.

Those years when the children were born were marred by a series of bereavements. Other than the death of her uncle William, and later her brother John when she was eighteen, Martha had experienced fewer deaths in the family than most people at that time. Daniel, for example, as related earlier, had lost his mother, two older siblings who died as babies, his sister Fanny, and his father.

While the death of her father-in-law probably caused her few pangs, Martha now suffered a number of other losses in quick succession. Daniel Parke Custis II died in February 1754, at the age of two. He was buried at Queens Creek in the family graveyard with his grandmother Frances. His tombstone was ordered from England. In September 1756, Martha's father, John Dandridge, was taken ill while on a visit to his niece Mary Spottswood in Fredericksburg and died suddenly of apoplexy on a hot day while attending a horse race. In the September heat, his funeral had to be held and the burial performed quickly. New Kent was several days' ride south of Fredericksburg, and Martha was unable to attend the funeral. Presumably her mother, who had given birth to Martha's youngest sister Mary in April that year, was not able to attend either. Martha tended her father's grave in Fredericksburg in later years.

In April 1757 four-year-old Frances died suddenly and was buried with her brother and grandmother at Queens Creek. Shortly after Frances's death an itinerant English painter, John Wollaston, stayed at White House and painted portraits of the surviving members of the family. Daniel may have hoped this would divert Martha from her grief. There is a portrait of Daniel, a portrait of Martha, and a portrait of their two surviving children, Jacky and Patsy. Though the family was bereaved, it was not a frivolous or uncaring gesture to have portraits painted at such a time. It is likely that all of Martha and Daniel's friends had lost children, because it was such a common experience, and that fact may have supported them in their grief, as well as helping them to see death as a manifestation of God's will. They undoubtedly hoped and expected that nature would take its course and that there would be more children.

In the Wollaston portraits, the medium seems to have been the message, because the subjects of all his portraits look suspiciously alike. The message was that here were people grand enough to have their portraits painted. He and his clients must have thought that was enough. His practice was to keep a supply of canvasses painted with a stock male or female figure, on which he superimposed the subject's head. The grander the sitter, the larger

"Martha Dandridge Custis," by Charles Willson Peale 1757. Courtesy of Washington and Lee University.

the canvas. However, in many cases he seems to have painted identical heads and faces as well. All Wollaston portraits, male and female, are noticeably characterized by slightly protruding, strangely froglike eyes. The Wollaston portrait of Martha is virtually indistinguishable in both dress and figure from Wollaston portraits of other women, notably a woman named Anne Harrison Randolph of Wilton Plantation on the James River, and a portrait of George Washington's sister Betty Washington Lewis of Kenwood. Only the poses and hairstyles are slightly different in each one. Martha's portrait shows she had a widow's peak and wore pearls in her hair and is shown plucking a blossom. This may have been intended as an allusion to her recently deceased child, or it may have been an allusion to her fondness for gardening. Otherwise it holds few clues to indicate what she really looked like at twenty-six.

Daniel's portrait shows a man whose features, though masculine, are very similar to Martha's. Here the head is superimposed on a body whose most prominent feature is a rounded stomach straining at a satin waistcoat. In fact, Daniel was said by his own father to closely resemble his grandfather Daniel Parke. "If Colonel Parke had lived to see my son," John Custis wrote to a friend in 1731 when Daniel had just turned twenty-one, "he would

"Daniel Parke Custis," by Charles Willson Peale 1757. Courtesy of Washington and Lee University.

have seen his own picture to greater perfection than ever Sir Godfrey Kneller could draw it." There is a painting of Daniel Parke, painted in 1705 by John Closterman. The face in the Closterman portrait is a handsome one, and it bears no relation to the Wollaston portrait of Daniel Parke Custis.

Wollaston tried to be more original with the portraits of the children, Jacky and Patcy. Children rarely had their portraits painted, and Wollaston may not have had the same stock of bodies, heads, and expressions ready. Jacky and Patcy were painted as a single portrait—two chubby, solemn toddlers whose grown-up, English-made clothes bespoke their father's wealth and position. Patcy is shown sitting down in miniature hoop skirts with a ribbon in her hair and a rose on her lap, a proper little miss. At the time she was probably just beginning to walk.

Jacky, on the other hand, seems to be the one character in the family to have inspired the artist to capture something of the sitter's personality. Three-year-old Jacky, looking very much the heir-expectant to the Parke Custis fortune, is shown standing with a small hawk perched on his arm, exuding all the confidence of a young master. Later, as a young man, Jacky possessed great charm, but never lost the self-confidence of a boy born to

"John Parke Custis (Jacky) and Martha Parke Custis (Patcy)," by Charles Willson Peale 1757. Courtesy of Washington and Lee University.

expectations of a large inheritance. Wollaston could not possibly have known that at the time, but the portrait hints at the cocksure problem child who would drive Martha to distraction by focusing his energies on hunting, racing, and girls rather than his books. In fact, Jacky at age three looks far more imperious than his forty-five-year-old father.

As only the most privileged members of society people could afford to have portraits painted at all, it seems to have mattered little that Wollaston's portraits were painted to a formula that made everyone—men, women, and children—look alike, but they spoke volumes about the sitter's status.

Wollaston was at White House in June and may have been there when Jacky was taken ill on June 12. Having buried little Frances in April, his parents were alarmed enough to send for medicine from a Williamsburg doctor, Dr. Carter. Martha obviously felt this was beyond her skills. Then on July 4 Daniel was taken seriously ill, and once again, medicine was sent for. Daniel continued no better for several days, so Dr. Carter himself traveled the twenty-five miles from Williamsburg, with a vast array of medicines.

Daniel died on July 8, possibly of a heart condition, at age forty-five. A story about Daniel's last moments, which had been passed down in the family, was related by his grandson George Washington Parke Custis many years later:

> It is related of this amiable gentleman, that, when on his death-bed, he sent for a tenant, to whom, in settling an account, he was due one shilling. The tenant begged that the colonel, who had ever been most kind to his tenantry, would not trouble himself at all about such a trifle, as he, the tenant, had forgotten it long ago. "But I have not," rejoined the just and conscientious landlord, and bidding the creditor take up the coin, which had been purposely placed on his pillow, exclaimed "Now all my accounts are closed with this world," and shortly after expired.[8]

Dr. Carter stayed at White House a few more days because Jacky grew no better. Having lost both her daughter and her husband in such a short space of time, Martha must have been terrified that Jacky would die too. Grieving for Daniel and Frances, she was in a state of suspense over Jacky for weeks, before Jacky recovered.

Immediately after Daniel died, a local dressmaker was summoned, and mourning clothes were ordered for Martha and the children. The summer heat meant a body had to be buried quickly, and whatever her sorrow, Martha had to make arrangements for a swift funeral. Less than three months after burying Frances, a funeral procession again wound its way to the graveyard at Queens Creek, this time with a black walnut coffin bearing Daniel's body. Martha later ordered a gravestone from England, specifying "One handsome tombstone in the best durable marble to cost about £100 with the following inscription and the arms [of the Custis family] sent in a piece of paper on it to wit 'here lies the body of Daniel Parke Custis, Esquire who was born the 15th day of October 1711 and departed this life the 8th day of July, 1757. Aged 45 years.' "[9] Late in the nineteenth century Daniel's tombstone was moved to the graveyard at Bruton Parish Church in Williamsburg, together with the tombstone of his unhappy mother and his and Martha's two children, Frances and Daniel.

It was considered the positive duty of a Christian to bow to God's will and not to repine or murmur at the dispensations of Divine Providence, but Martha had had more opportunity in the seven years of her marriage than in all her previous eighteen years of girlhood to practice this precept. Frances Dandridge had known that her daughters, if they survived to have families, were certain to suffer a constant string of such bereavements in adulthood, even if they had not as children, hence the need to equip them with the only antidote to the grief that would otherwise overwhelm them. Like many sorrowing women of the time, Martha now clung to the twin supports of religion and her sense of duty.

CHAPTER 4

The Widow Custis

For a time it seemed religion and duty might fail her. In the month following Daniel's death Martha became ill enough to require the services of Dr. Carter herself. On top of mourning her daughter and husband, there was the strain of Jacky's prolonged bout of illness, which might mean she was on the verge of losing another child. She also knew there was an overwhelming task ahead of her in running the plantation and coming to grips with the management of her own and the children's property.

During her marriage Martha had had too many domestic duties to be regarded as an idle woman, but by the standards of the day she had been a pampered wife. Daniel had dealt with the business side of the plantation. But time did not stand still on plantations, and in the aftermath of Daniel's death someone had to deal with pressing practical matters. Bereaved or not, Martha's own fortune and that of the children depended on tobacco, and the tobacco crop still had to be cultivated, harvested, cured, insured, and shipped to England. The factors in London had to be informed of Daniel's death, and for the time being Martha would have to deal directly with them herself in all matters of business. She would be responsible for ordering replacement equipment and farming tools necessary for the efficient running of the plantations, as well as other items—medicines, laundry bluing, spices, cloth, thread, sugar, salt, gunpowder, medicines, cloth for the slaves' clothing, and many other items that were essential to the running of a large estate. She could ill afford to abandon herself entirely to grief, illness, or spiritual contemplation, but it is little wonder that she collapsed under the strain.

By August 7, 1757, a month after Daniel's death, thirty-year-old Robert Carter Nicholas, burgess for York County and treasurer of the colony, wrote to Martha a letter of condolence and advice. He commended her fortitude in the face of her loss and strongly urged the necessity of getting someone to administer her affairs:

Madam   Williamsburg, 7th August, 1757

It gave me no small pleasure to hear with how great Christian patience and resignation you submitted to your late misfortune; the example is rare, though a duty incumbent upon us all; therefore I cannot help esteeming it a peculiar happiness when I meet with it. My late worthy friend from a very short acquaintance with him, had gained a great share of my esteem, which would naturally continue towards his family, had I been an utter stranger to them. How greatly this is increased by the pleasure of even a slight acquaintance with you, I shall leave it to time to evince, as it might savor of flattery were I to attempt the expression of it. . . . As it will be absolutely necessary that some person should administer upon the estate and no appear so proper as yourself, I would recommend it to you, and that so soon as it may be done with convenience, I dare say your friends will ease you of as much trouble as they can; and since you seem to place some confidence in me, I do sincerely profess myself to be of that number. I imagine you will find it necessary to employ a trusty steward; and as the estate is very large and very extensive . . . you had better not engage with any but a very able man, though he should require large wages, nothing appears to us very material to be done immediately, except what relates to your tobacco; if it is not already done, it will be necessary that letters be wrote for insurance and that we, or some other of your friends should be acquainted with the quantities of tobacco put on board each ship that we may get the proper bills of lading. If you desire it, we will cheerfully go up to assist in sorting your papers, forwarding invoices, etc, and any other instance that you think I can serve you, I beg that you will freely and without any reserve command me. I congratulate you upon your little boy's late recovery, and am madam your hearty well-wisher and obedient humble servant,

Robert Carter Nicholas[1]

This reminder of her Christian duty and offer of help had a galvanizing effect in recalling her to her responsibilities. Martha pulled herself together enough to begin attending to estate business. In the following weeks and months she paid the overseers on several of the Custis plantations, as well as tradespeople such as the seamstress who had hastily made mourning clothes for the family after Daniel's death. She paid John Wollaston for the three family portraits he had painted shortly before Daniel died. She paid the bills for items ordered by Daniel before his death, such as kegs of vinegar, lumber he had ordered to be sawed into boards, and a river schooner Daniel had had built. She signed a power of attorney to enable the courts in England to appoint agents from one firm of the Custis's factors in London to collect all outstanding debts due to Daniel in that country. She lent money to her brother Bartholomew and her uncle Lane Jones, her mother's brother. Benjamin Waller, a lawyer in Williamsburg, wrote a power of attorney and letters of administration that were needed to enable Martha to draw the interest and dividends from the Bank of England stock she had inherited. The first draft was lost. She signed another. She dealt with taxes. Her uncle Lane Jones was the deputy sheriff of New Kent County and, as such, issued Martha with tax receipts.

Martha personally wrote to two firms of factors in London that had traditionally handled the Custis tobacco, Robert Cary and Company and John Hanbury and Company (which would on the death of a partner there soon change its name to Capel and Osgood Hanbury):

> Gent.   Virginia 20th August 1757
>
>   I take this Opportunity to inform you of the great misfortune I have met with in the loss of my late Husband Mr. Custis, your Correspondent
>
>   As I now have the Administration of his Estate & management of his Affairs of all sorts, I shall be glad to continue the Correspondence which Mr. Custis carried on with you.
>
>   Yours of the 16th of March Mr Custis rec'd before his Death with his Account Current inclosed wch I believe is right; and he had put on board the Ship King of Prussia Capt. Necks 28Hnds of Tobacco and wrote to you for Insurance for it, I now inclose the bill of Lading for the Tobacco which I hope will get safe to your hands, and as have reason to believe it is extremely good. I hope you will sell it at a good Price, Mr Custis's Estate will be kept together for some time and I think it will be proper to continue his Account in the same manner as if he was living. Please to send an Account Current when the Tobacco is sold I am gentlemen Your very hbl Servt
>
>   Martha Custis
>   To Mr John Hanbury & CO
>   Merchts in London[2]

She sent a similar letter to Robert Cary and Company.

Although historians have dismissed Martha's intellectual capacities and her formal education, the way Martha rose to the occasion and shouldered the business of the estate suggests the opposite. She was clearly familiar with the practical aspects of tobacco growing and shipping, and when she said she believed the quality of her tobacco was good, she was speaking from experience, because she had known tobacco from an early age. She also consulted Daniel's lawyers over the Dunbar Suit. She may have taken the advice of friends, consulted her brother Bartholomew, or referred to Daniel's file of correspondence to assist her, but she wrote as good a business letter to her London factors as any planter. She showed herself to be shrewd, capable, and efficient. Clearly Martha did not simply sigh helplessly and fall into the arms of the next available man willing to deal with it all on her behalf.

It would have been perfectly acceptable for her to do so. The society she lived in would not have censured her had she chosen to remarry within months of being widowed. In Virginia, with more men in search of wives than women to fill the bill, few widows could expect to wither on the vine.

Instead, Martha concentrated on business. On top of her domestic responsibilities and the children, there was plenty to occupy her time. Daniel had died intestate. In the absence of a will, his heirs were automatically Martha and their two children. By law Martha, Jacky, and Patcy each inherited one-third of Daniel's estate, a vast one by Virginia standards. It comprised 17,779 acres of land in a string of plantations, including White House, spread over six counties, with all the associated farming equipment and livestock, nearly 300 slaves, lots in Williamsburg, Six Chimney House, and over £23,000 in money, as well as bank stock in England. Martha now had sole responsibility for the children and direct responsibility for an immense, widespread estate, and over 250 slaves.

Dividing up the estate and apportioning a third share in it to each of the three heirs would be a complex and time-consuming exercise. One advantage of being a woman was that Martha would not be required to undertake the onerous preliminary task of making an inventory of the huge estate. The court would have to appoint prominent male members of the community to carry out an inventory of all the assets in the estate—each kettle, slave, bed, horse, painting, hogshead of wine, plow, and so on. They would then have to assess a value for each item. The Bank of England stock and the property, such as the Williamsburg lots, would also be valued. The complete inventory and its valuation would then be submitted to the scrutiny of the Virginia court for approval before being apportioned into thirds. Obviously each different element of the estate could not be divided neatly into thirds—it was impossible to have a third of a cow, a third of a slave, or a third of a house. The estate would be apportioned in thirds of value.

It was typical of the period that a daughter's inheritance from her father was normally calculated in terms of the value of goods, chattels, and cash, she may have inherited as opposed to an outright bequest of land, because anything that a woman owned or inherited in her own right went automatically to her husband when she married. To keep land in the family, it was normally left to the sons, if any. In the case of Daniel's estate, Jacky would eventually inherit much of the actual land, together with some slaves, to a third of the estate's value; Patcy would receive mainly money and shares to a third of the estate; and Martha would inherit land, money, bank stock, and slaves to a third.

Using one of the smaller Custis plantations in Hanover County as an example of assessing assets and their value, the inventory prepared for that plantation itemizes the value of equipment and livestock, such as "1 old bay horse £5. . . . 4 Working Steers £8 together with a grind stone, a wheat sieve, a new hoe, and an ox cart," and other equipment, which totals £55.17.6 (fifty-five English pounds, seventeen shillings, and six pence), then goes on to include the human property and its value:

Matt	£45	John	£20	Sam	£45	Paul	£23
Sarah	£30	Patrick	£15	Moll	£35	Davy	£12
Jenny	£40	William	£6	Kitt	£40	Hannah	£25
Morris	£25	Alice	£25	Bob	£25	Jenny	£8
						Negroes	£419[3]

The total value of the Hanover County property was therefore £474.17.6. In New Kent County, where White House was situated and Martha and the children lived, the value of the property was much greater. At White House there were listed 155 slaves with a total value of £4,769.1.6., and this sum was added to the land at the White House estate, the valuation of the contents of White House and its barns and other buildings, and livestock.

Responding to Martha's letters of August, the London factors, John Hanbury and Company and Robert Cary and Company, sent their condolences, hoping Martha would be pleased to continue with them. They were Quaker firms, but Virginia planters had no real control over any of their distant factors. In a few months Martha would begin to suspect they were cheating her.

Shouldering the burden of unaccustomed responsibilities, missing Daniel, and aware she could not afford to break down as she had in the early days of her widowhood, Martha blamed her late father-in-law for driving Daniel to an early death. Beneath her capable exterior, Martha, never a high-strung or temperamental woman, seethed with resentment foreign to her nature. Although her grandson Wash remarked that Martha had a quick temper when roused, her naturally sunny disposition usually reasserted itself quickly, and all her life people who knew her were struck by her equanimity and even temper, often in the face of difficult or uncomfortable circumstances. But at some point following Daniel's death, Martha gave vent to her feelings.

Sometime after Daniel's death in 1757, possibly as late as 1761, Martha went to Williamsburg and cleaned out Six Chimney House, where most of John Custis's fine furniture, paintings, and family heirlooms were kept. Martha and Daniel had used it sporadically over the years to participate in the social life that attended "publick times"—balls, dinners, parties, concerts, and plays—and it must have held some happy memories for Martha.

Yet Martha, who had inherited the house and its contents and would under normal circumstances have preserved it and its Custis heirlooms for her children, put most of the contents up for auction, including 135 pictures and family portraits. She is believed then to have smashed John Custis's collection of hand-blown wine bottles in the well, defacing his seal quite badly on at least one. She also smashed a collection of rare delftware tea bowls and sixteen early fine wineglasses. After the house was empty, it was eventually rented to her younger brother Bartholomew, who was training to be a lawyer.[4] It was satisfying to think that the man who had sneered at "John Dandridge's daughter" would be turning in his grave with John Dandridge's son living in his precious house.

The Dunbar Suit remained an ongoing source of worry. The Virginia courts had dismissed the Dunbar claim against the Custis estate, but there had been an appeal to the English court of the Privy Council (which even today still acts as the court of final appeal in cases in the British Commonwealth). The Privy Council had sent the case back to the Virginia court for a rehearing. By December 1757 Martha was writing to John Hanbury and Company that what she called "the Cause" had been remitted back to the Virginia courts, and she was presently taking lawyers' advice in Virginia. She instructed John Hanbury to pay the English lawyers who had been involved and to send her a detailed account of their costs.

John Mercer, one of the Williamsburg attorneys who had been acting for the Custis family in the Dunbar Suit, began to put pressure on Martha, asking for payment on account. During all the time Mercer had acted as the Custises' lawyer, during John Custis's lifetime and later for Daniel and Martha, he had received only a few small payments, because both he and the Custises expected that a final determination of the case by the court either in England or Virginia was imminent. Mercer and his clients intended that a full account would be drawn up for professional services rendered when that happened. However, as time dragged on without the case being settled, Mercer was owed money for the work he had done. In the interim, the Custises had made Mercer a number of loans, and when Daniel died, an issue arose as to whether these loans were intended to offset Mercer's legal fees or whether Mercer actually owed repayment of these loans to Daniel's estate.

Mercer was an aggressive courtroom lawyer and may also have been aggressive outside it, but the man was out-of-pocket and he had reason to push for recovery of his fees. Dealing with Mercer was yet another problem for Martha to wrestle with, and she made a trip from White House to Williamsburg to consult her brother Bartholomew. Bartholomew advised her to begin by obtaining a full accounting from Mercer.

By early January 1758 Mercer faced growing personal debt, and there was no resolution of the Dunbar Suit in sight. The letter he wrote to Martha expressed his view that they would eventually lose the Dunbar Suit, and sought payment of legal fees for his past sixteen years' involvement. Mercer claimed that various promises had been made to him by Daniel vis-à-vis his retainer, referred to loans made to him by Daniel, and his expectation of being remembered in Daniel's will. It was clearly not the first attempt on Mercer's part to recoup some of what he believed the Custises owed him for his long-term professional services. Writing to Martha in January 1758, Mercer enclosed a letter from Daniel, written to Mercer just before Daniel's death in July. The letter from Daniel made reference both to Mercer's claims and to the grave financial implications for Daniel if the Dunbar Suit eventually went against him:

> Dear Sir
> I . . . am sorry to hear you are so involved as you say you [are]. I thought or at least hoped I had satisfied you that I have not near the quantity of money as you & some others imagined, I am sure I have not increased my flock much since, & I have the same Complaint to make as you have having a great Sum of money out & cannot get any in. There are several Gentlemen that have very lately applied to me for Money one of which is of the Council, [these gentlemen who owed money to Daniel included Martha's brother-in law, Anna Maria's husband, Burwell Bassett], which made me make very solemn Declaration that I would never meddle with one farthing I have in England until my Law suit here was over, which if it should go against me, all that I have in the whole World wou'd scarce do.[5]

In his letter to Martha, Mercer suggested it would be a good idea if Martha would let him "have the Use of the Principal Sum" sought by the Dunbar claimants until Jacky and Patcy came of age. Failing that, Mercer continued, "I should be obliged to you to let me have four thousand pounds at Interest for four or five years in which time you could not want to call it in."[6]

If Daniel took the view that a successful Dunbar claim would wipe out all his assets, John Mercer's request that he be allowed to "have the Use of the Principal Sum" sought by the claimants for the next nineteen or twenty years until Jacky and Patcy came of age is an outrageous impertinence. The four thousand pounds he suggested Martha lend him as an alternative was an enormous sum. It amounted to about a quarter of the currency in the estate. As the estate had not yet been inventoried, valued and divided up, it would have been impossible for Martha to agree to lend him so much money.

In April 1758 Mercer wrote again:

> Dear Madam　　　　　　　　　　　　　　　　　　　　　　April 24, 1758
> I have yet heard nothing mentioned of Dunbar or his Cause which I imagine I should have done had he come to a Resolution to have gone on with it.

He may proceed not withstanding, but it is very plain he is not so sanguine as Mr Hanbury represents. . . . Should he proceed I am of Opinion that your Resolution of having a Guardian appointed for your Son is a very prudent one, but much will depend upon the Choice of a proper one. It must not only be a Man of Fortune and Character but a Man of Interest and reputation in England. Few men would answer your Expectations that way better or do more for your Son's Interest than the Speaker [meaning John Blair, speaker of the Virginia Assembly]. . . . I spoke to him about my account which he said he would undertake to settle if you would signify your Consent to him. . . .

The principal Reason however of this Trouble is to know, Madam, whether you have yet come to a Resolution what sum of money you will supply me with. Whether Sterling or currency [Virginia money which was worth nothing outside the colony and in any case less than English sterling] and when I may have it. The sooner it could be the more Service it will be to me.[7]

Mercer's appeal met with some success, because the Custis estate eventually made him further loans in May and November 1758 to the value of £1,500 sterling.

On top of everything else, as a single woman Martha probably had trouble managing both her slaves and the Custis overseers. Slaves resisted their situation by every means at their disposal in the best of times. Aside from running away, field slaves worked as slowly as possible, availing themselves of opportunities to break equipment, neglect animals, and malinger. House servants often burnt food, ruined household implements, stole, and performed household chores as slowly and sullenly as possible. Suspicious "accidental" fires were common, and there were many instances when slaves tried to poison planters and their families. Superstitious planters occasionally believed slaves' spells and voodoo had the power harm them.

Overseers dealt directly with all but the household slaves, but overseers, the middle management between the planter and the slaves, were frequently brutal, lazy, and drunkards themselves. A planter had to exercise close supervision over his overseers, who otherwise either badly mistreated the slaves out of fear, which exacerbated existing tensions with the slaves or provoked them into running away or even attacking the overseers, or they lost control altogether, allowing the slaves to slack off, which affected productivity. Reining in the overseers from their worst excesses while keeping them up to the mark required a firm hand, and Martha may not have been up to it.

In New Kent, there were over 150 slaves, though obviously only a few worked in or around White House, and their hostility may have been palpable. Martha had every reason to be concerned for her children, herself, her estate, her children's inheritances, the tobacco revenues, and, in view of her recent bereavements, everyone's health. In early February 1758 there was another death in the family. At Chestnut Grove, Martha's thirteen-year-old sister Frances died.

By the spring of 1758, the young Widow Custis was surrounded by pressures, not the least of which was the need to appoint a guardian for the children, which she had delayed doing. Her mind must have turned to remarriage, both as a personal preference and because she needed someone who could deal with her affairs, but given the size of the Custis estate, it was important that anyone she chose be both capable and honest. It is hard to imagine that someone like the widowed Martha—attractive, popular, and rich—lacked for suitors. Since she stood to inherit a third of one of the largest fortunes in the colony, it must have taken some determined maneuvering on Martha's part to avoid the hopefuls, especially in a society where far-flung neighbors used any excuse for a social gathering. Martha had at least one suitor, who, like her late husband, was a representative of one of the most prominent families in Virginia. He was Charles Carter of Cleve, a member of the House of Burgesses and the son of the immensely wealthy Robert "King" Carter of Corotoman in Lancaster County Virginia.

Like Daniel Parke Custis, Charles Carter was considerably older than Martha, at least twenty-four years her senior. He had already been married twice, and in a strange twist of fate his second wife had been Anne Byrd, the one time object of Daniel Parke Custis's affections. Anne's father William Byrd II had once noted in his diary that Daniel had been visiting at their home at Westover and had come courting "to make love to Annie." Though Charles Carter was undeniably wealthy and socially a suitable match for the widow Custis, there was a drawback in addition to his age. He already had twelve children by his previous wives, and the prospect of dealing with twelve step children as well as Jacky, Patcy and any future babies may have daunted even Martha's maternal instincts. It is a matter of history that Martha did not marry Charles Carter, but she must have begun to feel that sooner or later she was going to have to marry someone.

All that changed suddenly. In March a chance meeting with young Colonel George Washington of the Virginia Militia at the home of friends led to an engagement by June 1758, less than eleven months after Daniel's death. The marriage was speedily arranged, on the strength of three meetings or fewer between the widow and the colonel.

There is an "official," rather florid, version of the meeting that led to this engagement. It was written by Martha's grandson Wash Custis many years later. Wash probably based his account on his grandmother's fond reminiscences some forty years or so after the event. He was a great romanticist and given to the flowery, sentimental turns of phrase so much in vogue during the Victorian period. As described earlier, Wash also had a political reason to embellish it. By the time he was writing to describe their meeting, George and Martha were long dead, but history had elevated George to a pedestal as the father of his country, a hero, and a demigod. Wash's object in recording the story of the meeting between the hero and the woman who became his wife was to confirm a suitably near-mythical "match made in heaven."

It was in 1758, that an officer, attired in a military undress, and attended by a body-servant, tall and *militaire* as his chief, crossed the ferry called William's, over the Pamunkey, a branch of the York river. On the boat touching the southern or New Kent side, the soldier's progress was arrested by one of those personages, who give the beau ideal of the Virginia gentleman of the old *regime,* the very soul of kindness and hospitality. It was in vain the soldier urged his business at Williamsburg, important communications to the governor, etc. Mr. Chamberlayne, on whose domain the *militaire* had just landed, would hear of no excuse. Colonel Washington (for the soldier was he) was a name and character so dear to all the Virginians, that his passing by one of the old castles of the commonwealth, without calling and partaking of the hospitalities of the host, was entirely out of the question. The colonel, however, did not surrender at discretion, but stoutly maintained his ground, till Chamberlayne bringing up his reserve, in the intimation that he would introduce his friend to a young and charming widow, then beneath his roof, the soldier capitulated, on condition he should dine "only dine" and then by pressing his charger and borrowing of the night, he would reach Williamsburg before his excellency could shake off his morning slumbers. Orders were accordingly issued to Bishop, the colonel's body-servant and faithful follower, who, together with the fine English charger, had been bequeathed by the dying Braddock to Major Washington, on the famed fatal field of the Monongahela. Bishop, bred in the school of European discipline, raised his hand to his cap, as much as to say, "your honor's orders shall be obeyed."

The colonel now proceeded to the mansion, and was introduced to various guests (for when was a Virginian domicile of the olden time without guests?), and above all to a charming widow. Tradition relates they were mutually pleased on this their first interview, nor is it remarkable; they were of an age when impressions are strongest. The lady was fair to behold, of fascinating manners, and splendidly endowed with worldly benefits. The hero, fresh from his early fields, redolent of fame, and with a form on which "every god did seem to set his seal, to give the world assurance of a man."

The morning passed pleasantly away. Evening came, with Bishop true to his orders and firm at his post, holding his favorite charger with one hand, while the other was waiting to offer the ready stirrup. The sun sank in the horizon, and yet the colonel appeared not. And then the old soldier marvelled at his chief's delay. "'Twas strange,'twas passing strange"—surely he was not wont to be a single moment behind his appointments, for he was the most punctual of all men. Meantime, the host enjoyed the scene of the veteran on duty at the

gate, while the colonel was so agreeably employed in the parlour; and pro-
claiming that no guest ever left his house after sunset, his military visitor was,
without much difficulty, persuaded to order Bishop to put up the horses for
the night. The sun rode high in the heavens the ensuing day, when the enam-
ored soldier pressed with his spur his chargers side, and speeded on his way
to the seat of government, where, having dispatched his business, he retraced
his steps, and, at the White House, the engagement took place with preparations for the marriage.[8]

While it was true George and Martha seemed to have reached a remarkably
quick "understanding" and became engaged after two or three meetings in
the spring of 1758, there was more to the story than immediately appears
in Wash's account.

First of all, Martha and George probably knew each other already, having met in Williamsburg during "publick times" while Martha was married
to Daniel. Though the Washingtons were not part of the Williamsburg social
scene at the time Martha was making her debut and the story of John Custis's
opposition to Daniel's choice of bride was the talk of the town, George
appeared in Williamsburg several years later, at least by 1754. Thanks to the
patronage of the wealthy Fairfax clan who were his neighbors in northern
Virginia, George had become a colonel and commanding officer of the local
defense force, the Virginia Militia. He was often in Williamsburg on business with the governor. By then Martha was a prominent young matron, and
George was edging into Williamsburg society, on the verge of becoming a
hero on the frontier and cutting a very fine figure in a dashing blue and red
uniform. George and Martha would almost certainly have frequented the
same gatherings, probably met, and possibly even danced together.

By the time he was twenty-one George had not only been appointed to
command the Virginia Militia and fought with the British army in the North-
west in the French and Indian Wars, but he had acquired a hero's reputation for gallantry and courage. This was not for any remarkable military feat
but rather because he had led the survivors of a disastrous rout by the
French and Indians, known as Braddock's defeat, to safety. He had then
been assigned to protect settlers in the western part of Virginia against brutal attacks by the Indians.

George took his duties seriously, and he did his best to counter the
Indian attacks with his disorganized militia, which was inadequately supplied and funded by the assembly in Williamsburg. The western border
was a sensitive area and vulnerable to encroachment by the French, who
were pushing to link their territories in Canada with their southern lands
in Louisiana by gaining control of the Mississippi River. England, the governor, and the assembly were mainly concerned to keep settlers in situ on
the western borders beyond Fredericksburg to act as a buffer zone against

the French. The harrowing tales the settlers told of attacks, murder, and scalpings and burning of homes, on the other hand, genuinely moved George.

Back in Williamsburg George's reputation as the gallant defender of the settlers was enhanced by his obvious enjoyment of the pleasures Willamsburg afforded. He was extremely fond of dancing and the theater, and seized every opportunity to attend balls and performances in Williamsburg. He became, if not an intimate of the governor's, someone who regularly visited the palace with dispatches and on whom the authorities depended for information.

Martha was not an impressionable girl to be swept dizzily off her feet at the Chamberlaynes in March. With her children and their fortunes at stake, she was unlikely to have acted impetuously in engaging herself to George Washington. First of all, Martha must have sensed instinctively that she could trust him as the children's guardian, which was not surprising, because all his life people trusted George. He inspired confidence. Furthermore, George himself must have been an attractive proposition in Martha's eyes. He had undeniable sex appeal. He was nine months younger than Martha, with a dramatic physical presence that all his life acted like a magnet for women. He was a tall, rugged outdoorsman, an upright, spare figure over six feet three inches tall, with a ruddy weathered complexion and reddish hair. He rode superbly well and was described as the best horseman of his age by a contemporary. Even in the sitting room George exuded vigor, the reckless good-old-boy courage he displayed on horseback, in the hunting field, or riding into a hail of enemy bullets. He had a tendency to be tongue-tied that sometimes caused him to withdraw behind a façade of impenetrable dignity, but at the same time he was physically courageous to the core, lacking any sense of personal fear. He made an awesome impression on his Indian enemies, who believed he was protected by the spirits and could not be killed by human means. Wash later wrote a play based on that legend, called *The Indian Prophecy.*

Even so, George was blessed with a rather endearing and inherent gallantry toward women, and pretty women had an effect on him. Since boyhood he had made a self-conscious effort to acquire the manners of polished society in order to appear the gentleman, not only in the company of the fair sex, but in polite society generally. Although George had grown up in rustic circumstances, by the time Martha met him, his rough edges had been smoothed away. Like all other members of the society in which he meant to move, George was passionately fond of fine clothes, and he wore them well on his huge frame. In a society that judged by appearances, George and Martha shared an instinctive understanding of the message clothes conveyed. The man Martha met in the Chamberlaynes' house appeared to great advantage, very attractive, yet well mannered and well dressed.

At the same time Martha may have been touched by George's underlying vulnerability. Outward appearances notwithstanding, George was an ambitious and largely self-taught man, and painfully self-conscious about how he appeared to others. His courteous manners cloaked a deep-rooted sense of social insecurity, lest he not appear the gentleman. The different aspects of his personality were sometimes at odds with each other and gave his manners an air of studied reserve and sometimes gravity. This impression of gravity was exacerbated by lifelong problems with his teeth. The main remedy of the day for dental problems was extraction, and by the time George met Martha at the age of twenty-six, he had lost many of his teeth to what must have been excruciating sessions of eighteenth-century dentistry.

Everything she knew of his reputation and observed of Colonel Washington personally confirmed his suitability as a potential husband and a perfect candidate to act as Patcy and Jacky's guardian. All of this must have been reinforced by his growing reputation in the colony and his connections with the powerful Fairfax family, who were his patrons and neighbors. Had Martha had any doubts, she would not have decided so quickly to entrust her own fortune to him, much less the children's.

As far as George's own finances went, he had nothing except for a large estate north on the Potomac at Mount Vernon, which he was then renting from his elder half brother's widow. In their few, but probably intense, meetings in the spring of 1758, George must have spoken of Mount Vernon and his plans. In describing it to Martha, he was probably inadvertently carried away by the subject, because Mount Vernon was the greatest passion in George's life. He had begun a careful program to improve and beautify the house and estate two years earlier. For such a masculine man, his hunger for beautiful surroundings in his home and gardens and his finely tuned aesthetic sense was an unexpected dimension to his character. Mount Vernon, restored and open to the public, still impresses a visitor as one of the loveliest houses in the country, and reflects Washington's timeless appreciation for graceful architecture, fine decoration, and handsome furniture. Martha, who never showed any similar inclinations toward home improvements, must have divined his passionate attachment to Mount Vernon and his plans to use her money to develop it. If so, it presented no drawback from her point of view. Instead, it meant she would be mistress of a fine home, and Mount Vernon would one day be inherited by their son.

The pros were more readily apparent than the cons. There were four things to be said against George: he was in debt, a fortune hunter, in poor health, and hopelessly in love with another woman.

While the first two considerations tend to ring alarm bells today, they were unlikely to have given anyone in colonial Virginia pause for thought. Brought up in that pragmatic society Martha was unlikely to be worried about being married for her money. In the colony everyone discussed everyone else's affairs, and she had probably heard gossip about George's financial position just as George would have heard gossip about hers. Few people thought of marrying for money as anything but sensible, and the most sensible of all were matches that combined money and land. While it was true George was in debt, it was the kind of debt that afflicted many Virginia planters, and Martha would have been familiar with George's land-rich/cash-poor situation. He had also, like other planters, spent money he had not yet realized from his crops by placing recklessly extensive orders with his English factors not just for farming equipment required at Mount Vernon, but also for furniture, paints, fabrics, bricks, and glass as well. He had great plans. The factors in England were only too willing to fill his orders and ship the goods, and allow George to pay later. Acting as banks to their planter clientele, factors lent money at high rates of interest against future crops if the proceeds from the latest crops were insufficient to cover, and many planters built up huge arrears this way.

George had done this in the spring of 1757, while Daniel was still alive and there was no indication that a year later a Widow Custis would be on the marriage market. At the time George was serving as a poorly paid colonel commanding the colonial Virginia Militia, and while Mount Vernon grew some tobacco, the small income this produced reflected the fact that his military duties prevented his giving the estate his full attention. With a blinkered approach characteristic of many planters, George had little idea what the extent of his debts in England actually were or how he was going to meet them when, inevitably, he would have to pay the piper.

Martha's money—or that of some wealthy bride—was essential if he was to avoid this trap, hang on to Mount Vernon, and make it profitable. George desperately needed a wealthy wife, because for all his industry, there was simply no other way to obtain a quick infusion of cash to develop Mount Vernon or any of his property. There was no prospect of income as an officer in the British army. The regular English army held the colonials and the colonial militia in contempt, and colonials were not considered English officer material, as George knew from many frustrated attempts to win a commission. His military career as an officer of the colonial militia was hardly lucrative and, in any event, was nearly finished. That left only surveying, but income from surveying could never provide capital on the scale he needed.

Martha knew that if she remarried she would automatically surrender her Custis inheritance to her new husband to use during her lifetime, but the offsetting advantage was that George would take over the onerous responsibility of acting as the children's guardian and trustee, managing the children's large estates, as well as relieving her of the management of her own share of the estate, her slaves, the tangled Dunbar Suit, and the necessity of fending off importunate lawyers seeking to encroach on the Custis capital.

As for George's health, all Martha had to do was look at George to see that he was perhaps not at his best. He was only just recovering from a six-month bout of dysentery contracted fighting in the French and Indian Wars in northwestern Pennsylvania. Dysentery, graphically called "the bloody flux," had nearly finished him the previous autumn, when he had languished for months on sick leave with fever and pains in his chest, unable to walk or stand. In fact, he had been so ill and feeling so low he had begun to suspect he had also contracted the "family disease," tuberculosis, which had carried off his elder half brother and which was endemic in Virginia.

In January 1758 a debilitated George had set out from Mount Vernon to Williamsburg to present his accounts for his command of the Virginia Militia on the western frontier of the colony, to report to the assembly on the state of hostilities with the Indians on the border, and to consult a doctor who specialized in the bloody flux, expecting to be told he was dying. In any event, George was too ill to complete the trip that time and returned to Mount Vernon. On March 5 George left Mount Vernon again. This time he did make the trip to Williamsburg, though he probably did not do so by way of the ferry near the Chamberlaynes en route. That would have been nineteen miles out of his way, and in view of his apprehensions about his health, he would have been unlikely to go courting.

By March George was finally on the mend, and Dr. Amson in Williamsburg did not believe he was dying of tuberculosis or anything else. The return journey must have been made with a lighter heart and in a more energetic physical condition. In that frame of mind George diverted his journey to pass by Richard Chamberlayne's house at Poplar Grove, where near neighbor Martha Custis happened to be visiting her old friends. George may have stayed a day or more in mid-March with the Chamberlaynes and Martha, but he was back in Williamsburg by March 18.

How much Martha may have known, heard, or guessed about the fourth matter is debatable. At the time of his meeting with Martha at Poplar Grove, George was hopelessly in love with another woman, the wife of his good friend and benefactor on the Potomac, George William Fairfax. There is no record of any rumors making the rounds of the colony about George and Sally Cary Fairfax, but if there had been, in that gossipy society they must have reached Martha's ears. She was no fool. Colonial planters' wives, unlike aristocratic Englishwomen of the period, were a straitlaced lot. They had a great deal to do and did not tend toward the brittle artifice and extramarital liaisons of their English counterparts. Gossip could have ruined Sally if anyone suspected she had had an extramarital affair. But if Martha knew or suspected she had a prior rival for George's affections, it did not affect her decision.

On March 25 George visited Martha a second time, this time at White House. Family tradition says the house slaves were expecting him. He may have visited White House once more in April By April at the latest they were engaged, and a date for the wedding was set for after Christmas for several practical reasons. As colonel of the militia George was bound for a final tour of duty on the western frontier that summer and fall, after which he would resign from military life to concentrate on Mount Vernon, and Martha clearly wanted time to plan her wedding.

As it was, she had no time to spare in dispatching orders for her wedding clothes. To be sure of having her wedding clothes in time for a winter wedding, it would have been essential to place an order for them to coincide with the spring sailing of vessels to England. She also sent her favorite nightgown back to England to be dyed and ordered a fashionable suit of clothes to be "genteel and not mourning." If all went smoothly, that allowed three months for the order to reach the English factors, be filled and sent back to the colony with the autumn sailing.

George called again at White House on June 5, but it was a quick visit because he left again that same day. He had ordered a ring from Philadelphia, probably Martha's engagement ring, and he may have made the trip to give it to her. Soon afterward George left for the western frontier to command his militia troops for the last time. Martha did not see George again until shortly before the wedding, on January 6, 1759.

Daniel Parke Custis had been a known quantity, a neighbor and Martha's godfather. Martha did not know George nearly so well. She had seven months to think about it.

CHAPTER 5

George Washington, His Family, and His Friends

Her forthcoming marriage would separate Martha from her family and all her Tidewater connections. She would have to make a new life in a different close-knit society among George's family and friends in northern Virginia. In terms of the distance and traveling time, three or four days' ride to the north, it may as well have been another country. She had seven months to learn what she could about her future in-laws and the people who would be her neighbors. Fortunately, Virginians took a great interest in their own and everyone else's family—who was descended from whom, who someone's "people" had been, who they were now, who had married whom, who owned what property, who was known for his or her peculiarities, who had built what home, how many slaves they owned, whose children were whose, and who the children had married. This kind of information was rountinely passed on in the course of visits and social gatherings.

In the absence of firsthand information, Martha probably gleaned information from this informal grapevine, which still thrives in southern states, to fill in the gaps of what she already knew or what George himself had told her, and form some idea of what lay in store. Local knowledge would have told her about the Washingtons' English connections and her widowed mother-in-law's difficult personality, that George had inherited Mount Vernon from his half brother, who had served in the British navy at the same time as Martha's uncle William from Elsing Green, that George was close to the grand Fairfax family at Belvoir Plantation, Mount Vernon's closest neighbors, and that he was on good terms with the famously eccentric Lord Fairfax, the closest thing to a feudal lord in the colony, who disliked women and avoided society.

The Washington family had been settled near the Potomac and Rappahanock Rivers and Fredericksburg for four generations. On George's paternal side, the Washingtons traced the family line to landed proprietors in Durham, Cumbria, and Westmoreland in medieval England, when they had been the "De Wessyntons." By the sixteenth century the family name had become "Washington." Many Washington men had made advantageous marriages to brides with property, both in England and later in Virginia. In 1530 one of George's direct ancestors, Lawrence Washington, had married the wealthy widow of a wool merchant. With her money he acquired an estate and house called Sulgrave Manor in Northamptonshire, England.

Sulgrave Manor is regarded today as the family seat of the English Washingtons. It dates in part back to Tudor times and is standing today, preserved and restored by money raised jointly by public subscription in England and the Colonial Dames of America. Two centuries after Lawrence Washington established himself at Sulgrave, George's marriage to Martha enabled him to establish an even grander family seat in America by the same means as his ancestor.

In the sixteenth and seventeenth centuries the Washingtons had connections to the royal court and prospered as country gentry in England until the English Civil War, when their support for the Royalists brought them into conflict with Cromwell's Puritan government. One of George's ancestors, another in a series of Lawrences, was the Oxford-educated Reverend Lawrence Washington. By 1633, he made a wealthy living as rector of Purleigh, in Essex, but a few years later the victorious Roundheads declared this ancestor of the hero of the American Revolution as a "Malignant Royalist," confiscated his living, and ejected him from the parish. Reverend Washington died in poverty in 1652, leaving behind a widow and several children, among them sons named John and Lawrence. About the time the first Custises were gaining an ever-larger foothold in the southern part of the colony, these two Washington brothers went to Virginia to make their fortunes.

Like the Custises, the Washington ancestors in northern Virginia energetically set about making the most of their opportunities. George's great-grandfather John arrived in Virginia in 1657. He soon owned land on the Potomac and acquired seven hundred more acres in the dowry of his wife, the daughter of a neighboring landowner. He also made money importing indentured servants. John had two sons, Lawrence and Augustine, names that cropped up with confusing regularity through many generations of Washingtons. The fortunes of the Washington family in Virginia peaked with the elder son, first-generation Lawrence Washington, George's grandfather, who married another well-connected and wealthy woman and lived the life of a country gentleman, even taking a honeymoon in England. He and his wife had three children, one a son named Augustine.

When Lawrence died at the age of thirty-seven, his widow inherited his estate, remarried, and took her three children back to England with her new husband. Her son Augustine, or "Gus" as he was known, and his brother were sent to Appleby School in Cumberland. An English education was a real mark of distinction in the colony, the ultimate status symbol of its day, but in England Virginia colonials were regarded with disdain. The English found the second- and third-generation colonials a crude lot and dismissed them as bumpkins, even if they were occasionally rather rich bumpkins. However much land they might own in Virginia, however rich and prominent they might be there, the boys discovered that status in Virginia did not translate intact to England. Gus and his brother must have been tempted to abandon their embarrassing colonial connection, remain in England, possibly attend Oxford where their ancestor had attended Brasenose College, and simply try to melt back into English society before it was too late. It was only by a fluke that George Washington's father, Gus, returned to the colony at all.

Gus Washington was obliged to return to Virginia as a young man after his mother's death because Washington relations there contested the disposition of some land in his mother's will. He was a tall, fair-haired boy, supposedly known for his great strength and easygoing ways. In 1715 he came of age and inherited an estate of seventeen hundred acres, married a sixteen-year-old heiress named Jane Butler, and purchased more land. In 1726 or 1727 Gus moved to a farm he had acquired on Pope's Creek. The house he built there is indicative of the status of the Washingtons as well as Gus's own aspirations. The foundations, which are all that remain on site, show it was an irregular, U-shaped structure of brick, nearly fifty-eight feet long. There is evidence it was surrounded by the usual plantation outbuildings like a kitchen and a smokehouse. The house had four rooms downstairs and probably a second story.[1]

In 1726 Gus's younger sister Mildred transferred to him an estate called Epsewasson, or Little Hunting Creek, consisting of about twenty-five hundred acres on the banks of the Potomac. This tract would form the core of the Mount Vernon estate.

Gus and Jane Washington had three children, two sons, one named—inevitably—Lawrence and a second named Augustine after his father but always called Austin, and a daughter, another Jane. Gus took his sons back to England to attend Appleby, his old school in Cumberland. He returned from England to find that his wife had died in his absence.

Gus soon married again. His bride was an orphan named Mary Ball, born in Lancaster County, on the Northern Neck of Virginia, who was still single at age twenty-three. This was unusual, particularly as Mary had a reputation as being a handsome, if headstrong, woman and an heiress with money and property, which adjoined some of Gus's. She also knew a good horse when she saw one. These undoubted attractions aside, there was more to Mary than met the eye. At best she was said to have had a strong will.

Martha probably picked up some of the details about Mary Ball Washington and the decline of the family's fortunes, which coincided with Gus's second marriage, from gossip that had filtered down into the Tidewater. The decline might have occurred despite the marriage. Gus seems to have been too easygoing to be successful, and though he acquired land, he never quite made it pay. Mary Ball Washington may have exacerbated the situation. She was a curious character with whom history has not dealt kindly, but she was undeniably a significant figure in George's life. In nineteenth-century Washington hagiography Mary features as a formidable matron, an off-putting character combining strict piety, rigorous economy and moral rectitude—a hero's mother perhaps, but also a thin disguise for a termagant. In her later years she was said to have smoked a pipe and embarrassed her son with her blunt ways, unpolished manners, querulous complaints, and demands for money.

But Mary was the parent with the greater influence on her son George in his formative years, and she may have transmitted enough of her own social insecurities to feed George's own deep-rooted anxieties about how he was regarded by the rest of the world. George himself perceived Mary's influence as negative, and most historians have taken their cue from him. Evidence suggests that George's relations with his mother were strained, even cold, if dutiful, all his life. His letters to her address her formally as "Honored Madam." Though George always saw to it that his mother was provided for, when possible, he kept his distance.

Martha was Mary's antithesis in most respects. One of George's reactions to his mother was to gravitate to women who were as unlike her as possible. Certainly all the women who attracted George were not only likely to inherit money but also confident of their place in the social hierarchy. Before Martha, George had courted, unsuccessfully, several other young women, all heiresses from prominent families, and all with a reputation as attractive girls. Martha fit into the pattern.

Inevitably, Mary has been compared unfavorably with her dainty, vivacious, popular daughter-in-law Martha Custis. But the comparison is unjust because the circumstances of the two women were very different. If Martha was a happier and more pleasant person than Mary, her upbringing was probably happier than Mary Ball's, having grown up in a loving family with relatives nearby, under the close supervision of a mother she always referred to as "dear Mamma." Whatever motivated John Dandridge to spend lavishly on clothing for Martha to enjoy a fling as a debutante in Williamsburg, it must have had something to do with a father's wish to indulge his daughter with a brief interlude of fun between girlhood and the onerous responsibilities of marriage, as much as with putting her in the way of a good husband.

If John Custis insulted Martha and her family by letting Williamsburg know she was not good enough for his son, the readiness of Daniel's prominent friends to intercede in her favor must have soothed her wounded feelings. Humiliating as the public insults must have been, the experience did not noticeably dent Martha's self-confidence or sour her personality.

Mary, on the other hand, either regretted marrying Gus Washington or grew up with a chip on her shoulder. She was the child of an elderly merchant, Colonel Joseph Ball of Epping Forest, in Lancaster County, and his short-lived marriage to a second wife, a woman who had been widowed at least once and possibly twice. The Balls were an old and prominent family who had settled near the Potomac, but some kind of shadow has always hung over Mary's mother. Generally, a man's second marriage was too common an event to attract any comment. Joseph Ball's did, because Mary's mother had been his housekeeper and possibly an indentured servant.

Today it hardly matters one way or the other whether Mary Ball Washington's mother was an indentured servant or not, but despite her good looks and inherited property, Mary seems to have had a deep-rooted sense of social inferiority, which she masked with a domineering character. It is difficult to imagine what was responsible for this particular combination. While Virginia was a class-conscious society, it was also a hardworking and highly mobile one. With marriageable girls in such short supply, a girl with property, and a pretty one to boot, would normally have been too much sought after to nurture a full-blown inferiority complex.

Why did indentured servitude carry such a taint? The practice of indentured servitude existed from the colony's earliest days in Jamestown and was intended to facilitate the movement of surplus skilled and unskilled labor in England to meet a rising demand for workers in the colony. Anyone who could not afford the passage could bind himself or herself to a period of contractual labor to pay for the transportation across the Atlantic, and once there, as described earlier, the purchaser of the contract for indentured labor paid the passage and provided room and board for the person bound to work for him for the term of the contract, normally seven years. In a society where even great planters and their wives worked hard, hard work itself carried no stigma. Yet by the time Joseph Ball married his second wife, about 1707, indentured servants had come to be regarded with contempt by the better-off inhabitants of Virginia, though that did not prevent those better off from making use of them.

In England advertisements promising a fine life in the New World induced many laborers, both skilled and unskilled, to indenture themselves, as did active efforts to recruit passengers by ships' captains or their agents. Many people with no prospects in England answered the call. On their arrival in the colony they and their skills would be advertised and they would be "bought" for their period of servitude. Young women might advertise themselves as seamstresses, housekeepers, or cooks, while men were prepared to undertake nearly every trade, from wig making and weaving, to bricklaying and plastering to farm work. Both the Dandridge children and the Washington children probably received their formal education from an itinerant tutor who was an indentured servant.

Those fleeing religious persecution, famine, and war in Europe, and orphaned children swelled the numbers of indentured servants. There were also a significant number of criminals either escaping justice or dispatched to Virginia to relieve English jails. Eventually so many criminals and unwilling victims of press gangs (press gangs were literally gangs who roamed England and "impressed" or "pressed" their kidnapped victims into some form of service for which the gangs received a bounty) were transported to the colony and sold into indenture that all indentured servants were tainted with a criminal connotation. In 1751, the *Virginia Gazette* complained "Robberies, the most Cruel Murders, and infinite other Villanies perpetrated by Convicts transported from Europe. . . . In what can Britain show a more Sovereign contempt for us than by emptying their jails into our settlements."

During the term of indenture, these servants had a status almost indistinguishable from that of slaves. They could be savagely disciplined without any legal sanction, though not killed in the process, as slaves could be. Most led a wretched existence.

The courts of Virginia had the power to extend a term of indenture or to impose a penalty by making an offender an indentured servant for a fixed period. As described earlier, among these offenses, in the case of white women, was that of bearing a mulatto child. Imposing a period of servitude as a legal sanction was intended to prevent a woman and child from becoming a charge on the parish system as well as to punish the sin of lewdness. The woman was effectively "sold" to someone for the duration of her penalty with the parish taking the money that was paid for her. Sanctions were rarely imposed on men who fathered bastards. Chillingly, when a woman was convicted of bearing an out-of-wedlock child, mulatto or not, the court usually ordered the child to be bound as an indentured servant too, often up to the age of thirty-one years. This usually separated the mother and child.

Indentured servants often fraternized with slaves and, like slaves, often ran away to escape their term of bondage and the harsh conditions that went with it. Those to whom they were indentured advertised for runaway servants just as they advertised for runaway slaves. The wording of one such advertisement in the *Virginia Gazette* in 1774 is revealing: "To those used to the smell of servants just from a ship, they will be easily discovered unless they have procured new clothes." Aside from any connection with indentured servitude, the only other rumored shortcoming of Mary's mother was that she was illiterate. Little, however, can be inferred from this, because that would have been true for most women in the colony.

Mary's mother remarried a third or fourth husband who died soon after, and she inherited property from each of her husbands before dying herself before her daughter's thirteenth birthday and passing on the accumulation to Mary. Mary was then pitched from pillar to post in the way of many colonial orphans, between the homes of various relatives and later possibly the home of an elder half sister who attempted to teach her sewing and other feminine accomplishments. She had a legal guardian, George Erskine, a prominent man in the colony.

Mary and Gus Washington married in 1730 or 1731, and their first child, George, was born at Pope's Creek on February 11, 1732, going by the calendar then in use. In 1752 England officially adopted the new-style Gregorian calendar used by the rest of Europe. Using the new calendar, the old date of February 11 became February 22. Mary probably named her firstborn son George after her guardian.

Only one surviving anecdote provides some insight into Mary's reputation for strange behavior. As a young woman Mary had a traumatic experience when a young female friend sitting next to her at dinner was struck dead by lightning during a thunderstorm. This may have taken place while Mary was pregnant with George, and the experience left Mary, whose reputation suggests she would not have feared the devil himself, terrified of thunderstorms ever after. She was also curiously timid about traveling, for a woman supposedly so strong-minded.

Augustine and Mary had five more children in the next eleven years. Elizabeth (called Betty), Samuel, Charles, John Augustine, and Mildred, who died in infancy. When George was three, his teenage half sister Jane died. He was much attached all his life to his sister Betty, and of his brothers, he was closest to John Augustine.

As his family grew, Gus continued to acquire land until he owned nearly ten thousand acres in a string of seven farms. What he failed to do was make it prosper. He grew tobacco, but he failed to make a fortune out of it, possibly because he did not have enough slaves or the necessary capital to buy more slaves and equipment. On one tract of land thirty-five miles from the home on Pope's Creek, Gus discovered deposits of iron ore, and he tried mining. When George was seven, Gus moved the family to another house he bought at Ferry Farm, further south near Fredericksburg, to be closer to his mining venture. The house at Ferry Farm was literally at a ferry crossing on the Rappahannock River, a great advantage because it made it possible to transport agricultural produce by water.

On the strength of his combined assets, Gus should have been a greater colonial success story than John Dandridge, who had an equally large family and far less land. Yet despite having land, farms, plantations, river frontage, and between thirty and seventy slaves at various times and at least one indentured mulatto servant, Gus failed to thrive. His plantations were not profitable, and the ore-mining business never prospered in line with his expectations, despite there being a large demand in England for iron. His son George absorbed an early lesson about the consequences of letting opportunity slip away.

The relationship between Mary and her husband progressively soured and kept him away from home for increasingly longer periods. Mary seems to have had a much stronger and more forceful personality than her husband. With her growing brood of children, Mary may have been irritated by her husband's ineffectual management and lack of drive, as well as by the fact that Gus was putting together substantial estates for the two sons of his first marriage, Lawrence and Austin, who had nearly completed their expensive English educations. One estate was composed of a large tract at Pope's Creek and included the house that had been Mary's first married home. The other was the property at Little Hunting Creek. As Gus mapped out plans to benefit the sons of his first wife, Mary may have felt he was not doing enough for hers.

Mary's stepsons Lawrence and Austin were out of the way at Appleby School in England for the first six years of her marriage to their father. Lawrence was first to return to Virginia in 1738, when George was six and Lawrence was around twenty. Lawrence had a kindly disposition and charmed the younger children. In George's adoring eyes, his elder half brother was a hero. Gus soon gave Lawrence possession of the Little Hunting Creek house and estate.

Lawrence had acquired English manners and polish with his education and moved easily in polite society. He was soon able to swashbuckle before his younger half brothers and sister in a dashing uniform, too. When war broke out in 1739 between England and Spain in the Caribbean, England expected a quota of four hundred men from Virginia to join the British troops. There was no colonial army at that time to furnish such a number, but because there was always the possibility of Indian depredations from the western frontier and the ever-present specter of a slave rebellion, British law obliged Virginia householders to arm themselves, and each county to maintain a militia of armed inhabitants. But because Indian attack had ceased to be a problem in the eastern counties near the coast, these militias had come to have a more social than military orientation. Rank was honorary, a reflection of social standing, and had nothing to do with military expertise. Membership in the militia accounts for the bewildering number of "colonels" in the colony, such as Colonel John Custis, Colonel Daniel Parke Custis, Colonel Joseph Ball, and Colonel John Dandridge.

With the prospect of a real war, the well-born young men of Virginia competed for the few precious commissions in the regular British forces on the Caribbean expedition. It was a rare opportunity for social and professional advancement for a Virginian, because the British were reluctant to commission "colonials," whom they regarded as untrained and undisciplined rabble. Gus had some influential friends, and in keeping with the local tradition of appointing military officers on the basis of social position, they persuaded the governor of Virginia to appoint young Lawrence Washington one of four company commanders in the navy, despite the fact that Lawrence was only recently returned from school and had no military training. Lawrence was posted south, to the West Indies, where the British fleet besieged the Spanish-held port of Cartagena.

The military exercise was a disaster. The colonial troops who were finally mustered to fill Virginia's quota were mostly convicts, strangers to military discipline and battle and unmotivated to fight. These inexperienced colonial troops and their untrained officers proved to be a hopeless nuisance to the British. Lawrence wound up serving as a captain of marines on board the British fleet's flagship, commanded by Admiral Vernon. He may have made the acquaintance of another British officer from Virginia, Martha Dandridge's uncle Captain William Dandridge of Elsing Green.

Lawrence spent months on board outside Cartagena, while conditions on the ship deteriorated in the heat, becoming more and more uncomfortable and unhealthy. By the time he was released from duty, he had contracted tuberculosis. The colonial troops suffered badly. Over half of them died, mostly of yellow fever on board the ships and from beatings and other ill treatment. Survivors were often drafted into the British navy to replace dead British seamen.

When he returned to Virginia in 1742 from this inglorious episode, Lawrence was appointed the adjutant commanding the Virginia Militia. In spite of his miserable experience at the siege of Cartagena, Lawrence had greatly admired the man who had commanded his fleet during the siege, Admiral Vernon, and in his honor Lawrence renamed his property at Little Hunting Creek after the admiral—Mount Vernon.

Gus must have taken satisfaction in having set up his eldest son with an English education, an estate, and military credentials. The time had come to make Austin's estate at Pope's Creek over to him, and then to turn his attention to providing for his and Mary's children. But he had no time to do so. In April 1743 eleven-year-old George was summoned home from a visit to cousins. Gus had been taken ill with what doctors described as "gout of the stomach," a vague diagnosis of a disease that does not exist, a reflection of both the level of medical knowledge of the day and the dubious abilities of colonial doctors. He died, not yet fifty, leaving his wife and seven children from his two marriages.

An inventory of the contents of the Ferry Farm home taken about this time gives some indication of the Washingtons' lifestyle at the time Gus died. The walls were painted, and there was a mirror in the hallway. The furniture consisted of two tables, eleven chairs with leather bottoms, some china, not especially fine, some silver spoons, and occasionally linen on the table. There were beds in all the rooms of the house. There were presumably pots and other domestic utensils, but nothing in the way of luxuries or fine furnishings. The contents were valued at twenty-five pounds and ten shillings.

Gus left the Pope's Creek estate to Austin, and Ferry Farm and ten slaves to George. The remaining children inherited the residue of slaves and property, and Mary was to manage Ferry Farm until George came of age, then receive the income from other property. A curious provision in Augustine's will read, "It is my will and desire that my said four sons [George, Samuel, John Augustine, and Charles] estates may be kept in my wife's hands until they respectively attain the age of twenty one years, in case my said wife remains so long unmarried."[2] In other words, if Mary wanted to remarry, she would have to find a guardian to manage her sons' estates.

The will left Mary in no position to attract another husband. It must have rankled, because she had brought land and money into the marriage, and as she knew, her own widowed mother had remarried at least twice and been left property by her husbands. The circumstances of Mary's widowhood made a sharp contrast to those of her son's fiancée, the Widow Custis, years later, a point unlikely to have escaped Mary, left in reduced circumstances with five children under the age of twelve to raise and educate on her own.

Evidently Mary was not a person who attracted scores of friends wanting to help her. In contrast, Martha, her future daughter-in-law, had been the cherished wife of a happy marriage when she was widowed. Nearby, she had her mother, brothers, and sisters to comfort her, good friends and neighbors like the Chamberlaynes to visit, two pretty children and slaves to help her with them and keep her from becoming overwhelmed with their care. She also had house servants, plenty of money, property and slaves to work it, homes at White House and Six Chimney House, fine clothes, and powerful friends in Williamsburg anxious to be of assistance. If Martha had a sweet temper and was popular, she certainly had everything to make her so. Mary manifestly did not.

The circumstances at Ferry Farm must have been grim. Mary must have struggled to make Ferry Farm productive—strong-willed as she was, she was not an innovative or overly successful farmer, though she must have done her best. She has been described as a conscientious mother of rigid morality and formidable piety by historians anxious to say something good about her. Mary's household comprised few books, other than her Bible and a copy of Reverend Matthew Hale's ponderously titled *Contemplations Moral and Divine.*

An anecdote about Mary recorded by George Washington Parke Custis in his *Memoirs and Recollections of Washington,* was told to him by one of George's cousins, who was often invited to stay at Ferry Farm and remembered the impression made by George's mother:

I was often there with George, his playmate, schoolmate and young man's companion. Of his mother I was ten times more afraid than I ever was of my own
parents. She awed me in the midst of her kindness, for she was, indeed, truly
kind. I have often been present with her sons, tall proper fellows too, and we
were all as mute as mice; and even now when time has whitened my locks, and
I am the grandparent of a second generation, I could not behold that remarkable woman without feelings it is impossible to describe. Whoever has seen
that awe-inspiring air and manner so characteristic in the Father of his Country, will remember the matron as she appeared when the presiding genius of
her well ordered household, commanding and being obeyed.[3]

Following her husband's death Mary Ball Washington turned to her eldest
son for support and assistance on the farm. Today single mothers are often
warned against relying on the eldest child to fill a partner's shoes, but even
so, many an eldest son of a widowed or divorced mother finds himself suddenly "man of the house." George did not want to be man of the house at
Ferry Farm, and like most teenage boys he was desperate to untie himself
from his mother's apron strings.

Circumstances connected with his eldest half brother's marriage
opened the door to his escape. A few months after his father's death in 1743,
Lawrence Washington married his fifteen-year-old Mount Vernon neighbor, Anne Fairfax. Gus would have been overjoyed. Lawrence could hardly
have made a more prestigious alliance. Anne Fairfax Washington was a
member of one of the most powerful clans in Virginia. Her father, William,
was a cousin of Thomas, Lord Fairfax, the sixth Baron Fairfax of Cameron,
and acted as Lord Fairfax's agent in managing the family's extensive property in the colony, a five-million-acre tract of land between the Potomac and
the Rappahannock Rivers. The Fairfaxes were a family of immense wealth,
influence, education, and culture, both in England and in Virginia. The family seat in England was Leeds Castle, in Sussex. Anne's father had built their
Virginia home, Belvoir Plantation, just down the Potomac from Mount Vernon. The two houses were in sight of each other, although at that stage they
did not bear comparison. The house at Mount Vernon was a basic one-and-
a-half-story affair, with four rooms separated by a wide passageway on the
ground floor, while Belvoir was a grand and handsome brick house of at least
nine rooms, with a library, fine furniture, mirrors, wallpaper, musical instruments, and fine fabrics all imported from England. Lawrence and Anne
divided their time between Mount Vernon and Belvoir.

As George grew restive at Ferry Farm with his mother, his elder half
brothers came to the rescue. Austin, who had married well into the Aylett
family, was busy improving the estate he had inherited at Pope's Creek into
Wakefield Plantation. He and his wife were happy to have George with them
at Wakefield, as were Lawrence and Anne Fairfax Washington at Mount

Vernon. George began spending less and less time at Ferry Farm with his mother and younger siblings, and alternating between the homes of his half brothers.

The Fairfaxes liked George, and aware of the benefits to George from such distinguished society, Lawrence and Anne often had George to stay with them. When George was at Mount Vernon, he spent much of his time at Belvoir. He was self-conscious and anxious to fit in with what he regarded as a socially superior crowd, and equally anxious not to be sent home. He made it his business to copy out a Jesuit manual of manners and proper behavior in order to learn how to conduct himself in such exalted company. He took to heart advice such as admonitions not to fidget, pick his nose, or scratch himself in the presence of others, as well as the need to observe distinctions in rank, of giving everyone present their due, not putting himself forward, behaving in a grave deferential manner to his betters, and so on. The maxims in the manual also fostered a keen awareness of the nuances of social position and the behavior they dictated, for example:

> Rule 37. In speaking to men of quality do not lean nor look them full in the face, nor approach too near them; at least keep a full pace from them.
> Rule 85. In company of those of higher quality than yourself, speak not till you are ask'd a question then stand upright, put off your hat and answer in a few words.[4]

With his lanky form, large hands and feet, and doing his best to practice these maxims with stilted newfound gallantry, the adolescent George must have seemed like an overgrown, earnest puppy to the polished Fairfaxes, but his earnestness was appealing and he became a favorite with the whole family. What particularly swayed Lord Fairfax in his favor was George's horsemanship. Lord Fairfax was a man's man, very fond of foxhunting and horses. George could ride any horse and rode hell-for-leather in the hunting field. He did not know the meaning of fear.

Lawrence appreciated the value of such an influential and powerful connection, and he impressed George with a sense of their superiority, leading by example in showing a proper deference to his wife's family.

George in his turn must have been repeating Lawrence's advice when he wrote to his younger brother John Augustine several years later, advising him to make the most of this grand connection when John Augustine was staying at Mount Vernon: "Live in Harmony and good fellowship with the family at Belvoir, as it is in their power to be very serviceable upon many occasion's to us as young beginner's: I would advise your visiting often as one Step towards the rest, if any more is necessary, your own good sense will sufficient dictate; for to that Family I am under many obligation particularly to the old Gentleman."[5]

Mary Washington, who believed that George should be helping her run the farm and raise the younger children, soon realized the difficulty of competing for George's time or affections. Ferry Farm, teeming with children and a library consisting of the Bible and a book of sermons, came a poor second to Lawrence, his well-connected wife, Anne, and the glamorous world of the Fairfax family. It was an opportunity for George to move in grander circles than what Mary could offer, and she knew he had to seize every opportunity to better himself, because his education was sketchy and there was no possibility of George following Lawrence and Austin to Appleby.

With a ten-year age gap between them, Anne's brother George William Fairfax became George's close friend and mentor at Belvoir, and George offered a steady contrast to George William's exuberant, troublesome half brother Bryan Fairfax. A willing pupil of all there was to learn at Belvoir, George copied the Fairfaxes' elegant manners, learned to dance, read their books, and acquired some of their social polish.

That Lawrence married quite so well is a bit curious. Lawrence may have had a kind and courteous nature, an English education, and an estate of about seventeen hundred acres with a house at Mount Vernon, but by the time he returned from Appleby School, the Washingtons were sliding a bit down the social scale. He also had a stepmother who was a strong-minded woman at best and at worst may have been the daughter of an indentured servant. The location of Mount Vernon, high above the Potomac, was impressive, but the soil was poor. Lawrence had been educated as an English gentleman from a young age and probably knew less about farming than George, who had observed the running of his father's farms since boyhood. As successful planters could have told him, turning a profit from plantation crops required a hands-on approach, either by the planter or experienced farm managers, and preferably both. Agriculture is a hard taskmaster. He was also in poorer health on his return from Cartagena than he had been before he left.

As the cousin of Lord Fairfax, Sixth Baron Fairfax of Camerar, the only resident peer in the colonies, Anne Fairfax might have expected to make a far grander match than Lawrence Washington, son of a failed planter, unless there were other factors at play. In fact, the Fairfaxes may have been so anxious to marry Anne off to any passable husband that they repaid what they regarded as a debt to Lawrence by energetically "taking up" both Lawrence and his younger brother George.

There are two possible reasons why this unlikely marriage was sanctioned so enthusiastically by the Fairfaxes. First, Anne's father, as an eldest Fairfax brother, had a reasonable expectation that the law of primogeniture would ensure that that he and his son would eventually inherit both the baronetcy and the estate on two continents that that went with it. His cousin Lord Fairfax was unmarried and had no heirs. The fact that Anne's father built Belvoir suggests a greater degree of autonomy and independent fortune than he actually had. In fact, the family at Belvoir was dependent upon Lord Fairfax's whim, with more expectations than cash to give Anne as a dowry.

Second, an unresolved question about the racial background of Anne and her brother George William's mother, their father's first wife, was a matter that the English branch of the Fairfaxes had never determined to their satisfaction. There is some evidence that Anne, Martha's predecessor as mistress of Mount Vernon, may have been of mixed race and the descendant of an African slave. As a young man Anne's father had been the British governor of the Bahamas. At that time the Bahamas had quite recently been a lawless place and a haven for pirates. While governor of the Bahamas, Anne's father had married a woman named Sarah Walker, a captain's daughter. The murky history of Barbados led the English Fairfaxes to believe, rightly or wrongly, that Sarah Walker herself had African blood, based on speculation that her mother was either black or a mulatto. If so, Anne and her older brother George William Fairfax, born in 1724, also had African blood. This would have implications for the way the title would pass down in the family.

George William's father was transferred from the Bahamas to Massachusetts, where he was appointed chief customs officer for the Crown. Sarah and George William accompanied him, and in 1728 Anne was born in Salem, Massachusetts. In 1729 the records of Marblehead, Massachusetts, record the baptism of a five-year-old boy, "William, negro child of William Fairfax Esq, baptised February 26th 1729." It may have been a record of the baptism of a slave, named William and not George William, though it would have been unusual to baptize a slave. Certainly George William was five years old at this juncture, and it has been suggested that George William was so clearly interracial that he was automatically recorded as being a "negro child" on being baptized. Sarah died in 1731, and rumors of her mulatto blood persisted in the Fairfax family.

George William and Anne's father remarried a widow from Salem named Deborah Clarke, who later became the mistress of Belvoir.

When George William's mother died, his father wrote to his own mother in England seeking help in educating his "eldest son George . . . a poor West India boy . . . especially as he has the marks on his face that will always testify his parentage."[6] It is unclear whether this meant that George William, who was born in the West Indies, looked African or that he bore a strong resemblance to the family in England.

Concern among the Fairfaxes about George William's possible African ancestry later became an issue connected with the Fairfax inheritance and title in England after George William married in 1748. After a very brief courtship George William Fairfax married Sally Cary, eldest of four Cary sisters of Ceelys plantations, when she was eighteen. It brought a feminine presence to Belvoir for the first time since Anne had married and moved away three years earlier. Anne and George William's stepmother Deborah had been dead for years.

The new young mistress of Belvoir was a lively, well-educated young woman, who often had her equally lively, attractive, and well-educated younger sisters Mary, Anne, and Elizabeth Cary to stay. A copy of a lost portrait of Sally in the naïf style shows a dark-haired, square-jawed young woman holding a flower. Sally had a reputation for wit and cleverness, which has survived, as well as a reputation for ambition. For a colonial girl to marry a future peer of the realm was unknown, and Sally must have found the prospect intoxicating. The Fairfaxes were rather intellectual, and the atmosphere at Belvoir, with its library and paintings and witty conversation, was now enlivened by amateur theatrical performances with classical allusions with which the Belvoir family amused themselves. Sally's arrival introduced George, who was only two years younger, to a pleasant new feminine element. He had a romantic streak and, like most teenage boys, was, by his own

"Sally Cary Fairfax," by Duncan Smith in 1915, copy of a lost original by an unknown American artist. Courtesy of The Virginia Historical Society.

description, "susceptible to the fair sex." He mooned after a girl he called his "lowland beauty," probably Lucy Grymes, who would later marry one of the Lee family, but he enjoyed the presence of Sally's sisters in the house, too. Sally fell in with the family's treatment of George as a kind of pet, teasing and bantering with him as with a younger brother.

At the time she married George William, his father appeared likely to inherit the Fairfax title from his childless cousin, the sixth Lord Fairfax, to become the seventh Baron Cameron of Fairfax. Lord Fairfax was unlikely to surprise everyone by marrying late in life and producing a legitimate heir to confound everyone's expectations. He had taken refuge from the world of women at Greenway Court because he was a man disappointed in love— jilted traumatically at the altar, in fact—who had carried a grudge against women ever since. In the absence of a legitimate son, the title would in the normal course of things pass to his cousin, the father of Anne and George William, and in turn to George William himself.

What happened to the title in later years sheds an oblique light on the issue of Anne and Lawrence Washington's marriage, and the way the Fairfax connection, invaluable to George, came to pass. Though after his mother's death George William had been raised by the family in England, who ought to have been in a position to decide based on their own acquaintance with him, in later life he would make several trips back to England for the sole purpose of demonstrating he was not "a negro's son." On his return to Virginia he ordered a portrait to make him look as white as possible to reinforce his case with the unconvinced Fairfax relatives.

But following Lord Fairfax's death in 1781, the title bypassed George William. Many years later his widow, Sally, would write a letter to a nephew explaining why George William's father had not inherited the Fairfax title and estate on the death of the sixth Baron Fairfax: "[the estate] went in fee simple to . . . eldest son Henry Fairfax, who would have left it to your uncle William Henry Fairfax [father to Anne and George William], but from an impression that my husband's mother was a black woman, if my Fairfax had not come over to see his uncle and convinced him that he was not a negroe's son."[7]

But it seemed he was not convinced enough. What the letter does not make clear is that in order for the title to go to George William, his father had to have been acknowledged as the cousin entitled to inherit the title. Although George William's father died in 1756, he nevertheless had to be acknowledged as rightfully next in line to the title in order for it to then pass to his living son. What is particularly strange is that George William's younger half brother Bryan Fairfax, Deborah's son, eventually inherited the title. George William was pointedly skipped over. If, as the Fairfaxes clearly believed, George William was the child of a mulatto, so was his sister Anne. The relevance of George William's racial status as perceived by the English

Fairfaxes became relevant to George Washington and by extension, to Martha, at a later stage.

In Virginia in 1743 the issue of Anne Fairfax's racial inheritance mattered far more than it did in England, and for a different reason, one that may explain why Lawrence Washington was able to marry so well. Virginia laws traced legal status as slave or free from a mother. If Anne's maternal grandmother had been a slave, by Virginia law her mother, even if part white, was legally a slave. If Anne was indeed of mixed race she must have been at least three-quarters white, but still, like her mother, a slave. If that were the case, the family may have been eager to see Anne married into a family not grand enough to have English connections who knew about the Fairfax reservations about Sarah Walker, and who stood to benefit from the Fairfax connection to such an extent that they would ask no questions in Virginia.

The connection with the Fairfaxes had a powerful effect on George Washington, not only because it smoothed his rough ways and rustic habits, but because it gave George his first glimpse of a world of beauty and elegance and kindled a desire to enter it in his own right, as a planter with a fine estate and an elegantly furnished home of his own. The Fairfaxes began to interest themselves in their young friend's future, and George's prospects as poor Gus Washington's son brightened considerably as he became the Fairfax protégé.

In 1747, the Fairfaxes and Lawrence cooked up a plan to help George get away from home to start a career of his own. They arranged for George to go to sea as a midshipman on a British naval vessel. At Ferry Farm Mary Washington gave her reluctant consent. It is a mark of the unfair treatment Mary has often received at the hand of historians that she was castigated for what she did next as being the act of a typical domineering, overpossessive mother, hell-bent on keeping her son at home to help on the farm. In fact, it was eminently sensible.

Having no husband to turn to, Mary wrote to her half brother Joseph Ball, now in London, asking his advice as to whether she had made the right decision about sending her fifteen-year-old son to sea. George's ship, a vessel-of-war, was standing in the Potomac ready to sail, with George's luggage on board, when Mary received Joseph's reply:

I understand you are advised and have some thought of putting your son George to sea. I think he had better be put apprentice to a tinker, for a common sailor before the mast has by no means the common liberty of the subject; for they will press him from a ship where he has fifty shillings a month and make him take twenty three, and cut, and slash, and use him like a negro, or rather like a dog. And as to any considerable preferment in the navy, it is not to be expected, as there are always so many gaping for it here [in England] who have interest, and he has none. And if he should get to be master of a Virginia ship (which It is very difficult to do), a planter that has three or four hundred acres of land and three or four slaves, if he be industrious, may live more comfortably and leave his family in better bread than such a master of a ship can. . . . He must not be too hasty to be rich, but go on gently and with patience, as things will naturally go. This method, without aiming at being a fine gentleman before his time, will carry a man more comfortably and surely through the world than going to sea, unless it be a great chance indeed. I pray God keep you and yours,

Your loving brother,
Joseph Ball[8]

Mary understandably—and wisely—withdrew her consent, and the ship sailed without George. The experience may have made her wary of Lawrence and his grand Fairfax connections and their plans for George. Certainly the worlds of Mount Vernon and Ferry Farm did not overlap, and now that George had discovered his ambition to be a fine gentleman, he needed to find a way of achieving it.

George had inherited his father's set of surveying instruments. Gus had probably shown George how to use them, and George would have known that surveyors played a vital role in the colony. As settlers acquired land, it became a matter of utmost importance to mark out accurately the boundaries of landownership. Frequently there were disputes as settlers and planters laid claim to the same piece of land. A proper survey was the only means of establishing who owned what. During his father's lifetime George must have accompanied Gus on surveying expeditions of his extensive property and absorbed the need for precision, accuracy, and method. These were lessons he never forgot.

With George's naval career stalled before it could begin, the Fairfaxes found another job for him. It started with Lord Fairfax's plan to build himself an estate further inland in the distant Shenandoah Valley, and to withdraw from the social whirl of Virginia. He needed a surveyor to mark the boundaries of the estate he proposed to establish there, and given the size of the Fairfax holdings in the western part of the colony, there would be a great deal more surveying to be done beyond that. Who better than the young Fairfax favorite with his surveying tools? By the time George was sixteen, thanks to Lord Fairfax, he was regularly employed surveying the western portion of the Fairfax lands in Virginia beyond the Blue Ridge Mountains. It was an opportunity to get away from his mother, and he was well paid. George made the most of it, becoming an experienced frontiersman in the process. He was young and hardy enough to survive the rough living conditions and ever-present dangers of the job—flea-ridden inns, snow-covered mountains, icy rivers, Indian attacks, treacherous guides, and

wild animals. Anxious to please his benefactors, he also developed his surveying skills and honed his ability to do precise painstaking work.

This backwoods life could not have been more different from the
refined elegance of Belvoir, where he would often return when staying with
Lawrence at Mount Vernon. From time to time he went to dances, ordered
himself some fine linen, and fell in love. But George worked whenever possible, which meant whenever the seasons allowed—anything to escape the
claustrophobic world of Ferry Farm.

While the drama of Martha Dandridge's courtship by Daniel Parke
Custis was being played out in Williamsburg in 1748 and 1749, her future
second husband was shivering on the frontier, hoarding the generous payments from the Fairfaxes and dreaming of an estate of his own to rival Belvoir.

By 1751, when George was twenty, he realized that while surveying
brought him an income, it was not large enough for his aspirations and he
hoped that, like his brother Lawrence, he might be able to obtain a commission in the British forces. Otherwise he was at a dead end, possibly even
doomed to return to Ferry Farm.

Lawrence, however anxious he was to help George, was in no position
to help promote his military plans. By 1751 Lawrence was far from well. He
was suffering from tuberculosis, contracted on board Admiral Vernon's ship
at Cartagena years before. Lawrence went to a spa at Berkeley Springs, a
place now known as Warm Springs, West Virginia, but the damp air there
probably made him worse. Then in September 1751 George made the only
journey abroad of his life when he accompanied Lawrence to Barbados in
hopes that the warmer climate there might restore him. In Barbados George
contracted a mild case of smallpox, from which he recovered easily. It was
actually a great stroke of luck because it meant he was immune to the disease thereafter in an age when smallpox was endemic and a great killer.

The Washington brothers found the weather of Barbados monotonous
but tried to keep their hopes up for Lawrence's recovery. Doctors advised
Lawrence to try England if the climate of Barbados failed to restore him to
health. Lawrence grew worse and returned to die at home at Mount Vernon in the summer of 1752. He left Mount Vernon to his widow, Anne, for
her lifetime and after that to their infant daughter, Jenny. In the event Jenny
did not survive to inherit, the property was to go to George. Before 1752
was out, Anne had remarried, to George Lee; Jenny had died; and since
there were no other surviving children to inherit the property, Anne agreed
to rent Mount Vernon to George.

Lawrence had been adjutant of the Virginia Militia, and with his death
the post became vacant. Since militia officers were appointed on the basis
of their social status, George stepped into Lawrence's boots, as it were, and
became Major Washington through the influence of the Fairfaxes. By late
1752, now a major and master of a rented estate, George was in love again,

this time with a fifteen-year-old girl named Betsey Fauntleroy. He proposed to her, but her wealthy parents did not believe George's prospects were good enough for their daughter. About this time George's younger brother John Augustine also escaped Ferry Farm, coming to keep George company at Mount Vernon, where George tried to introduce him to the beneficial influences of Belvoir.

In 1753 George's prospects took a new turn when the Fairfaxes persuaded the governor to appoint him to lead a delicate diplomatic mission to confront the French on Virginia's western frontier and warn them politely but firmly to stay out of the Ohio Valley, which many of the leading families of the Northern Neck were seeking to exploit under a joint venture known as the Ohio Company. By this time George not only knew the route and how to negotiate with the Indians along the way, but he also had enough social skills to parley with the French.

The mission under Major Washington turned into a disaster. George mistakenly ambushed the French as they camped, killing their aristocratic commanding officer. In the aftermath, he was somehow persuaded to sign an admission of responsibility, which sparked a diplomatic crisis that soon escalated into the French and Indian Wars.

George, having no idea at first of the crisis he had precipitated, wrote home enthusiastically that he had "heard the bullets whistling" and that there was "something intoxicating in the sound." The story made its way back to England and was repeated to the king, George II, who responded tartly that "he will not think so when he has heard many of them."

Not surprisingly, the British authorities, both in Williamsburg and in England, were not pleased with George. The incident helped put an end to any prospects of a career with the British army, confirming the English view that untrained colonial officers were an unreliable lot. Yet even though the governor and authorities now regarded Major Washington as a loose cannon, he remained more of an asset than a liability because of his experience in the wilderness. Having surveyed along the frontier, George knew his way over the mountains and had a firsthand knowledge of the Indians who lived there.

As hostilities with the French escalated on the northwestern frontier, professional English troops led by General Braddock arrived in the colony. The British were in no doubt of their superiority as a disciplined fighting force, and their confidence persuaded them they knew the best way to fight in the colonial wilderness. They insisted on maintaining control of the military logistics and delegated administration and supply to the colonials. It should have been the other way round.

The colonials knew how to travel, fight, and survive in the wilderness but were utterly hopeless at organizing supplies, men, uniforms, weapons, equipment, horses, or transport, all the things the British delegated to their control. Braddock ignored the advice of Washington, who knew the best route west, and insisted on cutting new roads and hauling heavy British cannon over the mountains. Driven to distraction by the inability of the colonial powers to supply his troops adequately, he also ignored George's advice on military logistics. Certainly Braddock and his troops were experienced, but on the battlefields of Europe. They had no idea what armed combat involved on the frontier and against the Indians. Inevitably, relations with General Braddock were strained, but George had no choice but to find a way to work with him.

In the chaotic and unsanitary conditions of the military camps, notorious breeding grounds for a range of diseases that felled many troops, George contracted a bad case of dysentery. When an advance party of British and colonials finally clashed in a disastrous battle with the French and their Indian allies on the Monongahela River in July 1755, he was so ill he had to be carried by litter. The tightly regimented British troops were totally unsuited for the surprise attack from the French and their Indian allies who had hidden in ravines on either side of the road.

The British and the colonials were in confusion; when the colonials took cover behind trees to fire at the enemy, the British forces, assuming they were deserting, fired on them. After having five horses shot out from under him, General Braddock was fatally wounded. George later reported that the British "behaved with more cowardice than it is possible to conceive" and fled "as Sheep pursued by dogs" while "the Virginia Troops shewed a good deal of Bravery and were near all killd."[9] George, ill as he was, continued on the battlefield and, on General Braddock's orders, somehow rode through the night back to find reinforcements. General Braddock was borne off the battlefield, badly wounded, to die in agony a few days later. The general was buried quickly on the road; his grave was then trampled over to prevent its being found and his body dug up and desecrated by the Indians. Many of the dead, wounded, and dying who had fallen were scalped. Braddock's Defeat has since figured as one of the great military disasters, and, at the time, news of it shocked and alarmed Virginia.

George, on the other hand, emerged from disaster a hero for leading the survivors back. Of the fourteen hundred troops, both British regulars and colonial militiamen, nearly nine hundred were killed or wounded. According to one of the British officers, Captain Robert Orme, George acted with "the greatest courage and resolution," a view reinforced by the fact that Braddock had bequeathed George his fine horse and his manservant, Bishop.

The incident also gave rise to the first myth about George Washington: his superhuman invincibility and the Indian belief that George could not be killed by human means. Washington biographer Jared Sparks repeated what he had heard from Martha's grandson Wash: "During the battle of the

Monongahela he [the chief] had singled him [Washington] out as a conspicuous object, fired his rifle at him many times and directed his young warriors to do the same, but to his utter astonishment none of their balls took effect. He was then persuaded, that the youthful hero was under the special guardianship of the Great Spirit, and ceased to fire at him any longer.... [Washington] was the particular favorite of Heaven, and who could never die in battle."[10]

George had, in fact, had a near-miraculous escape. Although he reported he had had four bullets through his coat and two horses shot from under him, George escaped without a scratch. He was to have similar near-miraculous escapes throughout the Revolution. The governor congratulated him on his gallantry and suggested that George might undertake a further expedition to the frontier, but did not offer George a regular commission.

By way of compensation the governor made twenty-three-year-old George a colonel of the Virginia forces and dispatched him to defend the thin line of English settlements on the frontier, which were under continual attack and harassment from the Indians, instigated by the French. For the better part of the next three years George did his best, hampered by the lack of effective support and supplies and weapons, and leading a sparse militia composed of unwilling souls, many of whom had been forced into service.

George was now the ranking officer in Virginia, but it was the worst of both worlds, because as a colonial officer he was both poorly paid and too poorly equipped and manned to do his job properly, and his orders could be countermanded by those of any lower-ranking officer in the regular British army. It was humiliating and frustrating. He could not bring himself to quit, however, because he worried about what would happen to the settlers if he did.

This unsatisfactory cycle made him a hero in the colony, but it became clear to George that even as commander of the Virginia militia, his prospects of advancing in the regular British army were poor to nonexistent. The British officers regarded the local militias as a necessity to defend the colonies, but believed them to be composed of undisciplined rabble. His former comrade at arms Captain Orme advised George to give up his fight for a British commission and retire to concentrate on planting at Mount Vernon. Putting it as tactfully as he could, Orme told George, "American Affairs are not very well understood at Home."

Early in 1756, in a final attempt to obtain a commission, George went north to Boston to confront the ranking English general there and then on to New York. George was put off with meaningless concessions. On his way back he stopped in New York, where he had met an heiress named Mary Phillipse, who owned a large stretch of land on the Hudson. George supposedly courted her, but somehow failed to propose, and Mary did not become the mistress of Mount Vernon. Curiously, her fate crossed with that of George on a later occasion. She married a staunch Tory named Robert Morris, and they had a fine mansion on the Harlem River. Over twenty years later, George would seize the mansion to use as his headquarters in the course of the Revolution, while Mary and her husband were described as "enemies" to the American cause.

Back at Mount Vernon, where George returned during the breaks between his military duties, the part sister-and-brother, part-flirtatious relationship he had enjoyed with Sally Fairfax for years crystallized into a full-blown love affair. They had long been on corresponding terms, with George William's knowledge, while George was away with the militia. As George William's wife, Sally had the upper hand in the relationship, both because of her status as a married woman and mistress of Belvoir, and because she was a girl two years older than the still-adolescent George. In camp, he pined for letters from Sally. However, something occurred to shift the balance of his fondness for Sally as a pretty flirtatious neighbor, because by the time George Washington proposed to Martha Custis in the spring of 1758, he was passionately in love with Sally.

There had been at least one very good opportunity in the long months of autumn 1757 for the relationship between Sally and George to take a new turn. At the end of the summer George had again become so gravely ill with dysentery that he was forced to return from the frontier to Mount Vernon to recuperate. By that time his brother John Augustine had married Hannah Bushrod and moved to Bushfield Plantation, many miles away. George William Fairfax's father had died, and George William had departed for England to put in his claim as his father's eldest son and rightful heir, which meant an absence from Belvoir for many months. Sally visited Mount Vernon frequently to look after George in his illness. Even before that she was having George's shirts made by her own seamstress at Belvoir. Had Sally and George wanted an opportunity for privacy they certainly had one during those months. It was this bout of illness that kept George bedridden for six months and convinced him that he was dying of the "family disease," tuberculosis. His desire to consult Dr. Amson in Williamsburg in the spring of 1758, as well as the need to deliver some dispatches to the governor, prompted him to set out in March on the trip that took him past Richard Chamberlayne's home on the return journey, and the meeting with the Widow Custis.

However, another view of the Fairfax/Washington friendship has suggested that the Fairfaxes—or at least George William and Sally—may have had an ulterior motive in their relationship with George, in that they may have hoped George would father a child for them and save the Fairfax title for George William. After nearly ten years of marriage, Sally had not produced a male heir, or indeed any child, which seriously jeopardized George

William's prospects of inheriting the Fairfax title and five million acres of Virginia, not to mention the estate in England. This lack of a child may itself have been connected—in the minds of the English branch of the family— with the rumors that the mother of George William and Anne Fairfax had either been an African slave herself or had mulatto blood. Lord Fairfax, a blunt man, had had plenty of opportunity to get to know Sally and George William and may have sent negative reports about both back to England. His nephew Bryan Martin had come over to Virginia in 1751 to act as Lord Fairfax's right-hand man, despite the fact that at Belvoir George William's father was ostensibly his agent and George William would have been at Lord Fairfax's disposal, precluding the need for Bryan Martin. At the best of times Lord Fairfax did not much care for women, and he may not have liked Sally or he may have been critical of her failure to produce an heir.

The family in England may have believed the issue of George William's supposed mulatto blood was connected to his lack of offspring. The term "mulatto" derives from the Spanish word for "mule," a species of animal in which the male cannot reproduce its own kind. In Virginia there was evidence before everyone's eyes that mulattos could and did reproduce — planters often had mulatto slave mistresses with whom they fathered children. But in England, the Fairfaxes may have subscribed to a theory of genetics of the period that held that a "mulatto" was, like a mule, somehow defective and unable to reproduce.

The Fairfax clan, especially Lord Fairfax at Greenway Court, may have been watching to see whether George William would have children and, if so, what racial characteristics they would exhibit. George William and Sally may have been growing desperate, and George Washington was not only a fine physical specimen, he was also clearly "English," with reddish hair and a fair complexion that sunburned easily.

There was yet another reason why George may have seemed a likely choice to Sally and George William. Though George Washington never fathered a child with Martha, there are rumors he may have fathered several children over the course of his lifetime. Rumors of the first child dated from George's younger years, and the Fairfaxes may have heard the story, because it involved George and Lucy Posey, wife of John Posey, one of Lawrence's neighbors at Mount Vernon, and a child, Thomas Posey, born in 1751. George later appointed Thomas Posey a general during the Revolution, and Posey eventually became territorial governor of Indiana. He was said to bear a striking resemblance to George. The rumor of Thomas Posey's paternity has been supported with the allegation that George accompanied Lawrence to the Bahamas in 1751 in part because he was anxious to escape the scandal he had caused in the neighborhood.

These rumors aside, all his life George ascribed to a rigid code of personal integrity; he was the last man to cuckold his best friend and powerful patron. If he did have a sexual affair with Sally, the situation made him miserable: not only was Sally married and unattainable, but his love for his best friend's wife would have conflicted with his strict sense of personal honor. Cuckolding a friend was something George would not have taken lightly, and cuckolding his patrons, the Fairfaxes, and risking their enmity would have been folly.

While Sally's letters have been lost, several of George's to her have survived. What is undeniable is that on the eve of his wedding George was writing love letters to Sally that reflect real anguish. Two letters to her that survive were written between his engagement in the spring of 1758 and his marriage in January 1759. Sally was evidently teasing him about the "animating prospect of possessing Mrs. Custis," but she could hardly have been in doubt about George's feelings for her. The letters George wrote suggest that either there had been an affair, there was still an active ongoing relationship between them, or that he was steeling himself to put the affair and Sally behind him.

Following his engagement, George had taken leave of Martha early in June 1758 and ridden west for his last stint with the Virginia militia, to camp at Fort Cumberland on the Ohio. It was at the end of that summer, while George William was busy supervising a program of improvements to Mount Vernon on George's behalf and to George's precise specifications, that George wrote one of the surviving letters to Sally. Clearly there had been no breach of friendship with George William, who was taking a good deal of trouble on George's behalf, riding over from Belvoir nearly every day and sending George progress reports. Although Mount Vernon's productivity had suffered from his prolonged absences at the front, George had ordered lavishly from his English factors a long list of materials and furnishings and furniture—panes of glass, bricks, paint, carpets, beds, material, and bed hangings. Now Sally's husband was supervising their installation to prepare the house for Martha.

On September 12, 1758, George wrote to Sally:

> Yesterday I was honored by your short but very agreeable favor of the first inst—how joyfully I catch at the happy occasion of renewing a correspondence which I feared was disrelished on your part, I leave to time, that never failing expositor of all things—and to a monitor equally faithful in my own breast to testify. In silence I now express my joy. Silence, which in some cases—I wish the present—speaks more intelligently than the sweetest eloquence.
>
> If you allow that any honor can be derived from my opposition to our present system of management, you destroy the merit of it entirely in me by attributing my anxiety to the animating prospect of possessing Mrs. Custis—when—I need not name it—guess yourself—should not my own Honor and country's welfare be the excitement? 'Tis true, I profess myself a votary of

Love—I acknowledge that a lady is in the case—and further I confess that this lady is known to you.—Yes, Madam, as well as she is to one who is too sensible of her charms to deny the Power whose Influence he feels and must ever submit to. I feel the force of her amiable beauties in a thousand tender passages that I could wish to obliterate, till I am bid to revive them,—but what experience, alas! sadly reminds me how impossible this is,—and evinces an opinion which I have long entertained, that there is a Destiny, which has the Sovereign control of our actions,—not to be resisted by the strongest efforts of Human Nature.

You have drawn me, dear madam, or rather I have drawn myself, into an honest confession of a simple Fact—misconstrue not my meaning—doubt it not, nor expose it—The world has no business to know the object of my Love—declared in this manner to you—when I want to conceal it. One thing above all things in this world I wish to know, and only one person of your acquaintance can solve me that or guess my meaning—but adieu to this till happier times, if ever I shall see them. The present hours are melancholy dull, neither the rugged toils of war, not the gentler conflict of A [??] B [??}s is in my choice. I dare believe, you are as happy as you say. I wish I was happy also. Mirth, good humor, ease of mind and—what else? Cannot fail to render you so and consummate your wishes.

He then went on to give Sally news of pretty Mrs. Spottswood, who was the toast of the camp and ends with a wish for the ladies of Belvoir "the perfect enjoyment of every happiness this world affords." Couched as it is in guarded and roundabout terms, there still seems no room for any interpretation other than as a declaration of George's hopeless love for Sally and not, as has been suggested, as a reference to Martha as the object of his love. On September 25 George wrote another letter to Sally, again echoing his tortured sentiments.

Sally may have been unhappy too, torn between duty, affection for her husband, ambition, and her feelings for George. She kept this letter of September 12 all her life, and, after she died, childless, widowed, infirm, and impoverished in Bath, England, in 1811, it was discovered in one of her trunks.[11]

CHAPTER 6

A Twelfth Night Wedding

There was almost no wedding. George came within a hairbreadth of being killed by Indians on the Ohio frontier shortly before his tour of duty ended. A month later he relinquished his hopes of becoming a British officer, formally took leave of his troops, and began the journey back to Virginia with mixed feelings over the finality of leaving military life and his forthcoming wedding. Resigning his militia post meant an end to the rugged, hard-living existence in the wilderness that George had come to enjoy. Full-time civilian life was a tame prospect in comparison. He kept his militia colonel's uniform for old times' sake.

On a personal level, writing love letters to Sally while engaged to Martha and despairing of ever seeing happier times did not betoken a man looking forward to his wedding. On the ride home from Ohio George had time to reflect on the step he was about to take with a woman he had not seen for seven months. His engagement to Martha had been quick, but he was too disciplined a man to act merely on impulse. He was the last man in the world to "marry down" or to choose a pretty but dim woman, nor would he have married a plain or graceless one. All of his life George appreciated pretty women, but he was a man of deliberation in important matters. He knew he needed a wife of financial, social, and practical substance, as well as personal attractiveness.

More significantly, it has been said of George that all his life he had an "eye for quality," whether in horses, hunting dogs, wine, architecture, silver, or people. If he had decided on the strength of a few meetings to propose to Martha, it suggests he recognized "quality" in her beyond her money. He was self-conscious enough to be anxious that "Mrs. Washington" would command respect, just as he wanted his home to impress.

Starved by an early domestic life with a mother not noted for her feminine graces, he knew how to value those Martha possessed. He did not want a shrew at home. If marriage to Martha offered a rare opportunity for him to climb Virginia's invisible social ladder and found his own family dynasty at Mount Vernon, the omens were also favorable for their domestic happiness. If George considered his marriage objectively, Martha was an ideal choice in every respect.

He had another agreeable prospect ahead of him, one that marked his upward transition in society. He had been elected to the House of Burgesses as the member for Frederick County in the summer of 1758 while he was away on the Ohio frontier. His election had cost him a lot of money because while success depended partly on what the electorate thought of the candidate personally it also depended on "persuading" the electorate with drink. His election agent had spent £39/6 shillings for alcoholic refreshments for voters, which was quite a big sum.

As he continued on his return from Ohio, George stopped at Mount Vernon to see for himself how the improvements had been carried out before beginning the final leg of his journey south to New Kent and his wedding.

Despite this being the bride's second marriage, the wedding was not planned as a quiet family affair or a subdued occasion. It was intended to make a statement about the couple, their position in plantation society, and their aspirations for the future. The lengthy engagement had allowed time for the bride and groom to order their wedding clothes from England, and for Martha to organize all the details. A superb hostess, Martha planned her wedding with care, both to ensure her guests were well provided for and to send a message that she and George were beginning life together on a positive note.

The date chosen for the event had its own significance. January 6, also known as Twelfth Night, was the perfect date for a winter wedding, because it had its own festive connotations.

In Virginia, as in England, Christmas itself was kept as a religious festival until Queen Victoria's reign introduced more exuberant German customs in the mid-nineteenth century through the influence of her German-born husband. While visions of a "colonial Christmas" complete with stockings, presents, towering Christmas trees lit in the square in Williamsburg, and carol singers dance like sugarplums in the popular imagination today, eighteenth-century Christmases were restrained. People hung greenery around the house—pine boughs, mistletoe, and holly—and went to church to hear sermons, but there were no stockings, Christmas trees, or orgies of gift giving. However, because the holiday was traditionally a religious feast day, it was celebrated with a special dinner. A poem in the *Virginia Almanack,* published in Williamsburg, sets the tone:

Christmas is come, hang on the pot,
Let spits turn round, and ovens be hot,
Beef, pork and poultry, now provide,
To feast thy neighbors at this tide;
Then wash all down with good wine and beer
And so with mirth concluded the YEAR.

Twelfth Night harked back to more ancient traditions. It was a time for letting the hair down in a riotous midwinter celebration firmly rooted in pagan
times. Shakespeare's play *Twelfth Night* captures the spirit. The characters
are in disguise, a Twelfth Night tradition, and in the atmosphere of baccha-
nalian revelry the characters interact in a festive muddle of confused identities until order and clarity are restored by a return to normal life. Virginia
settlers had kept alive the Twelfth Night customs brought with them from
England, and in the colony it had become a popular time for parties, balls,
and weddings.

Whether the Custis-Washington wedding was held at nearby St. Peter's
Church or at White House has been a subject of debate over the years. Both
practical considerations and historical evidence point to a home wedding at
White House. Family tradition recounted by descendants of Martha's
granddaughter tells that "it was a tradition in the family that all marriages
were performed at home," and an entry from a family Bible concerning a
daughter of James Anderson, one of George's farm managers, notes that on
November 28, 1806, "Margaret Anderson was united in marriage with
Richard Young. . . . The marriage was performed in the very room where
Washington was married to the charming widow Custis."[1]

A well-known painting of the wedding, "The Marriage of Washington"
by the nineteenth-century artist Julius Brutus Stearns, shows the wedding
taking place in church, but it is a version that draws generously on artistic
license and gives a misleading impression of the event. Not only is it wrong
in showing the wedding in church, but in almost every factual detail, from
the identities of many of the guests to their costumes. The painting post-
dated the wedding by nearly a century, having been painted in 1849. The
artist had a political message to convey that transcended factual accuracy,
in that he wanted to show that George Washington's marriage had been sanctioned by heaven. To convey that message and underline the subtext of family values to a nineteenth-century viewer, it was necessary to show the
marriage taking place in church. It is a telling example of the way the Washington myth has been exploited by a Victorian version of events. The real
wedding would have been quite different.

The wedding was probably a very robust affair. Most social occasions
in the Tidewater were. Martha would have known what to expect and would
have made meticulous preparations in advance to feed and accommodate a

houseful of guests who would be cooped up together in the house for an indeterminate number of days. Plantation weddings went on for a long time, and once guests had made the trip over bad, frozen, or snow-covered roads or up the icy Pamunkey River to White House, they would have had no inclination to go home quickly. Advance preparations must have involved making up endless sleeping pallets; preparing bedding; stocking up with firewood, extra soap, and candles; and an orgy of roasting, smoking, and baking; not to mention provisioning with cordials, brewing of beer, and ordering plenty of wine, Madeira, port, rum, brandy, and whiskey. Colonials were a notoriously hard-drinking lot. And in keeping with the custom of the time, Martha probably decorated White House with pine boughs, holly, mistletoe, and ivy.

The only eyewitness account of the wedding is found in Wash's *Recollections and Private Memoirs of Washington*. Wash, obviously, was not present on the occasion, but he recorded the recollection of an elderly Mount Vernon slave who was. In Wash's flowery version:

> And much . . . hath the biographer heard of that marriage of Washington, from the grey haired domestics who waited at the board where love made the feast and the Virginia colonel was the guest.
>
> "And so you remember" I said to old Cully, my grandmother's servant, when in his hundredth year—"and so you remember, when Colonel Washington came a-courting your young mistress?"
>
> "Ay, master that I do" said Cully. "Great times, sir, great times—shall never see the like again."
>
> "And Washington looked something like a man—a proper man, hey, Cully?"
>
> "Never seed the like, sir—never seed the like of him, though I have seen many in my day—so tall, so straight, and then he sat on a horse and rode with such an air! Ah sir he was like no one else! Many of the grandest gentlemen, in the gold lace, were at the wedding; but none looked like the man himself."[2]

Behind this picture of contented domestics sharing the masters' joy in the nuptials lurked a variety of issues, both for the bride and groom and for their slaves. When the bride and groom stood before Reverend David Mossom to take their vows, they had between them Martha's dead husband, George's hopeless passion for his good friend's wife, two rich overindulged children who badly needed a guardian, his difficult mother, her legal problems, his financial problems, his love of hunting, and her fondness for clothes, to name the most obvious concerns.

But the couple must have struck an irresistibly romantic note. Conscious of the image they wanted to present as a couple, Martha and George did what the English call putting the best foot forward. George radiated a kind of good-old-boy sex appeal while simultaneously looking grave and dignified. Martha was pretty and demonstrably affectionate. They were both dressed to convey wealth and status, and Cully was probably right in recalling that George had looked well.

George was always a fastidious, sometimes dashing, dresser. He was a tall, athletic man who wore clothes well; at six feet three inches, he towered protectively over Martha, who was about five feet tall. It is said he wore a suit of blue cloth with a white satin waistcoat, with gold buckles on his knee breeches and shoes, and gloves on his large hands. It is likely his clothes were uncomfortably tight on that occasion, because they often were. He complained that though he sent his exact measurements to England, the English tailors seemed to have difficulty making clothes large enough to suit his build, possibly not believing that the measurements of such a colonial giant of a man could be accurate. Nearly a century later Nathaniel Hawthorne wrote that while Washington knew a good-looking woman when he saw one, "Martha herself had an eye in the right vein"[3] in choosing a fine specimen of a man for her husband.

Family tradition and the recollections of guests who were present differ slightly about what Martha wore. One account says that for a wedding ceremony at 10 A.M. she wore a glazed calico dress, and then a handsome silk brocade gown for the 3 o'clock dinner that followed. According to the family of Martha's second granddaughter, she wore a somewhat more elaborate costume of a gold damask dress trimmed with lace, over a petticoat of fine white fabric decorated with silver threads, or possibly of a fabric known as silver tissue, along with purple satin slippers embellished with silver metallic thread and sequins, and pearl jewelry. The slippers probably had high heels. It was also customary for a bride to have a special "second day" dress.

Although one recollection places the wedding at 10 A.M., evening weddings were very popular at the time and still are in the southern states. Like the wedding of Martha's granddaughter Nelly Custis at Mount Vernon many years later, they often took place at twilight, "just after the candles were lighted." Any bride would look her best by candlelight.

It is likely that Cully's description of the wedding to Wash was rosier than the way the slaves actually perceived it. First of all, the slaves would have had a heavy burden of extra work to prepare for the wedding; ever the perfectionist in housekeeping matters, Martha must have kept all the house slaves hard at it. Second, major events like marriages and deaths in a planter's family often had ominous implications for the slaves. Since on marriage a woman's property automatically became her husband's, Martha's remarriage meant her Custis slaves would be at the disposal of a new master, and those inherited by the Custis children would likewise be property for their guardian and stepfather George to deploy or dispose of as he thought most profitable for their estates. George could decide to use the Custis slaves on different plantations, his own, or Martha's, or sell some outright to raise money, separating husbands, wives, parents, and children, and if there was a need to raise money quickly, sending any selected for sale to the auction block and an uncertain fate elsewhere.

The wedding, a happy event for George and Martha and their friends and families, may have been a deeply worrying occasion to the slaves, whose fates now depended on George. In the kitchen and barns and rudimentary cabins, the Custis slaves must have anxiously discussed what lay ahead for them. The Custis property was spread throughout the Tidewater, and Mount Vernon was a three- or four-day ride away in northern Virginia. It might as well have been on the moon for all the opportunity slaves would have to maintain contact between those who went and those who stayed behind.

The following account by an escaped slave, Francis Fedric, describes the fate the Custis slaves would have feared might befall them at any moment:

> The slaves are in general the first property parted with, a dozen likely niggers bringing in a round sum . . . a trader was seen talking to my master. The slaves were in a state of consternation, saying "Is it me? Is it me? Who'll go next?" . . .
>
> The slaves were all taking their dinners in their cabins about two o'clock. My master, the "trader" and three other white men walked up to one of the cabins, and entered one of them. My master pointed first to one, then to another, and three were immediately handcuffed, and made to stand out in the yard. One of the slaves had a wife and five children on another plantation, another slave had a wife and three children, and the other had a wife and one child. My master, the dealer and the others then went into another large cabin, where there were eight or nine women feeding the children with Indian-meal broth. My master said "take your pick of the women." The poor things were ready to drop down. The tracker said "I'll give you 800 dollars for that one." My master said "I'll take it." The trader touching her with a long cane said "walk yourself out here and stand with these men" She jumped up and laid her child out of her arms in an old board cradle, and walked to the chained men. . . .
>
> The trader spotted another woman, also buying her for 800 dollars. . . . She laid her child in one of the women's arms and said "Take care of my child if you please."
>
> The three men and two women were driven out to the gang on the highway, and chained together, two and two. We never heard from them again. . . . A slaveowner finds the sale [of slaves] the readiest mode of extricating himself from any pecuniary difficulty.[4]

Beyond Cully telling Wash what he knew he wanted to hear about the wedding, Wash may also have recalled the event in a cheerful light because it was typical of the few occasions when slaves were permitted a brief respite from their labors and given a few treats. The relentless harshness of their lives was lightened briefly at Christmas or when there was a wedding or christening in the owner's family. It was common practice on plantations to give the slaves some rum or brandy at these times, often of poor quality, and sometimes, intentionally, enough to allow the slaves to become extremely drunk. Allowing the slaves to drown their sorrows briefly was a method of convincing both the slaves and their owners of, first, the owners' benevolence and, second, of their moral and physical superiority over slaves who, when given drink, simply became incapacitated. Slaves were also commonly allowed leftovers of the special food prepared for the festivities. House slaves came off best in this arrangement, as they were closest to the food and drink and might even have been given an item of castoff clothing or provided with a new item of clothing to enable them to make a good appearance when serving the guests. Such small indulgences cast the system of slavery in a benevolent but misleading light and helped preserve the status quo. The old slave Cully may have had fond recollections of Washington as a bridegroom, because the yoke of slavery sat a little lighter on his shoulders that day when the slaves were allowed a share in the celebrations.

There is no comprehensive list of wedding guests, but between them Martha and George had plenty of family, friends, and on George's side, political and military connections. The wedding could easily have been a large party. At least two local families, the Macons and the Atkinsons, were present, and probably Governor and Lady Fauquier, who were now friends of George. Also probably among the guests were Martha's mother and her favorite sister and brother-in-law, Anna Maria and Burwell Bassett; her younger sisters Elizabeth, age nine, and Mary, not quite three years old; plus her brothers Bartholomew and William. George's half brother Austin and his wife may have come from Wakefield, several days away, and his favorite brother John Augustine and his wife Hannah from Bushfield may have been present. Also likely to have been in attendance were George's sister Betty, now Betty Lewis, and her wealthy husband Fielding Lewis, who lived near Fredericksburg.

Whether George's mother saw her son marry is a moot point. There is a sense that she was absent from the festivities. By all accounts Mary Ball Washington grew ever more plain-speaking with age, spent little time in society, polite or otherwise, and disapproved of anything frivolous. Had she attended the wedding, Martha would have behaved as charmingly and hospitably as she habitually did to company under her roof, while it is likely Mary would have tried to prove to the cream of Tidewater society that she could still assert a mother's authority over George. And, it is fair to conclude that she probably would have made George acutely uncomfortable. Another factor that may have prevented Mary from attending was that White House was a long way from Ferry Farm, particularly in winter, and Mary was never much of a traveler.

The Custis children Jacky and Patcy, aged about five and three, would have been present, probably under the supervision of their slave nurse, most likely a young slave named Molly. Other guests may have brought their children, and since small children always rush around at times of excitement, they must have added to the chaos. There were plenty of other neighbors, friends, and relatives to have swelled the numbers, but it is not known whether the Fairfaxes were among them.

In keeping with traditions of local hospitality, White House was probably bursting at the seams, with some of the male guests accommodated in rooms over the stables or other outbuildings. Guests would have arrived over several days, dressed in traveling clothes for the cold dirty journey by terrible roads and river barges, and would have needed to change at White House. They would have brought their best English clothes, carefully transported to White House. Getting dressed and primping for the festive event in the crowded house must have presented a challenge, with a great crush of ladies vying for the looking glasses as they made their toilettes, and ladies maids' and planters' valets rushing about with hair powder and water to sponge off the dirt of traveling, and overexcited children underfoot everywhere.

The Reverend David Mossom from St. Peter's Church, using the Church of England service from the prayer book, performed the ceremony. At dinner in mid-afternoon and throughout the festivities, the couple and their guests would have feasted on food available at that time of year or traditionally prepared especially for Christmas celebrations, such as cured hams, oysters, river fish, crayfish, crabs, wild turkeys, spiced fruit, gingerbread, and plum cake. The occasion would have called for a long series of toasts, preceded by the customary loyal toast to their sovereign, King George II. This custom of a loyal toast to the monarch is still observed today in England at all formal dinners. Following the toasts to the bride and groom, and then toasts to everyone and everything else possible, the party, now much the worse for the toasts, would have moved on to the entertainment. As Martha and George were both fond of music and the whole colony loved dancing, it was almost certainly part of the entertainment, as were parlor games such as "Pawns for Redemption."

The wedding conjures up a picture of the hybrid English and New World culture of which the bride and groom were a part. Deep in the New Kent countryside, in many respects the celebration resembled a wedding breakfast in England in Suffolk or Sussex following a wedding at a local church. Though performed at home, it had been an English wedding service. There was English finery, English-style food, and English dances and music.

The main differences were the black faces in the background and the likelihood of English decorum giving way to colonial exuberance as the evening wore on. An evening typically began with formal minuets and quadrilles, in the English style, but soon moved on to livelier reels and country dancing, which everyone much preferred in Virginia. The dancing would have been fueled by wine, Madeira, punch, whiskey, and rum in abundance. Deep in the Tidewater wilderness White House must have been cozy and thick with the smells of log fires, wax candles, pine boughs, spices, food, spirits, snuff, and sweating bodies, lightly overlaid with violet-scented hair powder. As the festivities lurched on, the slaves probably snatched at the surreptitious opportunity to enjoy the food and drink.

The happy couple at the center of a plantation wedding could expect little privacy beyond their bedroom, as their guests remained to celebrate the wedding for days. Consequently, Martha had to have at least a "second day dress" for the days following the wedding. The Washingtons spent some, if not all, of their honeymoon period at White House with well-wishers. There is a local tradition that part of the honeymoon was spent at a cottage at nearby Rickahock Plantation, which was owned by Martha's brother Bartholomew. If so, the children Jacky and Patcy must have gone too, because Martha hated being parted from her children.

Between the wedding and the opening of the assembly session in Williamsburg, which George would attend as the new member for Frederick, Martha and George stayed in New Kent. It was the custom for newlyweds to make a round of postnuptial wedding visits—as if Virginians needed an excuse for visiting—and they may have paid such formal visits to members of Martha's family, including the Bassetts. Beyond the social calls, Martha had a good deal to do in organizing the move for herself and the children from White House to their new home at Mount Vernon.

Several days before February 22, when the assembly was due to open, George, Martha, and the children traveled to Williamsburg and probably moved into Six Chimney House, taking some of the house slaves with them. George took his seat in the House of Burgesses for the first time on his twenty-seventh birthday, where he rose to his feet, tongue-tied and self-conscious, to hear a formal vote of thanks for his service on the frontier. Only one record survives of the new burgess and his wife attending a ball in March, but as both were popular and of a social disposition, they must have enjoyed a great many other social occasions.

The assembly was still in session in April 1759 when George decided to leave for Mount Vernon, presumably because it was time to begin the spring sowing. They returned to White House briefly, and on April 5 George sent a thoughtful message to his estate manager and former body servant

John Alton. He wanted Martha's first impression of Mount Vernon to be welcoming. As transcribed, the message read:

> You must have the house very well cleaned, and were you to make fires in the rooms below, it would air them. You must get two of the best bedsteads put up, one in the hall room and one in the little dining room that used to be, and have beds made on them [before] we come. You must also get out the chairs and tables and have them very well rubbed and cleaned; the staircase ought to be polished in order to make it look well.
>
> Inquire about the neighborhood and get some eggs and chickens and prepare in the best manner you can for our coming.[5]

The household goods from White House were sent by water, which was far easier than hauling furniture over rough roads. Martha, the children, and the Custis slaves who were being brought to Mount Vernon, along with light luggage, came by coach and wagon. Because George hated being cooped up in a carriage when he could be on horseback, he rode alongside the carriage. It took Martha and George and their entourage of children and slaves five days to make the trip from New Kent to Mount Vernon. They went via Fredericksburg, probably calling briefly on George's mother at Ferry Farm and his younger sister Betty Lewis and her husband, Fielding Lewis, at their home, Kenward, in Fredericksburg. It would have been considered polite for George and his new wife to call on Mary, particularly if she had been unable to attend the wedding.

George was fond of Betty, a tall woman who resembled George so closely that she could dress in George's hat and cloak and be mistaken for him. Martha also liked Betty, and, being Martha, she would have done her best with Mary. Oddly, there is no record of what Mary and Martha Washington made of each other. In a world where close family ties counted for everything, it is strange that so little is known of the relationship between Mary and her daughter-in-law.

Mary may have felt herself sidelined by Martha. There is something sad about Mary, even if she was as irascible, possessive, and difficult as her worst detractors believe. George was moving up in the world, with his estate, his wallpapers, his Chippendale chairs, his rich society wife, and his grand friends, leaving Mary, her plain ways, abrupt manners, and her rigid piety to the lonely comfort of her pipe and book of sermons at Ferry Farm.

Martha always invested a great deal of her time and energy in her extended family connections, keeping up with everyone's concerns, health, and news, and forever sending presents such as sewing silk, fans, handkerchiefs, food, and medicine she thought people might like. The one person in the family with whom Martha was never involved in this way was her mother-in-law. Martha may have sensed George's ambivalent attitude toward

Mary early in their marriage, if not his actual dislike, and Mary may have experienced mixed feelings about the woman whom she saw as taking her place in George's affections. George's well-dressed bride, with her two pampered children and household slave retinue in tow, must have been an exotic, frivolous creature in comparison to plain-speaking, plain-living, plain-dressing Mary, whose life as the Widow Washington had been so much harder than that of the Widow Custis. Under the circumstances, Mary may have initially taken a sour view of Martha.

After leaving Fredericksburg, Martha first saw the place that would be her home for more than forty years in early April 1759. The timing for her first sight of Mount Vernon was well chosen, and probably deliberately chosen, by George, who had an instinct for the dramatic. Mount Vernon, which he was anxious to show off to its greatest advantage, was at its best. Many years later Martha's granddaughter Nelly Custis agreed, writing to a Philadelphia friend that Mount Vernon was at its loveliest in April, when the trees were in blossom and the green of the new grass and budding leaves made everything look fresh.

The arrival of a bride at her new home provided another excuse for a party. On such occasions it was the custom in Virginia for the neighborhood to hold an "infaring" party to welcome a new wife, and Martha probably met many of the surrounding families for the first time at her own infaring. Guests could have been neighbors like the Masons from Gunston Hall, the Fairfaxes from Belvoir, the Thurstons, the Lees, Denis McCarty, and the Poseys.

When Martha first saw it, the Mansion House at Mount Vernon, as they called it, was a smaller house than it later became, but it was still imposing, sitting high above the Potomac with a sweeping view of the broad river. George once described Mount Vernon as "most pleasantly situated in a high healthy country; in a latitude between the extremes of heat and cold, on one of the finest rivers in the world—a river well stocked with various kinds of fish at all seasons of the year, and in the spring with shad, herrings, bass, carp, sturgeon, etc. in abundance. The borders of the estate are washed by more than ten miles of tide-water."[6]

The location high above a broad river was fresher than the low-lying New Kent, which quickly became steamy and muggy in spring. Martha, obsessed as she was with her children's health, would have appreciated that its "high healthy aspect" was a less likely breeding ground for the diseases and fevers that killed so many young children in the Tidewater. It would be a safer place for Jacky and Patcy, as well as for her and George's future children. The original modest one-and-a-half-story house, where George and his younger brother John Augustine had kept house together following Lawrence's death, was now two and a half stories high, with four rooms on the first floor and four rooms on the second. Like most new construction work, it was slightly raw in the newer parts, but it was a big house, comparing favorably with neighboring Belvoir, which had nine principal rooms.

Already George's aspirations to grandeur were evident. There was a wide, high-ceilinged hallway that ran from the east-facing river side of the house through to the entrance on the west. It was a feature as welcome in its day as air conditioning is in our own, because this shady through-hallway allowed cross breezes to cool the house in summer. Such large central hallways were a practical feature of many of the houses in northern Virginia They were used as a dining room in the summer, and on hot days as a comfortable place for the ladies to gather with their endless sewing.

Much depended on appearances in the colony, and George was anxious to appear the gentleman, not least to his new wife. He was beginning in the way that he meant to go on. Martha must have been charmed to find how attractively George had fitted out Mount Vernon. In fact, even in the early stages of the many improvements George would carry out over the years, her new home was probably grander and handsomer than the one she had left behind at White House. The White House inventory had listed a vast number of useful items, such as cooking equipment, bedding, a few looking glasses and chairs, some china and tea things, and quantities of dressmaking materials such as silk and damask; but most of the valuable items, such as furniture and paintings owned by the Custises, had been used at Six Chimney House. Martha had auctioned off many of these after Daniel's death, and the Moodys still had the Custis silver.

Comparatively speaking, White House had been a comfortably functional working plantation house, but George had already begun to turn Mount Vernon into a colonial palace. In 1757, influenced by the elegant lifestyle of Belvoir, George had ordered what he had learned were the proper trappings for a gentleman's country house from London, specifying "fine" porcelain, "fine" china serving dishes and soup plates, a Chinese porcelain tea service, which was considered extremely fashionable, a "fine" mahogany tea table, and "fine" Wilton carpets. He had also ordered a large four-poster bed with "Mahogany Carvd & fluted pillars for feet posts . . . yellow Silk and Worsted Damask [bed] curtains," and a "Fine neat Mahogany Serpentine Dressing Table." Finally he had ordered silver cutlery embossed with the Washington coat of arms and an elegant silver cruet stand.

The downside was that all this newly bought elegance for the house came at a huge price. In addition to the bills he had run up for the house, the agricultural side of the Mount Vernon estate, which was run-down in comparison to the house, needed a large infusion of capital. Although tirelessly industrious, with great plans for developing his estate, George's enforced absences during his military career between 1753 and 1759 had prevented his giving the estate the attention it needed to be both productive and profitable. Fences were broken, fields had been left uncultivated, outbuildings and barns were in poor repair, and new equipment was needed. While he did ship some crops to London while engaged in his military activities, Mount Vernon had not been productive in George's absence. Additionally, the soil was poor, and tobacco was becoming hard to grow profitably there.

George arrived home keen to expand, improve, experiment, develop, and innovate, all at once. Before his marriage George had either lost track of whether the income from Mount Vernon had been enough to cover the orders for the farm equipment he needed if he was to carry on at all, let alone the paint, glass, bricks, wallpaper, furniture fabrics, and silver, or he had simply ignored the unpleasant reality that he was in debt to his factors. Putting Mount Vernon on a sound financial footing with Martha's capital and slaves was an urgent priority if he was not to follow his father's example.

From Martha's point of view, the trickiest aspect of adjusting to her new home must have been the proximity of the Fairfaxes. No one knows what, if anything, George told Martha about Sally, and aside from George's letters alluding to something between them, no one knows what Sally's feelings were for George. Yet there was clear evidence from George's letter to Sally months before his wedding that he was in love with her, as well as a strong hint that something had been going on between them.

On the bare facts, it is hard to imagine that the situation did not generate pronounced emotional undercurrents, and it seems equally unlikely any woman in Martha's position would have been unaware of them. Any woman finding herself face to face with a husband's former lover needs all the restraint she can muster. While reining in any instinctive reactions of jealousy or hurt feelings is often the best policy, it requires great reserves of self-control. Martha was a sensible woman, and her instincts were always governed by a firm sense of her duty. If she sensed anything that caused her pain, she was likely to have reminded herself that George was now married to her, she was in charge as mistress of Mount Vernon, and she would have to trust that it would work out. The least sensible course of action with someone like George would have been to behave with outraged possessiveness like his mother had done.

A short time proved her right. Months after his marriage, George wrote contentedly to a friend and possible relation Richard Washington in London: "I am now I beleive, fixd in this Seat with an agreeable Consort for life, and I hope to find more happiness in retirement than I ever experienced amidst wide and bustling World."[7]

CHAPTER 7

Halcyon Days

Although George was less demonstrative about his feelings than Martha, there were clear signs of his affection for her from the beginning of the marriage. George called Martha "Patsy" and "My Dear" and formally, "Mrs. Washington," when he mentioned her in his diary. Before her marriage Martha had ordered a pretty English songbook *The Bull Finch,* and when it arrived, George inscribed her name, "Martha Washington," boldly on the frontispiece. According to Wash Custis, George had a miniature of Martha he wore in a locket round his neck throughout their married life.

Martha settled happily into her new life at Mount Vernon. Benson Lossing, one of George's nineteenth-century biographers and a contemporary and friend of Wash Custis, left a picture based on neighborhood hearsay but consistent with firsthand accounts of people who met her later, describing Martha in the early years of her marriage as

> a small plump, elegantly formed woman. Her eyes were dark and expressive of the most kindly good nature; her complexion fair; her features beautiful; and her whole face beamed with intelligence. Her temper, though quick, was sweet and placable, and her manners were extremely winning. She was fond of life, loved the society of her friends, always dressed with scrupulous regard to the requirements of the best fashions of the day, and was in every respect, a brilliant member of the social circles which, before the revolution, comprised the vice-regal court at the old Virginia capital.[1]

This rosy view glosses over the fact Martha had the opportunity to move in vice-regal circles at Williamsburg only once, or at most twice, a year, and not every year at that. Like all planters' wives in her circle, Martha's life

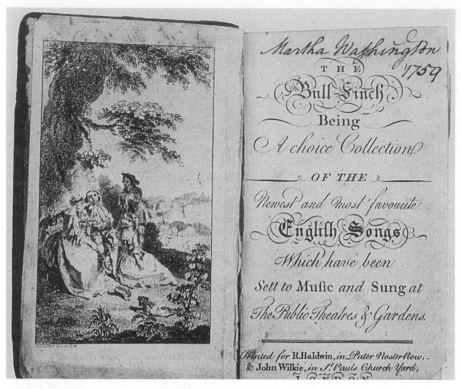

"The Bull Finch," a songbook belonging to Martha Washington, with her name inscribed by George Washington in 1759, the year of their marriage. Courtesy of the Mount Vernon Ladies' Association of the Union.

revolved around the less glamorous, more mundane, concerns of housekeeping and family life.

Both George and Martha had long and active days. As described earlier, the seasons governed plantation life, which revolved around preparing ground for planting, digging in manure or river silt to fertilize the poor soil, sowing seeds, tending crops, harvesting, caring for and breeding livestock, seeing the animals fattened and slaughtered, and keeping barns and outbuildings in repair, fences mended, and poachers off the property. The couple kept country hours and soon established a daily pattern, which they kept to for the rest of their lives at Mount Vernon and adhered to as nearly as possible elsewhere.

George rose early, around 4 A.M. He would shave and dress himself, put on the clothes laid out the night before, then go to his study to spend several hours before breakfast dealing with correspondence and plantation business, reading or working on plans for the estate. He knew the days of profitable tobacco growing were numbered, and his financial position allowed him no time to waste in finding alternative ways of making Mount Vernon pay. To improve the soil at Mount Vernon and introduce new crops more profitable than tobacco, he sent for books on agricultural methods from England, invented new farm implements, experimented with seeds and plants, recorded the results, and designed new moneymaking enterprises like a fishery, a distillery, and a mill. He also had charge of managing the Custis estate, which was much larger than his own and widely spread over several counties to the south, as well as the Custis slaves and their overseers. He had to keep accounts for the different Custis plantations and deal with the Custis factors in England in addition to his own. Two years after Daniel's death the official appraisal and division of the Custis estate between Martha and her children had not been completed, and George had to keep precise records of his dealings with Custis estate property. If time allowed, George liked to pay a prebreakfast visit to the stables.

Martha rose slightly later, around dawn, dressed, and gave her housekeeping orders to the slaves. She then unlocked the stores where food was kept and the chests containing coffee, tea, or spices to allocate what was required for that day. She was also responsible for doling out rations to slaves around the Mansion House, including both the house slaves and those who worked nearby in the barn, stables, kennels, and garden. She probably saw that the bulk of the rations for the field slaves were portioned out and delivered to the overseers for distribution on the individual farms.

Breakfast was at seven in summer, eight in winter. There were often guests who had stayed the night at the meal. George famously took a light breakfast of what were called Indian cakes, a kind of pancake made of cornmeal, with butter and honey, all of which he washed down with a few cups of tea.

George exercised remarkable restraint. Breakfast at Mount Vernon was a lavish affair. The Reverend Andrew Burnaby, traveling in Virginia, visited at Mount Vernon in the early years of the Washingtons' married life. He described a typical breakfast: "In several parts of Virginia the ancient custom of eating meat at breakfast still continues. At the top of the table, where the lady of the house presides, there is constantly tea and coffee; but the rest of the table is garnished out with roast fowls, ham, venison, game and other dainties. Even at Williamsburg, it is the custom to have a plate of cold ham upon the table; and there is scarcely a Virginia lady who breakfasts without it."[2]

As well as the Indian cakes and the spread described by Reverend Burnaby, plantation breakfasts often included eggs, a sweet bread, butter, gingerbread, spoon bread, hominy, molasses, beaten biscuits, tea with cream, and so on. A plantation diet was clearly not for the weight-conscious. An eighteenth-century English visitor to Virginia, Nicholas Cresswell, noted in his diary that many women seemed to have bad teeth, which he attributed to the custom of serving hot bread at every meal. Martha had lovely teeth, but the hot bread, a Virginia speciality to this day, probably had some effect on her figure. Cresswell also noted that most Virginia women were tall and shapely, generally inclined to go without stays.[3] Martha, who inherited a genetic predisposition to plumpness, bolstered by a short stature and four pregnancies, and who was fastidious about her appearance and slightly self-conscious about her height, probably wore stays most of the time to look slimmer. However, when she sent for stays from England, she asked they be "easy made, and very thin," probably because she planned to wear them even in hot weather. Headgear was an important item of clothing in the colony, and ladies wore high caps most of the time. There were caps for everyday wear while going about household tasks, night caps for sleeping, and fancy beribboned, lace-trimmed, or pleated caps for "best." A fetching cap could cover a multitude of sins. Martha was always vain about her caps, and she had a tendency to wear rather high, bouffant ones to make her look taller.

The Washingtons were typical of the period in that they spent little time alone. There was either a steady stream of company at Mount Vernon, or the Mount Vernon family visited friends. In addition to overnight guests at breakfast, there were nearly always guests at dinner. In the morning George was courteous but businesslike, eating breakfast quickly and anxious to be out on the plantation, leaving guests to the newspapers, their choice of books, or Martha.

After breakfast, in good weather or bad, George rode out on the estate to supervise the slaves and indentured servants' work in progress, from manure spreading and fence building to plowing, sowing, and harvesting, often covering as much as fifteen miles on horseback. He was a stickler for detail and gave the minutest attention to every aspect of production at Mount Vernon. Since his property comprised some four thousand acres spread out over five farms, supervising was a time-consuming business but he was desperate to make Mount Vernon profitable.

The field slaves who lived on the farms had harder lives and more Spartan living conditions than those attached to the Mansion House, and unless forced, none worked willingly, and most worked as slowly and inefficiently as possible. Consequently George went out to check that his overseers were literally driving the slaves to work productively. The slaves' working day began at dawn and ended at dusk six days a week. George would watch slaves at their tasks, and use his watch to time them to see how efficiently they were working and to see who was slacking. It was the overseer's job to make them stick to it. George had the usual problems other planters had with their overseers. Many drank heavily, and they alternated between those brutal enough to motivate the slaves through fear and those so ineffectual that the slaves under their management performed little work. The women slaves were worked almost as hard in the fields as the men, performing tasks like spreading manure and hoeing the ground.

While George went out to the fields, Martha always retired to her room for an hour's private devotions after breakfast, providing her with an iron-clad excuse not to dawdle indefinitely at the table. She read her Bible and sermons and prayed. No one was allowed to disturb her.

Afterwards Martha went back to work, overseeing the house slaves in the kitchen, the still room, the smokehouse, and other outbuildings, galvanizing any of her reluctant household staff who appeared to be slacking or dawdling, keeping a sharp eye for theft or any unauthorized consumption of food by the slaves, tending to any domestic problems, and dosing anyone who was ill with medicine. She oversaw the kitchen garden, and a seemingly bottomless sewing basket with family sewing and mending always awaited her attention when she had a chance to sit down. Then there were the children to teach and play with.

George returned home each day punctually at quarter to three, cleaned himself up, powdered his hair, and presented himself for dinner. His diary frequently mentions arriving home from a day's hunting or work on the estate to "find" that people had arrived for dinner, which suggests he was not expecting them—though this did not mean they were unwelcome. Martha had to be constantly ready for unexpected company to appear at this meal, as well as the invited guests. The common assumption that simply because there were slaves, there was little for the mistress to do is wrong. Though the house slaves at Mount Vernon may have taken the initiative to make the necessary adjustments to accommodate extra guests, in general there were few incentives for slaves to exert themselves to do anything they were not specifically ordered to do. This meant that Martha would have had to personally supervise whatever was necessary to provide for unexpected guests.

The main meal of the day was dinner at three o'clock. Since meat, game, and fish were plentiful, they were the mainstay of the colonial diet, and it was common to serve several dishes of whatever meat, poultry, and fish were in season, as well as vegetables and fruits and the ubiquitous hot bread. The hot bread appeared in many forms, from waffles and pancakes to biscuits, the risen, cakelike "Sally Lunn," or spoon bread, which was cooked in a dish and had to be spooned out. All meals had to be expandable in case of last-minute arrivals. The custom was to have all the food on the table at once. Plantation food was hearty, and George was particularly fond of fish, possibly because fish was easier for his troublesome teeth to chew. Fish were plentiful in the Potomac, and one of his favorite meals was said to have been salmon with mashed potatoes. Dinner was washed down by port and Madeira.

A guest who dined at Mount Vernon after the Revolution left an account of dinner, which probably did not vary greatly from dinners before it. He wrote: "The dinner was very good, a small roasted pigg, baked leg of lamb, roasted fowles, beef, peas, lettice, cucumbers, artichokes, etc. puddings, tarts, et. etc. We were desired to call for what drink we chose."[4] The drinks to choose from ranged from George's favorite, Madeira, to port, canary, peach brandy claret, and sparkling porter.

When this substantial meal was over, the ladies would retire and the men would sit for a while, drinking and cracking nuts if there were any available. Martha would spend the rest of the afternoon entertaining her guests, visiting, gardening, or sewing. A few hours later, around eight, there would be a light meal of tea and toast. The family retired at nine.

Martha did not keep diaries—or if she did, she burned them or they have been otherwise lost—but for most of his life George did. The terse, businesslike entries in his daily diary, the orders sent to the factors in England, and a few surviving letters written by Martha are good indicators of the life they led on the plantation and the subjects that occupied them. George recorded the weather and the crops he planted and experimented with, as well as keeping notes on dog breeding, visitors, visiting, church attendance, the occasional ball, dinners, foxhunting, Jacky Custis's schooling and Patcy Custis's health, and trips to Williamsburg and Alexandria and, occasionally, to Fredericksburg to visit Mary Washington.

The fact that much of their social life revolved around such country pursuits as foxhunting and race meetings kept Martha busy catering for large parties of men in hunting boots. Like his neighbors, George was a horses-and-dogs man, a fearless rider, and he adored foxhunting at breakneck speed. He had a favorite hunter named Blueskin, high-strung and strong, and he was very proud of a fine pack of hunting dogs that he had bred himself. Martha may have hunted in her youth, but hunting at Mount Vernon seems to have been an exclusively male pastime. According to George Washington Parke Custis's memoirs: "The habit was to hunt three times a week, weather permitting: breakfast was served on these mornings at candle-light, [George] always breaking his fast with an Indian-corn cake and a bowl of milk."[5]

Though only the men seem to have participated in foxhunts, a dinner party for everyone invariably followed. Indeed, plantation life was an endless succession of dinners, with few days without guests at Mount Vernon or, alternatively, the Washingtons traveling to have dinner at Belvoir or with other neighbors, such the Masons at nearby Gunston Hall. In 1760 George William and Sally Fairfax left for a trip to England, on yet another mission to resolve the vexing question of whether or not George William had Negro blood, but the intimacy with Belvoir continued with George William's half brother Bryan Fairfax, who lived there with his wife, Sally Cary Fairfax's younger sister Elizabeth. Lord Fairfax was sometimes a visitor at Belvoir, and he and Bryan continued to be George's hunting companions.

During the day, when she was not entertaining and could steal time away from her many responsibilities, Martha visited her neighbors. If she had received a formal call, etiquette demanded she repay it by the third day. Both out of fondness and to maintain his image, George saw to it his wife traveled in style. He kept a chariot—a carriagelike vehicle—and four horses for Martha's use when she went to church and on the constant round of socializing. Martha was driven by a slave coachman in the Washington livery, white with red collar and cuffs, and often attended by four postilions, also in livery. George accompanied the chariot on horseback. Like many of the other planters whose homes were on the river, George kept a barge at Mount Vernon on its own landing below the house. The barge was used to transport crops on the Potomac, but it was also used by the family for visiting and social outings.

Aside from the work of the plantation, George had civic responsibilities commensurate with his position as a prominent planter, serving as a vestryman of both his local Pohick Church, seven miles from Mount Vernon, and Christ Church in Alexandria, as well as acting as a local magistrate. And as he continued to be reelected as a burgess, twice a year George made the three-day trip to Williamsburg, where assembly business could detain him for weeks. Occasionally Martha and the children kept him company, for it meant Martha could visit the Bassetts and the rest of her family en route. Because Six Chimney House had been rented out and most of its contents auctioned off, the Washingtons stayed in lodgings in Williamsburg.

Martha's brother Bartholomew had married his cousin Elizabeth Macon and now lived at Pamocra Plantation in New Kent. Martha's widowed mother, Frances, and her younger sisters, Elizabeth and Mary, still lived at Chestnut Grove. Her brother William, who was serving in the British navy, was also sometimes there. Judging by Martha's concerned queries in letters to Anna Maria, Frances Dandridge suffered from a variety of ailments, and Martha's little sister Elizabeth [Betsy] was becoming a headstrong teenager who, in Martha's opinion, was getting her own way far too often. Martha and George usually stayed with the Bassetts at Eltham. Even when Martha did not accompany him, George would spend a night or a few days with Anna Maria and Burwell Bassett, and call on his mother-in-law. He got on well with Martha's family, and far better with Frances Dandridge than with his own mother.

Martha was close to her family, but did not see as much of them as she would have liked. In September 1763, George wrote to a Dandridge uncle of Martha's who lived in London, "I live on the Potomac River in Fairfax County, about ten miles below Alexandria and many miles distant from my wife's relations, who all reside upon the York River and whom we seldom see more than once a year, and not always so often."[6]

A year after the wedding George found his lifestyle required the services of a valet. He wrote to his former servant, the free black Thomas Bishop, who had served General Braddock until Braddock's death in the disastrous Monongahela campaign of 1755. He was the servant the dying general had left to George's protection, and Bishop had been in George's service until George married. Bishop had been the servant left holding the horses in Wash Custis's account of George's first meeting with Martha at the Chamberlaynes, when George forgot the time. Bishop had since returned to the British army in Philadelphia but answered George's summons and came to Mount Vernon, where he lived for the rest of his life.

The goods George ordered from London reflected their lifestyle at Mount Vernon and his changed circumstances after the marriage. Now that George was a family man, with Martha and the children in residence and money at his disposal, George's orders swelled. A life "in retirement" on a plantation demanded an extensive wardrobe for everyone, not only for Martha and George but also for the children and even for the house slaves, who wore the Washington red and white livery. At Mount Vernon, the clothing of the house slaves distinguished them from the field slaves. The field slaves wore rough pants, shirts, and shifts, while in and around the Mansion House the butler, waiters, postilions, and coachman had white livery with scarlet collars and cuffs ordered from London. The children's teenage body slaves and the household maids and seamstresses wore nicer clothing and shoes ordered from London, as did Martha and George's personal servants. On one occasion silver earrings were ordered for the housemaids.

A typical order George sent to London in September 1759 speaks volumes, not only about what the Washingtons believed they needed to cut a good figure in society, but what was essential for the house, kitchen, estate, and slaves to keep the estate up and running. However, compared with the extravagant orders for clothing she placed when she was Mrs. Custis, Martha's order was notably restrained.

Typically, the order specified a huge range of clothing, farm equipment, sewing items, comestibles, luxuries, decorative items, necessities, and treats, indicating what colonial Virginians needed—or thought they needed—and depended on obtaining from England:

> A light Summer suit made of Duroy or by the inclosed measure
> 4 pieces best India Nankeen [a kind of corduroy]
> 2 best Beaver hats
> 1ps of Irish Linnen
> 1ps of black E Sattin Ribbon
> . . .
> 1 Salmon-colored Tabby [plain-woven fabric] of the enclosed pattern, with Sattin flowers; to be made in a sack and coat.

1 Cap, Handkerchief, and Tucker [a swatch of lace or linen pinned to the top
of a woman's stays] Ruffles of Brussells lace or Point . . . to be worn with
the above negligee
1 piece Bag Holland [linen]
2 fine flowered Lawn [sheer linen] Aprons . . . a puckered petticoat of a fashionable color a silver Tabby petticoat . . . 1 black Mask

Also ordered were perfumed hair powder, violet-scented snuff, which was
popular with ladies, and which Martha probably took, ordinary snuff for the
men, mitts and stays, stay laces, plain handkerchiefs for everyday use, and
"most fashionable Cambrick handkerchiefs" for dressing up, cotton stockings as well as silk, linen shoes, satin pumps, kid gloves, bonnets and ornaments, and ribbon and trimming for dresses. Since there was a great deal of
sewing done at Mount Vernon, the orders included items such as sewing
scissors, sewing silk binding tape, thread, embroidery silk, sewing pins, and
hair pins.

Food and drink were also ordered, some of which came from England
only because the items had made a roundabout trip there from the Caribbean or other parts of Europe. England's restrictive trade laws prevented
the American colonies from trading directly with other countries, with the
bizarre effect that some of the items ordered may have already gone back
and forth across the Atlantic and added to the expense. A typical Washington grocery list included anchovies, capers, olives, salad oil, bottled man-
goes, a large Cheshire Cheese, green tea, raisins, almonds in the shell, a
hogshead of best Porter [wine], loaves of sugar [which would have to be broken into pieces or pulverized for use in tea or cooking], mustard, sacks of
salt, sugar candy, and barley sugar.

There were requests for equipment to be used on the estate, from hal-
ters and snaffle bits for horses to handsaws, axes, a plow, compasses, nails,
paintbrushes, joiners' tools, a vice, lanterns, gouges, saws, chisels, and so on.
There were lists of material and other items for clothing the slaves, such as
strong stockings, coarse shoes, knee buckles for livery, postilions' caps, coarse
linen, woollen cloth from which to cut blankets for the slaves, coarse duffel
cloth, buttons, and shoe-making materials.

Another substantial part of the order consisted of medicines or items
to be used in treating a wide variety of illnesses in humans and animals.
While Martha would have been responsible for treating any of the family or
slaves ill at the Mansion House, the slaves on the further parts of the estate
would have been treated by the overseers. George and the overseers would
also have treated any animals. The items specified indicate the kinds of conditions that afflicted people and livestock.

Among the medicines were Turlington Balsam for treating wounds and
abrasions, Spirit of Lavender for menstrual problems, powdered Ipaca,

which was mixed with opium to treat diarrhea, sago jelly from the sago palm, which was used with milk to make a nourishing food for invalids, Sal Volatile for fainting, laudanum for pain relief, anise seeds for stomach disorders, "sweet mercury" for the circulation, alum to stop bleeding, cinnamon water to clean wounds and cuts, and a variety of horse medicines.[7]

Because George wanted Mount Vernon to emulate the elegant style of Belvoir, it was George's, rather than Martha's, requirements and taste that swelled the orders with decorative objects and furniture for the house. In May 1759 George ordered more knives, forks, and glassware and "4 fashionable China Branches, & Stands, for Candles," as well as detailed, color-coordinated furnishings for one of the upstairs bedrooms:

> 1 tester bedstead 7½ feet pitch, with fashionable blew or blew and white Curtains to suit a room lind. wt. The Incld paper Window Curtains of the same, for two Windows; with either papier Mache Cornish to them, or Cornish covered with the Cloth 1 fine Bed Coverlid to match the Curtains 4 Chair bottoms of the same; that is as much Coverings suited to the above furniture as will go over the Seats of 4 Chairs (which I have by me) in order to make the whole furniture of this Room uniformly handsome and genteel.[8]

Another order specified busts of Alexander the Great, Julius Caesar, King Charles XII of Sweden, and the King of Prussia, as well as busts of Prince Eugene and the Duke of Marlborough and some figures of "Furious Wild Beasts." The factors, Robert Cary and Company, wrote back that there were no busts of the personages specified, all of whom were military men and may have been intended to allude to George's military past. Instead, Cary offered busts of literary figures such as Homer and Locke, but they were no substitute, and George declined them.

There would always be an uneasy relationship with the London factors on whom he was so dependent. The large, costly orders dispatched from Mount Vernon were not being filled to George's satisfaction. In the autumn of 1760, a year after his marriage, he complained to Robert Cary and Company that they sent him outmoded goods, "Articles . . . that could only have been used by our Forefathers in the days of yore," and it was "needless for me to particularise the sorts, quality or taste I would choose . . . unless it is observed."[9] Martha and Daniel had made similar complaints to Robert Cary about their orders being carelessly filled with inferior goods. This did not stop George from placing similar orders regularly. George had never had money in any sizable amount before, and now that he was realizing his ambition to live on a par with the Fairfaxes, he seems to have been unable to restrain himself.

As the Washingtons settled in Mount Vernon, staying well themselves and keeping family and slaves healthy were major preoccupations, as indicated by the orders for large supplies of medicine. Maintaining health was a major issue in plantation life. As William Byrd II at Westover Plantation had done in his secret diaries two generations earlier, George's notes record just how precarious everyone's health seems to have been on a constant basis. Martha's letters also focus on matters related to her own health and that of her family. There is a litany of illnesses and indispositions, doctors being called, the patients being bled and dosed with various medicines and dire-sounding treatments, from purges and "vomits" to Jesuit, or Peruvian bark, a form of quinine, which George took when he suffered from one of his recurrent bouts of malaria, which at the time was also known as "ague and fever."

Martha probably spent a good deal of time nursing and doling out medicines, restoratives, purges, medicinal teas, and so on, because people of the period were often "poorly." Aside from the big diseases like smallpox, cholera, malaria, and tuberculosis, which were often fatal, there was a whole range of lesser indispositions, among which stomach upsets, worms, vomiting, diarrhea, fevers, and jaundice featured prominently, especially in hot weather, and in the winter there were colds and sore throats. In an age with no antibiotics and doctors who were inclined to bleed everyone for everything from sore throats to miscarriages—or even to prevent fever or miscarriage—a lesser ailment might suddenly turn fatal, either in spite of, or because of, the treatment. Martha had watched her two eldest children die, followed by their father, all after brief illnesses. In her eyes even the slightest indisposition in Jacky or Patcy could be the first step toward the grave, and as a result Martha positively hovered over the children. She kept an eye on George, too, who from early on in their marriage was inclined to brush her off if she fussed, though his painful teeth and gums troubled him incessantly and he lived in the constant expectation he would contract the "family disease," tuberculosis.

Martha was no more immune herself to common ills. She spent her first wedding anniversary, January 6, 1760, miserably bedridden. Five days earlier George had returned home to find she had broken out with measles. She was so ill that George contacted a local clergyman, Reverend Charles Green at Pohick Church, who also had medical training. It was not as odd a combination as it sounds. In the colony clergymen often combined medicine with their pastoral duties because those literate enough to read theology could also read weighty medical textbooks.

George noted in his diary that a number of the "family" caught measles too. Even that did not stop the visitors, who now came to cheer Martha up on her sickbed. Visitors must have played a significant part in passing around anything contagious. A neighbor, Mrs. Barnes, called on Martha and had to be sent home in the chariot because the weather was so bad. Sally Cary Fairfax called at Mount Vernon as soon as she heard the news. A pregnant Anna Maria

Bassett traveled up from her home at Eltham in New Kent to visit Martha, an ill-advised move given what is known today about the risks of measles to an unborn child. George escorted Anna Maria part of the way home again.

Martha was seriously ill again in April, and again George was worried enough to call a doctor. The doctor, not the Reverend Green on this occasion, arrived drunk. Useless in that condition, he stayed the night. The next morning, presumably in a sufficiently sober condition to do so, he bled Martha. Judging by a letter to her sister Anna Maria, dated June 1, 1760, written to congratulate her on the birth of a daughter, Martha had had recurrent bouts of ill health since winter but had recovered sufficiently to enjoy a visit from Burwell Bassett, Anna Maria's husband, and to worry about Anna Maria's recovery from childbirth and reports of their mother's indifferent health.

Martha added: "The children are now very well and I think myself in a better state of helth than I have been in for a long time and don't dout but I shall present you a fine healthy girl again when I come down in the fall which is as soon as mr W-ns business will suffer him to leave home . . . give our Blessing to the dear little children and each of them half a Dozen kisses and hope you will not imagin that yourself and Mr Bassett is forgot by dear nancy your sincere and loving sister."[10]

Was here a note of envy for Anna Maria's new baby? Affectionate, maternal Martha was naturally preoccupied with the idea of pregnancy. Any woman in those days of no birth control, with large families the norm, would have been. She and George must have been living in the monthly expectation that she would become pregnant. George's desire for a son to inherit the estate he was building up would have been as firmly rooted as his love of Mount Vernon. Martha would have been equally anxious to give him an heir, though her anticipation of another baby was probably tinged with anxiety, because she had had a very difficult time with Patcy's birth.

As for her daughter, four-year-old Patcy had taken a sickly turn that year, which must have been worrying. In September 1760 Martha wrote to her friend, the vicar's wife, Margaret Green: "I have the pleasure to tell you my dear little girl is much better she has lost her fitts & fevours both and seems to be getting well very fast we carried her out yesterday in the chariot and the change of air refressed her very much."[11]

The following spring, in March 1761, whooping cough struck. Martha had it so badly she could not leave the house for four weeks, and the children had it too. In April Martha canceled a visit to Anna Maria because neither she nor the children were up to traveling, and considerately, she did not want to expose her sister and the children at Eltham to whooping cough. Campaigning for reelection as a burgess in May, George caught a bad cold he could not shake for months. His condition was made worse by a recurrence of either dysentery or malaria, and for months he grew no better. The specter of tuberculosis cast a shadow over the spring, and in August he took himself off to Berkeley Springs, where he lived in a tent and drank the waters. Against his expectations he recovered.

Then Martha suffered another long bout of ill health, and Burwell Bassett was ill enough at Eltham to prevent Anna Maria's visiting Mount Vernon as planned in the spring of 1762. In April Martha seized the chance to send a letter to Anna Maria via Mount Vernon neighbor John Poscy. Aside from George, everyone was in poor health.

> Dear Sister   Mount Vernon   April 6, 1762
>   . . . it was a very great disappointment to me your not comeing as we had so long expected you. . . . I have had the pleasure of hearing of you by several that has come from below but had no opportunity to write or would not neglect it as it is the only pleasure absence can afford me—I have had a very dark time since I came home. [Martha had probably traveled through New Kent with George on their way to the previous autumn's session of the assembly at Williamsburg.] I believe it is owing to the severe weather we have had . . . the only comfort was that Mr. Washington and my children have had their health very well. I think Patcy has been hardier than Ever she was till lately they have both had colds and fevers—. . . I am very sorry to hear my mamma is still complaining and her staying home so much as she doz I believe is a great hurt to her I hope she is happier at home than she seemed when I was down I never think of her but with concern. . . . I shoud be glad if you would take care of Betsy [their thirteen-year-old sister Elizabeth] and keep her in proper order she has her own way so much at home I am affraide she will be quite spoild.[12]

Always a stickler for good manners and decorum, Martha was always very strict with young women under her care. This lack of sympathy expressed in the letter for Betsy's hoyden ways would show in all her dealings with her young female relatives.

It was a side of Martha that made a vivid impression on one of her young relations. Elizabeth Jones was the daughter of Martha's cousin Frances, who was herself the daughter of Martha's uncle Lane Jones. (This cousin Frances had, confusingly, married another, unrelated man also named Jones so she remained Frances Jones even after her marriage.) Frances was nine years younger than Martha, but they became close friends as they were growing up, and later, when both cousins had married, Frances often visited at Mount Vernon, bringing Elizabeth with her. As an old lady, Elizabeth told the following story when asked by her grandson why she always referred to Martha Washington as "Aunt Martha" when the exact relationship was that of second cousins:

> Well, you see, I was quite a small girl and she was older than my mother,—I suppose she thought it a more dignified form of address, from a child, than

"Cousin" would be. She was a great stickler for dignity. . . . Oh yes: she had to scold me occasionally, of course, but she once gave me a great shaking which surprised and mortified me greatly. We were spending part of a summer at Mount Vernon, and one day it was planned to go into Alexandria early the next morning to do some necessary shopping. The next morning my mother had one of her bad headaches, but insisted she be left to rest quietly, and the shopping be attended to. Aunt Martha agreed, and said I and my maid should go with her. When all were ready the coach was driven to the back door, as there was no company. It was the fashion then to drive four horses and to go very fast. The cushions were of red morocco leather, smooth as glass, and the maid and I had the front seats facing Aunt Martha. When the driver started, for some reason he lashed one of the horses which caused them all to spring forward suddenly, giving the coach a jerk which thrust me off the seat into Aunt Martha's lap, rumpling and disarranging her handsome gown and laces. Seizing me by the shoulders and giving me a good shake she scolded: "Child, can't you keep your seat like a lady? Do you wish people to believe you are not in the habit of riding in coaches?" But before we left town she gave me a beautiful doll and said "You must let her apologize for your Aunt Martha's impatience."[13]

More than a year after the marriage, in October 1760, the Custis estate was finally apportioned in three equal parts as to value and divided between Martha, Jacky, and Patcy by the General Court of Virginia. Martha's share included much property that had been part of the Parke estate, and therefore it was property at risk of being lost if the Dunbar Suit succeeded. It comprised all 2,880 acres of Custis land in King William County, 1,000 acres of land comprised of Bridge Quarter, and Ship Landing Quarter at Queens Creek Plantation on the road to Williamsburg, a mill in York County, Six Chimney House on Francis Street in Williamsburg with all its contents, and a third of the lots owned by the Custis family at Jamestown, about eighty-three slaves worth £2,986, and livestock. She also received, as did each of her children, £1,617.18 in British sterling and £7618, 7 pence and 11½ shillings in Virginia currency.[14]

The following year the court appointed George the official guardian of Jacky and Patcy. This meant George's duties vis-à-vis the Custis estate were slightly different from what they had been on his marriage, because he now had to administer and keep separate accounts for each of the children's separate estates as distinct from Martha's. During her lifetime, Martha's property was by law her husband's to use as he pleased. On her death, however, what was known as Martha's "dower" estate—that is, property including slaves she brought to the marriage as part of her Custis inheritance—would go to her Custis heirs, Jacky and Patcy and their children. John Mercer advised George that the children's estates would each have their own separate accounts with the London factors for the sale of tobacco and anything else produced and shipped for sale to England. Anything ordered for them from London would therefore be charged against their estates. All of Martha's account in London would now be charged to George.

Martha was fortunate in having a husband prepared to spend so much of his time looking after the children's estates. George took his responsibility toward his wards seriously. He was genuinely fond of his stepchildren, as well as conscious that they needed to be prepared to assume the responsibilities that came with their fortunes. Both could expect to marry well and, in due course, to be responsible for managing large households and properties. For that reason he grew concerned that despite her strictness in matters of manners and deportment, Martha spoiled the children and over-protected Jacky to an extent that was unsuitable for a boy. It is probable that George privately thought Jacky needed toughening up and that both children ought to have an education appropriate to their status. Patcy's domestic education could safely be left to Martha, but George knew it was up to him to ensure Jacky was able to manage his vast Custis estate when he came of age.

In 1761 George hired a resident tutor named Walter Magowan to give the children their lessons. Jacky was a lazy student and prone to indispositions that would send Martha into a protective flurry, interrupting lessons until he was feeling better. Magowan found teaching Jacky to be an uphill battle, as would all of Jacky's tutors.

Meanwhile the steady stream of orders from Mount Vernon to London continued, now including schoolbooks as well as a lavish assortment of clothes, toys, silver-topped riding whips, and sweets and gingerbread for the children; books, schoolroom paper, silver shoe and knee buckles for eight-year-old Jacky, plus livery in the Custis colors for Jacky's fourteen-year-old body servant. Patcy, at age six, required a "Persian quilted coat," feather headdresses, satin shoes, a silk coat, a child's prayer book and Bible, a doll, child-size sewing implements, and a spinet.[15] All these items were charged to their separate accounts in London.

Martha was reluctant to go anywhere for long without the children. She tried it once when they were small, going to visit George's younger brother John Augustine and his wife Hannah at Bushfield Plantation, taking only six-year-old Patcy and leaving Jacky at Mount Vernon. It was not an experiment she wished to repeat. She wrote to Anna Maria:

> My Dear Nancy   Mount Vernon August 28, 1762
>   I had the pleasure to receive your kind letter of the 26th of July just as I was setting out on a visit to Mrs Washingtons . . . where I spent a week agreably I carred my little patt with me and left Jackey at home for a trial to see how well I coud stay without him though we ware gone but wone fortnight I was quite

impatient to get home if I at any time heard the dogs barke or a noise out I thought thair was a person sent for me I often fansied he was sick or some accident had happened to him so that I think it is impossable for me to leave him as long as mr Washington must stay when he comes down [to Williamsburg for the Assembly session] . . . I assure yourself nothing but my childrens intrest shoud prevent me the sattisfaction of seeing you and my good Friends I m always thinking of and wish it was possable for me to spend more of my time amongst . . .

We all injoy very good health at preasent I think patty seems to be quite well now Jackey is very thin but in good health and learn thaire books very fast I am sorry to hear you are unwell.[16]

Martha did not need any incentive to lavish more attention on her own children, but she was already torn between her duty to bring the children up properly and an overwhelming urge to indulge her two precious surviving darlings. Of the two Patcy was the more fragile, and Martha's anxieties about her daughter must have grown keener when Martha's youngest sister Mary, only a year younger than Patcy, died at Chestnut Grove, aged seven, in September 1763. Nothing illustrated the battle between common sense and her inclination to spoil her daughter more than the colonial litmus test, the issue of clothes. On the one hand, ordering a little girl's clothes from England was fantastically extravagant, but it was a way Martha could share her own fondness for clothing with her daughter. To compensate Martha gave a nod in the direction of "frugality." One of her surviving letters was written to an English dressmaker:

To- Mrs Shelbury-Milliner Dean Street Soho. London
Madam   August-1764
    In an invoice to Mr Cary I have directed all the goods for Miss Custis's use to be got from you as I approved your lat years choice- Such things as Misses of her age usually wear here I have sent for; but if you can get those which may be more genteel and proper for her I shall have no objections to it, provided it is done with frugality, for as she is only nine years old a superfluity, or expence in dress would be altogether unnecessary-. . . .[17]

In addition to their lessons with Walter Magowan, the children had music lessons from a traveling music master named John Stedlar. Patcy learned the spinet and flute and Jacky the violin. Jacky's reluctant practicing must have been excruciating for anyone within earshot. Martha took music lessons too for a time. The children also attended dancing classes with an itinerant dancing master named Mr. Christian. These dancing classes were held in turn at different plantations in the neighborhood and provided an excuse for a dance involving everyone. Philip Fithian at Nomini Hall wrote an account of one of Mr. Christian's classes, which, typically, occupied most of a weekend.

> On the Friday, company arrived, as did Mr. Christian, and a dance was held at the house. On Saturday after breakfast everyone retired into the dancing room, and the young people had lessons individually, then all danced minuets together. The whole company then joined in country dancing. Dinner was eaten at 3:30, and afterwards it was back to the dancing room. A bemused Fithian, whose ascetic New England upbringing had not run to dancing lessons, described Mr. Christian as "punctual and rigid in his discipline . . . he struck two of the young misses in the course of their performance, even in the presence of the mother of one of them . . . when the candles were lighted we all repaired for the last time, into the Dancing Room: first each couple danced a Minuet; then all joined in as before in the country Dances, these continued till half after seven." Then the guests played games, including Pawns for Redemption, a kind of gambling game with buttons, followed by supper.[18]

The daily bustle of early risings, household occupations, the children, company, visiting, hunting, family concerns, and orders to England made up the fabric of the first fifteen years of Martha and George's life at Mount Vernon, and Martha would later look back on this time as a kind of halcyon period. Martha's only surviving letter to George, written seven years after her marriage, reflects contentment in the relationship.

> My Dearest   March 30 1767
> It was with very great pleasure I see in your letter that you got safely down. We are all well at this time but it is still rainney and wett. I am sorry you will not be home so soon as I expected you. I had reather my sister [Anna Maria] woud not come up so soon as May woud be much plasenter time than April. We wrote you last post as I have nothing new to tell you I must conclude myself
> Your most Affectionate
> Martha Washington[19]

CHAPTER 8

Uneasy Times

In the halcyon years that followed the wedding, the pattern of domestic life at Mount Vernon suited both Martha and George. It was a family-oriented life balancing the hard work of the plantation with the pleasures of a lively social life among friends, neighbors, and families. In 1761 Anne Fairfax Washington Lee died, and George now owned Mount Vernon outright. However, there were always underlying concerns with the potential to disrupt their tranquil existence, and even from the early days of the marriage clouds occasionally trailed a shadow across the sunny landscape at Mount Vernon. As in many families, finances and children lay at the heart of the concerns.

In 1760 their London factors, James Gildart and Capel and Osgood Hanbury, wrote that the Washington tobacco crops shipped to England that year were of poor quality and fetching less than expected at auction. In addition, a ship carrying Washington tobacco was lost in the Bay of Biscay and another was taken by three French privateers. Fortunately the latter was recaptured by the British a week later, but it was a troublesome, time-consuming, and expensive business.

Martha also had things on her mind. For one thing she failed to become pregnant. No one knows why George and Martha never had children, but at the time Martha's failure to conceive a child by George must have surprised them, because she had borne four children in quick succession during her first marriage. Family tradition suggests that Martha had suffered some form of internal damage during Patcy's birth that may have left her unable to have more children.

That tradition is supported by a note included by the editors of the Confederation Series of the Papers of George Washington: "Eugene E. Prussing reported that a tradition persisted in Masonic circles that Martha

Washington would have required corrective surgery to conceive children after her marriage to GW (memorandum of Charles C. Wall, 24 Jan 1975 ViMtV)."[1]

Though corrective gynecological surgery must have been unknown in Martha's lifetime, it is strange there should have been any mention at all of Martha's obstetric problems "in Masonic circles." George was the one person who was both a Mason and in a position to know whether Martha had a condition that prevented her conceiving, but it is hardly a subject he would have discussed with his fellow Masons. Other historians have suggested George was sterile, although at the time he was supposed to have fathered at least one child. The cause is irrelevant, but the initial disappointment at a lack of children of their own must have become dismay as time passed. They lived in a society where landownership was paramount, and inheritance of land depended primarily on male heirs. Devoting so much of his time and energy, not to mention Martha's money, to building up his estate, a continually unfulfilled expectation of children must have been distressing for George. Both George and Martha had strong parental instincts, which over time they increasingly focused on the wider family network of nephews, nieces, Martha's grandchildren, and the children of their friends and neighbors.

To add to their other financial pressures, the cost of living at Mount Vernon was expensive. By 1763 George had run through all the money Martha had brought to the marriage, and there had been several bad growing seasons. The quality of George's tobacco crops compared unfavorably with those grown on Jacky's estates in the southern counties. Jacky's tobacco could fetch twice the price in England that Washington tobacco did.

This by itself was not absolutely alarming to Martha. She had been familiar all her life with being land-rich and cash-poor, which had also affected Daniel Parke Custis and probably struck her as perfectly normal. An English traveler, Nicholas Cresswell, noticed this was the prevailing relaxed attitude among the Potomac planters. Writing about his visit to Mount Vernon, he observed in his journal: "A great number of pleasant Houses along the River, both on the Virginia and Maryland side. All Tobacco Planters, some of them people of considerable property . . . it appears to me there is a scarcity of cash amongst the people of all ranks here. They Game higher, Spend freely, and Dress exceedingly gay, but I observe they seldom show any money, it is all Tobacco notes."[2]

These "tobacco notes" were drafts on London factors, often used as people today use checks, in an age when there was no common colonial currency. Each colony had its own "specie," or form of currency, while English sterling was good everywhere but in short supply. The lack of a common currency was one of the factors hampering intercolony commerce, helping to ensure that planters made their purchases from English merchants rather than colonial ones.

As previously noted, George had spent much time devising alternative moneymaking schemes—a fishery, a flour mill, a distillery. He did implement some of these schemes profitably. He caught huge quantities of herring in the Potomac, which he salted and exported; ground his own and his neighbors' wheat in the mill; and made whiskey. His plans to diversify out of tobacco into other enterprises would have been the stuff of dinner table conversation and George must have discussed his plans at length with Martha and their friends and neighbors with whom they kept constant company. As a planter's daughter Martha would also have appreciated his concerns about the effects of frost, flood, drought, and poor soil on Mount Vernon's profitability. In 1763 George wrote to his brother-in-law Burwell Bassett that his wheat crop had been badly affected by rust and the corn and tobacco harvest were poor because of heavy rain. It was not just expenditure on luxury items that drained the finances. Implementing new projects required an investment of capital and equipment before it turned a profit.

Despite his efforts to diversify at Mount Vernon, they were not enough to reverse his ebbing finances, and in the main George's approach to financial pressures was consistent with that of other planters—he ignored them. Even had Martha wanted to economize by curtailing their lavish lifestyle, she would have had a difficult job persuading George. It was more likely Martha shared George's blinkered attitude. It was deeply ingrained in many Virginians who would survive the Revolution and in later years pose an obstacle to Alexander Hamilton's economic policy geared toward creation of a central federal bank. Many Virginians—though not Washington, who was by then president—were appalled. Their reaction was summed up neatly by historian Joseph Ellis:

> A significant percentage of Virginia's landed class . . . were heavily in debt to British and Scottish creditors, who were compounding their interest rates faster than the profit margins in tobacco and wheat could match. One cannot help but suspect the beleaguered aristocracy of Virginia saw in Hamilton and his beloved commercial elite of the northern cities the American replicas of British bankers who were bleeding them to death. The more one contemplates the mentality of the Virginia planters—the refusal to bring their habits of consumption and expenditure into line with the realities of their economic predicament, the widespread pattern of denial right up to the declaration of bankruptcy—the more likely it seems that an entrenched and even wilful ignorance of the economic principles governing the relationship between credit and debt had become a badge of honor in their world. These were simply not the kind of concerns that a gentleman of property should take seriously. In a sense, they took considerable pride in not having the dimmest understanding of what Hamilton was talking about.[3]

Having finally attained a position in the higher echelons of the planter class, visibly retrenching would have been humiliating for George. If he had been cavalier about spending money to improve the Mansion House in 1757 when he was merely renting, he now seemed to throw caution to the winds. No matter how much the upkeep of Mount Vernon absorbed, George continued to order items he wanted for the house with reckless abandon: porcelain dishes, silver and enameled wineglasses, cut-glass decanters, and a fine saddle, along with continuing large orders to his tailor and boot maker, or such items as a hunting coat with gilt buttons and a matching waistcoat in scarlet cloth trimmed in gold lace and silver spurs. For Martha there were bonnets, shoes with her name inside, ivory combs, lace, reams of dress-making fabrics, and a gold seal for Martha's watch. There were also orders for pipes of wine and Madeira and rum and spices and tropical fruits. All these were charged against George's account, where they were not offset by income necessary to pay for them.

At the same time, the lavish orders sent on behalf of his stepchildren, for clothing, toys, books, and sweets, charged against the children's individual accounts with their London factors, were well within the children's means, underlining the contrast between the Custis financial position and the Washington one. It was another incentive for him to keep up appearances. Though his debts in London had begun to mount from 1765 on, George continued to entertain lavishly at Mount Vernon, at one point bemoaning the fact that even though the estate had one hundred cows, he still had to buy butter for his household.

The expense of the orders for Mount Vernon was compounded by two factors. One was that ships from England tended to ply either the York River in the south, where the Custis goods had traditionally been directed by the English factors, or the Potomac, which was where George wanted most orders delivered to Mount Vernon's own wharf. The London factors nevertheless often put Mount Vernon orders for the Washington and Custis accounts on ships bound for the York River, because historically that was where Custis goods had always been sent. If so, George had the expense and trouble of arranging for them to be transported north from the Tidewater, often by careless boatmen in small vessels who delivered the goods in a damaged, wet, or pilfered state. The other factor that added to George's frustration was that buying English goods often amounted to throwing money away, thanks to the perennial problem of the poor quality or damaged condition of so many of them. George continually complained that his clothes and shoes were not made large enough, that farming equipment arrived minus essential parts, and that casks of wine arrived with a spigot having been inserted for the refreshment of the sailors en route. Martha was annoyed by shoes that disintegrated because they had been made without lasts. As a result the steady flow of orders from Mount Vernon was followed by a steady stream of ineffectual complaints.

Yet in 1768 George perversely ordered a very expensive status symbol from England. The old chariot, which had carried Martha and the children about the country for years, had worn out on the rough country roads, and George had a new one custom-made. He specified it should be "in the newest taste, handsome, genteel and light," green in color, with gold trim, leather upholstery, and blazoned with the Washington coat of arms. He also ordered carpet on the floor, an interior painted with flowers, glass windows, and blinds, a "Rolls Royce" among chariots. Within months of its arrival, the new chariot proved to be a typically disappointing example of "colonial" merchandise. The wooden panels on the sides had not been properly cured and soon warped, making the grand chariot all but unusable. As ever, George complained to London, to no effect whatsoever.

The Washingtons' experiences were common to most of the planters they knew, bolstering a growing sense of personal grievance at Mount Vernon and elsewhere about the one-sided benefits of English control of trade in the colonies. In fact, the Virginia colony had been established in 1607 for the sole purpose of remitting colonial wealth to England, and that purpose had been accomplished. Many English merchants now depended heavily on the lucrative trade with the colonies, in everything from tobacco and slaves to a range of goods, commodities, and luxuries like those ordered for Mount Vernon.

Though concerned about keeping up appearances, George was too much of a self-made man and a new arrival in the upper levels of Virginia society to have been quite as unconcerned about his worsening financial position as his ongoing expenditures suggested. Worried, he cast about for solutions, spurred on by the fact that by 1768 even he acknowledged he was in debt and his English factors had outraged him by writing dunning letters for money they were owed.

Martha must have known he was anxious. She saw him disappear for months at a time to investigate other schemes. One was a plan to drain Dismal Swamp—a vast marshy area in the Tidewater—and reclaim the land for development. This never came to fruition. Another was a project to take up grants of land in the Ohio Valley, and here George was more successful. In 1754, Governor Dinwiddie had promised George and other Virginians serving in the British army on the western frontier in the French and Indian Wars that they would be offered bounty lands there for their service.

The grants had never materialized because the Indian tribes were actively hostile to further encroachment by white settlers. To pacify the Indians, in 1763 the British government had passed an act prohibiting settlement beyond the Appalachians, nullifying Dinwiddie's promise at a stroke and bearing out the advice George's friend Captain Orme had once given him that "American affairs are not very well understood at Home." George felt the colony was bound to expand westward. Needing to explore every avenue for making money, he actively involved himself in a struggle with the authorities to pursue his own and other veterans' claims. In fact, he bought up many of the claims of fellow veterans and, in the end, obtained title to twenty thousand acres of land in western Pennsylvania and Ohio.

As moneymaking schemes went, it was bound to take some time, but in Virginia settlers had already pushed the colony's boundary relentlessly west in their hunger for land. George was sure they would continue to do so and his western lands would increase in value. He envisaged renting or selling them. Neither he nor Martha entertained thoughts of moving there themselves. George enjoyed expeditions to explore them and appreciated the rich soil and the potential, but for both of them it was the back of the beyond in terms of a place to live.

The Washingtons' finances were unraveling in a greater context. Mount Vernon's increasingly precarious situation was linked, like those on all plantations, with the wider picture of England's restrictive trade laws. Of all the parties in the economic chain from production on the plantation to sale in England, the planters drew the short straw. If things were getting tight for the Washingtons at Mount Vernon, the same was true for many of their neighbors.

England's economic stranglehold on the American colonies had a long history, but it had begun to tighten significantly in 1764 when England had passed a series of Stamp Acts, imposing a new form of taxes in the American colonies. The tax was a stamp duty, payable on a variety of documents, including land transfers, wills, passports, liquor licenses, almanacs, and newspapers, which now required a formal stamp to be legal. England had just concluded a long and ruinously costly war with France, and the English government of the day, headed by Lord North, passed the measure to offset the ongoing cost of keeping a protective military force in the colonies.

The measure provoked mixed but passionate responses on both sides of the Atlantic. The cost of defending the American colonies had hitherto been borne by the English taxpayer, and many Englishmen felt the measure was just in principle. There were other factions in England who had little sympathy for the slave-owning colonies and were therefore sufficiently anti-colonial to support the measures. However, a significant element in England was opposed to the Stamp Acts. English merchants were alarmed, foreseeing a hostile reaction from the colonies that would directly impact on their trade interests. Members of Parliament argued at length as to whether or not the tax was "constitutional" in the sense of the unwritten English constitution, using terms like "traditional liberties." One pro-American member of Parliament, Isaac Barre, even used the term "sons of liberty" in a speech.

In the colonies people long aware of the one-sided benefits of the trade monopoly imposed by England were also polarized by the English constitutional issues at stake. Broadly speaking, they divided into two camps. The distinction was not between those who were for or against the Stamp Acts—nearly everyone was opposed. The difference was between those factions prepared to abide by the rule of law, even unpopular laws that clearly infringed on the traditional English right not to be taxed except by Parliament, where the Americans had no representatives, and those hotheads who were prepared to resist the laws by whatever means possible.

The latter were the more active and vociferous. Flags were flown at half-mast in New York the day the Stamp Acts were due to take effect, marking "the death of American liberty," and an effigy of the New York governor was burned. In New England ad hoc vigilante groups calling themselves the Sons of Liberty took to the streets to prevent the tax from being collected—tarring, feathering, vandalizing property, and generally terrorizing His Majesty's tax collectors and making it impossible to enforce the Stamp Acts. In Virginia the assembly fulminated and protested, and righteous indignation and talk of embargoes rather than tarring and feathering was the order of the day. Social gatherings in Williamsburg and on the plantation social circuit provided a forum for the exchange of information and discussion. Martha, married to a burgess and with the opportunity of attending "publick times" to hear the matter debated by everyone in Williamsburg, was well placed to keep up with events.

Lord North and his government were stunned by the force of the reaction, and Parliament voted to rescind the Stamp Acts within months. There was a proviso to their withdrawal, however, in that nearly all members of Parliament agreed that the doctrine of parliamentary supremacy (meaning that Parliament can do anything) meant that England retained the right to tax the colonies, and that the colonies were bound by English legislation. The proviso attracted little attention in the colonies at the time.

In 1767 that proviso gave birth to a new set of measures, the Townshend Acts, which provided for a tax on four items in the colonies—lead, glass, paint, and tea—to be collected at ports by customs officers. The last item, tea, was the most popular beverage in the colonies, and at the time there was a surplus of tea building up in the warehouses of the East India Company. The tea was already subsidized, but taxing its sale would have two benefits. Because there was so much of it, even with a nominal tax, the glut meant it could be sold at a lower price to colonial consumers, which should simultaneously result in more tea being sold and more tax revenue to Britain. It was a scheme to benefit everyone.

Tea became the central issue for the colonists, possibly because many prominent merchants such as John Hancock in Boston did a thriving business smuggling both tea and Madeira into the colonies. Flooding the market with cut-price English tea, even with a nominal tax, would actually have resulted in cheaper tea for the colonists but would have seriously undercut the tea smugglers' profits. A storm of protest was orchestrated over the tax on tea, with the Sons of Liberty in the vanguard, rumored to be funded by the smugglers. The English were, on the whole, astonished at the illogic of protests about cheaper tea. "Taxation without representation is tyranny" bellowed colonial broadsides. More tarring and feathering followed.

By this time widespread support was growing for a semiofficial embargo on the taxed goods. George wrote his factors that as he and other burgesses had signed a nonimportation agreement, he did not expect embargoed goods to be included in his orders.

While women were largely excluded from the political process, what happened next stunned both colonial men and the British. In a militant and spontaneous response, ladies up and down the colonies began forming themselves into groups known as the Daughters of Liberty. Their purpose was to highlight not only their own boycott of tea, but they took it on themselves to boycott English clothing—so dear to Martha's heart and that of her contemporaries—until the Townshend Acts should be withdrawn.

An anonymous poem appeared in the Pennsylvania *Gazette* in 1768: [Grenville was George Grenville, the king's chief minister]

> Since the men, from a party or fear of a frown,
> Are kept by a sugar-plum quietly down,
> Supinely asleep—and depriv'd of their sight,
> Are stripp'd of their freedom, and robbed of their right;
> If the sons, so degenerate! the blessings despise,
> Let the Daughters of Liberty nobly arise;
> And though we've no voice but a negative here,
> The use of the taxables let us forbear:—
> (Then merchants import till your stores are all full,
> May the buyers be few, and your traffic be dull!)
>
> Stand firmly resolv'd, and bid Grenville to see.
> That rather than freedom we part with our tea.
> And well as we may love the dear draught when a-dry,
> As American Patriots our taste we deny—
> Pennsylvania's gay meadows can richly afford
> To pamper our fancy or furnish our board;
> And paper sufficient at home we still have,
> To assure the wiseacre, we will not sign slave;
> When his homespun shall fail, to remonstrate our grief,
> We can speak viva voce, or scratch on a leaf;
> Refuse all their colors, though richest of dye,

When the juice of a berry our paint can supply,
To humor our fancy—and as for our houses,
They'll do without painting as well as our spouses;
While to keep out the cold of a keen winter morn,
We can screen the north-west with a well polished horn;
And trust me a woman by honest invention,
Might give this state-doctor a dose of prevention.

Join mutual in this—and but small as it seems,
We may jostle a Grenville, and puzzle his schemes;
But a motive more worthy our patriot pen,
Thus acting—we point out their duty to men
And should the bound-pensioners tell us to hush
We can throw back the satire, by biding them blush.

Daughters of Liberty groups sprang up in Boston, Providence, and New-port and spread down the East Coast to Wilmington, North Carolina. The women held gatherings at which they spun thread and wove cloth as a sub-stitute for British material, and ostentatiously partook of a beverage known as "Liberty Tea," made from a variety of leaves and flowers—sage, raspberry leaf, and rosehips, among others. Prominent ladies made public pledges not to buy tea or English clothing until the Townshend Acts had been repealed.

In Boston, General Thomas Gage, commander of the British forces in America, struggled to avoid provoking the colonists, but as one contempo-rary noted, "General Gage found it difficult to deal with the Sons of Liberty and even more difficult to deal with the Daughters of Liberty."[4]

Women were steadfast in their support for the sentiments espoused by the Daughters of Liberty, and they were aware that they were taking on an active political role. Within a few years, Abigail Adams would write to her husband, John, who was by that time a delegate to the Continental Con-gress, which had been formed in Philadelphia: "If the men are not able to perform their duty to their country, the enemy will find the women to be a veritable race of Amazons."

Martha was not part of the feminine movement to boycott British goods. Her substantial orders to London for clothing for herself and Patcy contin-ued and grew as Patcy became a young woman with greater requirements for pretty things. In July 1772, by which time English clothing was being boy-cotted widely, Martha wrote to a London milliner complaining about the price and quality of a suit made of Brussels lace she had ordered for Patcy. Notwith-standing her dissatisfaction, Martha placed another order for a "suit at ye price of £40 . . . —and ye othr things sent last yr for myself &ca were 5 gauze Caps w. Blond Lace bordrs. at a Ga [guinea, unit of English currency slightly more than a pound] each . . . I have now sent for 2 Caps for M. Custis, & 2 for myself of Mint. Lace . . . hers to suit a Person 16 yrs old mine one of 40." Martha also added a tippet and cap for Patcy to match the lace suit.[5]

Patcy was growing into a pretty, though frail, girl, who had been nick-named the "Dark Lady" because of her dark hair and brunette complexion. As Miss Custis, Patcy would be a rich young woman when she came of age and, with her good looks, bound to marry well. Given her social position, it was important she be "finished" as a young lady. In addition to lessons with her tutor Walter Magowan, her lessons on the spinet with Mr. Stedlar, and learning to dance at Mr. Christian's classes, Patcy's education would have included, at her mother's hand, a thorough indoctrination in housekeeping skills, so necessary when she became mistress of her own establishment.

Martha was never one to neglect her duty, but Patcy may not have been strong enough to benefit from such teaching. The "fitts," which Martha had first written about in 1760, continued as Patcy grew older. Martha was devoted to her surviving daughter, and George was touchingly protective. In contrast to her brother Jacky, Patcy obediently studied her books, fol-lowed instructions in her music and dancing lessons, and kept close to Martha's side; Martha probably excused her from having to do anything strenuous in the kitchen, laundry, dairy, or garden until she was better. Martha could see Patcy was not very well, but judging by contemporary accounts, people seemed to be forever "unwell" in those days of no refrig-eration for food and no antibiotics for infections. Martha trusted Patcy would get over it, whatever "it" was.

George noted in his diary that Dr. Rumney had called at Mount Ver-non to see his stepdaughter in February 1767 when she was eleven. The doctor had stayed the night and prescribed powders, "nervous drops," and valerian.[6] The treatment must have worked, because in August and Sep-tember 1767 Martha and George went on a holiday with George William and Sally Cary Fairfax, now returned from England, to Berkeley Springs for a few weeks, leaving fourteen-year-old Jacky and twelve-year-old Patcy behind at Mount Vernon. Martha must have been confident that both were fine, and Patcy, especially, in robust health, because she would never have left the children for so long if she had had any qualms about their well-being in her absence.

Berkeley Springs was a very rudimentary resort, about ninety miles from Mount Vernon. People came to take the spring waters as a cure for nearly everything, as for example, Lawrence Washington had done for his tuberculosis in 1751 and George in 1761 from a bad cold caught while cam-paigning. On this occasion there is no record of anyone being ill, and the Washingtons and the Fairfaxes seem to have gone with no object in mind but a pleasant excursion. They took the family cook and probably Martha's maid, as well as George's valet Bishop, who accompanied George when hunting and most other places as well. They took their own supplies of food, including a quarter each of veal and venison, butter, eggs, squash, corn, cucumbers, watermelons, peaches, and apples.[7] They lived in tents at the springs.

It would be a short-lived carefree interlude. Within months George's journal was recording more and more doctors' visits, and his accounts showed more prescriptions for Patcy. The odd behavior of earlier generations of Custises and Parkes had not been forgotten, and as Patcy's condition became more widely known there was muttering about the "bad Custis blood" coming out.

In the spring of 1768 Dr. Rumney visited Mount Vernon on several occasions to treat Patcy. An order to England that spring included harpsichord music for her, as well as surveyor's instruments for Jacky. In April George and Martha took her and Jacky to a ball in Alexandria as a treat, and a few weeks later the whole family set off for Williamsburg, this time with Billy Bassett, Anna Maria's eldest son, who had been visiting at Mount Vernon, in tow. They stayed overnight at an inn south of Fredericksburg and may have called on Mary Washington and Betty Lewis.

In June Dr. Rumney stayed the night and gave Patcy "a large julep," probably a nonalcoholic soothing drink. Then, on June 14 Dr. Rumney was again sent for, urgently this time, as Patcy was, in George's words, "seized with fits." This time he bled her and dosed her with valerian and "nervous drops." A week later he was called back.

Preoccupied with her daughter, Martha probably neglected Jacky, who had learned as little as possible from Walter Magowan. The tutor left Mount Vernon for good in December 1767. No one raised the issue of Patcy's further education, but by now Jacky frankly worried George, who had been conscientious in shipping Jacky's tobacco and keeping an eye on the children's accounts and had nearly doubled the value of Jacky's estate by his good management. George could see he was enjoying greater success in building up Jacky's assets than in his efforts to raise Jacky with enough sense to manage them. Having had to seize the few opportunities he had had as a boy to better himself, Jacky's laziness at his books and general complacency irritated George. The surveyor's instruments he had ordered for Jacky in the hopes of passing on lessons taught him by Augustine Washington lay unused.

As the Custis heir, Jacky had the status of a little prince and grew up with an undeniable fund of sly charm. George was a very shrewd judge of character, and he must have sensed that Martha's coddling and indulgence exacerbated something weak about Jacky. His redeeming qualities were that he shared George's passion for all things to do with horses, dogs, and hunting.

Still, Jacky needed to be educated if he was to hang on to his estate when he came into his inheritance. George was increasingly involved in an uphill battle to accomplish it. After five months when Jacky had no lessons following Walter Magowan's departure, George heard of a small, select school run by the Reverend Jonathan Boucher in Caroline County, Maryland, that looked like the answer for a spoiled fourteen-year-old boy. Though concerned at the prospect of parting with Jacky, Martha deferred to George's judgment in the matter. Reverend Boucher was delighted at the prospect of having the Custis heir as a pupil. On June 28, 1768, George and Jacky left with Jacky driving two horses, his body servant Julius in livery in attendance, and endless luggage.

Jacky made a docile first impression on Boucher, who wrote the Washingtons in August in honeyed terms: "Yr son came to me teeming with all ye softer virtues; but then I thought possessed as he was of all ye Harmlessness of ye Dove, He still wanted something of ye wisdom of ye Serpent."[8]

Once at school Jacky was indisposed with a variety of complaints. Subsequent letters from Boucher minutely detailed the state of Jacky's health, noting with concern that his new pupil was excessively fond of fruit and particularly cucumbers. In fact Boucher swiftly discerned Jacky was lazy and thick, but he was clearly the most prominent pupil a struggling schoolmaster could wish for.

Dr. Rumney paid several more visits to Patcy in July, now prescribing musk, believed to be an antispasmodic, as well as more valerian.

In August Jacky was allowed a holiday with the family, who paid a round of family visits, first to George's brother Samuel Washington and afterwards to George's favorite brother John Augustine Washington at Bushfield. There Jacky fell ill with fever and vomiting, and Martha insisted he come back to Mount Vernon to recover before returning to Reverend Boucher's.

Martha was so occupied with her daughter she was unable to visit her family that November. George attended the session of the assembly on his own and came back to Mount Vernon to find Dr. Rumney there, giving his stepdaughter more musk and "drops." In December 1768 the Washingtons hired a white housekeeper named Mary Wilson, possibly because Martha was distracted from her normal routine.

In January 1769 Patcy was so ill the Washingtons called in another Washington friend and neighbor, Dr. Hugh Mercer, for a consultation with Dr. Rumney. Mercer had studied medicine at the University of Aberdeen. The two doctors consulted and decided on a new treatment with mercurial pills, purging pills, and ingredients for a "decoction."

These proved no more effective than earlier treatments. Patcy continued to have alarming "fits," finally diagnosed as epilepsy. It is just possible her condition may have been triggered by catching measles when Martha and other members of the Mount Vernon household had them in 1760. At this remove in time it is impossible to diagnose measles or any other possible cause, such as delivery complications at Patcy's birth, or a later injury to the head, for certain. It seems that Patcy's seizures were intermittent at first and became worse at puberty.

Epilepsy was a mysterious and terrifying condition and probably rare. The doctors knew only what the medical textbooks said, and that was not enlightening. "The Epilepsy," read one treatise, "appears so surprising in many Respects, that in former Ages it has been attributed to the particular Operation of the Gods, devils and Witchcraft and other supernatural events." The treatise then suggested seizures were caused by heredity, a local disorder in and about the brain, wounds, bruises, "Sharp Lymph in the Other Parts of the Body," worms, teeth, curdled milk, drinking, eating, exercise, menopause, and pains. All these were subject to aggravation by motion, heat, drunkenness, gluttony, venery, passions of the mind, fright, grief, and vexation. The entire human condition, in fact. The medical profession suspected some connection with the brain and believed medicine for epilepsy needed to be in small enough particles to reach the brain.[9] Beyond that they had no idea.

In fact, epilepsy is defined in a modern work as "a disturbance of the nervous system that abruptly interferes with behavior, perception, movement, consciousness or other brain functions"[10] Today it can be controlled with medication, but there is still no cure.

This definition would probably have left no one the wiser as far as treatments were concerned in the eighteenth century. Another contemporary medical text in Patcy's day recommended bloodletting, purgatives, something called "Issues and Setons" on the nape of the neck, and abstinence. It recommended Peruvian bark and metallic tonics such as those containing tin, iron, and copper, and arsenic, which was obviously dangerous. It suggested peony and valerian and cold baths. Some of the doctors who saw Patcy recommended barley water, a light diet, and keeping the body cool.[11] The girl was tormented with bloodletting and probably many another popular remedy in the form of purges and "vomits."

Patcy's condition, as mysterious and terrifying as an evil visitation, must have had its effects within the family. Martha would have been on edge, hoping the last drops, remedy, or doctor might have succeeded in halting her seizures, but always on guard in case they did not. Today families with an epileptic child are counseled to guard against the natural inclination to overprotect him or her, as well as the dangers of focusing their attention on the child with a disability at the expense of other children in the family. Modern advice probably identifies a pattern Martha experienced:

> Children with epilepsy often have trouble developing relationships with other children. They tend to be isolated from their peers but inordinately dependant upon their mothers. The parent lacks confidence the child can manage outside the family if a seizure occurs and a seizure can occur at any time. The child adopts this parental attitude and clings to the family.

Unless the parents are unusually well-informed, they are likely to worry that they will inadvertently make the epilepsy worse. Even if they know their every action and remark will not significantly affect the disorder, each severe attack will stir up the notion that the child might have fared better if they had behaved differently.

All family activities may be fashioned around the child's limitations.[12]

George and Martha tried everything. While George's diary is full of entries about doctors and medicines, they tried at the same time to give her a normal life. The Washingtons bought Patcy presents—songbooks and clothes—and young people in the neighborhood came to Mount Vernon for dancing classes. One of Patcy's best friends was Milly (Amelia) Posey, a daughter of neighbor John Posey, who was a ne'er-do-well and who owed George a large sum of money. She was the younger sister of Thomas Posey, who may have been George's son. Martha took Milly under her wing, and she continued to be a favorite at Mount Vernon even though George's relations with John Posey had grown strained.

George's diary recorded that in one particularly bad three-month period Patcy had seizures on twenty-six days. By then Martha must have been desperate. George noted in his diary that in February 1769, Joshua Evans, clearly a quack, had called at Mount Vernon and fitted Patcy with an iron ring. It was a remedy that had its origin in a fourteenth-century superstition that "cramp rings" on a finger could relieve epilepsy. The design of these rings varied, but their ability to ward of attacks depended on the blessing or inscription engraved inside. Though he did not say so in any of his papers, this kind of voodoo must have annoyed the rationalist George. However, because he was acutely conscious of being "only" a stepparent and guardian to Patcy and Jacky, he generally deferred to Martha in most matters regarding her children's welfare.

In July 1769 George and Martha took Patcy to Berkeley Springs, which really was a last resort, in every sense of the word, for anyone with an incurable illness. Patcy grew no better there, and they returned home in September.

In November the Washingtons tried a different tack. They took Patcy to Eltham, where she was visited and examined by an eminent Williamsburg doctor, Dr. John de Sequeyra, a Sephardic Jew. He called to see Patcy on six occasions. She may have been a little better because the family spent several weeks there, joined by Jacky. George went back and forth to nearby Williamsburg for sessions of the assembly, spending many nights there on his own. He noted giving both children and Martha spending money, and on at least one occasion the whole family went to Mrs. Campbell's lodging house, where George usually stayed, and ate oysters.

On December 13 the burgesses gave a ball for the governor and ladies and gentlemen of Williamsburg. Williamsburg was brightly lit up for the occasion, and over a hundred ladies of Williamsburg seized upon the occasion to demonstrate their boycott of imported British clothing by attending the ball in homespun gowns. George paid a subscription of £3 for the ball and may have attended. Martha probably did not, both because her daughter was not well and because Martha was the last woman in Virginia who would willingly have attended a ball in homespun.

Jacky returned to Reverend Boucher's, and George, Martha, and Patcy made a leisurely trip back to Mount Vernon, stopping for Christmas in Fredericksburg at Kenmore, the home of Betty and Fielding Lewis. George met with his mother's overseer while they spent one night with Mary.

In March 1770 Patcy was well enough for one of Mr. Christian's weekend-long dancing classes to be held at Mount Vernon. Aside from Millie Posey, who would likely have been invited, Patcy seems to have had few friends her own age, though young girls visited Mount Vernon with their parents or other relatives. What is also striking in this context is that nowhere in George's diaries is there any mention of young men coming to call on Patcy or paying her any special attention. This seems surprising, given that she was a pretty girl, judging by a portrait painted when she was fifteen or sixteen, and that she would inherit a great deal of money. Normally such a girl would have been sought after. Patcy was not.

Meanwhile, two years had passed since Jacky had first graced Reverend Boucher's educational establishment. Boucher had struggled to contain Jacky's penchant for life's pleasures and his profligate spending habits, as well his total disinclination for any kind of academic endeavor. In the interim the school had moved to Annapolis, which to country-bred Jacky, was a dazzling metropolis promising many pleasures.

Even Boucher, keen to make allowances for youth and privilege and desperate to hang on to his rich prize pupil, was driven to distraction. Jacky had taken up with the gilded youth of Annapolis, most of whom saw little point in books when there were horse races to bet on and balls and theater performances to attend. Jacky had a wonderful time and, to Boucher's horror, soon became involved in scrapes with females, involving in one case an actress and in another, a Miss Galloway, sister of a fellow pupil and daughter of a man who had seen better days and could hardly afford his son's school fees. Boucher was scandalized and worried that the young heir for whom he was responsible could be caught in the clutches of a gold digger. He wrote George that Jacky was behaving like an Asiatic sybarite. Fifteen-year-old Jacky was also running up immense bills for clothes and doctors and, on occasion, keeping his own kitchen boy to prepare his food.

Boucher tried another tack. In May 1770 he wrote to George to persuade him that what Jacky really needed was to make a grand tour of Europe, with Boucher as his guide. George was skeptical about the benefit Jacky was likely to derive and believed the scheme was too expensive. George's reply in July speaks volumes about his own grasp of Jacky's limitations, Martha's attitude toward her son, and Patcy's health:

> Before I ever thought myself at liberty to entertain this plan, I judged it to be highly reasonable and necessary that his mother should be consulted. I laid your first letter and proposals before her and desired that she would reflect well, before she resolved, as an unsteady behavior might be a disadvantage to you. Her determination was, that, if it appeared to be his inclination to undertake this tour, and it should be judged for his benefit, she would not oppose it, whatever pangs it might give her to part with him. To this declaration she still adheres, but in so faint a manner, that I think, with her fears and his indifference, it will soon be declared he has no inclination to go. . . . Several causes, I believe, have concurred to make her view his departure, as the time approaches, with more reluctance than she expected. The unhappy situation of her daughter has in some degree fixed her eyes upon him as her only hope.[13]

In June 1770 at Williamsburg the burgesses drafted a nonimportation agreement, which was signed by 164 men, including George. Of interest to Martha and Patcy was the fact that it was now permissible to order previously embargoed items, like sugar, trinkets and jewelry, from England although this did not really dent the initiative of the Daughters of Liberty, who continued their highly publicized unofficial boycott of English clothing, materials, and all items of dress.

At the end of July Patcy became dangerously ill, the misery of her seizures compounded by "ague" and fever. Over the course of the next eighty-six days Patcy had seizures on twenty-six of them. They took Patcy to Williamsburg in August, probably to consult doctors and buy more medicine. To cheer her up they bought her silk embroidery thread and earrings.

In the autumn of 1770 Martha spent nine weeks alone at Mount Vernon with Patcy while George went on an extended trip to the Ohio frontier.

In January 1771 Dr. Rumney arrived with the Peruvian bark thought to be good for epilepsy as well as malaria, and more pills, powders, and drops. In February George wrote Reverend Boucher asking him to buy some ether for Patcy.

In April 1771, Martha was persuaded to allow Jacky to have a smallpox inoculation by a Baltimore specialist. The procedure was illegal in Virginia because it involved infecting people with what was always intended as a small dose of the disease. Many people died as a result. Jacky got cold feet and, believing he had changed his mind, Martha went to Williamsburg with George and Patcy. While she was gone, Jacky changed his mind again and went ahead with the inoculation. Jacky's new body slave Joe was inoculated at the same time. Both were helped on their way to recovery with violent purges. George and Jacky kept the inoculation a secret from Martha until all danger had passed and it was clear the inoculation had "taken," that is, there had been a few pustules. George and Jacky believed doing it in secret had spared Martha unnecessary anxiety, and by the time Martha found out, Jacky was fully recovered.

Jacky came home in July for another holiday. In September George went to Ferry Farm to move his increasingly infirm mother into a house in Fredericksburg near Betty and Fielding Lewis.

In 1772 Charles Wilson Peale came to Mount Vernon to paint the family's portraits. He painted a grand portrait of George in his Virginia Militia uniform, with the king's gorget about his neck, and a miniature of Martha, painted at Jacky's express request, a sweetly dignified portrait of a middle-aged woman in lace and pearls. Jacky was shown in miniature in a beautifully worked waistcoat, looking complacent and plump, and there was an exquisite miniature of Patcy, wearing pearls in her hair, possibly the same Custis pearls that Martha had worn in her hair when she married George. Significantly, Patcy is depicted with heavy dark eyebrows. According to Philip Fithian, the Carter family tutor at Nomini Hall, these were regarded as a great mark of female beauty in the colony.

Testaments to wealth and prominence, good looks, and great expectations, the portraits capture each member of the family looking his or her best, in a moment of calm. For all of them, in different ways, it was the proverbial calm before the storm.

CHAPTER 9

Sudden Changes and Milestones

Jacky's adolescence was wearing everyone out. Relations between the Washingtons and Reverend Boucher grew strained over Boucher's failure to control Jacky or teach him anything. Horrified respectively by the prospect of Jacky cut loose on the world in his resolutely uneducated state and the prospect of losing a pupil able to afford the fees, both parties battled on, trying to maintain cordial relations in the interests of keeping Jacky in school. Today the family of a troublesome pupil at a select private school might meet in the headmaster's study for "a quiet word." In September 1772 Martha, George, and Patcy set out to accompany Jacky back to Annapolis to school for the same purpose. They visited the Bouchers and dined at their home together with a fellow parent, Benedict Calvert of Mount Airey near Baltimore, whose son Charles was also at Boucher's school. With Benedict Calvert were two of his daughters, Betsy and Eleanor Calvert.

The cordial meeting over the dinner table might have soothed relations between the Washingtons and the Bouchers, but it failed to have any impact on Jacky. By early 1773 an exhausted Boucher wrote to the Washingtons that if Jacky were not to make the grand tour he might derive more benefit from attending another institution of learning. Martha left the decision to George, though she leaned toward William and Mary College because it was closest to Mount Vernon. In fact, William and Mary was notoriously full of students just like Jacky, and with its rowdy reputation and lax college discipline it was the last place George was prepared to consider. Boucher, a staunch loyalist throughout the furor over the tax acts, begged Jacky not be sent to the college at Princeton, a stronghold of Patriot sympathizers. George considered King's College in New York to be the soundest option. Its president, Dr. Myles Cooper, was a staunch Tory. Martha was unhappy Jacky would be so far away from home, but decided that George knew best.

Jacky had other plans. In April he returned home from his final term at Boucher's and dropped a bombshell at Mount Vernon, announcing to his mother and stepfather that he was engaged to fifteen-year-old Eleanor Calvert. As heir to one of the largest fortunes in Virginia, Jacky was a prize catch for some girl and undeniably the best match Eleanor Calvert could have made. From the Washingtons' point of view, Eleanor was far from unsuitable in a social sense. She was one of ten children of Benedict Calvert of Maryland, himself a natural son of Lord Baltimore. But, despite her grand connections, as one of so many children, she could not expect to have much settled on her by her father when she married. She was an exceptionally pretty girl, but she came in for high praise on other counts as well, and from an unexpected quarter, the Reverend Boucher.

Worried that he would be blamed for a development that had taken place almost under his nose, an agitated Boucher promptly wrote to the Washingtons:

> I hardly remember ever to have been more surpris'd than I was a few days ago on being informed by the Governor of the Engagement that had taken place between Mr. Custis and Miss Nelly Calvert: and, I beg Leave to assure You, on my Word of Honour, that, never till that moment, had I the most distant Suspicion of any such Thing's being in Agitation. It has given me great Uneasiness to learn, from the same Authority, that You think Me, in some measure, to blame.

Going on to note that he always thought Jacky had a preference for Betsy Calvert and that Jacky had failed to consult him just as he had failed to consult the Washingtons, Boucher continued, looking on the brighter side:

> I should belie my real Opinion, were I not to say, that, I think, it had been better for Mr. Custis not to have engag'd Himself: but since This could not be, I should hardly belie it less, not to own, that I think He cou'd nowhere have entered into a more prudent Engagement. Miss Nelly Calvert has Merit enough to fix Him, if any Woman can: and I do, from the Fullness of a warm heart, most cordially congratulate his Mother & Yourself, as well as Him, on the Happiness of his having made this most pleasing of all Connections, with this the most amiable young Woman I have almost ever known. I know her well and can truly say, She is all the Fondest Parent can wish for a darling Child. . . . I can almost persuade myself to believe, that the Advantage which may be deriv'd to his Morals from this Engagement, rash as it has been, are enough to compensate for the ill Influence it may be supposed to have had on his intellectual Pursuits.[1]

In fact, this echoed Martha's view of the matter. She was a champion of matrimony and a firm believer in young people settling down. She also

"Colonel George Washington in his uniform of the Virginia Militia," by Charles Willson Peale 1772. Courtesy of Washington and Lee University.

remembered how unpleasant it had been when John Custis opposed her engagement to Daniel. Distracted as she may have been with Patcy, Martha was not unaware that Jacky's behavior was in part a result of her spoiling him and would, if allowed to continue, eventually lead to serious problems. She was devoted to her son, and engagement to a steady girl struck her as the best means of halting his slide into dissipation and focusing him on his responsibilities. The Calverts were a desirable family connection for the Washingtons, and as strict as Martha was about manners and proper behavior, when fifteen-year-old Eleanor was invited to visit at Mount Vernon, she passed that test with flying colors and made a good impression. Though Eleanor was well brought up, it is fair to say that there was something about Martha that always put young people on their best behavior. At the same time, Martha was always warmly affectionate, and she made Eleanor very welcome.

George was less sanguine. He was exasperated, believing Jacky's impetuous and irresponsible behavior would lead to an embarrassing mess with the Calverts because privately he doubted Jacky had the staying power to keep to the engagement. He felt bound to write to Benedict Calvert, setting out

"Miniature of Martha Washington," by Charles Willson Peale 1772. Courtesy of the Mount Vernon Ladies' Association of the Union.

his concerns in a tactful way and saying something equally tactful about marriage settlements. However warmly Martha welcomed the engagement, George was less convinced that marriage at that stage would be good for so young a couple, and advised waiting until Jacky was almost of age. The letter that follows is revealing not just for the way he sets out his concerns to Benedict Calvert, but in that it sets out George's views on the serious nature of marriage. It is the first of several letters George would write in the course of his life to relatives and friends contemplating marriage. If none of the Washingtons' personal correspondence survives to shed light on their relationship, George's letters on marriage to others offer insight into his own experience of matrimony.

Mount Vernon, April 3, 1773
Dear Sir,
    I am now set down to write to you on a Subject of Importance, and no small embarrassment to me. My Son in Law and Ward, Mr. Custis, has, as I have been informed, paid his Addresses to your Second Daughter, and having made

some progress in her Affections has required her in Marriage. How far a union of this Sort may be agreeable to you, you can best tell, but I should think myself wanting in Candor was I not to acknowledge, that, Miss Nellie's amiable qualifications stands confess'd at all hands; and that an alliance with your Family will be pleasing to his.

. . . permit me to add Sir, that at this, or any short time, his youth, inexperience, and unripened Education, is, and will be insuperable obstacles in my eye, to the completion of the Marriage. As his Guardian, I conceive it to be my indispensable duty (to endeavor) to carry him through a regular course of Education, many branches of which, I am sorry to add, he is totally deficient of; and to guard his youth to a more advanced age before an Event, on which his own Peace and the happiness of another is to depend, takes place; not that I have any doubt of the warmth of his Affections, nor, I hope I may add, any change in them; but at present I do not conceive that he is capable of bestowing that due attention to the Important consequences of a marriage State . . . and am unwilling he should do it till he is. If the Affection which they have

"Miniature of Martha Parke Custis 'Patcy,' " by Charles Willson Peale 1772. Courtesy of the Mount Vernon Ladies' Association of the Union.

avowd for each other is fix'd upon a Solid Basis, it will receive no diminution in the course of two or three years, in which time he may prosecute his Studies, and thereby render himself more deserving of the Lady . . . If unfortunately, (as they are both young) there should be an abatement of Affection on either side, or both, it had better precede, rather than follow after, the Marriage.

Delivering my Sentiments thus will not, I hope, lead you into a belief that I am desirous of breaking off the Match; to postpone it is all I have in view; for I shall recommend it to the young Gentleman with the warmth that becomes a man of honour, (notwithstanding he did not vouchsafe to consult either his Mother or me, on the occasion) to consider himself as much engaged to your Daughter as if the indissoluble Knot was tied; and as the surest means of effecting this, to stick close to his Studies . . . by which he will in great measure, avoid those little Flirtations with other Girls which may, by dividing the Attention, contribute not a little to divide the Affection.

It may be expected of me perhaps to say something of Fortune . . . I shall inform you that Mr. Custis's Estate consists of about 15,000 Acres of Land, good part of it adjoining to the City of Williamsburg, and none 40 Miles from it; several Lotts in the said City; between two and three hundred Negroes; and about Eight or ten thousand pounds upon Bond, and in the hands of his Merchants. This Estate he now holds Independent of his Mother's Dower, which will be an acquisition to it at her Death. . . .

At all times when you, Mrs. Calvert, or the young Ladies can make it convenient to favor us with a visit we should be happy in seeing you at this place. Mrs. Washington and Miss Custis join me in respectful Compliments.[2]

Benedict Calvert must have been holding his breath to see what the Washingtons' reaction to the engagement would be. The couple was very young, Jacky was going to be very rich, and there was a chance the Washingtons would feel, as John Custis had so long ago about Martha, that it was not a grand enough match for Jacky. He was immensely relieved and gratified by George's letter, responding:

I am truly happy in your Approbation of [Jacky's] future Union with my Second Daughter. I would be dead to parental feelings were I untouched with the polite manner in which you are pleased to compliment Nelly's Qualifications; Being her father, it would illy become me to sound her praise, perhaps I might be deemed partial—I shall therefore only say, That it has ever been the Endeavor of her Mother and me, to bring her up in such a manner, as to ensure the happiness of her future Husband, in which I think, we have not been unsucccessfull.[3]

He went on to agree that it would be advisable to postpone the wedding, accepting George's invitation to visit Mount Vernon and reciprocating with

"Miniature of John Parke Custis 'Jacky,'" by Charles Willson Peale 1772. Courtesy of the Mount Vernon Ladies' Association of the Union.

an open-ended invitation for the Mount Vernon family to visit at Mount Airey. As Benedict Calvert put it, he would be "happy in bringing my family to wait on Mrs. Washington." In fact, it was considered a gesture of courtesy to visit and "wait upon" someone.

Eleanor soon became a frequent and welcome visitor at Mount Vernon, occasionally with her mother and a sister or two. Both Martha and Patcy grew attached to her. Martha may have welcomed her all the more because she was company and a friend for poor Patcy, as well as Jacky's fiancée.

That same spring Martha and the two girls had a happy time unpacking a large order George had sent for the previous summer. It was a treasure chest of pretty things for Patcy, though Martha was too considerate and thoughtful a person not to have made sure that Eleanor had a share of them: handkerchiefs, a shawl, dresses of silk and lace, silk slippers in gold and another pair in silver, a fan, mother-of-pearl quadrille counters in a mother-of-pearl box, amber beads, a handsome velvet collar with an Indian pearl bow, a satin bonnet, a necklace and earrings, garnet shoe buckles, a silver thimble, hairpins set with garnets and diamante, leather shoes with her name inside, a powder box and puff, silk gloves, lace caps, an embroidery frame, a new prayer book with silver clasps, silk stockings, and *Lady's Magazine,* together with more workaday items such as thread, pins, hairpins, and laces. The Daughters of Liberty, who had renounced such English frippery and taken to homespun with a vengeance, would have disapproved, but as the organization had not caught on as strongly in northern Virginia and Maryland as it had elsewhere, it is unlikely Martha, Patcy, and Eleanor worried what people would think.

In April there was news from New Kent. Martha and Anna Maria's youngest surviving sister Elizabeth, at the relatively ripe old age of twenty-four, married John Aylett. Frances Dandridge, who had moved in with her son Bartholomew, a lawyer, and his second wife, Mary, at Pamocra, gave Elizabeth a Bible to mark the occasion. Martha's brother William Dandridge was still in the British navy, but continued to make his home with his mother and brother when in New Kent. From Eltham there was sadder news. Patcy's cousin, Anna Maria's fourteen-year-old daughter Betsy Bassett, had died.

In May George took Jacky north to resume his studies in New York. Jacky had been entered at King's College, later to become Columbia University. To this day, Columbia College lists "John Parke Custis" as one of its alumni. George and Martha had no wish to keep Eleanor and Jacky apart unnecessarily, and with their approval Jacky left Mount Vernon a few days before George for a farewell visit at Mount Airey. George, too, stopped at Mount Airey on the way, to "wait on" Mrs. Calvert and collect Jacky.

In New York, George attended a farewell dinner for a former colleague, British general Thomas Gage, who was resigning as commander of the British forces in the colonies. George and General Gage had served together on the frontier in the French and Indian Wars. George was also looking forward to an extended tour of the western lands along the Ohio River with his friend Governor Dunmore, which the two men had planned while the assembly was sitting in March. Feeling he had done his duty by Jacky and relishing the prospect of an excursion to the frontier, George returned to Mount Vernon early in June to prepare for it. There he found Patcy enjoying what was turning into an unusually long spell of good health. Joining the happy family party were Eleanor and a Miss Reed, a Calvert family servant, not a slave, who was paid by the family and acted as a kind of governess and chaperone to Eleanor. His favorite brother John Augustine was also there with his wife Hannah and their two children.

With the exception of the John Augustine family, who had left for Bushfield, the whole party was there enjoying dinner on a sunny Sunday afternoon, June 19, when tragedy struck. George's daily diary entry stated, "At home all day. About five oclock poor Patcy Custis Died Suddenly." The next day a deeply affected George wrote to Burwell Bassett an account of what had happened:

yesterday removed the Sweet Innocent Girl into a more happy, & peaceful abode than any she has met with in the afflicted Path she hitherto has trod. She rose from Dinner about four Oclock in better health and spirits than she appeared to have been in for some time; soon after which she was seizd with one of her usual Fits, & expired in it, in less than two Minutes without uttering a Word, a groan or scarce a Sigh. This Sudden, and unexpected blow, I scarce need add has almost reduced my poor Wife to the lowest ebb of Misery.[4]

Patcy's funeral took place Monday, the day after her death. It was a hot, overcast thundery day. The Reverend Mr. Massey was summoned from nearby Pohick Church to read the funeral service, and Patcy was laid to rest in the old Washington family vault, which was about two hundred yards south of the main house, down a slope. It must have been a small funeral. Jacky was in New York, unaware of his sister's death, and there would have been no time for the New Kent relatives to be informed or to get there. Probably those present were George and Martha, Eleanor, Miss Reed, and Sally and George William Fairfax, who came from Belvoir. Some, if not all, of the Mansion House slaves must have been present too. Afterward the Fairfaxes left, and Mr. Massey stayed to dinner and the night. The suddenness with which death had struck at the peaceful dinner table must have left everyone shocked and traumatized.

As well as writing to his brother-in-law at Eltham the day of the funeral, George wrote to Governor Dunmore to cancel the Ohio trip. On July 3 the governor replied:

> I am most exceedingly sorry to learn by your last that you have so good a reason for chainging your resolution, & I do sincerely condole with you and poor Mrs. Washington for your loss, tho as the poor young Lady was so often Afflicted with these fitts. I dare say she thinks it is a happy exchainge.... I thought if it would not be disagreeable to Mrs. Washington I certainly would do myself the Honor of calling upon you, but if it should not be agreeable to Mrs. Washington to see company I hope I shall have the pleasure of meeting you at some of your Neighbor's which will oblige.[5]

People came to keep a stricken Martha company. John Augustine and his wife returned from Bushfield as soon as they could and stayed a few days, though they, with Eleanor and Miss Reed, were dispatched to Belvoir to dinner while George stayed home with Martha. Eleanor was joined a few days later by her father and her eldest sister Betsy, who paid their respects and took Eleanor home on June 28. The next day George and Martha went to dine at Belvoir.

Martha must have been striving with all her might to submit to God's will, but years of strain and worry about Patcy had taken their toll. She was bereft and struggling, overwhelmed with her grief. George did what he could to comfort her. He often took Martha with him when he took his daily tour of the plantation and work in progress. He spent whole days at home and welcomed friends and neighbors to dinner.

On July 8 George William and Sally Fairfax came over to say goodbye. They were going to England in connection with George William's inheritance of a Yorkshire estate at Towlston. As noted earlier, Lord Fairfax had replaced George William as his agent with another Fairfax relative, a dissipated spendthrift named Robert Bryan Martin, who now lived with Lord Fairfax at Greenway Court. With their source of income cut off, George William and Sally had seen their prospects in Virginia shrink despite the fact that they still had Belvoir, and in the prevailing political climate, with Virginians outraged over taxes and trade embargos, they were among the significant numbers of Virginians who remained resolutely Tory and regarded resistance to the king and Parliament as amounting to treason.

On July 9 Martha and George went to Belvoir in the afternoon to see George William and Sally sail from the Belvoir wharf. Although Bryan Fairfax, who had married Sally's younger sister and built a home called Mount Eagle, remained in Virginia, George was given power of attorney so he could rent out Belvoir during Sally and George William's absence.

By this time a letter from George had reached Jacky in New York, informing him of his sister's death. Jacky waited five days before sending Martha a curiously insensitive, self-centered letter that dealt at length with his own concerns at the college before turning to the subject that he must have known had prostrated his mother:

My Dear Mama   Kings-College July 5
    I have at length the pleasure of informing you that I am settled in every respect according to my satisfaction. There has Nothing been omitted by the professors, which could be in any means conducive to my happiness and contentment . . . and I believe I may say without vanity that I am looked upon in a particular Light by Them all, as there is as much distinction made between me and the other students as can be expected. I dine with them (a liberty that is not allow'd any but myself) associate and pertake of all their recreations . . .
    It is now time to give you a short plan of my apartments and my way of living. I have a large parlour with two Studyes or closets, each large enough to contain a bed, trunk and a couple of chairs, one I sleep in, & the other Joe calls his, my chamber and parlour are paper'd with a cheap tho' very pretty paper, the other is painted; my furniture consists of Six chairs, 2 Tables, with a few paultrey Pictures; I have an excellent bed, and in short everything very convenient & clever. I generally get up about Six. . . .
    Things My dear Mother were going on in the agreeable manner, till last Thursday, the day I receiv'd Pappa's melancholy letter, giving an account of

my dear & only Sister's Death. . . . My confusion & uneasiness on this occasion is better conceiv'd that expresst. Her case is more to be envied than pitied, for if we mortals can distinguish between those who are deserveing of grace & who are not, I am confident she enjoys that Bliss prepar'd only for the good & virtuous, let these considerations, My dear mother have their due weight with you and comfort yourself with reflecting that she now enjoys in substance what we in this world enjoy in imagination & that there is no real Happiness on this side of the grave. . . . my Nature could not bear the shock . . . sunk under the load of oppression . . . this letter is the first thing I've done since I received the melancholy News. . . . I put myself and Joe into deep Mourning & shall do (all) Honor in my power to the memory of a deceas'd & well belov'd Sister, I will no longer detain you on a subject which is painful to us both but will conclude with begging you to remember you are a Christian and that we ought to submit with patience to the divine Will and that to render you happy shall be the constant care of your affectionate and dutiful son

John Parke Custis[6]

Hoping it would distract and comfort Martha, George asked Martha's mother, Frances Dandridge, to move to Mount Vernon. It seems that Frances agreed. He wrote to Burwell Bassett: "I was master of arguments powerful enough to prevail upon Mrs. Dandridge to make this place her entire and absolute home. I should think as she lives a lonesome life (Betsy being married) it might suit her well, and be agreeable, both to herself and my Wife, to me most assuredly it would."[7]

George's invitation to his mother-in-law was made because he really would have been happy to have her living with them at Mount Vernon. But in the end Frances must have changed her mind because she did not move to Mount Vernon, remaining with Bartholomew and his wife Mary and their children at Pamocra, which was also close to the Bassetts and to Elizabeth and her new husband. There is no record that Frances ever paid George and Martha a visit at Mount Vernon, though she saw the Washingtons and her Custis grandchildren when they came south to visit the Bassetts and go to Williamsburg. Frances may have felt her health was not strong enough to allow her to travel so far.

It was a sad autumn at Mount Vernon. Eleanor came to visit, often with a member of her family, and there were other visitors, though fewer than before. With Sally and George William away there was an end to the daily visits between Mount Vernon and Belvoir. Martha's good friend Anne Mason, wife of George Mason at Gunston Hall, died. George went about Mount Vernon business, still taking Martha with him sometimes, and otherwise hunted foxes from time to time.

In October Jacky came home on holiday, bringing letters of commendation for his attention to his studies and praise from Dr. Cooper for "the purity of his morals." His mother and stepfather had little time to congratulate themselves on this evidence of Jacky's unprecedented academic success, because Jacky announced he did not intend to return to college and wanted only to get married. Martha was in favor of the plan, and this time George capitulated. George still believed Jacky was too young and immature to be a husband and dismayed that just as he was beginning to earn praise for making headway in his studies he had abandoned his academic career for a life that would allow him unlimited freedom to do what he liked. None of this mattered to Martha, who took the view Jacky should be allowed to marry if that was what he wanted. Between them they wore George down. It sounds as if Jacky and Martha may have dragged Jacky's grandmother and his aunts and uncles in New Kent into the argument too, because George groaned inwardly and wrote to Dr. Cooper:

> Revd. Sir　　　　　　　　　　　　　　　Mount Vernon December 15, 1773
>
> In the favourable account you was pleas'd to transmit me of Mr. Custis' conduct at College, gave me very great satisfaction; and I hope to have felt an increase of it in his continuance at that place under a gentleman so capable of instructing him in every branch of useful knowledge, as you are: but these hopes are at an end; and at length, I have yielded, contrary to my judgment, and much against my wishes, to his quitting College; in order that he may enter soon into a new scene of Life, which I think he must be fitter for some years hence, than now; but having his own inclination, the desires of his mother, and the acquiessence of almost all his relatives, to encounter, I did not care, as he was the last of the family, to push my opposition too far, and therefore have submitted to a Kind of necessity.[8]

Buried in the last sentence is a point that probably weighed heavily with both Martha and George—that Jacky was the last of the Parke Custis line. For all of Jacky's newfound "purity of morals" at King's College, he seemed the type to go astray again before long, and Martha may have felt the best thing to do was to get him married to a respectable girl as soon as possible in the interests of producing legitimate Custis grandchildren with the right sort of wife. In the months that followed Jacky went back and forth between Mount Vernon and Mount Airey, making trips in between with George to the estate he was about to inherit in the southern counties.

Later in October Martha went south with George to Williamsburg and paid an extended visit to her family. She remained at Eltham with the Bassetts through most of this session of the assembly, though occasionally she joined George in Williamsburg. George dined with his friend Governor Dunmore at an estate Dunmore had bought outside Williamsburg, called Porto Bello. In December the Washingtons made their way back to Mount Vernon, stopping briefly to call on Mary Washington en route. Christmas was spent quietly, with only the company of George's old companion at arms, Dr. James Craik, who spent Christmas Eve and left after breakfast the next day.

About this time news filtered slowly south of an incident in Boston that had taken place just before Christmas. In November a consignment of tea had arrived at Boston Harbor and the governor of Massachusetts insisted it would be unloaded ashore. Following a tumultuous public meeting by aggrieved Bostonians, on the night of December 16 a group of men dressed somewhat unconvincingly as Mohawks gathered and advanced on the ship crying, "The Mohawks are come!" and "Boston Harbor a teapot tonight," and then proceeded to empty 35,000 pounds of tea into the water. The event triggered the seizing and dumping of British tea elsewhere, and a group of patriotic ladies in Edenton, North Carolina, declared their solidarity with the Bostonians by taking a public pledge never to drink English tea or wear English clothes again. A troublesome customs official in Boston was tarred, feathered, and beaten up. In London, people were shocked by such violence. Samuel Johnson declared the Americans were "a race of convicts . . . rascals robbers and pirates."

At Mount Vernon Jacky was unconcerned by tea and taxes and was busy getting ready for his wedding. In January 1774 George gave him money for his wedding clothes. Martha was still grieving. She wrote a note to a young woman friend named Elizabeth Ramsay, eldest daughter of some Washington friends who lived near Williamsburg, inquiring halfheartedly about some black clothes in silk and satin, possibly thinking to wear them for the wedding.

Jacky and Eleanor were married on February 3 at Mount Airey. Jacky was eighteen and Eleanor was fifteen. George went up for the ceremony and stayed the next day, but in the end Martha could not face attending the wedding. Fearing she would make too mournful an appearance at a happy event, she stayed at home. A young woman named Nancy Carlyle, a niece of Sally Cary Fairfax and a frequent visitor at Mount Vernon, came to stay and keep Martha company.

There is some controversy surrounding a note Martha supposedly wrote and sent via George, to hand to Eleanor after the ceremony. The whereabouts of the original are unknown today, if such a letter ever existed. The note was supposedly copied from the original by Wash's friend Benson Lossing, who claimed to have seen it at Abingdon, the home of Jacky and Eleanor Custis a few years later. Lossing quotes it in his book *Mary and Martha, the Wife and Mother of Washington*, published in New York in 1886, on page 26:

> My dear Nelly:
>   God took from me a Daughter when the June Roses were blooming. He has now given me another daughter about her age when winter winds are blowing, to warm my heart again. I am as happy as one so afflicted and blest can be. Pray receive my benediction and a wish that you may long live the loving

wife of my happy son and a loving daughter to your affectionate mother,
M Washington

This letter is like nothing else that survives of Martha's writing, in terms of
style, punctuation, or spelling, and the phrases have a florid Victorian ring.
If the letter existed, it is unlikely that Martha wrote it and more likely that
it was the product of someone else's overwrought imagination. What is true
however, is that Martha was exceptionally close to her daughter-in-law all
her life, and the letter probably does reflect Martha's feelings on the occasion that she was gaining a daughter.

Because people lived very much within the wider family network—
which makes the Mount Vernon family's distant relationship with George's
mother so curious—a girl did not automatically expect to be at loggerheads
with her mother-in-law. Martha had always had a motherly attitude toward
little girls, probably as a result of having had four younger sisters. She had
been very close to Patcy, and it has been said that for the rest of her life she
unconsciously sought out surrogate daughters. Complex psychological
insights aside, it was a fact of life in colonial society that many young girls
were motherless by the time they reached their teens due to high maternal
death rates.

Though her views of manners and propriety were strict, Martha was
always fond of young people, and all her life she instinctively took many
motherless young women under her wing. It was mutual, because younger
women, whose mothers were often either dead or distracted with the
responsibilities of a large family, gravitated to Martha, responding to her
maternal nature. Not only did Martha welcome Eleanor as another daughter from the time of her engagement to Jacky, Eleanor probably enjoyed
feeling special. As one of ten children, Eleanor could not have been the center of her busy mother's attention at Mount Airey to the extent that she was
the center of Martha's at Mount Vernon.

A month after the wedding, while the happy couple were embarked on
the traditional round of wedding visits, financial pressures arose in a form
that was impossible to ignore. Mount Vernon's debts in London had accumulated to the point that Robert Cary and Company sent George a dunning
letter. It was an alarming development, even for Martha and George, who
were normally inclined to disregard the precarious aspects of their financial
position. They had to take this new development seriously, however, because
planters' debts carried a lucrative interest rate for the factors, and factors
were loathe to cut off such a lucrative source of income. When the factors
decided to cut off the credit line, it was a sure sign things were at a crisis
point. George received the letter in June, coinciding with an unseasonably
late frost that destroyed a thousand acres of wheat he had expected to sell
for a good price.

As it happened, Patcy Custis had, like her father, died intestate, and by law her share of the Parke Custis fortune was divided in half between Jacky and Martha. Much of Patcy's inheritance had consisted of cash and Bank of England stock. Martha's share of Patcy's estate automatically went to George, who averted disaster by using it to pay off the London factors, though payment was not actually made until after the Revolution. The Dunbar Suit had yet to be resolved, but as the years passed less and less had been heard about it, and Martha and George, having more pressing financial problems, had largely ignored it.

George continued to correspond with the Fairfaxes in England. They now wrote they had no plans to return to Virginia, and George arranged for an auction to dispose of Belvoir's contents. George bought a number of things, including some of Sally's personal furniture.

Jacky and Eleanor divided their time between Mount Vernon and Mount Airey, and as the months passed, George recorded the usual stream of visitors stopping for breakfast, paying calls on Martha, staying to dinner, and spending the night. The Calverts, including Eleanor's elder sister Betsy, frequently came and went as well. George dispatched a party of slaves and white indentured servants to the land he had acquired along the Ohio, to begin cultivating it, but within two months hostilities with the Indians put an end to the undertaking. The overseer of the expedition sold the contracts of most of the indentured servants to other settlers and came back.

In April Martha had the pleasure of a long visit from the Bassetts. Anna Maria's company was always cheering, but at the same time, Martha's younger sister may not have been very well. At about the same time, it became apparent that Mary Washington was no longer capable of coping with Ferry Farm, so George sold his boyhood home to a friend. Though he had been happy to invite Martha's mother to move permanently to Mount Vernon, he did not extend the same invitation to Mary. Instead he went to Fredericksburg to install her in a small house she had chosen and that he had bought for her in Fredericksburg within walking distance of Betty and Fielding Lewis at Kenwood.

By the spring session of the assembly, George's considerate treatment of her, the prospect of Jacky settling down, the pleasure she derived from her daughter-in-law, and the visit from her family had helped to ease the pain of Patcy's loss, and Martha gradually resumed her social life. "Publick times" were late that year, beginning early in May and running into June; Martha went to Williamsburg with George to participate in the official celebrations planned to welcome Governor Dunmore's wife and daughter, who had just arrived from England.

Besides visiting the family in New Kent and friends in Williamsburg, George and Martha dined several times with the Dunmores at Porto Bello. Their friendship soon became strained following developments in Boston.

Almost as soon as the burgesses arrived, news came that the British had closed the port of Boston in retaliation for the tea dumped into the harbor. Because the harbor was Boston's commercial lifeline, the burgesses were appalled at such heavy-handed and punitive tactics on Britain's part.

The burgesses reacted by voting to have a day of prayer and fasting in solidarity with Boston's beleaguered inhabitants. This plan had taken shape even while George was being entertained at Porto Bello, conceived by a group including Thomas Jefferson, Richard Henry Lee, and Patrick Henry. Martha did not disapprove of prayer and fasting, but she disliked Patrick Henry, who she thought was crude and brash and inclined to ill-advised, hotheaded speeches. Patrick Henry was indeed edgy, but he was a man laboring under a burden of personal pressure. His wife, Sarah, whom he had married when she was sixteen, had developed mental problems so severe that she was kept locked in the basement of his home. After this unhappy woman's death, Patrick Henry would marry one of Martha's relatives. Governor Dunmore was infuriated by the motion in favor of the day of fasting, and regarded support for the Boston rebels as treasonous. He promptly dissolved the assembly and called for new elections to be held for the burgesses.

With the assembly dissolved, the burgesses regrouped across the street to the Raleigh Tavern, and continued their discussions in open defiance of the governor. The political picture was now complicated by social considerations. The grand ball to welcome Lady Dunmore was scheduled for May 27. There was some debate among the ladies about the proper etiquette in this trying situation. Some ladies felt they ought to shun the ball altogether, but for most it went against the grain to snub Lady Dunmore, whatever their husbands were doing. George and Martha attended, because even though she no longer danced, Governor Dunmore was a friend and it would have been the polite thing to do. Martha was not the woman to abandon good manners in the interests of politics. On June 10, as part of the celebrations, there was a splendid display of fireworks.

After the Washingtons returned to Mount Vernon, George went to Alexandria to run for burgess in the new elections which had become necessary following the governor's dissolution of the Assembly. Nicholas Cresswell was there and observed:

> Thursday, July 14th, 1774. An Election for Burgesses in town. . . . There were three candidates, the Poll was over in about two hours, and conducted with great order and regularity. The members Col. George Washington and Major Bedwater. The candidates gave the populace a Hogshead of Toddy (what we call Punch in England). In the evening the returned Member [George] gave a Ball to the Freeholders and gentlemen of the town. This was conducted with great harmony. Coffee and Chocolate, but no Tea. This Herb is in disgrace with them at present.[9]

A Virginia Convention of Burgesses was held in Williamsburg in August, which George attended and where he was nominated as a delegate to a Continental Congress scheduled to take place in Philadelphia the following month. The object of the Continental Congress was to allow representatives from the different colonies to meet and consider ways to resolve the growing dispute with England. The view in Virginia at that time was, on the whole, conservative. Planters like the Washingtons and most of their neighbors, bound by cultural and economic ties to the mother country, not to mention their social aspirations, felt their loyalty to the Crown transcended nonimportation agreements and solidarity with Boston. The Virginians were far more restrained than their New England counterparts. When they spoke passionately about their traditional "liberties," they meant the traditional rights of Englishmen vis-à-vis the Crown.

At the end of August a Mount Vernon neighbor, Edmund Pendleton, and Patrick Henry, also delegated to the Congress, called at Mount Vernon, stayed for dinner, and spent the night. The next morning George left with them. According to an account left by Pendleton, Martha was a "plucky little woman," who told them to stand firm, because she knew George would.

In Philadelphia, simultaneously described as the largest and most elegant city in the colonies and as a sink of iniquity, the delegates met between sessions and canvassed each other's opinions, weighing their options. They went to dinners and balls and the theater and church, played cards and paid calls, and were entertained by the large Whig—soon to be called "Patriot"—faction, though there was also a staunch Tory presence in Philadelphia. George developed an acquaintance with a short, rotund Massachusetts delegate named John Adams, a lawyer. John Adams's wife, Abigail, had remained at home like Martha and the other delegates' wives, but from their farm in Braintree she passionately followed developments, and John wrote faithfully to her what he observed. He also struggled to maintain his New England asceticism amidst the social whirl. He was not entirely successful. Writing Abigail about one of the dinners, disapproval fought a losing battle with enjoyment: "A most sinful feast again . . . curds and creams, jellies, sweetmeats of various sorts, twenty sorts of tarts, fools, trifles, floating islands and whipped syllabubs . . . turtle and every other thing, flummery . . . wines most excellent and admirable. I drank Madeira at a great rate"[10]

Accustomed to Martha's lavish table, and the Madeira he regularly ordered by the cask for the Mount Vernon cellar, George was less impressed by curds and flummeries.

George was away for two months and, on his return to Virginia in November, was asked to command a local group called the Fairfax Militia, forming in Alexandria. Up and down the colonies similar ad hoc militias were forming and spending a great deal of time and effort "drilling," though it was not entirely clear for what purpose. These were uncoordinated efforts, and the militias could hardly take on the might of the British army piece-meal. Both Martha and George had grown up surrounded by local militias, whose original function in the seventeenth century had been to protect set-tlers against Indian attack. By the time Martha was old enough to know what a militia was, they had become a kind of men's social gathering, with a mainly ceremonial, rather than military, function. From Martha's point of view and probably from that of most Virginia women, these new "militias" were another male pastime, more an extension of the hunting fraternity than a precursor of intensifying hostilities.

There was, however, someone on the scene whose presence was an indi-cator of the serious turn events were taking, chiefly because he had a keen nose for trouble. In December an odd character named General Charles Lee visited Mount Vernon. No connection to the huge Virginia Lee family, he was an Englishman who had obtained a commission in the regular British army and then become a soldier of fortune, serving as a mercenary in various Euro-pean conflicts. He was an experienced military man, and he came and spent six days with George, discussing the situation. It was a visit that must have tried even the Washingtons' hospitality. Charles Lee was a tall thin man, slovenly in his dress and not fond of washing or shaving. His language was foul. He was accompanied everywhere by his pack of badly behaved dogs, even indoors and at meals, where they prowled and lunged around the table. He, his habits, and his dogs drove the fastidious Martha wild. At the end of the six days he borrowed £6 from George before departing.

In January George went to Alexandria to review and drill the Fairfax Company and to organize a Committee of Safety. Martha watched George become increasingly involved, supplying ammunition at his own expense. Nicholas Cresswell, still traveling in Virginia and Maryland in spring of 1775, summed up the overwrought atmosphere: "It is as much as a person's life is worth to speak disrespectfully of the Congress. The people arming and train-ing in every place. They are all liberty mad."[11]

Neither George nor Martha could be remotely described as "liberty mad" in the spring of 1775. George and most of his fellow planters were conservatives, still persuaded that though there were legitimate grievances to be addressed, reconciliation with the Crown was the only way forward. George's fellow burgess Patrick Henry, however, had in late March made an inflammatory speech from the pulpit of St. John's Church in Richmond, about Americans, chains, and slavery and had exclaimed, "Give me liberty or give me death." It was stirring rhetoric, although the irony of this use of the slavery metaphor in the largest slave-owning colony went over the heads of most Americans. In London Horace Walpole quipped dryly, "The souls of the Africans hang heavy on the swords of the Americans." To Martha this speech merely confirmed her view that Patrick Henry was a hothead, but he may have been particularly agitated because his wife, Sarah Henry, died that year.

Rising political tensions had another effect. The slaves throughout the colonies were growing restless as the population polarized into Tory and Whig, or Patriot, factions, and the Tories suffered increasing intimidation and reprisals at the hands of the Sons of Liberty, or any vigilante mob. Slaves watched the persecution of the Loyalists, often by Patriot slave owners, and decided their interests lay with the British. A rumor spread among the slaves that the British would free them, and indeed by this time there was a vociferous antislavery movement in England. In April 1775, a delegation of slaves was emboldened enough to call on the governor in Williamsburg, offering to take up arms for the British in exchange for their freedom.

Lord Dunmore did not accept their offer, but it dawned on him that the slaves might effectively be used against the rebellious colonists if the need arose. Late in April, upon hearing of the clash between the colonials and British troops at Lexington and Concord, Governor Dunmore seized the powder store kept in Williamsburg against the long-expected slave uprising and transported it onto a warship in the James River.

It was a move designed for maximum impact. The slave-owning populace was alarmed, so much so that prominent citizens of Williamsburg were prepared to eat humble pie. The *Virginia Gazette* carried a public appeal to the Governor for the restoration of the powder:

> My Lord
>   We his Majesty's dutiful an loyal subjects, the Mayor, Recorder, Aldermen and Common Council, of the City of Williamsburg, . . . humbly beg leave to represent to your Excellency, that the inhabitants of this city were this morning exceedingly alarmed by a report that a large quantity of gunpowder was . . . removed from the public magazine. . . .
>   We further beg to inform your Excellency, that, from various reports at present prevailing, in different parts of the country, we have too much reason to believe that some wicked and designing persons have instilled the most diabolical notions into the mind of our slaves.[12]

Dunmore refused to return the powder, using the excuse that because he had heard of a slave insurrection in the next county, he had taken the powder to a safe place. His response provoked threats of reprisals from armed groups collecting throughout the colony, and Patrick Henry actually led an armed contingent toward Williamsburg to wrest the powder back. He did not get far. Dunmore paid the colony for the powder and kept it, and condemned Henry as an outlaw and a troublemaker.

Just as George was preparing to depart Mount Vernon to attend the Second Continental Congress in Philadelphia in May, the governor decided the political situation warranted sending Lady Dunmore and his children onto a warship for safety. He was now confronting a real dilemma—how he could manage to maintain the upper hand and continue to perform his duty as the king's official representative in the absence of sufficient military support to back him up. He wrote Lord Dartmouth that he was thinking of arming his own slaves and offering freedom to any others who came to his defense.

CHAPTER 10

"Mrs. Washington, a Warm Loyalist"

While the furor over the seizure of the Williamsburg powder store swept through the now decidedly uneasy colony, one of the Williamsburg papers carried this welcome report:

> Williamsburg, April 21, 1775
>   By Capt. Taylor, from Liverpool, there is advice that things had taken a sudden turn in the House of Commons, in favour of America; and that it was expected that Lord North [author of the odious taxation measures] would resign in a very short time.[1]

If the report had been accurate, things might well have calmed down throughout the colonies. There were two factors that could have been brought to bear on strained Anglo-American relations, allowing differences to be resolved by negotiation. Though the report of Lord North's resignation was untrue, there was a distinct pro-American faction in opposition in Parliament who agreed with the colonists' objections that the taxation measures adopted by the government infringed upon the rights the colonists enjoyed under the unwritten English constitution. On the American side, Washington and many of his influential fellow planters, for all the drilling and arming of local militias, still believed in the spring of 1775 that the way to proceed was to present a petition to the king setting out the colonies' grievances, which could then be properly addressed by Parliament. One such diplomatically worded petition had already been sent, fully supported by most Virginians, who remained, on the whole, fairly conservative.

It is difficult to pin down any single precipitating cause of the American Revolution, but at the time, for Martha and probably for many other women, particularly of her social class, and even more particularly, of her social class in Virginia, the slide into political upheaval was so gradual that the full import of what was happening was slow to register. In June just the previous year George and Martha had been dining with their friend Governor Dunmore and his wife on friendly terms. By May 1775 the governor was all but barricaded in Williamsburg, his wife and daughter under the protection of the navy, and the colony fearful that a slave revolt was on the verge of erupting.

Disturbing as the seizure of powder was to the whole colony in these circumstances, from Martha's point of view George's departure for the Second Continental Congress in Philadelphia in May 1775 was business as usual. It was nothing new for George to be gone for weeks. He had been away many times attending the assembly sessions when she could not go with him. He had made several lengthy trips to the Ohio frontier and Dismal Swamp, investigating land options and schemes to reclaim swampland in southern Virginia. And he had spent two months the previous fall in Philadelphia. Normally, he was unwilling to be away from Mount Vernon during the harvest season, a crucial time for the plantation's finances, when he devoted most of his time to making sure that his overseers were sober and maintaining discipline and that the slaves were working to capacity. This time George left his cousin Lund Washington in charge of Mount Vernon. Lund was honest but nowhere near as capable as George.

Expecting him back in a matter of weeks, Martha waved goodbye to George, who was wearing his old Virginia Militia colonel's uniform and attended by his valet Will Lee. She had other things on her mind. Sixteen-year-old Eleanor was pregnant with Martha's first grandchild, and there was the house to run and the usual company.

The couple wrote to each other after George departed. Martha's letters conveyed news of the family, the plantation, and everyone's health, especially with Eleanor pregnant, and included a shopping list. Though Martha was not a political firebrand like Abigail Adams, George did write to her about developments as they unfolded in Congress and in Philadelphia. At the end of June a letter arrived from George saying he did not expect to be back before the fall. The letter was couched in terms suggesting he knew the news would exasperate and worry Martha. George and Martha wrote each other hundreds of letters over the course of their marriage, but the only two surviving letters from George to Martha were written by George from Philadelphia in June 1775. At the time neither of them appreciated their far-reaching import. The first letter read:

My Dearest   Philadelphia June 18, 1775

I am now set down to write you on a subject which fills me with inexpressible concern—and this concern is greatly aggravated and increased, when I reflect upon the uneasiness I know it will give you. It has been determined in

Congress that the whole Army raised for the defence of the American Cause shall be put under my care, and that it is necessary for me to proceed immediately to Boston to take upon me the command of it.

You may believe me my dear Patsy, when I assure you, in the most solemn manner, that, so far from seeking this appointment I have used every endeavour in my power to avoid it, not only from my unwillingness to part with you and the family, but from a consciousness of its being too great for my capacity, and that I should enjoy more real happiness in one month with you at home than I have the most distant prospect of finding abroad, if my stay were to be seven times seven years. But as it has been a kind of destiny that has thrown me upon this service, I shall hope that my undertaking of it, is designed to answer some good purpose. You might, and I suppose did perceive, from the tenor of my letters, that I was apprehensive I could not avoid this appointment, as I did not pretend to intimate when I should return. . . . It was utterly out of my power to refuse this appointment without exposing my character to such censures as would have reflected dishonour upon myself and given pain to my friends. This I am sure could not, and ought not, to be pleasing to you, and must have lessened me considerably in my own esteem. I shall rely therefore, confidently, on that Providence which has heretofore preservd and been bountiful to me, not doubting but that I shall return safe to you in the fall. . . . my unhappiness will flow from the uneasiness I know you will feel at being left alone. I therefore beg that you will summon your whole fortitude, and pass your time as agreeably as possible. Nothing will give me so much sincere satisfaction as to hear this, and to hear it from your own pen. My earnest and ardent desire is, that you would pursue any plan that is most likely to produce contentment and a tolerable degree of tranquillity; and it must add greatly to my uneasy feelings to hear that you are dissatisfied or complaining at what I really could not avoid.

George went on to say he was enclosing a draft will and explained what its provisions were for Martha, before signing himself "with unfeigned regard my dear Patsy your affectionate [George Washington]."[2]

George then added a postscript that he had bought her some muslin she had asked for.

From a post-Revolution perspective, the letter is held up as proof of Washington's exemplary conduct as a thoughtful husband. Martha, in a pre-Revolution frame of mind, may have felt more like the woman who listens to her husband make lame excuses about why he "had to" go to the bar, on the hunting trip, to the races with his buddies. Since she knew George had attended the Congress wearing his old uniform, she was unlikely to believe he had not courted the military appointment. Even George betrayed discomfiture about her probable reaction, by trying to fend off "complaints" in advance.

Martha had good reason to be exasperated. It is hard to see what George had in mind if not a military appointment. George was no public speaker, so he had not worn his old uniform to lend gravitas to his contribution to the debate. Furthermore, no one was more sensitive to the nuances of appearance than George, and he knew he cut a commanding figure. The other contender for the position of commander in chief was John Hancock, president of the Congress and the wealthiest man present. Hancock had no military experience but assumed as a matter of course that the distinction of commanding any new colonial army naturally fell to him. His face fell in disappointment and disbelief at the announcement that George Washington had been chosen to lead the army.

However, many at the Congress appreciated that in order to bring Virginia, the richest and largest colony, fully into the effort, it was essential to choose a Virginian. According to John Adams, who lobbied heavily for George's appointment, Washington was the only choice to lead the new army on the strength of his "skill and experience as an officer, whose independent fortune, great talents, and excellent universal character would command the approbation of all America."[3]

Historian and Washington biographer Rupert Hughes elaborated: "Compared to Washington, no other American officer had so much wealth, such social distinction and such manifest freedom from personal ambition. His head was remarkably level, and above all he was a Burgess from that vital colony of Virginia, where his influence was evident since so many of the rapidly forming military companies had paid him honor."[4]

No one needed to spell out the reasons for appointing George to Martha, who knew better than anyone that much of George's social distinction and perceived wealth could be traced directly to her Custis fortune. Unlike what John Adams thought, she knew George's short-lived military career had ended in failure, and that had been part of the reason he married her. Martha also knew that their debts in England were multiplying and were not yet paid off with Patcy's stock, that last year's promising wheat crop had failed, and how important George's close attention to all details of Mount Vernon production was. With Lund Washington in charge, Mount Vernon—and all their fortunes—might suffer irreversibly while he went off to play soldier. Martha was a supportive wife, but she was a realist. Under the circumstances, the muslin may not have pacified her.

A week later George wrote again as he was leaving Philadelphia to tell Martha he hoped to meet her sometime in the fall and to tell her, "I retain an unalterable affection for you, which neither time nor distance can change.... Yr. Entire Go. Washington."[5]

George was clearly worried about how much Martha would miss him. At the same time that he wrote to her, George also wrote to Jacky, urging him and Nelly to spend as much time as they could with Martha, and to his brother John Augustine and his wife, Hannah, asking them to visit Martha, as she was likely to be lonesome.

In Fredericksburg Mary Washington is said to have taken her usual independent view, complaining, "Is there to be more fighting, more bloodshed? Surely it will all end in the halter." It was an eminently reasonable thing to say under the circumstances.

There was nothing Martha could do about George's absence. In late August or September she went to Mount Airey, where Eleanor was awaiting her confinement. In September Eleanor had a baby girl who died at birth, and she was ill and low for months afterwards.

The Bassetts came to Mount Vernon in September, and Martha planned to travel down with them to New Kent with Jacky and Eleanor. As it was, the Bassetts left without the Mount Vernon party. Martha stayed behind, probably on account of a threat from an unexpected quarter, her old friend Lord Dunmore. According to Benson Lossing:

> Nothing of importance, aside from the routine of plantation life, occurred at Mount Vernon after the summer 1775, until 1781. At the former period, Lord Dunmore and his marauding followers, ascended the Potomac as far as Occoquan Falls, with the intention of making Mrs. Washington a prisoner, and desolating the estates of Gunston Hall and Mount Vernon. The Prince William Militia gathered in large numbers to oppose him, and these aided by a heavy storm, frustrated his lordship's designs, and he sailed down the river, after destroying some mills and other property.[6]

Lund Washington was frightened enough to begin packing, and he wrote George that he was worried about Mount Vernon and Martha's safety. Martha thought the rumors were nonsense, but on receiving an urgent message from George Mason at Gunston Hall begging her to leave Mount Vernon, she did, but she stayed away only two days before returning home.

As it had become obvious that George would be tied up with his army for the foreseeable future, Martha had broached the subject of joining George in camp. Now that Dunmore was raiding up and down the Potomac, her suggestion took on a new urgency. The local Committee of Safety, a sort of home guard, had hastened to offer Martha their protection, yet it was not a very reassuring offer. The members of the Committee of Safety were often the worse for wear due to drink, and neither Martha nor Lund could have counted on them in a crisis.

Martha finally left Mount Vernon for Eltham on October 17, taking Jacky and Eleanor, and going by way of Fredericksburg. Because she took six days to reach Eltham, Martha probably called on Mary Washington to try to pacify her as much as possible, and on Betty and Fielding Lewis. Before she left, a letter had come from George inviting her to join him in

Cambridge, but she carried on with her plan of going south first. In fact, Martha did not make up her mind to go north until she reached the Bassetts at Eltham.

Soon after her arrival at Eltham, Lord Dunmore occupied Norfolk on October 26. A few days later Dunmore followed up by issuing a proclamation offering freedom to any slave and an end of the contract of servitude to any indentured servant who took up arms for the British.

Lund wrote George warning that the Mount Vernon slaves found the promise of liberty "sweet" and that "there was not a man of them but woud leave us, if they belivd they could make their escape." All over Virginia, slaves could and did make their escapes, with a number of the Mount Vernon slaves going to the British, including a cook named Deborah Squash and her husband Harry. The planters panicked. Some executed any absconding slaves who were caught, lest they "infect" fellow slaves with nonsense about "liberty." Others got together to insert an article in the *Virginia Gazette* addressed directly to their slaves, denying that they, the slave owners, were responsible for the practice of slavery and warning any slaves thinking of bearing arms for the English that they should be "content with their situation and expect a better condition in the next world." Why the slave owners thought an appeal through the medium of the press would work is difficult to understand because most slaves were illiterate, a result of the laws that made it illegal to teach them to read and write.

In any event, the slaves were unpersuaded by the planters' appeal. About eight hundred joined Governor Dunmore and, duly armed, took an active part in raiding coastal plantations, frequently freeing other slaves in the process. According to historian Ira Berlin, "After a British raid up the James River, a prominent clergyman reported that 'the families within the sphere of this action have suffered greatly. Some have lost 40, others 30, every one a considerable part of their slaves.' Few of the great Chesapeake planters—the Carters, Harrisons, Jeffersons, Nelsons and Washingtons—survived the war without losing at least part of their slaves. Indeed British raiders took special delight in liberating the slaves of the great Patriots."[7] Martha and Mount Vernon were obvious targets.

At Eltham Martha weighed the pros and cons of joining George. On the one hand, she wanted to go. On the other hand, Eleanor was still suffering the effects of losing her baby, and Martha was convinced that she could face down Governor Dunmore should he return, and that, if the slaves were restless, she ought to stay. The media forced her hand. Burwell Bassett showed her a newspaper clipping: "Mr. Washington we hear is married to a very amiable Lady, but it is said Mrs. Washington, being a warm Loyalist, has separated from her husband since the commencement of the present troubles, and lives, very much respected in the city of New York."[8]

It was a report that could have had serious repercussions for George, struggling as he was with the seemingly hopeless task of turning into a viable army a motley band of sixteen thousand or so free-spirited souls described by historian Henry Commager as "a haphazard collection of volunteers, skilful enough in the use of a musket or rifle, but almost wholly without experience or training, disrespectful of officers, fiercely resentful of discipline, ignorant of the rules of hygiene, wasteful and disorderly."[9]

This was the raw material to be pitted against the most highly trained and effective fighting force in Europe, and it looked increasingly likely that the life of George and other prominent members of the Congress would depend on whether the colonial forces were able to fight effectively. George's personal position, like that of all the other leaders of the rebellion in the colonies was increasingly precarious. Under English law, which continued to apply in the colonies, the taking up of arms against a monarch was the capital offense of treason. A recently resurrected statute, dating from the time of Henry VIII, provided that any English person accused of treason against the English Crown on foreign soil could be arrested and transported back to England for trial. The penalty for anyone found guilty was to be hanged, drawn, and quartered, a grisly and lingering death, which had recently been the fate of Irish insurgents tried in London.

Because George and the other insurgents were now guilty of treason in the eyes of the law, they, as outlaws, could be captured and transported by the British authorities under the statute. Mount Vernon was also at risk of confiscation, and if George was lucky enough to escape the British, his only option would have been to take refuge in the inhospitable western lands along the Ohio. All that stood between George and capture, death, or ruin, were the shabby volunteers of the grandly named Continental Army. Shaping them into an effective military force looked almost impossible, and the last thing George needed was to have his authority undermined by the suggestion that his wife was a Tory.

It was not the first media attempt to undermine George. In August there had been a press smear, known subsequently as the "Washerwoman Kate Affair." It had presaged the undercurrent of sexual scandal that would follow George for the rest of his public life.

The "Washerwoman Kate" scandal has hovered in the background, never entirely quashed despite two notable attempts to refute it, first by John C. Fitzpatrick, former keeper of manuscripts in the Library of Congress, and, second, by the Massachusetts Historical Society in 1935. What is curious is that the Massachusetts Historical Society prefaces its report, written by Allen French, with the statement that "many good Americans are unaware that there is a series of tales about George Washington, involving him, by implication, with women at various times of his life,"[10] thereby hinting there were others.

This particular scandal arose from a letter that Benjamin Harrison, a member of the Continental Congress in Philadelphia, had written in late July 1775 to George at Cambridge. The letter had been intercepted by the British, along with two others from John Adams. It was published soon afterwards in the *Massachusetts Gazette and Boston Weekly News-Letter* on August 17, 1775. Harrison was writing to George about supplies the army needed in Cambridge, and included the following passage:

> As I was in the pleasing task of writing to you, a little Noise occasioned me to turn my Head round, and who should appear but pretty little Kate the Washerwoman's Daughter over the Way, clean, trim and Rosy as the Morning: I snatch'd the glorious Opportunity, and but for that cursed Antidote to Love, Sukey [Mrs. Harrison], I had fitted her for my General against his Return. We were obliged to part, but not till we had contrived to meet again; if she keeps the Appointment I shall relish a Week's longer stay—I give you now and then some of these Adventures to amuse you, and unbend your Mind from the cares of War.[11]

The passage was probably a forgery, added by the British for propaganda purposes, but it brought home to George and Martha the fact that anything they wrote was subject to interception and damaging alteration for the purpose of British propaganda. It also made it imperative that the Washingtons present a united front. There is no record of George writing to Martha about the Washerwoman Kate business, but it would have been typical of him to have handed her a copy and told her straight out that this was the kind of attack they could expect as British propaganda. From Eltham Martha wrote in late October to tell Lund she had decided to go to Cambridge. Lund was concerned by her delay in making the decision and wrote George on November 5:

> The Inclos'd I expect will inform you that Mrs. Washington intends to come to you—she informs me she will leave Colo. Bassetts tomorrow & lose no time getting home where she will Stay but a few days, before she sets out for the Camp—I think her stay in New Kent so long after she had your invitation to come to you, was rather ill judg'd, & will I fear occasion her haveg a very disagreeable journey—I suppose one way or the other she will make it near the 20th before she will set off—I will do all I can to get her off sooner if Possible.[12]

Martha arrived back at Mount Vernon around the tenth of November. Lund was anxious about her traveling just as winter weather was setting in, at a time when armed slaves were roaming and the threat of kidnap by the British along the road could not be discounted. Preparations to leave were made as quickly as possible. Martha planned to be away for months, but knew that anything could happen. She took a number of house slaves with her. Although there is no list of what else she took, as a practical woman, she undoubtedly took medicines, sewing equipment, and provisions including as many of her own cured hams as she could manage. The slaves would have emptied the contents of the smokehouse soon after she left. Both George and Martha were generous to the needy, and both made some arrangements to continue their practice of helping their less fortunate neighbors in their absence. From Eltham Martha sent a note to a Mr. Devenport, who may have been an overseer on one of the Washington farms, about a Mount Vernon neighbor, Mrs. Bayley, whose husband was too ill to work his farm. Martha left instructions with Mr. Devenport to provide Mrs. Bayley with "corn or wheat as she may want it . . . and a fat hog."

George also wrote to Lund Washington after Martha left:

> Let the Hospitality of the House, with respect to the poor, be kept up: Let no one go hungry away. If any of these kind of People should be in want of Corn, supply their necessities, provided it dos not encourage them in idleness; and I have no objection to your giving my Money in Charity, to the amount of forty or fifty Pounds a Year, when you think it is well bestowed. . . . You are to consider that neither myself nor my Wife are now in the way to do these good Offices.[13]

Martha, Jacky, and Eleanor left on November 16 or 17. They set out in the Washington coach with the coat of arms on the door and with a slave coachman and four postilions smartly dressed in the Washington livery, white with red collars and cuffs. By now Martha was at pains to explain that although the livery was made from English material, it had been ordered before the nonimportation agreement.

The report about Martha's Tory sympathies had spread. It was not altogether unbelievable for several reasons. First, many Virginians, like the Washingtons' close friends the Fairfaxes, remained loyal to what was still the legitimate government of King George III. Second, Martha's uncle William Dandridge and two of her brothers had served in the British navy, as had George's half brother Lawrence. Mary Washington, conservative to the core, was believed to have Loyalist leanings. Martha had been a member of "the Williamsburg court." And finally, Martha had voiced no views like those of the Daughters of Liberty—no public pledges about eschewing English clothing for example. In fact, she had been a walking testament to the opposite. There is anecdotal evidence that as she began the long trip north she was booed and the epithets "traitor" and "Tory" followed the carriage.

The travelers were on a diplomatic offensive. As they stopped along the way, they let it be known that the highly conspicuous entourage contained "Lady Washington and her family, on their way to join the General at Headquarters." Martha, and probably Eleanor for good measure, wore homespun gowns. Martha stopped powdering her hair. Though the carriage and livery were very fine, the occupants were down-to-earth, especially the short plump lady. It was a neat piece of what we call "spin doctoring" today, and it worked. The fact that she was making this long trip in the dead of winter also helped swing public opinion in Martha's favor.

Reaching Philadelphia on November 28, Martha's carriage was escorted ceremoniously into the city by the First Troop of Philadelphia City Cavalry. She stayed at the home of wealthy Patriots, the Reeds. The ladies of Philadelphia were promptly thrown into a social dilemma. Though visiting among neighbors in Virginia had been a way of life, and "waiting on" someone at any time was regarded as courteous behavior, it was an era when a rigid etiquette governed the paying of formal calls among ladies in New York and Philadelphia. The pattern of call paying among ladies was dictated to some extent by the political allegiances of their husbands or fathers. Tory ladies, who in less acrimonious times might have called on Mrs. Washington of Mount Vernon, could hardly pay a formal call on the wife of treasonous General Washington, the man now regarded by Loyalists as public enemy number one, especially now that Lady Washington, as Martha was beginning to be known, was making such a public show of her support.

As far as the Patriot ladies were concerned, there was another, delicate, problem. A great ball had been planned in honor of Lady Washington. However, in their enthusiasm for doing public honor to the commander in chief's wife, the organizers had forgotten that a resolution had been passed banning frivolous entertainments in this time of crisis. Political feeling had been whipped to such a pitch that militant Patriots threatened to wreck the New Tavern where the ball was to be held, if it went ahead. This distressing prospect caused an anxious group of prominent Whigs to wait on Martha and beg her to discourage the ball by letting it be known she would not attend. Martha's status as a Virginia aristocrat was better known than the true extent of her political sympathies, and the delegation was worried about offending her. While the commander in chief's wife seemed quite pleasant, no one quite knew how someone so grand as Martha reportedly was would react to the announcement that her ball was canceled. Martha's tactful reply that "the desires of your committee are agreeable to my own sentiments" brought sighs of relief all around.

In fact, having covered over 450 miles of terrible roads in four or five long, cold, bone-shaking days, with the prospect of more to come, Martha was only too happy to forgo the ball and rest, and Eleanor was still in a delicate condition.

Martha and her party stayed in Philadelphia a week. Her remarks about the ball were widely repeated and the initial favorable impression she had made grew. She, Eleanor, and Jacky now received and paid formal calls and were extensively entertained—though not with balls or tea drinking—before leaving Philadelphia for the next leg of the journey to Cambridge. Another general's wife, Mrs. Gates, joined them, as did Mrs. Warner Lewis, a relative of George's. The ladies were accompanied by a military escort part of the way and then by local gentlemen on horseback as far as Newark. Church bells now rang wherever they arrived.

This was quite a change from public reaction to Martha's departure. As one of Martha's biographers noted: "With George Washington's acceptance of the command of the Continental Army, his wife had become a public figure. Every move she made, everything she did and did not do, was held up to criticism by those all too eager to find fault with her."[14]

There were many people all too ready to undermine George through Martha. Allegations of Loyalist sympathies on Martha's part in the prevailing political atmosphere of 1775 would have been extremely difficult to refute directly and could easily have become George's Achilles' heel. Martha's sense of image and timing, demonstrated so successfully on the trip north from Mount Vernon, was both deeply ingrained and finely tuned. She instinctively fell back on the lessons she had absorbed from childhood about the importance of image, and to some extent the message of clothing. It was a peculiarly Virginian thing. Using a combination of carriage, livery, postilions, homespun, the family coat of arms, artlessly good manners, and a display of wifely devotion strong enough to carry her a thousand miles in the dead of winter, accompanied by her son and daughter-in-law in a show of family support, she enhanced the image of the commander in chief by showing herself to be a model consort.

CHAPTER 11

"I Doe My Dear Sister
Most Religiously Wish Thare
Was an End to the Matter"

Although they arrived in camp on a triumphant note, the realities of camp life brought Martha, Jacky, and Eleanor rudely back down to earth. They found that conditions in the Cambridge camp were dreadful, and that was after George had had six months to bring some order to the situation. On his arrival in Cambridge the previous July, George had been so appalled by the chaos that he swore that had he known the scale of the task he would never have accepted the command and observed that "I daresay the men would fight very well (if properly officered) although they are an exceedingly nasty and dirty people."

Armed with powers from Congress to flog and hang, he had set about organizing a disparate armed mob who had gathered from the thirteen sovereign states that made up American colonies, each with different loyalties, customs, laws, ethnic backgrounds, and religious orientations, united mainly by a general disinclination to take orders, into a semblance of an army. By early 1776 there were around seventeen thousand "soldiers" under George's command, though it was difficult to be precise. The size of his army fluctuated as men came and went at will, to see their families, visit their farms, and so on. At that stage the enlistment period was for one year, and after that the men expected to return home.

They had begun arriving in Cambridge in June. They had spread out over several camps, living in shelters ranging from tents to lean-tos of boards and sailcloth. The men and horses had stripped most of the surrounding fields and orchards of crops and firewood and churned up mud everywhere. When

George arrived in the summer of 1775, the camp and the "army" presented a squalid picture. The camp was a filthy unsanitary mess. There was no adequate supply system in place, ammunition was low, drunkenness was rife, and bored sentries frequently left their posts to chat with their equally unhappy and uncomfortable opposite numbers on enemy lines. Officers from different states refused to cooperate with each other, and a number of officers were arrested for drawing more pay and provisions than what they were entitled to. One of George's earliest measures was an order prohibiting "lewdness." The troops bathing in the river were "mooning"—and worse—the public at large, to the distress of "ladies of fashion" on the bridge above.

Relying heavily on his flogging powers, George eventually mobilized the men into digging latrines and fortifications, organized some supplies, and imposed on the camp some semblance of order and military discipline. But it was all relative; one observer summed up what he saw, confirming George's initial reaction:

> The army in general is not very badly accoutred, but most wretchedly clothed, and as dirty a set of mortals as ever disgraced the name of a soldier. They have no women in camp to do the washing for the men, and they in general not being used to doing things of this sort, and thinking it rather a disparagement to them, choose rather to let their linen, etc. rot upon their backs than to be at the trouble of cleaning 'em, themselves. And to this nasty way of life, and to the change of their diet from milk, vegetables, etc., to living almost entirely upon flesh, must be attributed those putrid, malignant and infectious disorders which broke out among them soon after their taking the field.[1]

Martha, Jacky, and Eleanor did not have to live amidst the squalor. George had made his headquarters in the Vassal House in Cambridge, which had been the property of Tory sympathizers who had fled Patriot reprisals to Nova Scotia. It was a handsome house that the Americans used partly as a hospital. It would later be home to Henry Longfellow. Even though Martha, Jacky, and Eleanor, still poorly after her confinement in August, were settled in relative comfort, the stark conditions in the camp brought home to Martha how drastically her family's circumstances had changed. It had been one thing to dismiss Governor Dunmore's threats to kidnap her. Martha always believed he would not dare, and small though she was, she could and did summon an air of formidable authority when necessary. People thought twice before crossing her, and Martha had been confident she could deal with Governor Dunmore on her home ground if necessary. But now, Mrs. Washington of Mount Vernon, who had lately dined with the governor and, as Wash wrote, "occupied the first circles in the colonial court of Williamsburg," had a different status as the wife of a treasonable insurgent with the death penalty hanging over him.

The prospect of George's colonials holding out against the largest and best-trained and -equipped army in the world struck many people as madness and doomed from the start. Nicholas Cresswell, who had been entertained at Mount Vernon and liked the Washingtons personally, believed George was being manipulated by Congress, and he opined, "Washington, my Enemy as he is, I should be sorry if he should be brought to an ignominious death"—even though there seemed every likelihood that was where it would all end.

If conditions in camp shocked Martha, they paled in comparison with the bad news coming from the north, which highlighted the extreme precariousness of the Washingtons' position. In the fall of 1775, while Martha was still in Virginia, George had dispatched eleven hundred men north to Canada under the command of two generals, Benedict Arnold and Richard Montgomery, in the first major offensive of the Continental forces. Their object was to block the British plan to sweep down from the north to attack the rebels.

By the time Martha arrived at Cambridge, reports were arriving at headquarters of the disaster that expedition had become, grimly highlighting a new set of problems that had to be addressed. There had been a total failure of supplies, leaving men whose homespun shirts had been worn to shreds pushing through the mountains to face the onset of winter in a ragged and half-clothed state. Many had worn out their shoes and were nearly barefoot, and there was so little to eat, the men went for days at a time with no food. There were times when they killed and cooked dogs and ate them— skin, entrails, and all—for lack of anything else. Many were too ill to march, and there were desertions and many deaths from the cold, hunger, and disease. And finally, those survivors advancing on Quebec had to contend with snowstorms and ground frozen too hard to dig shelter or fortifications. To add to these woes, smallpox spread rapidly among the troops.

In a camp disheartened by the news of setbacks and suffering from the north, Martha attended church on Christmas day, calmly taking her place in a prominent pew and bowing politely to the other ladies and wishing them "the compliments of the season" just as if she were home at Pohick Church. It would be typical of her behavior throughout the war to maintain a calm front, no matter how desperate conditions became, and it was an immense morale booster.

Despite her outward sangfroid, Martha was surrounded by brutality and misery on a vast scale. She wrote several letters from Cambridge that have survived and hint at the unbelievable position in which she now found herself. The first of Martha's letters was to her young friend Elizabeth Ramsay, whose parents were friends and neighbors of the Washingtons in Fairfax County. By this time it was necessary to be extremely careful about what she wrote, because the British might intercept any letter. Martha tried to sound positive, but her letter is more cheerful than circumstances warranted, and at the end a note of concern does creep in:

> Dear Miss   Cambridge, December the 30th 1775
>
> I arrived here safe, and our party all well . . . the weather proved fine all the time we were on the road. . . . I dont doubt but you have seen the Figuer our arrival made in the Philadelphia paper—and I left it in as great pomp as if I had been a very great somebody.
>
> . . . every person seems to be cheerfull and happy hear—some days we have a number of cannon and shells from Boston and Bunkers Hill, but it does not seem to surprise any one but me: I confess I shudder every time I hear the sound of a gun—. . . I just took a look at pore Boston and Charlestown—. . . thare seems to be a number of very fine Buildings in Boston but god knows how long they will stand; they are pulling up all the warfs for firewood—to me that has never see anything of war, the preparations, are very terable indeed, but I endever to keep my fears to myself as well as I can. . . .
>
> . . . thare are but two young Laides in Cambridge, and a very great number of Gentlemen so you may gess how much is made of them—but neither of them is pretty I think,
>
> This is a beautyfull country, and we had a very plasant journey through New england, and had the pleasure to find the General very well we came within the month from home to the Camp.[2]

Martha's letter must be read in the greater context, not just of life in Cambridge, where she now was, but vis-à-vis the broader picture, which from Martha's point of view was dark indeed. In the north, American generals Montgomery and Arnold knew British reinforcements were on their way. Deciding they could not afford to wait, they attacked Quebec on December 31 in a bad snowstorm, but failed to take it. General Arnold was badly wounded, and General Montgomery was killed almost at once. Montgomery, just recently married, left his young widow devastated by his loss. Having failed to take Quebec, the Continental army besieged it, but a large contingent of British troops was en route to relieve the city, accompanied by warships and heavy artillery under the command of General Burgoyne. So determined was the British captain leading the convoy that he rammed his ship through an ice field blocking his passage in the frozen St. Lawrence River. At Cambridge it was only a matter of time before General Burgoyne cut down the tattered besiegers at Quebec and moved south to fall on the rebels in Massachusetts and New York, with the intent of ending the rebellion once and for all.

There was better news from Fort Ticonderoga, where American general Knox had taken the fort and a quantity of enemy cannon and other supplies.

By the time Martha wrote Elizabeth Ramsay about "pore Boston," the British army had been under siege there for months, convinced they were surrounded by an army of savages, some of whom had killed and scalped British wounded after the battle at Lexington the previous year. Frances Wentworth, the wife of the English governor of New Hampshire, wrote to her cousin in England: "The King's troops have too mean an opinion of the Americans—they think them Fools and Cowards, but indeed my Lady, they are neither. Undisciplined and to be conquer'd they no doubt are, but they are far from the despicable set thought for—their numbers make them formidable and they take all possible pains to improve themselves in military skill."

Days later a mob of Americans attacked the Wentworths' home. Frances described her terror:

> Colonel Fenton had dined with us that day, and was sitting with the Governor when the rabble . . . came arm'd and insisted on Col Fenton's appearance. The Governor refused when their insolence became abominable. They stove at the House with Clubs, brought a large Cannon and placed it before the Door and swore to fire through the House. They were so cruel as to affirm no one person, man woman or child, shou'd escape with life. And when we found resistance was vain Col Fenton surrendered himself. . . . We got into the Boat with our poor Child . . . and hurried away. We had not time to get a hat or Blanket for him but thought ourselves fortunate to get him off alive. . . . They were so cruel as to say—If they could get the Governor's fat child they would split him down the Back and broil him.[3]

This was not an isolated incident. The mobs earned their nickname "Sons of Violence" by terrorizing real and suspected Loyalists at will—tarring, feathering, and generally mistreating those unfortunate enough to fall into their hands, and vandalizing or looting Loyalist property.

Chaotic and ill-supplied as the American troops at Cambridge were, things were far worse for the majority of the wretched English troops cooped up in Boston with little food and foul drinking water, which made everyone ill. It had been a cold and wet winter, hence the breaking up of the wharfs for firewood that Martha reported. Most of the inhabitants of Boston had fled, with only as many of their household belongings as they could carry, and their homes were pillaged and destroyed. Supplies of fresh food had all but dried up, because the Continental army blocked access to the city. The Americans would not let food in, and the Tory sympathizers trying to run the blockade risked reprisals. Frances Wentworth's sister and two small children were stuck in Boston, and Frances agonized over their plight and the fact that she was unable to help them.

What little food there was in Boston consisted mostly of salt meat, and cost more than the average British soldier could afford. The foot soldiers who cut such a fine figure from a distance in their ranks of red coats were a different animal up close. Many were felons or had been conscripted or lured with the promises of higher pay than they would ever receive. Out of their meager wages they often had to buy food, mend their boots, and off-set part of the cost of their uniforms. Punishments for breaches of discipline were severe. On January 3, 1776, there was an order in the British camp that

> Thomas MacMahan, private soldier in His Majesty's Forty-third Regiment of Foot, and Isabella MacMahan his wife . . . tried by court martial . . . for receiving sundry stolen goods, knowing them to be such, are found guilty of the crime laid to their charge, and therefore . . . the said Thomas MacMahan to receive a thousand lashes on his bare back with a cat-of-nine-tails . . . and the said Isabella MacMahan, to receive a hundred lashes on her bare back, at the cart's tail, in different portions and the most conspicuous parts of the town, and to be imprisoned three months.[4]

This mention of the unfortunate private's wife introduces a little-known aspect of the role of women in the Revolution. Though Martha and other officers' wives had joined their husbands at the American camp in 1775–1776 there were few other women there at that time. Most soldiers' wives and other female relatives had their hands full at home, keeping up with small holdings that barely provided a subsistence living in the best of times, planting and harvesting crops as best they could, and managing families until the men who had enlisted for only a year could come home. Martha and the officers' wives who arrived in camp were following a British practice of wives and families accompanying soldiers on military campaigns. Since the sixteenth century the British army had been joined by wives, children, and sometimes mothers and sisters, who nursed, laundered, cooked, hauled water for teams firing cannons, and took food to the troops. In return the women drew half rations.

Each company of each British regiment had its own allocation of women. British general Burgoyne's army of 7,200 troops in Canada had an allocation of 2,000 women.[5] Transporting whole families to the colonies was a costly business for the British authorities, yet they did it because the women played an indispensable supporting role in the work they performed. Most wives and family members, like poor Isabella MacMahan, suffered terribly in a variety of ways. Living conditions in camp were hard, and when the army marched, the women and children marched too. The trip across the Atlantic, however, must have been truly horrible, a wretched existence cramped and crowded below decks in the hold of a pitching warship. One noncommissioned officer who set out with British general Howe's army wrote home: "There was continued destruction in the foretop, the pox above—the plague below decks, hell in the forecastle, the devil at the helm."[6]

Many of the passengers died en route, and corpses were thrown overboard on a regular basis. The conditions were particularly hard on children. Not all the accompanying women were simple soldiers' wives, however. On General Burgoyne's staff was German general Baron Frederick von Riedesel, who had brought his wife, young Baroness Frederica von Riedesel, their two small daughters, two maids, and vast quantities of clothing and other necessities, such as dishes and silverplate for the family's use—as if the American campaign were a kind of camping expedition. Lady Harriet Ackland accompanied her husband, Major Ackland, in the same spirit.

By inviting Martha to join him at Cambridge and set an example for other officers' wives to follow suit, George may have intended to convey an image of confidence to the British. He did not anticipate that Martha and the other women would be a permanent fixture, believing it was appropriate for the wives to be there only during that period when both sides more or less withdrew into winter quarters and hostilities were halted by cold weather.

As far as the troops were concerned, George was ambivalent about the practice of wives following their men all year, though more and more women did so as the war dragged on and the men did not return home. It was useful—it got the army's filthy shirts washed, for example—but the women and children had to be allocated rations from the army's scarce supplies. Furthermore, the women were not subject to military discipline, and there was always a risk of their being spies. However, as the war drew on, Washington found it impossible to prevent the women from coming and, at one desperate point, admitted his men fought all the harder knowing their families were present.

Martha's immediate reaction to camp life was to try to alleviate some of the problems her husband was facing. While an anxious camp was bracing itself for the anticipated British attack from the north, Martha insisted she would celebrate Twelfth Night, which was also their wedding anniversary. George was against it because it seemed frivolous under the circumstances, but Martha got her way and had her party. In fact, she used the occasion as part of a pattern of socializing she introduced among the officers, which turned out to help George enormously.

With the constant struggle to obtain supplies from the Congress, and so much to do to set up a military chain of command, whip the camp into order, and enforce discipline and authority between the ranks, George had had little time for the finer points of military etiquette. Relations between his staff and other officers were riven with petty jealousies, as the officers jockeyed for position around their commander. Under impossible pressures, George admitted to Martha his own harassed manner often led to "unintentional offences" that at best undermined morale and at worst could lead to the formation of dangerous cabals that would jeopardize the fragile structure of military authority. It was a possibility that added immeasurably to George's difficulties. Martha, at home in social situations since childhood, began smoothing ruffled feathers. She made friends with the other officers' wives, among them Lucy Knox, the large, bossy, and rather loud wife of General Henry Knox, and Kitty Greene, the pretty but scatterbrained young wife of Quaker general Nathanael Greene.

That Martha was able to get along easily with these distinctly different women, who did not like each other, is a testament to her good nature and, when that was too sorely tried, to her good manners. Lucy Flucker Knox had been the only daughter of prominent and wealthy Boston Tories. Her father had been secretary of the province of Massachusetts. A statuesque, outspoken, strong-willed girl, she had fallen in love with an equally large man, Boston bookseller Henry Knox. The couple had married in the teeth of opposition from Lucy's parents, whose reaction to her marriage was to disown her and return to England. They were a noticeable couple, not least because of their size. Lucy Knox was described by one of Henry's fellow officers as "fat, lively and somewhat interfering . . . a general favorite."

Kitty Greene was a general favorite too, though she was the opposite of Lucy Knox. Born Catherine Littlefield, Kitty had been a famous belle of Providence, Rhode Island. A penniless orphan, she was brought up in the home of a woman she called Aunt Greene. She was bewitchingly pretty, and a good dancer, not very well educated and sweet natured, if rather dim. Her husband, General Nathanael Greene, had met Kitty at his aunt's home, and they had married in 1774. Nathanael was besotted with her, called her his angel, and worried endlessly about her when they were apart. Even Nathanael, however, was not entirely blind to the shortcomings in Kitty's education, once warning her to take special care about her spelling and grammar when writing to the other wives lest the well-educated, outspoken, and intimidating Lucy Knox sneer at her.

Never the type to sneer at anyone, Martha took Kitty Greene under her wing. She became quite fond of Kitty, who was one of many young women to become a surrogate daughter for Martha. She found Lucy Knox less congenial, but they managed to get along because Martha was used to being charming to everyone, and Lucy was anxious to be on good terms with the commanding general's wife.

Nathanael and Kitty's grandson wrote many years later:

> An intimacy sprang up between [Kitty Greene] and Mrs. Washington which, like that between their husbands, ripened into friendship and continued unimpaired through life. His [Nathanael's] first child still in the cradle, was named George Washington and the second, who was from the ensuing year, Martha Washington.[7]
>
> During part of the spring and summer [1776] [Kitty] was with him [Nathanael] in camp. Mrs. Washington and Mrs. Knox were with their hus-

bands at the same time and the pleasant intercourse of Cambridge appears to have been kept up between them all—dinner being still a favorite mode of bringing them together.[8]

Over time Martha became a catalyst among the different personalities of the women at camp, someone they could all relate to. The presence of two attractive, romantic young people, Jacky and Eleanor, helped. Jacky's lazy charm and good southern manners, Eleanor's poor health, and their extreme youth inclined the other wives to view the general's wife in a sympathetic light. With her knack of getting on smoothly with people, Martha unobtrusively managed to take the social lead without upsetting other women. Had she had a more abrasive personality, it would have elicited a different response from the other wives and simply exacerbated the existing tensions in camp.

Entertaining being second nature to Martha, she set up a rota to ensure that each of the officers and his wife, if present, would dine at headquarters on a regular basis. These "dinners" were hardly the style of dinners she was accustomed to at Mount Vernon, but everyone looked forward to them just the same. Though she had brought some of the Mount Vernon house slaves with her to cook and serve, there was relatively little to cook and serve. Yet everyone was so grateful for the diversion, the dinners made a welcome respite in an impossible situation.

Other officers began to entertain as well, and soon there was an established social life in the camp to offset the tension. Cards and gambling had been banned by George because they would lead inevitably to gambling debts and the problems they generated, but there was occasionally music, and Martha was a vivacious chatterer. Kitty Greene flirted, and Lucy Knox was irrepressible.

There were other ladies in camp with whom Martha became friends. One was Mrs. Morgan, a doctor's wife whose mother lived in Philadelphia. Mrs. Morgan wrote to her mother of her visits to the Vassal House headquarters, of tea (ersatz of course) drinkings, and praising Martha's kindness.

Another was a playwright, journalist, and historian, Mercy Otis Warren, a New England bluestocking and a great friend of John Adams's wife, Abigail, and a woman who was quite struck, as women often were, by George. An intellectual with strong political views, Mercy Otis Warren was not, on the face of it, someone with whom Martha would have had a great deal in common. That Mercy was won over by the charm of the Mount Vernon party reveals a curious trait, which other prominent New Englanders, including her friend Abigail Adams, would share. To those steeped in the Puritan traditions of New England, there was something irresistibly glamorous and exotic about Virginia planters. Although many northern women liked Martha, there was often just the faintest tinge of awe in their descriptions, as if they were quite determined to like her and anxious to establish that they were really quite at home with Lady Washington.

Mercy's friend Abigail spent most of her time back home on her farm in Braintree with her children. Feeling patriotic but out of things with her husband, John, away in Philadelphia, she longed to know what was happening elsewhere. Mercy obliged with this description:

> If you wish to hear more of this lady's character [Martha's] . . . I will tell you I think the complacency of her manners speaks at once of the benevolence of her heart, and her affability, Candor and gentleness, qualify her to soften the hours of private life or to sweeten the cares of the Hero, and smooth the rugged paths of War . . . Mr. Custis is the only son of the lady above described—a sensible modest agreeable young Man. His lady, a daughter of Colonel Calvert of Maryland, appear to be of an engaging disposition, but of so extremely delicate a constitution, that it deprives her, as well as her friends, of part of the pleasure, which I am sure would result from her conversation, did she enjoy a more perfect share of health. She is pretty, genteel, easy and agreeable.[9]

In fact, Abigail did meet Martha at some point at Cambridge, because she was invited to one of the headquarters dinners. Also present was the unwashed, foul-mouthed general Charles Lee, who insisted on introducing Abigail to his dogs.

George began 1776 facing a new and pressing problem in camp. His army was evaporating before his eyes. The one-year period of enlistment would soon be up for most of the troops, and the men were anxious to return to their farms. With difficulty George and the Congress were scrambling together enough incentives and propaganda to induce some departing enlistees to return and new ones to join. In the meantime, with the Continental forces dwindling by the day, the British were momentarily expected to take advantage of the situation and attack the camp at Cambridge. Mercy Otis Warren wrote to Martha immediately after Martha's Twelfth Night party to offer her a refuge in the Otis's home in Plymouth.

Martha's reply, though written in her own hand, sounds like it was dictated by George or one of his aides. In fact, much of Martha's correspondence written in an "official" capacity was either dictated or actually written by others over her signature. This letter is the first surviving example, clearly written in the knowledge it might be intercepted. Had this letter fallen into enemy hands, its measured tones give no hint of George's desperate predicament:

> Cambridge, January the 8th, 1776
> Mrs. Washington presents her respectfull compliments to Mrs Warren, and thanks her most cordially for her polite enquire, and exceedingly kind offer— if the Exigency of affairs in this camp should make it necessary for her to

remove, she cannot but esteem it a happiness to have so friendly an Invitation as Mrs Warren has given.[10]

The unruffled tone of this letter is belied by the one Martha wrote to Anna Maria at Eltham a few weeks later. By then news had reached Cambridge that Governor Dunmore had burned Norfolk because the townspeople refused to supply his troops. Martha had no way of knowing what this meant for her family not far away in New Kent. If they were writing to her, the letters had not arrived, and she was growing alarmed:

> My Dear Sister   Cambridge January the 31 1776
>   I have wrote to you several times . . . I am really very uneasy at not hearing from you and have made all the excuses for you that I can think of. . . . if I doe not get a letter by this nights post I shall think myself quite forgot by all my Freinds. . . .
>   The General myself and Jack are very well Nelly Custis is I hope getting well again, and I believe is with child . . . god knows where we shall be I suppose thare will be a change soon but how I cannot pretend to say . . .[11]

Martha's letter also makes it clear she was following developments elsewhere, and that she knew what military intelligence had informed George a few days previously, that British general Clinton had slipped away from Boston and gone south to New York, which was a Loyalist stronghold. She also knew that the strange mercenary General Charles Lee, now working for the Americans, had gone to intercept Clinton.

In Cambridge the situation changed markedly for the better. By February 1776, despite a flood of departures from the army, new recruits had swelled the force at George's disposal to seventeen thousand men. There were twelve thousand increasingly bored and ill-provisioned British troops barricaded in Boston. While their commander General Howe was awaiting ships to evacuate them, early in March the Americans seized the moment and attacked. The Americans had the advantage of occupying the high ground overlooking Boston, which made a counterattack by the British difficult. All prospect of a British counterattack ended when a fierce storm blew up, violently tossing the British warships moored in Boston harbor. Howe decided there was no option but to withdraw from Boston even though the additional ships he needed to do so had not arrived. No only did he have his own troops to evacuate, he now had a thousand Americans still loyal to the Crown to evacuate as well.

Martha and the other ladies went to watch their departure. In exchange for the Americans withholding their fire, Howe undertook not to burn Boston—or what was left of it after his men had destroyed most of the houses—and for ten days the British and their supporters were rowed out to be packed into the warships so overloaded that a number of small children were suffocated in the crush. The British finally sailed away—to regroup in Halifax.

In early April Mercy Otis Warren invited the Washington party to dinner, but they were all unable to attend. Martha wrote a note declining the invitation, again couched in stiffly formal sentences unmistakably composed by someone else but copied using her own spelling and punctuation. George was swamped with military affairs demanding his immediate attention, and Martha was busy helping him. Then Jacky took ill, and when George went south to New York in April, Martha stayed behind a few days to nurse him and keep an eye on Eleanor. When Jacky was better, he and Eleanor, definitely pregnant, left for Mount Airey. Martha joined George in New York, where he occupied the house of Abraham Motier, paymaster of the British army, at the corner of what are now Varick and Charlton Streets.

Martha did not stay long in New York, because by May she was en route to Philadelphia to be inoculated for smallpox. Martha may have been trying to persuade George that it would be beneficial for the army by undergoing the procedure herself. If so, it was a courageous gesture from a woman who was always anxious about matters of health. Curiously, Martha may have been more convinced than George of the advantages of inoculating the army.

Of all the perils of the Revolution, smallpox was the most deadly. John Adams said the pox was "ten times more terrible than Britons, Canadians and Indians together." It was a disease that spread like wildfire through closely packed camps, and though George could ill afford an epidemic that might render his army unfit for service, he was of two minds about the benefits of inoculation, fearing inoculation itself might trigger an epidemic. An overworked Massachusetts physician, Dr. Lewis Beebe, had recorded the devastating effects when smallpox had swept through the American forces besieging Quebec in 1775, when it struck down a large percentage of the troops. There was no provision to care for those who collapsed and lay burning with fever. Sufferers were tossed into a stinking makeshift hospital with no facilities and left to care for themselves. Even those who recovered were weakened and in no state to fight or march. It has been estimated that nine times as many Revolutionary War soldiers were killed by smallpox as by the enemy.

The practice of inoculating by deliberate infection was initially brought to the notice of a Boston doctor by his African slave Onesimus, whose tribe had practiced a form of inoculation. The person to be inoculated had his or her arm scratched, and fresh pus from a smallpox pustule on a sufferer from the disease was rubbed into the scratch. The person inoculated would then develop a—hopefully—mild case with a few pustules to indicate that the inoculation had "taken" and that the inoculate was now immune to the disease.

George, who had had smallpox many years earlier in Barbados, wrote his brother John Augustine that he doubted Martha would actually be brave enough to go through with the procedure. At that stage George was so concerned that inoculating the troops would trigger an epidemic that he made it a military offense to be inoculated. In fact, even while Martha was recovering, he issued a general order that any officer who voluntarily underwent inoculation would be discharged. But by the end of May George was in Philadelphia briefly and wrote his brother again: "Mrs. Washington is now under inoculation in this City; and will, I expect, have the smallpox favourably, this is the 13th day and she has very few Pustules; she would have wrote to my Sister [meaning John Augustine's wife, Hannah] but thought it prudent not to do so, notwithstanding there could be but little danger in conveying the infection in this manner."

By June 9 Jacky had already had a letter from George telling him that Martha was on the road to recovery. He wrote an affectionate, if slightly incoherent, letter to congratulate Martha, who was staying at Randolphs' Tavern in Philadelphia, and give her some family news:

My dear Mamma   Mount Airey June 9th, 1776
    your kind letter . . . gave Me the sincerest pleasure to hear You were in so fair a Way of getting faverably through the Smalpox . . . had releivd Me from much Anxiety, which I doubt less should have felt on the Innoculation of so dear a Mother:—I do with the truest affection congratulate you on and thank God for your recovery— . . . I propose leaving this Place for Williamsburg next Tuesday . . . [to] return . . . [to] be present at a certain Occasion which I believe is not far distant, as soon as the Lady recovers I shall carry her to Virginia, as the Family here is too large for ye House, and I believe the Province of Maryd. Will shortly be in a State of the greatest Confusion.[12]

Jacky then went on to allude to some kind of difficulty his father-in-law, Benedict Calvert, was having. The Maryland governor, Lord Eden, and his wife were on the point of leaving for England, and though many Loyalists were clamoring to be taken on his ship, the governor was refusing to give any of them a passage. There is a hint that Benedict Calvert may have been among their number. The governor's wife, Lady Eden, was Benedict Calvert's aunt and Eleanor's great-aunt. In Virginia Governor and Lady Dunmore had already left for England aboard a warship.

In July, the draft of the Declaration of Independence, prepared by Thomas Jefferson, was approved by the Congress. Congress declared that the term "United States" would replace "United Colonies." In England Samuel Johnson's response was to wonder publicly why "it is that we hear the loudest yelps for Liberty among the drivers of Negroes?"

Martha had remained sweltering in Philadelphia during the summer, hoping to rejoin George in camp. She had reason to believe he might send for her because there had been a spy scare in George's New York headquarters involving his housekeeper. An anonymous letter arrived there claiming Mrs. Mary Smith, a New York woman hired to act as housekeeper for the commander in chief, was a Loyalist sympathizer. Mrs. Smith had already left George's employment and soon fled to England, which made the allegations believable. It was an incident that confirmed George's need to be constantly on guard, as did an attempt to poison George later that summer, instigated by New York Governor Tryon. In London a pamphlet appeared alleging that George Washington kept a mistress named Mary Gibbon at a boarding house in New Jersey and visited her in disguise late at night.[13]

While she waited, Martha had her miniature painted again by Charles Willson Peale, who had come to Mount Vernon in 1772 and painted miniatures of Jacky, Patcy, and Martha and a large portrait of George. George spent the summer strengthening his defenses in New York, acutely aware that General Burgoyne was still a threatening presence in the north, and trying to impress Congress with the absolute necessity of adequate supplies for the army.

The letters George sent to Congress specifying what clothing was needed for the army sound as if he had first discussed the practicalities of clothing large numbers of people as cheaply, functionally, and warmly as possible with Martha. Uniforms would have been both expensive and time-consuming to make. The hunting shirts and leggings George finally requested were practical, comfortable, versatile, and cheap, and his militia had worn them on the frontier in the French and Indian Wars in the 1750s. Martha, acquainted with the practicalities of clothing large numbers of slaves and an expert seamstress herself, could advise on mass-producing these garments quickly for the troops. The following request specified not only what George wanted but the effect that the chosen attire was designed to have on the British. It was a very "Virginian" approach, in that George was using the clothing of his troops to make a statement:

> the General being sensible of the difficulty, and expence of providing Cloaths, of almost any kind, for the Troops, feels an unwillingness to recommend, much more to order, any kind of Uniform, but as it is absolutely necessary that men should have Cloaths and appear decent and tight, he earnestly encourages the use of Hunting Shirts, with long Breeches, made of the same Cloth, gaiter fashion about the legs, to all those yet unprovided. No Dress can be had cheaper, nor more convenient, as the Wearer may be cool in warm weather, and warm in cool weather, by putting on under Cloaths which will not change the outward dress, Winter or Summer—Besides which it is a dress justly supposed to carry no small terror to the enemy, who think every such person a complete Marksman.[14]

George was right. The British believed—with some justification—that "those hunting shirt fellows from the woods" could "hit button on [a] coat when they are in the humor of sharp shooting." It was another weapon in George's pitifully small arsenal.

In the end George decided he did not want Martha to come to New York. Momentarily expecting a British attack, George thought it was too dangerous for Martha, and he hired a second housekeeper in July, Mrs. Thompson. On July 22 George wrote to his brother John Augustine at Bushfield that: "Mrs. Washington is now in Philadelphia, and has thoughts of returning to Virginia as there is no prospect of her being with me any part of this summer."

The fact that Martha stayed on in Philadelphia throughout August indicates either the extent of her anxiety for George or the fact that it was not considered safe for her to leave, even with a military escort. The situation in Virginia was still precarious. Though Governor Dunmore was gone, there were still British raiding parties along the Potomac, and Jacky sent George an account of one of these. Alarming though it was, the incompetent response of the local militia was even more so:

> Mount Airey, August 8, 1776
> You have no doubt heard of the men-of-war coming up the Potowmack as far as Mr. Brent's, whose house they burnt with several outhouses and some stacks of wheat. A Captain James with sixty militia were stationed there who all got drunk, and kept challenging the men-of-war to come ashore, and upbraiding them with cowardice. Hammond [a British officer] sent one hundred and fifty men, who landed about ten o'clock under cover of a gondola and tender. The militia were asleep after their drinking frolic, and did not discover the enemy until they landed and their vessels began to fire. Captain James desired his men to shift for themselves and ran off without firing a gun. . . . Captain James is to be tried for cowardice.[15]

Nothing else could have kept Martha away from Mount Airey, where Jacky's baby was due in August. Her sole comfort that summer was to reflect that Jacky's marriage had turned out so well and that it had been wise to let him have his way and marry young. Jacky proved to be a surprisingly devoted husband to Eleanor and was in raptures over his new baby. He wrote to give Martha the good news the day she was born and share some of the obstetric details:

> My dearest Mamma   Mount Airey August 21st 1776
> I have the extreme Happiness at last to inform you, that Nelly was safely delivered this Morning about five o'Clock of a fine Daughter. . . . You would be much more pleased, if you were to see the strapping Huzze. . . . She is in short as fine a Healthy fat Baby as ever was born.

Poor Nelly had a very indefferent Time, her pains were two Hours long & very severe. She is now thank God as well as can be expected . . . I cannot pretend to say who the child is like, It is as much like Doctor Rumney as any Body else. She has a double Chinn something like His, in point of Fatness with fine black Hair, & Eyes, upon the whole I think It is as pretty & fine a Baba as ever I saw. This is not my opinion alone, but the Opinion of all who have seen Her— I hope she will be preserv'd as a Comfort, and Happiness to us all.[16]

It conjures up a picture of the whole Calvert family at Mount Airey making much of Eleanor's baby and relief on everyone's part that both were well. The baby was named Elizabeth Parke Custis, after Eleanor's mother Elizabeth. Martha and George were to stand as godparents.

In late August the British attacked New York, accompanied by stolid, hymn-singing Hessian troops. They outnumbered and outflanked George's troops, who retreated in panic. Taking New York, the Hessians, known as avid plunderers, were remarkably restrained. In contrast, the victorious British went on a rampage and distinguished themselves by the number of rapes they committed. According to one of their officers, Captain Lord Rawdon, they were like "deprived satyrs." He noted callously: "A girl cannot step into the bushes to pluck a rose without the most imminent danger of being ravished, and they are so little accustomed to these vigorous methods that they don't bear them with the proper resignation, and of consequence we have the most entertaining court martials every day."[17]

For Martha, forced to remain in Philadelphia, it was an anxious time, with the news almost all bad. The reports that reached Philadelphia of the American defeat and British atrocities, bad enough on their own, were exaggerated for propaganda purposes. A young spy named Nathan Hale was hanged by the British twelve days after he had volunteered to undertake a mission George had ordered. George was holed up in Brooklyn with his exhausted, demoralized troops, who had abandoned the bulk of their food, heavy artillery, equipment, and ammunition when fleeing New York. In the following weeks and months they would continue to retreat slowly with diminishing supplies as the British and the Hessians pressed their advantage, taking White Plains, Fort Washington, and Fort Lee. The American army began to retreat through New Jersey, disintegrating as men were taken prisoner or killed, or simply deserted.

For the first time in her life Martha was separated from everyone— Jacky in Maryland, her relatives in New Kent, and George away with the army. The mail was not reliable, often leaving messages carried in person by anyone coming from Virginia to Philadelphia as her only contact with her relatives. Added to that was a nagging worry over Anna Maria at Eltham and her mother at Pamocra. Anna Maria, who had three surviving children, Burwell Bassett Jr., John Bassett, and Fanny, had been increasingly unwell for two years, and at some point in 1776 Martha's brother William drowned in the Pamunkey. Martha's mother was sixty-five and often poorly. Virginia remained full of escaped slaves who had been armed by the British roaming the countryside, and Martha knew the risk they posed to isolated New Kent planters. Still in Philadelphia at the end of August, Martha wrote longingly to Anna Maria:

> My dear Sister   Philadelphia August the 28th 1776
>   I am still in this town and Noe prospects at present of my leveing it,— . . .
> I doe my Dear sister most religiously wish thare was an End to the matter that
> we might have the pleasure of meeting again—
>   My Duty to my Dear mamma—and tell her I m very well—I don't hear
> from you so often as I used to doe at Cambridge . . . please to present love to
> . . . my Brother and sisters my dear Fanny and the Boy [s] & Except the same
> yourself   I am my dear Nancy your
>   ever affectionate sister
>   Martha Washington[18]

CHAPTER 12

"General Washington's Lady, an Example of Persistent Industry"

There is no evidence as to when Martha finally left Philadelphia in 1776 or when she returned to Mount Vernon that fall. It may have been November before she arrived home, because she wrote to Lund Washington on October 23 asking him to give Patcy Custis's old playmate and friend Milly Posey five pounds in Virginia currency. It seems likely she went back by way of Mount Airey to see Jacky, Eleanor, and her first grandchild, Elizabeth, whom they called Betsy.

Mount Vernon presented a depressing spectacle when she finally did return home. By November 1776 George had been away for eighteen months, and Martha had been away a year. She had taken many of the house slaves north, and if any house slaves had been left behind, there had been no incentive for them to keep the house in order. Without Martha's direction the house had grown dusty and gloomy, with linen unaired and furniture and mirrors unpolished. Lund Washington was having to manage the estate with fewer slaves because a number of Mount Vernon slaves, both from the house and the surrounding farms, had disappeared in response to Lord Dunmore's offer of the previous November.

If Martha's heart sank at the state of things at Mount Vernon, there was little time to worry about them. First of all, she was extremely tired. Traveling between Virginia and Massachusetts was an exhausting business, compounded by the worry and pressure of the war, and the strain of keeping up a positive front. Though Martha usually held up remarkably well away from Mount Vernon, at forty-five, she was no longer a young woman, and the long trips she made north during the course of the Revolution and afterwards always took their toll on her return. Despite her longing to visit the family

211

in New Kent, she was far too exhausted to make a trip south, and once she was finally able to get up and take stock of the effects of her absence, there was a great deal to be done.

Although Martha's role at Cambridge had been largely social, she had observed George's frustration at Congress's inability to supply the army adequately with clothing as well as other necessities. Even before the war Mount Vernon had produced flax and wool cloth, and once back at Mount Vernon, anticipating Congress would remain incapable of meeting the army's needs in full, Martha stepped up production of material, setting sixteen slaves to work spinning thread and making cloth. She also set slaves to knitting stockings as well as sewing soldiers' shirts. She herself unraveled old silk stockings and silk cushion covers and wove the thread as stripes into homespun. Martha was very proud of this cloth and had a number of dresses made for herself from it during the Revolution.

Meanwhile, Martha followed developments from a distance. The outlook for the Continental army was still bleak. George and his disintegrating army had been steadily driven further and further from New York. Save for skirmishes, they had not engaged with the British in any actual battles since being overrun in New York. They simply retreated and retreated, one step ahead of the pursuing English army, withdrawing west and south. Public confidence in the commander in chief was ebbing. By December George's troops were licking their wounds in Princeton, and the seventeen thousand strong army George had had in February 1776 had dwindled to three thousand cold, ragged, hungry, ill-shod, and badly provisioned men, not all of whom were able-bodied enough to fight by the time December arrived. One observer called them "animated scarecrows." Desertion was rife. Men who had been absent for over a year wanted or needed to return to their farms. Many had heard the stories of British atrocities and feared for the safety of their women. The troops simply melted away.

Wash Custis said that George and Martha wrote many letters during the Revolution. Though Martha later burned virtually all their correspondence, it is reasonable to believe George kept Martha informed of the worsening crisis, while Martha waited for a summons to camp and prepared to leave. There was no reason for optimism in New Jersey or Mount Vernon.

Then in January came welcome news. The day after Christmas, George had taken Trenton while the drunken Hessian defenders were befuddled from their Christmas celebrations. A few days later George welcomed in the new year by routing the British at Princeton. Having so few men and so few supplies to transport had given him the advantage of mobility if nothing else. In a single night he had transported his army across the Delaware River, marched on Trenton, and taken it, together with a quantity of food, ammunition, and to his troops' joy, rum.

George's elation at the victory was tempered by the knowledge that his old friend and neighbor, Dr. Hugh Mercer, who had once treated Patcy Custis, had been severely wounded by bayonets at Princeton. Mercer had not been killed, however, and George was relieved to be assured by an army surgeon that Mercer would recover. But being a doctor himself, Mercer knew otherwise and, showing a wound from a bayonet thrust hidden beneath his arm, said that was the one that would prove fatal. He died on January 12.

The rejoicing of the army was cut short as a smallpox epidemic broke out almost immediately. Within days George had withdrawn his exhausted and now rapidly sickening troops into winter quarters at Morristown, unable to press his advantage any further for the moment. He decided the only way to contain the epidemic was to have the troops inoculated, and he reversed his orders of the previous summer against it, possibly influenced by the fact that Martha had recovered so well from her own inoculation. Military doctors were ordered to inoculate the men in the greatest secrecy, to prevent a British attack while the effects of the procedure temporarily incapacitated the army.

There was no "camp" at Morristown for the thousands of ragged, weary, sick soldiers, so George quartered them with local families and set up his own headquarters at Arnold's Tavern. If George had had his way, there would have been a much greater number of soldiers needing shelter, but the army was once again dwindling after the victories at Trenton and Princeton. In the surrounding countryside British and American troops foraged for food and fodder for their horses and fought skirmishes. Both sides terrorized civilians believed to be sympathetic to the enemy, and as elsewhere, many civilians were forced from their homes by marauding soldiers.

By the end of February 1777 George had not yet sent the military escort to bring Martha north to camp, but word reached her at Mount Vernon that George was extremely ill at Morristown, possibly with quinsy, a kind of putrid sore throat. Some of his staff expected him to die. There is anecdotal evidence—though no actual letter survives—that Martha wrote to camp saying if she did not hear at once of George's recovery she would leave for Morristown, adding that if there were no carriage available she would come on foot.

That turned out to be unnecessary, because Jacky sent his mother north in his carriage. This time he and Eleanor did not accompany her, as they were occupied with their new daughter. Jacky and Eleanor, who did not yet have their own home, had been alternating their time between Mount Airey and Mount Vernon, and now that their family was growing, they preferred Mount Vernon.

Martha arrived in camp in New Jersey in March, and the long trip in the coldest part of the year must have been more grueling and frightening than the year before. By the time Martha reached Pluckamin, George was better and well enough to come to meet her. There George waited at the house of a Mrs. Eliot. Mrs. Eliot watched the carriage arrive and a small plainly dressed woman alight, whom she took to be the great Lady Washington's maid. She was astonished, when the general stepped forward to embrace her, to find it was Martha.

A soldier's journal of the period remarks that "Mrs. Washington's arrival at camp was an event much anticipated."

By the time Martha arrived at Morristown, about March 15, the Continental army had been there for two months, and George was losing the battle for the hearts and minds of both his troops and the local residents. The impact of thousands of ill, ragged, starving men quartered on the town had been immense. The Presbyterian and Baptist churches had been turned into makeshift hospitals for the soldiers suffering from smallpox or those recovering from inoculation. The townspeople resented the measures, which quartered three or four men in their homes, particularly as the soldiers brought smallpox and dysentery with them. Before the winter was over, smallpox and dysentery killed a fourth of the inhabitants of Morristown. In the countryside farmers resented the depredations of foraging expeditions, and those soldiers well enough to complain grumbled at the poor conditions and lack of supplies.

On her arrival Martha was established in the unfinished upper story of the frame house where she and George were lodging. To make it as comfortable as possible, George sent some carpenters along to fit it out to Martha's specifications. Martha launched a charm offensive. The carpenters described Martha as a portly-looking agreeable woman of forty-five who told them, "Now young men, I care for nothing but comfort here; and should like you to fit me up a beaufet [a sort of cupboard] on one side of the room, and some shelves, and places for hanging cloths on the other." Every morning at eleven Martha came upstairs to inspect the progress and bring each of the workmen a glass of spirits. When the Washingtons had finished their very simple dinner in the room below, the workmen were called down to eat their dinner at the same table. Martha, not surprisingly, was a woman they wanted to please. They fixed smooth boards over rough and worm-eaten planks and stopped up the crevices in the walls. Martha professed herself delighted with the result and praised their work. The workmen left in a glow of goodwill to spread the word of the general's affable wife.

Congress had not managed to supply the army with nearly enough hunting shirts or footwear, and the soldiers had been ragged and often shoeless long before the battle of Trenton. Martha had brought material and wool from Mount Vernon, and soon she was busy sewing shirts and knitting stockings. She had not been in camp long before several prominent ladies did Martha the honor of "waiting" on her, despite the fact that so many of the townspeople now resented the army's presence. One of these local ladies, Mrs. Troupe, called afterwards on her friend Mrs. Tuttle. Mrs. Tuttle naturally wanted to hear what the general's wife was like, and Mrs. Troupe obliged:

> as she [Martha] was said to be so grand a lady, we thought we must put on our best bibs and bands. So we dressed ourselves in our most elegant ruffles and silks and were introduced to her ladyship. And don't you think, we found her *knitting, and with a specked apron on!*
>
> There we were without a stitch of work and sitting in state, but General Washington's lady with her own hands was knitting stockings. . . .
>
> And this was not all. In the afternoon her ladyship took occasion to say, in a way that we could not be offended at, that at this time it was very important that American ladies should be patterns of industry to their countrywomen, because separation from the mother country will dry up the sources where many of our comforts have been derived.[1]

Another lady present left a similar record of the visit:

> Yesterday with several others I visited Lady Washington at headquarters. We had expected to find the wealthy wife of the great general elegantly dressed, for the time of our visit had been fixed; but instead she was neatly attired in a plain brown habit. Her gracious and cheerful manners delighted us all, but we felt rebuked by the plainness of her apparel and her example of persistent industry, while we were extravagantly dressed idlers, a name not very creditable in these perilous times. She seems very wise in experience, kind hearted and winning in all her ways. She talked much of the suffering of the poor soldiers, especially the sick ones. Her heart seems to be full of compassion for them.

In a camp rife with sickness and teeming with ragged men foisted on a reluctant townspeople, Martha's diplomatic skills and practical abilities were immensely useful. The favorable impression Martha made on the local ladies affected how they, in turn, viewed the army's presence, and it helped to swing the opinion of an increasingly antagonistic public back behind George. The image of the general's wife hard at work on behalf of the troops boosted George's relations with the troops as well. Many of the troops owed what little alleviation of their suffering they received to Martha, who doled out her store of medicines and small comforts to the worst-off. If Martha despaired, she hid it well, because she was always seen to be resolutely cheerful in the most appalling circumstances.

In fact, Martha was behaving as she always had, adapting her normal way of life to different circumstances on a larger scale. She had been trained from childhood to look after large numbers of people, to sew, cook, and nurse, and to get along easily with strangers. She also applied her lifelong experience of hospitality and entertaining effectively to the exigencies of camp life.

As in the previous year, Martha initiated a social life to lighten the tedium and stress affecting everyone. There were other ladies in camp, again including Lucy Knox, and a number of the daughters of the late Judge Livingston. Among them was Janet Livingston Montgomery, the young widow of General Montgomery, who had died at Quebec, still stunned with grief at the loss of her husband. The Livingstons' lively cousin Kitty Stirling was also present, and the Washingtons made a point of entertaining the young people. Though Kitty Greene was not actually present in Morristown that winter, Nathanael Greene's grandson drew on his grandfather's recollections of life in camp when he described what happened in Morristown in 1777. In his biography of General Greene three-quarters of a century later, the general's namesake wrote "Mrs. Washington came to camp; and other ladies joining their husbands, a little winter circle was formed like the winter circle of Cambridge. There were sleigh rides . . . dinner parties at headquarters and now and then a subscription ball."[2]

In fact, with so few supplies available, these dinner parties were modest in the extreme and the "balls" took place in cramped and very unfestive conditions: the ladies wore homespun and the officers were beginning to be a bit frayed around the edges, but everyone made the most of these occasions. Martha behaved as if she were back at the governor's palace.

The wife who most enjoyed camp social life was unable to be present. Kitty Greene was back in Rhode Island, having given birth to a daughter in mid-March, whom she named Martha Washington Greene. Nathanael missed her and wrote her wistfully: "Mrs. Washington and Mrs. Bland from Virginia are at camp, happy with their better halves. Mrs. Washington is extremely fond of the general and he of her; they are very happy in each other."[3]

Martha's tireless example motivated many women to undertake some form of war work. Knitting and sewing circles were organized to make clothing for the troops or to roll bandages. In nearby Whippany, a farmer's wife, Mrs. Anna Kitchl, kept a soup cauldron boiling twenty-four hours a day to feed passing soldiers, and in Braintree Abigail Adams also ran a soup kitchen.

With the coming of warm weather, George prepared to move the army out of winter headquarters. Because there was no place for wives in the field, Martha left for Mount Vernon in June, where there was good news waiting for her. Eleanor was pregnant again. Life at Mount Vernon in the summer of 1777 was hardly back to normal with George still away, but Jacky and Eleanor and Betsy livened up the house.

Around this time Jacky and George took shares in a privateer as a commercial investment, intended to turn a quick profit. Privateering was licensed piracy, preying on ships of an enemy power. It is not generally known that the commander in chief and his stepson were involved in it, but in addition to making a profit, George hoped to capture ammunition and other supplies he needed.

This was as close as Jacky had come to any form of military involvement. Jacky had no inclination to join either a local militia or the Continental army, preferring to stay at home looking after Eleanor, his daughter, and Martha, but he was also about to come into his inheritance. Jacky and Eleanor were hunting for a suitable house conveniently located to both Mount Vernon and Mount Airey. Neither George nor Martha appears to have found anything untoward in Jacky's preference for civilian life. In fact, the vast majority of American men did not serve in the military. Jacky did inform George he intended to stand for election to the Virginia Assembly for New Kent. Jacky also consulted George about some land he wanted to purchase to add to his estate, and George offered to rent him a further parcel of land that was part of Martha's dower property in King William County to the south.

As well as consulting George about his plans to run for burgess and add to his property holdings, Jacky kept George up-to-date on the political situation in Virginia. He wrote George that wartime profiteering was on the increase in Virginia, as it was in Philadelphia, while political ardor in Virginia had cooled to the point that it was becoming increasingly difficult to recruit men either for the army or the militia.

News from the north that reached Mount Vernon was mostly bad, and the experiences of General John Burgoyne in Canada and northern New York illustrate why George was unwilling to have Martha with him. British-held New York was crammed with American Loyalist refugees. Foraging parties from both sides roamed in the outlying areas of New York, skirmishing and pillaging at will. Further north up the Hudson and in Canada, the British, commanded by General Burgoyne, had enlisted the help of some Iroquois tribes who scalped the settlers suspected of being Patriots as they were driven from their homes. In scenes reminiscent of recent Balkan conflicts, women and young girls were raped and civilians massacred as farms and homesteads were torched. Surrendering prisoners were bayoneted. Both sides were responsible for those and other atrocities, creating a wave of displaced, terrified civilians for whom there were few safe havens.

By July 4 Burgoyne had taken Fort Ticonderoga from its American defenders and was proceeding south toward Albany, pursuing an apparently successful military strategy of coming down on the Americans from the north, as one arm of a pincer movement. Broadly speaking, the plan was to link up with General Howe, who was en route to Philadelphia.

An aide-de-camp to General Burgoyne wrote a friend that they were being harassed by the Americans in Canada but hardly took it seriously. He went on to paint this cozy picture of camp life:

> One proof of the spirit of our army, the Ladies do not mean to quit us. Lady
> Harriet Acland graces the advanced Corps of the Army, and Madame Riedesel
> the German brigades. We have frequent dînées and constantly musick . . . this
> campaigning is a favorite portion of Life . . . none but stupid Mortals can dis-
> like a lively Camp, good Weather, good Claret, good Musick and the enemy
> near. I may venture to say all this, for a little fusillade during dinner does not
> discompose the Nerves of even our Ladies.[4]

General Burgoyne passed most nights, according to Frederica von Riedesel,
who was obviously kept awake, "singing and drinking and diverting himself
with his mistress . . . who was as fond of Champain as himself." The troops
were accompanied by their retinue of women and children, and people, baggage and supply wagons, and gun carriages made a formidable procession
traveling through the forests of New York. Forty miles from Albany, their
progress suddenly slowed to a crawl, obstructed by an American guerrilla tactic. The Americans had felled a vast number of trees across Burgoyne's route,
one every ten or twelve yards. The whole unwieldy baggage train ground to
a halt each time the path had to be cleared, and in addition they now had to
build bridges over creeks and marshy ground to allow the heavy baggage train
to go on. Burgoyne now found he could travel no faster than a mile a day.

Between the end of August and mid-October Burgoyne engaged with
the American troops many times and was successful in the main. However,
it was one thing for the British to take a fort with their superior guns and
numbers but an impossible task to secure the surrounding area full of rebel
snipers perched in trees who picked off slow-moving British and German
soldiers heavily encumbered with bulky uniforms and equipment. Then in
October American general Horatio Gates resoundingly defeated Burgoyne
in a fierce battle near Saratoga.

On this occasion the "Ladies" were brought quickly face to face with
the crude realities of war. The aide-de-camp who had written so blithely
about the joys of camp life was killed. The husband of pregnant Lady Ackland was wounded, and Baroness von Riedesel huddled with her terrified
children in a basement for six days as the guns pounded over her head. The
basement was used as a makeshift hospital, and the baroness and her children were surrounded by casualties, blood, amputations, and death.

Burgoyne formally surrendered to General Gates on October 17. As
his men marched out to lay their arms in front of the Americans, the smartly
uniformed British were astonished at the motley appearance of the rebel
troops, dressed in stained and torn shirts and some accompanied by pet rac-
coons and bears. Some were wearing wigs that looked, as one English officer noted, as if a whole sheep was being worn under a hat. Many of the
Americans seemed to be men in their fifties and sixties who were new to
military life.

Frederica von Riedesel and her children, now officially prisoners, were fortunate in the treatment they received. They were driven to the American camp, where they were kindly welcomed and fed by General Schuyler. The baroness was eventually reunited with her husband. The von Riedesels remained in the colonies as prisoners for some time, eventually meeting the Washingtons.

The women attached to the body of the defeated troops fared less well than the officers' wives. After Burgoyne's defeat, Hannah Winthrop wrote this letter to her friend Mercy Otis Warren about the women she saw following the defeated Hessian troops:

> Great numbers of women, who seem to be beasts of burden, having a bushel basket on their back, by which they were bent double, the contents seem'd to be Pots and Kettles, various sorts of Furniture, children peeping thro' gridirons and other utensils, some very young Infants who were born on the road, the women bare feet, cloathd in dirty rags, such effluvia filled the air while they were passing, had they not been smoking all the time, I should have been apprehensive of being contaminated by them.[5]

In fact, this is indicative of the plight of the majority of women who accompanied the troops on both sides. Martha and other officers' wives lived in spartan conditions at the American camps, but the women who began trickling in to join their men full-time in the Continental army lived in the same conditions of desperate squalor as their counterparts the Hessian women.

George had not been at Saratoga. He was anticipating an attack on Philadelphia, and he and his troops had experienced a string of defeats in Delaware in September, and Germantown, Pennsylvania, in early October, where American casualties had been high. With the British under General Howe drawing closer and closer to Philadelphia in September, the Continental Congress fled to reestablish themselves at York two weeks later. On September 25, the British occupied Philadelphia. For weeks afterwards Martha was ignorant of George's fate and frantic with worry until she finally received word early in November that he was alive and well and heading for winter quarters at Whitmarsh, fourteen miles north of Philadelphia. It was a serious blow to the Americans that the British now occupied their political center, a state of affairs that led a number of generals and members of Congress to question the military capabilities of their commander in chief.

From Mount Vernon Martha went to New Kent to visit Anna Maria and the rest of her family and returned with Anna Maria's two sons, Burwell Bassett Jr., age thirteen, and John Bassett, age eleven, who were to stay with her to be inoculated against smallpox and recuperate. In November Martha wrote to Anna Maria that she was sending them home with a Clairborne neighbor who lived near Eltham:

My Dear Sister   November the 18th 1777

I have the very great pleasure of returning,—you your Boys as well as they were when I brought them from Eltham—They have had the small pox exceeding light and have been perfectly well this fortnight past . . . —they have been such good Boy that I shall love them a great deal more than I ever did. . . .

The last letter I had from the General was dated the 7th of this month—he says nothing hath happend since the unsuccessful attack upon our forts on the Dalaware—the Boys bring the last papers down with them—

—Jack is just come over, he tells me that little Bet is grown fat as a pigg— Nell is not well her self—

I have often wished for my dear sister and Fanny, as the small pox was so trifling with the Boys— . . . I have had all thare cloths washed and rinsed several days—and do verily believe that they can bring no infection home with them—if you are afraide lett someone who has had the small pox put out thare cloths to air for a day or two in the sun—an Thomas [probably a slave from Eltham who accompanied the boys and was inoculated as well] has also been washed and his cloths changed—his cap & shoes he did not ware, when he was sick—I shall be glad you will lett me know how the Boys gett down. . . .

—I am my Dear sister your sincearly affectionate
Martha Washington[6]

With this letter Martha sent Anna Maria a piece of blue satin, probably precious imported dress material left over from pre-embargo days, and a piece of muslin for one of Anna Maria's neighbors.

Within a month of the boys' return to Eltham, a sad Martha was writing a letter of condolence to Burwell Bassett. Anna Maria, whom Martha called "the greatest favorite I had in the world" had died on December 17. The cause of her death is unknown, but according to this letter Anna Maria had been ill at least since 1774 and had lately been in enough suffering to make death seem a happy release.

My Dear Sir   Mount Vernon December 22nd 1777

I doe most sincearly lement and condole with you, on the loss of our dear departed Friend she has I hope made a happy exchange—and only gon a little before us the time draws near when I hope we shall meet never more to part—if to meet our departed Friends and know them was scertain we could have very little desire to stay in this world where if we are at ease one hour we are in affliction days . . .

—my dear sister in her lifetime often mentioned my taking my dear Fanny if she should be taken away before she grew up—If you will lett her come to live with me, I will with the greatest plasure take her and be a parent and mother to her as long as I live . . . my Dear sister for the last three or four years of her life could have but very little pleasure her health was such that must render her life a misere to herself and a very great affliction to her friends—which I hope will in some measure reconcile you to your very great loss of her . . . —I have often wished that fortune had plased us nearer to each other.

> My Dear brother your ever
> affectionate
> Martha Washington[7]

Martha longed to go to New Kent immediately, to comfort Burwell Bassett, the children, and her mother, and to bring Fanny back to Mount Vernon. Two circumstances prevented her doing so. One was that Eleanor Custis was pregnant and very unwell at Mount Vernon, about to give birth any day. She suffered terribly with each of her pregnancies. On December 31, Eleanor had another daughter, Martha Parke Custis, who would be known in the family as Patty.

The other reason was that she was waiting for George to summon her to camp. Whatever else was happening in Martha's family, that took priority. George did eventually write for Martha to join him in winter quarters. By January George had withdrawn to Valley Forge, a bleak hollow with a few houses, an iron forge, and a frozen creek. The troops there were worse off than ever. Many men were now shoeless, and the lucky ones had rags in which to wrap their feet. All were in tattered ragged clothing, and there were many ill and wounded. There was no shelter at Valley Forge, and George ordered the men to build themselves huts at once. In desperation George offered a prize of money for the most ingeniously designed hut, and he also offered money to the soldier who devised the best pair of shoes from bark. Even the desperate soldiers never managed much in the way of bark shoes, but the weary men were obliged to cobble huts together for protection from the weather. George lived in his tent until all the men had a hut of some kind. He was racked with sympathy for the soldiers' plight and wrote continually to Congress venting his frustration at Congress's failure to send the army the most basic supplies. There was no straw to insulate the cold earth floors of the huts, little firewood, no blankets, and almost no food. Horses were killed because there was no fodder. When a man was due to stand sentry, the men in his hut would pool most of their items of ragged clothing for him to wear in the biting wind.

On February 1, 1778, George wrote to Jacky:

Dear Sir: Valley Forge, February 1, 1778

I congratulate you upon the birth of another daughter, and Nelly's good health; and heartily wish the last may continue and the other be a blessing to you.

. . . . Your mamma is not yet arrived, but if she left Mont Vernon on the twenty sixth ultimo, as intended, may, I think, be expected every hour. Mead set off yesterday (as soon as I got notice of her intention) to meet her. We are in a dreary kind of place, and uncomfortably provided.

Martha and her entourage of eighteen slaves had a particularly arduous trip. The weather was so bad en route that when Martha stayed overnight at an inn on Brandywine Creek, the snow had made the road impassable for her carriage by next morning. Martha abandoned the carriage and hired a sleigh from a nearby farm to take her, and presumably her slaves, the rest of the way. The carriage and any other vehicles coming from Mount Vernon would have been packed with practical supplies—material woven there, scissors, thread, needles, pins, buttons, thimbles, knitting needles, skeins of wool, darning wool, food such as ham, salt herring, dried fruits, and cornmeal, and home-distilled spirits, bandages, and as many medicinal ingredients as Martha could pack in. The sleigh probably made many trips from Brandywine to Valley Forge to collect these precious supplies.

Martha reached the Valley Forge camp sometime between the fourth and tenth of February. In the dismal conditions there the arrival of the commander in chief's wife was a significant event, especially as she had had to battle her way through some very rough weather. Martha's presence lent moral support to George, but Martha had begun to enjoy a measure of popularity with the troops in her own right the previous year. It was said that when Martha arrived at Valley Forge the soldiers cheered, and she was welcomed by shouts of "God bless Lady Washington!"

CHAPTER 13

"A Dreary Kind of Place"

Georges's description of Valley Forge as a "dreary kind of place" was a masterpiece of understatement. Had the British grasped the full extent of his situation, they might have attacked and overrun the army camped there. Nothing could have prepared Martha for the squalid sight that met her eyes nor the hellish conditions of the camp. Contemporary descriptions of the Continental army's camp at Valley Forge are reminiscent of twentieth-century refugee camps.

By the time Martha reached Valley Forge in early February 1778, between ten and eleven thousand men, now joined by many of their women and children, had been there since the week before Christmas. Though it could be easily defended, Valley Forge was an inhospitable location and not George's choice as the ideal place to set up winter camp. But he had little choice. Pennsylvania's Supreme Executive Council had threatened to withdraw the Pennsylvania troops if the Continental army camped more than twenty-five miles away from Philadelphia, now occupied by British forces under General Howe.

The troops had arrived in an appalling state—wet, cold, sick, and hungry. The majority were in rags, their only protection from rain, sleet, and snow and the biting wind. A fortunate few had a piece of tattered blanket. The road to Valley Forge, which had been churned up into ruts and frozen many times over, cut open the many shoeless men's feet. Most men were bare-legged, their stockings long worn-out. One of the fortunate ones, a sixteen-year-old soldier, had procured himself a piece of cowhide and made himself some moccasins, but the hard leather never softened and rubbed his ankles until they were covered with bloody sores.

Food had been desperately short for months. Several contemporary diaries kept by the men in the camp during this period survive to paint a vivid picture of the suffering they endured. One wrote feelingly of the "cold hunger and other miseries" he and his fellow soldiers suffered, while gallantly trying to see a flicker of humor in their terrible situation:

> But lest the reader should be disgusted at hearing so much about "starvation" . . . While we lay there, there was a "Continental Thanksgiving" ordered by Congress. And as the army had all the cause in the world to be particularly thankful . . . we were ordered to participate in it. We had nothing to eat for two or three days previous, except what the trees of the fields and forests afforded us. But we must now have what Congress said, a sumptuous Thanksgiving . . . our country, ever mindful of its suffering army opened her sympathizing heart so wide, upon this occasion, as to give us something to make the world stare . . . it gave each and every man half a gill of rice [a few handfuls] and a tablespoon of vinegar![1]

The men were ordered to church to hear a Thanksgiving sermon before partaking of their rations.

In the winter fresh produce was always in short supply, and the men depended on whatever meat, the soldiers' staple, could be obtained. Such meat as was available was not always good. Another young soldier, Albigence Waldo, left this wretched account of conditions in Valley Forge in mid-December 1777:

> December 14 . . . The Army which has been surprisingly healthy hitherto, now begins to grow sickly from the continued fatigues they have suffered this Campaign . . . I am sick . . . Poor food—hard lodging—Cold Weather—fatigue—Nasty Cloaths—nasty Cookery—Vomit half my time—smoak'd out my senses . . . Here all Confusion—smoke and Cold—hunger and filthyness. . . . There comes a bowl of beef soup—full of burnt leaves and dirt, sickish enough to make a Hector spue. . . . December 21 [Valley Forge] preparations are made for huts . . . Provisions Scarce . . . my Skin and eyes are almost spoil'd with continual smoke. A general cry through the Camp this Evening among the soldiers, "No Meat! No Meat!"—the Distant vales Echo'd back the melancholy sound "No Meat! No Meat!"[2]

In the absence of meat the men were reduced to impossibly short rations consisting of nothing more than a little flour. This was mixed with water to make an "ash cake"—so-called because it was cooked on hot stone in the ashes—if enough firewood could be found to make a fire. One New England doctor called for the vengeance of the Lord to be visited on the commissary officers responsible for providing rations that "turned men's glutted guts to pasteboard."

The troops, many now accompanied by their families, were vulnerable to illness and infection from exhaustion, the relentless cold, and bad—or no—food and suffered miserably from a variety of diseases. In December many of the men had come down with an infection doctors called "the Itch," which left the body covered with itching scabs and the men suffering from it unfit for duty. Smallpox, dysentery, diarrhea, and putrid fever swept through the camp, and the cold wet weather brought on rheumatism.

Horses died or were killed because there was no fodder, and their corpses added to the sanitation problems arising from so large an encampment. Unlike Morristown, there were few houses, and the staff officers occupied these. George immediately set the men to building huts to specifications designed to provide a cramped shelter for a dozen men and their weapons, as well as larger huts fifteen feet by twenty-five feet, with a fireplace and a window, for use as hospitals. The latter were soon filled with patients, partly as a result of a new inoculation drive against smallpox. Problems arose when patients' clothing, ragged as it invariably was, was often stolen. George passed a general order requiring a patient's belongings to be itemized so they could be returned to him upon release from the hospital.

Martha arrived at a particularly low point, when George's army was on the verge of dissolving or dying before his eyes. The commissary general, Thomas Mifflin, had quit in November after an abortive attempt along with several other officers, including General Charles Lee, to have George replaced as commander in chief. George did not appoint another commissary general until March, when General Nathanael Greene temporarily took over the job. George held the Continental army together by the sheer force of his will and personal charisma, while Congress dithered over supplies and reinforcements, but there was still a high desertion rate, and many of those who remained were too weak and hungry and ill to be fit for active service.

George's one hope was that France, still smarting from defeat at British hands in the French and Indian Wars years earlier, could be persuaded to join the Americans against their common enemy. In fact, French agents had been in the colonies since the outbreak of the Revolution and had been supplying arms to the Americans. A nineteen-year-old French aristocrat, the Marquis de Lafayette, had turned up the previous summer to offer George his services and been commissioned a major general by a reluctant Congress, which had seen a great many unqualified soldiers of fortune come and go from Europe. The difference was that Lafayette was smitten with the concept of American "liberty" and worshiped George as a hero. He was also immensely rich and well connected at the French court and was doing his utmost to persuade the French government to join the American war in an active capacity, with the strength of the French navy.

Despite the terrible condition of his troops, there was nothing George could do but hold on, agonizing over the privations they were suffering, aware that in Philadelphia and elsewhere, the army's suppliers were profiteering at his men's expense. Shortly after Martha's arrival George sent a desperate plea to Governor Clinton about conditions at Valley Forge, setting out

> the present dreadful situation of the army for want of provisions, and the miserable, for, to form a just idea, it were necessary to be on the spot. For some days past, there has been little less, than a famine in camp. A part of the army has been a week without any kind of flesh, and the rest for three or four days. Naked and starving as they are, we cannot enough admire the incomparable patience and fidelity of the soldiery, that they have not been ere this excited by their sufferings, to a general mutiny or dispersion. Strong symptoms, however, of discontent have appeared in particular instances.[3]

By now half-naked soldiers were muttering audibly enough for the officers to hear "no bread, no soldier."

It is not surprising that the men cheered Martha into camp. With her supplies from Mount Vernon she was a one-woman relief agency. She found George harassed and anxious, but if she was worried, she gave no sign. She was conducted to the commander in chief's headquarters at an old stone house, known as the Potts House, where Martha and George had the use of two small rooms. The house also served as George's military headquarters and was extremely crowded, with staff officers, secretaries, papers, maps, slaves, and military paraphernalia everywhere. George soon ordered a log cabin extension built. Martha cheerfully adapted herself to this cramped accommodation. A letter reportedly written by Martha and possibly copied in the hand of another person—judging by the spelling and punctuation—about this time describes their lodging:

> The general's head-quarters have been made more tolerable by the addition of a log cabin to the house, built to dine in. The apartment for business is only about sixteen feet square, and has a large fireplace. The house is built of stone. The walls are very thick, and below a deep east window out of which the general can look upon the encampment, he had a box made . . . with a blind trap door at the top, where he keeps his valuable papers.[4]

In fact, compared to the huts occupied by the soldiers, described by Lafayette as "no gayer than dungeons," the Washingtons were living in luxurious comfort. Martha soon threw her energies into improving conditions as far as she could. She organized a sewing circle with the other wives in camp, who this year included Kitty Greene as well as Lucy Knox, Mrs. Clement Biddle, and Lady Kitty Stirling. The Knoxes were billeted in one of the few stone houses in the area, just outside camp, and Kitty and Nathanael Greene were in a tiny house three miles from camp. Both women had left their children at home.

A Mrs. Westlake, who was also at Valley Forge, recalled:

> I never in my life knew a woman so busy from early morning until late at night as was Lady Washington, providing comforts for the sick soldiers. Every day, excepting Sunday, the wives of the officers in camp, and sometimes other women, were invited to Mr. Potts' [house] to assist her in knitting socks, patching garments and making shirts for the poor soldiers when material could be procured. Every few days she might be seen, with basket in hand, and with a single attendant, going among the huts seeking the keenest and most needy sufferers, and giving all the comforts to them in her power.[5]

Martha had also had some unexpected help. Mrs. Elizabeth Ellet recounted a story about one person who was Martha's "attendant" on some of these errands of mercy:

> One day a seven-year-old black girl named Mary MacDonald appeared at headquarters and gravely announced to Mrs. Washington that she had come to join the army. Mrs. Washington took her to the general, who smiled and patted her on the head. Mary became a fixture at the log cabin annex. She would often go along with lady Washington on her daily visits to the soldiers' hospital and huts, proudly carrying the basket holding the bowl of soup or some delicacy.[6]

In the huts Martha found naked men lying on bare boards, shivering and huddled under ragged blankets. The troops were so short of anything to wear that the men of one hut would pool all their flimsy, tattered items of clothing for any one of their group standing sentry duty or sent on a foraging expedition. On sentry duty the shoeless men stood on their hats to keep their feet warm and out of the snow. There were many amputations for frozen limbs and, of course, no anesthetics. The men were extremely grateful for the stockings and shirts delivered by Lady Washington.

Years later, after the Revolution, a woman who had been present in camp as a young girl recalled accompanying Martha on her excursions as another of her attendants and remembered that it was Martha's habit to seek out the neediest sufferers to help and comfort. Sometimes there was nothing more she could do than pray with men who were dying, and this woman recalled a particular instance of Martha doing her utmost to comfort a dying sergeant and his frightened young wife.[7]

As in previous camps, Martha initiated a social life in the evenings with as much formality and gaiety as camp conditions allowed. On George's birthday, February 22, she found some musicians and organized a concert. There was no place for balls in Valley Forge, but there were "dinners" in the log cabin and other social gatherings. The dinners normally featured a small piece of salt fish, a potato or two, and spring water. Otherwise the officers and their wives were invited to headquarters for conversation, a cup of ersatz coffee, and singing. It was the best Martha could do, and those present recalled, "Everyone who *could* sing, *sang!*" The other ladies also pitched in. Lucy Knox, whose ebullience Martha privately found rather trying, was loud and good-humored and lively, while Kitty Greene was decorative, a terrible flirt, and fond of any kind of social occasion. The other women gamely joined in the pretense that the log cabin extension where they spent their days sewing became an elegant drawing room with the lighting of a candle.

It was extremely fortunate for the American army that General Howe was not disposed to pursue them the little distance to Valley Forge, because the Americans were in no condition to put up an effective resistance to any attack. With all the military circumstances favoring the British, it is extraordinary they did not attack. However, General Howe had been temporarily distracted to the point of ignoring his military advantage. He was having a splendid time that winter in Philadelphia and preferred to spend the cold months there enjoying the company of his mistress, Mrs. Loring, the wife of one of his officers. It has been said no patriot could have done more than Mrs. Loring to prevent a British attack when the Continental army was at its most vulnerable and that America has yet to acknowledge her invaluable contribution to the cause.

Thanks to the British occupation, Philadelphia was a merry, fashionable place that winter, full of wealthy Tories who found the dashing British officers a welcome addition to the social whirl. Speculators were making a handsome profit due to inflation of the Continental currencies, and Philadelphia presented a wealthy and gay appearance. There could not have been a greater contrast than that between the conditions of the British army in Philadelphia and those of the Americans in Valley Forge. One Philadelphia belle, a Miss Franks, wrote giddily to her dear friend Mrs. William Pace:

> You can have no idea of the life of continued amusement I live in. I can scarce have a moment to myself. I have stole this while everybody is retired to dress for dinner. I am but just come back from Mr. Blacks' hands and most elegantly am I dressed for a ball this evening at Smith's where we have one every Thursday. . . . I spent Tuesday evening at Sir Wm Howes where we had a concert and a Dance . . . the Dress is more ridiculous and pretty than anything I ever saw— great quantity of different colored feathers on the head at a time besides a thousand other things.[8]

In early March, with the situation in camp more desperate than ever, Martha wrote—or had drafted for her—a letter to her friend Mercy Otis Warren in Massachusetts. It is interesting because of its timing and content. A chatty letter, it contained the usual niceties, compliments to Mercy and her husband, comments on health, news that a man they both knew had accidentally drowned crossing the Potomac. Martha wrote that the general was very well and that her daughter-in-law Eleanor, whom Mercy had met at Cambridge, had given birth to a second daughter. Finally, in passing, she casually described the situation at Valley Forge: "The General is camped in what is called the great Valley on the banks of the Schuylkill officers and men are cheifly in which they say is tolarable comfortable; the army is as healthy as can well be expected in general—the General's apartment is very small he has had a log cabben built to dine in which has made our quarter much more tolarable than they were at first."[9]

Considered in context Martha's letter was probably more than just a friendly note, and probably part of the American propaganda effort. Lafayette and a number of American envoys had been lobbying hard in Paris to persuade Louis XVI to support the colonies against France's old enemy England. By early March George and his staff were desperate to buy time, anxiously awaiting news from France. Military advantage favored the well-equipped, well-supplied British a few miles away, hence he needed to hold them off a bit longer, concealing the desperate conditions at Valley Forge. Martha's letter does not allude to any of the horrors that were part and parcel of daily life in camp and must have been intended to camouflage American vulnerability.

American hopes were resting on French intervention, but there is a story that there was valuable help from another quarter at some stage during the Valley Forge winter—that the Oneida Indians supplied food to the American troops at a critical point. A recent account records a story kept alive for two centuries by the Oneida tradition of oral history:

> During the long winter at Valley Forge, when one-quarter of the soldiers died from lack of nourishment and exposure to the harsh winter elements, the Oneidas walked hundreds of miles south to Valley Forge to come to the soldiers' aid. They carried with them 600 bushels of corn and other goods to assist George Washington. When the Indians arrived, the soldiers, cavernous [*sic*] at the sight of food, attempted to eat the corn raw. However, doing so would have swelled the dry corn in their stomachs, and they would have died from their ignorance. Instead, the Oneidas held the soldiers back, cooked the corn, and showed the soldiers how to eat it gradually, so it would not harm their systems. One Oneida woman, Polly Cooper, stayed behind after the goods were delivered to help care for the soldiers and teach them how to cook and prepare the corn.[10]

Polly Cooper refused payment, which was offered to her when the war ended, but years later Martha, by then the wife of the president, invited Polly to Philadelphia, which was then the capital, and made her a gift of a bonnet and a fine shawl.

Martha was not so occupied with the concerns in camp that she failed to miss her family. Jacky wrote from Mount Airey in April that the new baby, Patty, had been inoculated three times, but it had failed to "take" and he and Eleanor were anxious about trying it a fourth time. Jacky was proving to be a surprisingly fond father, writing that Patty was a "dear Child . . . the finest Girl I ever saw and the most Good natured Quiet little Creature in the World." Jacky had obviously hoped Patty would be a boy, because Martha had teased him about his "Disappointment." Jacky now wrote, "I could not have loved It better if It had been a Boy." As for Betsy, Jacky bragged, "ms Bet has grown very much and is very saucy and entertaining. She can say any Word but Washington."

Jacky was elected delegate for Fairfax County to the Virginia General Assembly that spring. Sometime in 1778 he also bought Abingdon, an estate with a house and nine hundred acres of land on the west bank of the Potomac. He sold some of his Custis property to fund the purchase. Jacky also employed the brother of Millie Posey, his sister Patcy's old friend, to be an overseer on his Custis property in New Kent. This was a young man named John Price Posey. John Price Posey was the ne'r-do-well younger brother of Thomas Posey, the one believed by some to have been George's natural son, and currently an officer in the Continental army.

The Washingtons also caught up with news of the Fairfaxes. Their old neighbor, George William's younger half brother Bryan Fairfax, came to visit them at Valley Forge. Bryan Fairfax had grown serious with age and was no longer the feckless irresponsible boy Martha and George had known. Bryan had taken holy orders and was now the Reverend Bryan Fairfax. Married to Sally Cary Fairfax's younger sister Elizabeth he lived at his plantation, Mount Eagle in Fairfax County. He had also had at least one child, a boy named Toulston Fairfax, by one of his slaves, an experience that was causing him to question the system of slavery. Though Bryan had mild Tory sentiments, he was a pacifist and, on the whole, approved of the break from the Crown. Evidently neither George nor anyone else in camp regarded his presence as dangerous. Irascible old Lord Fairfax, back at Greenway Court, retained his strong loyalty to the monarchy throughout the war but was never troubled by the rebel forces, probably through the exercise of George's influence. Though Belvoir and most of the other Fairfax property in Virginia were confiscated, Greenway Court was not.

Like many American Loyalists who had fled to England at the outbreak of the Revolution, George William and Sally had felt the loss of the income from their Virginia property and were living in much reduced circumstances near Bath. Though they were staunch Tories, the Fairfaxes and George corresponded throughout the war, a state of affairs that attracted surveillance from the British authorities, who intercepted George's letters in England and suspected George William of being a spy.

Jacky wrote in April that Bryan Fairfax's teenage daughter, the namesake of her aunt Sally Cary Fairfax, had died. Jacky wrote often with news of his family, and as he had come of age, he had begun to consult George about his plans for managing his estate and property. Busy as he was, George went to considerable lengths to write and explain to his stepson the basic laws of economics, pointing out the drawbacks of selling property when the value of Virginia currency was diminishing.

As spring advanced, conditions improved slowly in camp. With warmer weather Congress was able to send supplies, and there was a run of shad in the river, on which the camp feasted for days. Gradually George was able to persuade local farms to supply three markets in the vicinity with pork, poultry, and some milk, food badly needed for the men who were hospitalized following their smallpox inoculations. This provided a source of food, but at a price, and soon soldiers' wives were hiring themselves for whatever jobs were available, such as cooking or washing, and Martha helped these women out when she could.

The thaw was a mixed blessing because as the once snowbound and frozen camp turned muddy, it was soon almost awash in sewage. It was said the ladies had to both mind their step and avert their eyes.

That spring several plays were performed for the entertainment of the whole army. The more puritanical members of Congress were outraged, when they learned of it, regarding plays as a breach of morals and religion. Congress passed an ill-advised resolution threatening to dismiss any soldier attending a performance.

In May came the joyful news that the French government had recognized the independence of the American colonies. Impressed by the American defeat of General Burgoyne at Saratoga the preceding October, France now formally declared war on England. The Americans and French signed a treaty, and at last, George had a powerful ally. He announced a day of celebration.

The whole camp turned out in the best outfits they could muster. Martha, Lucy Knox, Kitty Greene, and Lady Stirling presided as the army paraded and drilled as smartly as possible. There were games, races, and a meal of bread, beef, pork, beans, rum, and cider, with toasts, and cries of "Long live the king of France!"

In Philadelphia the British were also in a festive mood, preparing to leave Philadelphia in a display of pomp and pageantry. A young major named John Andre had collected over three thousand pounds from his fellow officers. The money was used to stage a medieval-style extravaganza called the Mischianza. There was a huge ball, with festively decorated barges on the Delaware River, costumes, jousts, and an elaborate dinner in a huge tent hung with mirrors. Public opinion in Philadelphia was divided over the wisdom of blatantly consorting with the enemy—as a great many Philadelphi-

ans had been only too happy to do on a social basis through the winter—
and a longing not to miss such a stunning event.

As Martha left Valley Forge in May, General Howe left Philadelphia,
and his army marched toward New York. The Continental army followed,
and the center of operations shifted to New York.

When she finally arrived home at Mount Vernon, Martha had some
hopes that George might be able to join her soon. Even if France's involvement did not bring the war to the speedy end they hoped for, it was still possible George might be able to come home for a visit. Exhausted herself by
the hardships of the preceding months, Martha knew the experience was
taking its toll on George. At the same time she was distressed that she was
no closer to bringing her motherless twelve-year-old niece Fanny Bassett to
Mount Vernon to live—as she had promised Anna Maria she would. Burwell Bassett, already a middle-aged widower when Anna Maria married him,
had not remarried. He could manage Fanny's two older brothers, but a
twelve-year-old girl needed a mother figure. Until Martha could take her,
Fanny would have to be farmed out to various relatives.

By the fall of 1778 it was clear that Eleanor Custis was pregnant again.
For Martha, who knew how ill Eleanor became with each pregnancy and
how poorly she was after each birth, and who would never willingly have
violated a promise to her dead sister, it required a painful ordering of pri-
orities. The prospect that Eleanor might die was a real one, and one that
would inevitably leave Martha with Eleanor and Jacky's children to bring
up, as Eleanor's mother at Mount Airey was in no position to cope with two,
and possibly three, young children.

But that wasn't the only consideration for Martha. At Valley Forge, it
had become clear that Martha had an important complementary role to play
beside George. Their combined effectiveness was tied up with image, a concept they both understood. If George was a heroic, larger-than-life commanding officer, Martha by his side was every soldier's mother, wife, or sister,
a sturdy patriotic figure in a homespun dress working tirelessly to clothe,
feed, nurse, and cheer both the officers and men. As Lady Washington, she
was not just popular, she was indispensable. Martha had to make a painful
choice, but in view of George's need to have her by his side, Fanny would
have to wait, and all she could do for Eleanor was give her advice and pray
for her well-being from a distance.

On November 2 she was still at Mount Vernon awaiting a summons
from George and the military escort he always sent for her. Prepared to set
off at any moment, she wrote to her brother Bartholomew at Pamocra in
New Kent, a letter alluding to the fact that she was torn between the responsibility she felt to George, her worries about her mother's declining health,
yet another concern weighing on her mind, and her need to travel at once
if she was to avoid the bad weather and a repeat of last year's experience

when her carriage had been halted by snowdrifts. She acknowledged that she was "very uneasy at this time—I have some reason to expect I shall take another trip to the northward." All she could do for her relatives in New Kent was to send shoes, probably bought in the shops in Philadelphia, to her mother and Bartholomew's daughter Patty, and her love to everyone.

Sometime after this Martha received a letter from George and soon after set off to meet him in Philadelphia. A journey from Mount Vernon to Philadelphia normally took five days, but on this occasion it took much longer. George, at his winter headquarters in Middlebrook, New Jersey, wrote to Jacky on December 17 that he had just learned of Martha's arrival in Philadelphia. The trip may have been slower on this occasion because of bad roads, bad weather, or the fact that Martha's coach was in poor shape.

The Washingtons stayed in Philadelphia about seven weeks. Compared to the previous winter, the general mood was optimistic. George had to meet with Congress, and the Washingtons were entertained by Philadelphia society, many of whom had enjoyed socializing with the British officers the previous winter. They attended dinners, and a ball was held in their honor at Trinity Tavern. At the end of January they set out for Middlebrook.

CHAPTER 14

Middlebrook and Morristown

The winter camp at Middlebrook in 1779 was a far less grueling experience than Valley Forge had been. George had chosen the Wallace House as his headquarters. It was one of the largest houses in New Jersey at the time, built by a wealthy Philadelphia merchant named John Wallace, who thought his chances of remaining neutral in the war would be improved by moving out of Philadelphia. In 1776 he had settled his wife, his elderly mother, and his three sons there, only to find the house requisitioned by the Continental forces in December 1778. The house had a dozen rooms spread over two wings, with a cellar and an attic, with slave quarters above the kitchen.

The winter was comparatively mild; the men were not in the desperate straits of the previous winter. There were no dead horses rotting and relatively little illness, and the camp was reasonably well supplied. Nathanael Greene was still in charge of the commissary, albeit reluctantly.

For Martha life at the Middlebrook camp began on a festive note. Shortly after the Washingtons arrived in February, a dinner and a ball were held to celebrate the anniversary of the treaty with France. Though news had not reached Valley Forge until May, the treaty had actually been concluded in Paris in February 1778.

General Henry Knox and his artillery company hosted the event. Martha had not danced in public for years, and George opened the ball with Lucy Knox. Nathanael Greene later noted, "Mrs. Knox is fatter than ever." George then danced for three hours without stopping with Kitty Greene, who adored dancing and was ready to dance all night, but even she, after three hours, finally declared herself breathless and had to sit down.

Both Kitty Greene and Lucy Knox had brought their young children with them to camp this year, instead of leaving them with relatives. They did not have to travel as far as Martha from their homes in Rhode Island and Massachusetts, and they were glad not to have to choose between supporting their husbands in camp and staying with the children at home, when they knew how important they were at headquarters. This year the fact that their husbands agreed to the children coming reflected a new mood of optimism in 1779, that possibly hostilities were nearing an end.

There was good reason to celebrate the alliance with France. The French dimension had set the war with England on a new footing; in addition to bolstering colonial forces, hostilities with France in the American colonies would inevitably extend into French/British rivalry in the West Indies. Since Burgoyne's defeat at Saratoga in October 1777, the English had known the American victory might be sufficient to persuade the French to enter the war. In the following months, anticipating that French involvement in the war was imminent, and reluctant to escalate an already costly foreign engagement to fight the French in the Caribbean as well as the Americans in the colonies, the British government had weighed the alternatives of an expanded military engagement against a policy of conciliation. Lord North, the prime minister, had drawn up a conciliatory plan, under which England would recognize the American Congress, give the Americans representation in Parliament, withdraw the Townshend Acts, and relinquish the right to tax the colonies. In exchange, all American property confiscated from Loyalists would be restored, all military commands not held from the king abandoned, all American trade be regulated by England, and the Declaration of Independence withdrawn.[1]

The olive branch, such as it was, had been refused by Congress in the summer of 1778. In England naval observers reported that the French fleet was sailing west, well provisioned, presumably for America by way of the West Indies. England saw no choice but to escalate the conflict and responded by dispatching more ships to increase its naval presence in the colonies as well as more land troops. Throughout the summer and autumn of 1778 the British and French had skirmished up and down the coast of New England and engaged in the West Indies. By the end of 1778, the focus of British attention had shifted to the South, and they landed troops along the coast of Georgia and the Carolinas. On December 29, 1778, the British had taken Savannah. In the South the British counted on support from two sources: a significant number of Tories and slaves seduced by British promises of freedom. The shift to the South removed some of the immediate pressure from George but raised fresh concerns about a British advance into Virginia from North Carolina.

In Middlebrook, where things were relatively quiet from a military perspective, Martha followed developments in the South and worried about Jacky and Eleanor. The baby was due anytime, and their silence was worrying. She wrote anxiously:

My Dear Children: Middlebrook March the 19th 1778 [misdated]

Not having received any letters from you the last two posts, I have only to tell you that the general and myself are well. All is quiet in this quarter. It is from southward that we expect to hear news. We are very anxious to know how affairs are going in that quarter. . . .

I hear so seldom from you, that I don't know where you are, or whether you intend to come to Alexandria [where Jacky had bought Abingdon] to live this spring, or when. The last letter from Nelly she says both the children have been very ill: they were she hoped getting better. If you do not write to me I will not write to you again till I get letters from you. Let me know how all friends below are; they have forgot to write to me I believe.

Remember me to all inquiring friends. Give the dear little girls a kiss for me, and tell Bett I have got a pretty new doll for her, but I don't know how to send it to her. The general joins me in love to you both, and begs to be remembered to all our friends that inquire after us. I am, with sincere love,

Your truly affectionate mother,
Martha Washington[2]

Jacky and Eleanor had in fact moved to Abingdon, and on March 21 their third daughter was born and named after her mother, Eleanor Parke Custis. This child would be called by her mother's nickname "Nelly." Eleanor was in such frail health for months after the birth that she was unable to look after the baby properly, and Jacky worried about them both.

That spring Martha's presence was less needed in camp than it had been the previous year, and though she was supportive of George, she may have felt she would have been more useful in Virginia. At Middlebrook Martha's role was mainly social, as many visitors came to the camp, including on one occasion a French minister. Important guests were treated to a review of the troops. By this time Martha had her own regiment, Lady Washington's Dragoons, with uniforms in white with blue trim. They were commanded by Lieutenant Colonel Baylor.

A letter dated May 15, 1779, purported to be from Martha to Eleanor is quoted in Benson Lossing's book *Mary and Martha*, describing one of these reviews in honor of some Delaware Chiefs. The letter does not sound like anything else Martha wrote, and if she did write it, it was probably heavily edited by someone else. It is included here to give the flavor of these reviews:

Yesterday I saw the funniest, at the same time most ridiculous review of the troops I ever heard of. Nearly all the troops were drawn up in order, and Mrs. Knox, Mrs. Greene, and myself saw the whole performance from a carriage. The General and Billy, [Will Lee, George's body servant now that Bishop was too old to accompany him] followed by a lot of mounted savages, rode along the line. Some of the Indians were fairly fine looking, but most of them appeared worse than Falstaff's gang. And such horses and trappings! The General says it was done to keep the Indians friendly towards us. They appeared like cutthroats all.[3]

At the end of May Martha went home. Finding Eleanor still ill and unable to feed Nelly, she took Nelly back to Mount Vernon and gave her to a wet nurse named Mrs. Anderson, a young Englishwoman who had lost her own child. While Martha and Lund Washington's wife, Elizabeth, looked after Nelly at Mount Vernon and Eleanor slowly recovered, it became clear to the Washingtons that Jacky was making some serious errors of judgment in managing his estate. It was to avoid such mistakes in the management of his property that George had fought an uphill battle to ensure that Jacky had a sound education and why George had steadily responded to Jacky's letters to him in camp. No matter how pressured he was, George had always taken time to give considered advice about the land and business transactions Jacky proposed. None of his efforts had made any difference, and having sought George's advice, Jacky then either failed to understand it or was too lazy to follow it.

In August George wrote to Jacky about the sale of some of the Custis property to buy Abingdon:

West Point, August 24, 1779

Dear Sir:

In answer to your letter of the 11th inst. I candidly acknowledge I am a loss what advice to give you, with precision, respecting the sale of your estate upon the eastern shore; but upon the whole, in the present uncertain state of things, should, were I in your place, postpone the measure a while longer.

Your own observation must have convinced you of the rapid depreciation of the paper currency in the past ten months, and this it will continue to do. . . . You must be sensible that it is not forty thousand pounds, nor four hundred thousand, nor any nominal sum whatever, that would give you the value of the land in Northampton. Instance your unfortunate sale of the York estate to Colonel Braxton for twenty thousand pounds, which, I suppose, would now fetch one hundred thousand pounds.[4]

The letter continued to point out the disadvantages of selling for currency at a time of runaway inflation in Virginia. Reading between the lines, we can guess that Jacky's feckless approach to his inheritance must have had George gnashing his teeth, but George made a valiant effort to give reasoned advice in the hopes it might be taken.

George continued in a hopeful vein about military affairs to Jacky, "Our affairs, at present, put on a pleasing aspect, especially in Europe and the

West Indies, and bids us, I think, hope for the certain and final accomplishment of our independence."[5]

By fall Eleanor was better, and Martha took Nelly back to Abingdon. Martha was consulted about Jacky's plans to rent some of her dower property in King William County, and though legally George controlled the dower lands during Martha's lifetime, Martha was shrewd enough not to agree to a bad bargain. George would not override Martha's objection in any case. He had already written Jacky that "it is not my wish to let it, for any longer term than your mamma inclines to, and at no rate, for her life, unless it is perfectly agreeable to her."

Jacky wrote to George in October:

Honored Sir   Mount Vernon, October 26, 1779
     I believe I shall be obliged to postpone settling the rent of your plantation in King William until that wished for period [a proposed visit to Washington's camp], as mamma seems to have some objections to renting it during her life, and it would not answer my purpose to rent it on any other terms. When I first wrote to you, I thought she had no objections; but since I have received your letter, I have talked to her on that subject, and it does not appear to be perfectly agreeable to her to part with the place entirely during life.[6]

Underlining these letters is a sense that Jacky was either alarmingly naïve in matters of business or that he was somehow trying to take advantage of Martha. Either possibility is borne out by a letter from George in November. It shows George exasperated, either by further evidence of stupidity on Jacky's part or an actual attempt by Jacky to cheat him. Two years previously Jacky had agreed to rent some of George's land, slaves, and cattle, with the rent fixed on a valuation of the whole. Jacky had now had the cattle culled, removing the healthy ones and leaving the rent to be fixed on the basis of the worthless remainder.[7]

If Jacky continued to deal so ineptly with his property, the Custis estate would soon dwindle into nothing. But Jacky and Eleanor had to be left to manage as best they could because George and Martha's hopes that the hostilities were nearly at an end were disappointed. In November Martha was preparing to go north once again, this time back to Morristown.

George had gone into winter quarters on December 1, and Martha set off at the end of November or early December. By the time she reached Philadelphia, bad weather stopped her from going any further until after Christmas. It was an ill omen. The winter of 1780 was one of the coldest ever, and conditions in the army had deteriorated to the point that the men looked back to Valley Forge with longing. Meanwhile they slept in the open on the ground, feet first to their campfires. Their clothes were worn out, and Nathanael Greene was finding it difficult to obtain food. George wrote that the men "ate every kind of food but hay." The starving tattered men cheered as they had before when Martha's carriage and entourage rolled in to camp at the end of December.

A few days later another snowstorm piled drifts four feet high. The risk of bad weather had not been enough to deter a heavily pregnant Kitty Greene from making her way to camp at the end of November. One account of Kitty had her battling her way through a blizzard. Kitty gave birth to her son Nat in Morristown on January 31.

George had established his headquarters in the home of the widow of a doctor named John Ford. Patriotic Mrs. Ford, recently bereaved, had a large house and insisted on squeezing herself, her children, and her servants into two rooms to leave the rest at George's disposal for offices and bedrooms. Living there were George, Martha, and a number of military aides, plus eighteen slaves from Mount Vernon who lived in two log cabin annexes George had built to serve as a kitchen and an extra office.

There is no record of which slaves Martha took north each winter, but it was probably most of the house slaves, unless a slave was too old and feeble to make the trip. Will Lee accompanied George as his valet throughout the Revolution, because Bishop had grown too old for the rigors of military life. George had made him an overseer on one of his farms, and late in life, Bishop had married. Though George had a housekeeper, Martha would have needed her personal maid; there was a great deal of domestic work to be done at headquarters, where Martha entertained and based her war relief efforts—cooking, washing, mending, carrying messages, looking after horses, and sewing. Another reason for bringing the slaves was to keep them from running away to the British.

Though there is no indication in George's surviving papers or those few papers Martha left, Martha's half sister Ann Dandridge may also have accompanied Martha on these trips. Though a free "sister of color," she was probably perceived as a slave. Martha and George and anyone else aware of the family relationship would have been likely to conceal it behind the usual veil of silence.

While Ann's whereabouts as a young woman can only be a matter of speculation, the possibilities seem narrow. With Martha prepared to offer her a home at Mount Vernon, she was unlikely to have gone to live in New Kent with any of her other half siblings such as Anna Maria Bassett at Eltham or Bartholomew Dandridge at Pamocra. It is possible she lived by herself in Alexandria or elsewhere, perhaps working as a seamstress. Martha would certainly have taught her younger sister to sew. However, Martha had taken responsibility for Ann and was unlikely to have parted with her. It was risky for a young woman to live alone, particularly if she was obviously of mixed blood, because even if legally free, she was at risk of being captured as a slave and sold south. Free blacks or free men and women of mixed race occupied a highly precarious position, and Martha was always protective of young girls. Ann did not vanish into thin air, because there is concrete evidence of her presence at Mount Vernon in 1780.

There is a record that in 1780 Ann gave birth to a son named William at Mount Vernon. The only mention of that child's father described him as a "white man from a prominent family," but his identity was never disclosed. Ann may have remained at Mount Vernon in Martha's absence to keep an eye on the house during that period and, in 1779, had a liaison with a prominent man in the neighborhood. That raises the question of which men might have been in the Mount Vernon neighborhood at a time when many, though not all, white men from prominent families were away fighting. Alternatively, if she had gone north, her baby's father may have been one of George's officers or another prominent man in camp.

While there is no proof of who the baby's father may have been, Ann eventually married a slave named Costin—of whom no record exists at Mount Vernon—and gave her son the name William Costin. William, of course, was legally free like his mother. Although three-quarters white, William Costin seems to have been obviously of mixed race, because in later years when he lived in Washington D.C., he and other members of his family were prominent in the city's Free Black community as teachers and church leaders. This suggests the possibility that although Ann herself had a white father and a half-African, half–Native American mother she may have been sufficiently dark to blend in with the slaves, especially those Mount Vernon house slaves who were also of mixed race. If Ann was indeed present among the slaves or as a companion, maid, seamstress, or servant, in camp in Morristown or elsewhere, her relationship to Martha was kept quiet, and for observers she simply faded into the background.

The Ford house was in Morristown proper, but the main camp and body of troops were several miles away. In fact, there were British outposts closer to George's headquarters than the main American camp was. A company of Life Guards—an elite handpicked body of men, all over six feet tall—was quartered in log huts in a nearby meadow to protect headquarters.

With the British so close, the alarm was frequently sounded in the middle of the night to warn of a possible attack. On these occasions Martha and Mrs. Ford were awakened by members of the Life Guard rushing into their bedrooms and throwing open the windows as five men with muskets positioned themselves at each window of the house. The ladies would hastily pull the bedclothes over their heads for modesty and warmth against the icy wind.

The conditions at Morristown did not improve with the arrival of spring. Anxiety mounted about military developments in the South in Savannah and Charleston, and headquarters were in a state of permanent alert against an attack from British troops stationed there. Warmer weather caused the snowdrifts to melt and turned the ground into a sea of mud. The ever-worsening supply situation once again had the soldiers muttering "no bread, no soldier" loud enough for their officers to hear. George's troop strength was now at fewer than ten thousand men.

In April two foreign emissaries from France and Spain visited camp, the Marquis de la Luzerne and Don Juan de Mirailles. As it was vital to make a good impression on two important allies, there was a review of the troops in their honor, followed by a ball. De Mirailles's enjoyment of the festivities was cut short when he suddenly fell ill. Martha nursed him herself at Mrs. Ford's.

On April 30 George wrote the governor of Cuba to "communicate . . . the painful intelligence of the death of Don Juan de Mirailles. . . . This unfortunate event happened at my headquarters the day before yesterday and his remains were yesterday interred, with all the respect due to his character and merit. He did me the honor of a visit in company with the minister of France, and was seized the day of his arrival with a violent biliary complaint, which after nine days continuance, put a period to his life."[8]

This "biliary complaint" was possibly food poisoning, hepatitis, typhus, or any one of a number of diseases that festered in crowded, unsanitary camp conditions now made worse by the deep mud.

Throughout the dreary winter and spring Martha battled on, doing what she could in camp, sewing, and visiting the worst-off. She took up her usual pattern of inviting officers and their wives, if in camp, to dinner at headquarters. There was a little light relief in Kitty's baby, and the fact that another young woman she had grown fond of, Betsy Schuyler, daughter of General Schuyler, was staying with her aunt at Morristown. To the amusement of everyone who knew him, Betsy was being courted by an obviously smitten Alexander Hamilton. Although there was no possibility of shopping to buy toiletries or anything pretty, it was Martha's habit, and a general custom among ladies, to give each other small presents to lift the spirits. For instance, when Betsy presented Martha with a pair of cuffs, probably "worked" or trimmed by Betsy, in exchange Martha sent her "some very nice powder."

On May 10 Lafayette arrived in camp, newly returned from France with news: his wife had given birth to a son they had named George Washington Lafayette and a fleet and six thousand men were on their way from France under General Rochambeau.

Even so, the military situation was getting worse. By May two regiments were near mutiny at the lack of provisions. On May 31 George received a blow in the form of news that General Cornwallis had taken Charleston. It seemed certain to be the beginning of the end if a British drive up toward Virginia, which was bound to follow, could not be stopped. George's present resources from Congress were inadequate to accomplish that.

Martha returned to Mount Vernon in June. In England, Horace Walpole said, "We look on America as already at our feet."

Martha did not reach home for weeks, and when she did she was too drained of energy to make a long-anticipated trip to New Kent. She also learned that Eleanor Custis was again pregnant and ill. The weariness comes through in a letter Martha wrote to Burwell Bassett:

> Dear Sir   Mount Vernon July the 18th 1780
>   I left the General about the Middle of June—the last I heard from him he was going up the North river—I got home on Fryday and find myself so much fatigue with my ride that I shall not be able to come down to see you this summer and must request you to bring Fanny up— . . . I am dr Sir your affectionate friend & hmble sert
>
>   Martha Washington[9]

Throughout the colonies women had been drawn into the war effort over the years, making clothing, sending blankets, operating feeding stations, and contributing pewter articles to be melted down for bullets. When Martha was recovered from her trip, she threw herself once more into organizing clothes for the troops. This time her efforts went beyond cloth production at Mount Vernon. She launched a wider clothing drive among her acquaintances in Virginia and Philadelphia, as well as a relief fund for the poorest soldiers. Many women sold their jewelry to contribute. The wealthy women of Philadelphia not only subscribed to the relief fund themselves but also collected money to buy linen, which they then made into shirts. Martha contributed too. George's account book notes an entry dated October 10, 1780: "Mrs Washington's bounty to the soldiers, £6000." Lafayette made a generous donation in the name of his wife, and another French noblewoman, the Countess de Luzerne, also contributed.

In aristocratic French circles it had become not only patriotic to support the Americans against France's traditional enemy, England, but it was fashionable as well. The American emissary Benjamin Franklin, in artfully scruffy clothing and a little fur hat, was the darling of Paris. Marie Antoinette dispatched a "valuable present" to Martha as a token of her admiration for Martha's contribution to the war. What the "valuable present" was remains a mystery, because the British sank the French ship believed to be carrying it in New York harbor.

At Mount Vernon Martha prepared for an early departure in November, probably with misgivings. At Abingdon in 1780 Eleanor had given birth to twin girls who died and, months later, was now pregnant—and ill—again. Martha's granddaughters Betsy, Patty, and Nelly were well, but Jacky was spoiling Betsy. Betsy was a willful, determined child, and because Eleanor was continuously either pregnant or ill, Betsy's behavior showed she was missing a mother's guidance. In later life Betsy, or Eliza as she became known in adulthood, left this account of raucous goings on at Abingdon when she was a small child:

> My father's house [Abingdon] was the resort of the Alexandrians, & all gen-teel strangers found a welcome at his board, among the number was an English Physician—whose name was Rumney—he play'd well on the flute, & took delight in making me sing—I soon attain'd excellence in this science, & was always lifted on the Dinner table to sing for my father's guests—I had a good memory, & learnt many songs—my father & Dr R taught me many very improper ones, & I can now rememr standing on the table when not more than 3 or 4 years old, singing songs which I did not understand—while my father & other gentlemen were often rolling in their chairs with laughter—& I was animated to exert myself to give him delight—the servants in the pas-sage would join the mirth, & I holding my head erect, would strut about the table, to receive the praises of the company, my mother remonstrated in vain—& her husband always said his little Bet could not be injured by what she did not understand that he had no Boy & she must make fun for him, until he had—he would then kiss her to make his Peace, & giving me a Nod my voice which was uncommon powerful for my age resounded through the rooms, & my Mother who could not help laughing, had to retire and leave me to the gentlemen, where my father's caresses made me think well of myself . . . all who saw me then know I had an uncommonly fine voice for so young a child.[10]

Martha was too great a believer in propriety and good manners to have been amused by the idea of her granddaughter singing bawdy songs at the top of her voice to a table full of drunk men. This passage is also revealing about Jacky's less pleasant side in amusing his guests at the expense of his daugh-ter. It also hints at the pressure there may have been on Eleanor to produce a son. Had there not been a war, Martha would have nursed Eleanor, taken Betsy and Patty in hand, and made a home for Fanny Bassett. But instead of looking after the girls, she faced another tiring trip north and what prom-ised to be a grueling winter in camp with George. In November Martha left for New Windsor, New York, in the teeth of more bad news. George had suffered a recent blow from the defection of one of his most trusted gener-als, Benedict Arnold, to the British. Bad as that setback was, there were omi-nous reports that that the British were firmly entrenched in South Carolina and encroaching into North Carolina.

CHAPTER 15

"We Look Upon the Americans
as Already at Our Feet"

M artha left for New Windsor, New York, in November, stopping in Philadelphia on the way to lend her support to the war relief work undertaken there by committees of women. By December Benjamin Franklin's daughter Sarah Franklin Bache, chairwoman of an association of patriotic Philadelphia ladies, wrote to George that the committee was sending 2,500 shirts they had made. A few weeks later a group of women in New Jersey sent 380 pairs of stockings they had knitted. By now George was depending heavily on such practical support from patriotic women.

In New Windsor the Washingtons settled into headquarters at a farmhouse that belonged to William Ellison. It was a terrible winter again, with both supplies and morale at an all-time low. The French, on whom such great hopes had been fixed two years earlier, were at Rhode Island unable to offer military support for the time being, insisting they would not be ready to fight the English for another year. One of the French generals, De Chastellux, who was at the New Windsor camp, met Martha at about this time. He liked her, describing her as looking younger than her years "about forty or five and forty, rather plump, but fresh and with an agreeable face."

Doing her best to cope with the general mood of pessimism in camp, Martha organized her usual relief effort and a women's sewing circle to sew, knit, mend, and patch. She also arranged the customary program of evening entertainments, inviting local people as well as George's officers and their wives to social gatherings at headquarters. To help George deal with the huge volume of military correspondence and copies that had to be kept, Martha occasionally also acted as George's secretary. Although he had a number of aides and secretaries at headquarters for this purpose, Martha's involvement, particularly with her spelling and punctuation, suggests his clerical staff was overstretched.

One of the Life Guards, Uzall Knapp, recalled a party given by the Washingtons at headquarters on Christmas Day 1780. Twenty people sat down to dinner, including two French officers and Governor Clinton and his family. Martha must have brought supplies of smoked, cured, and dried meats, such as beef, pork, and venison, and dried fruits with her from Virginia, because there was precious little to be had in the area around New Windsor. The headquarters cook produced a miraculous feast—platters of meat and vegetables, pies, puddings, apples, and hickory nuts. Will Lee, George's valet, waited at the table, and the Life Guards' band played in the hall. In the evening the village girls were invited to headquarters for a dance with the officers. Balls and dances in the military camps had to end early to ensure that the men were not too tired next day.

An anecdote has survived that one of the local girls invited to the festivities declined the Washingtons' hospitality, an almost unthinkable response among Patriots to an invitation from Commander in Chief and Lady Washington. Martha then discovered that the girl, possibly named Anne Brewster, was a dwarf, less than three feet tall. Conditioned by a lifetime of being an oddity, Anne Brewster believed she had been invited only to satisfy the curiosity of strangers at headquarters about the local dwarf.

The story went that on discovering the reason Anne had refused their invitation, Martha persuaded her to visit on another occasion and arranged for the other guests present to be small girls. The entire party, Martha included, took tea from doll-sized china, sitting on the floor. Whether or not the story is true, it reflects the popular perception of Martha's kind nature.

In late December Martha sent from camp to Philadelphia to have three miniatures painted by Charles Willson Peale to be set in bracelets. These were the portraits of Jacky and Patcy Custis done at Mount Vernon in 1772, and the miniature of Martha that Peale had painted in Philadelphia in the summer of 1776 while she waited until it was safe to return to Mount Vernon.

The request for the bracelets also included a mention of some diamonds, which Martha wrote, "may be set in a pin for the hair." These may have been a gift from George, although at a time when many ladies were selling their jewelry to donate money to the relief effort or to purchase material for shirts, to be ordering bracelets and hair ornaments strikes a frivolous chord. And given that homespun dresses were the order of the day for patriotic women, it is hard to imagine on what occasion Martha might have contemplated wearing diamond hairpins, as she would have done in happier days.

By the start of 1781, the immediate future looked increasingly bleak. At headquarters, the sewing circles, Christmas dinner, entertainments, and tea parties were the only light relief. Martha watched George and his officers grow increasingly strained as the situation grew worse and worse. Supplies of everything from food and medicine to clothing, blankets, and feed for the animals, never plentiful to begin with, had trickled to a halt. By now, even if there had been supplies available to buy, Continental currency was worthless. Foraging parties, which antagonized local inhabitants and left nothing in the ravaged countryside to eat, had stripped the surrounding New York countryside. And to add to the mounting tension, although it was foiled, there had been a plot to assassinate George.

The cold, hunger, sickness, lack of supplies, and a never-ending war were taking their toll on the morale of both officers and troops, while their farms and families, businesses, and trades suffered. Hostilities dragged wearily on as the focus of the war shifted to the South, where the Americans were suffering heavy casualties using hit-and-run guerrilla tactics, then retreating, pursued by the British. Neither side could be said to be winning. Along the coastal areas, the British had the advantage of naval support, numbers of men, ammunition, and supplies. But in the mountains and forests of North Carolina and Georgia, the Americans' lightweight clothing and ability to forage meant they could attack and melt into the wilderness. The British troops, encumbered by heavy uniforms, a heavy pack, and their supply train, were less mobile. It it was a strategy that might exhaust the British but could not be relied upon to win a war.

Alarming news came of British attacks in Virginia. Since betraying the American cause in the autumn of 1780, a vindictive Benedict Arnold had led British troops on forays into the colony. Wash Custis left an account of these events that added to the pressure on George in New Windsor, and that must have made Martha frantic for the safety of Jacky, Eleanor, their children, and her family in New Kent:

> Early in January 1781, Benedict Arnold, zealous in the cause of his royal purchaser, went to Virginia with about sixteen hundred British and Tory troops, and a few armed vessels. He went up the James River, as far as Richmond, and destroyed much public and private property.... In April he accompanied General Philips up the same river in a desolating expedition. They were joined in Petersburg by Cornwallis, who had invaded the state from North Carolina....
>
> The invasion of Arnold was more immediately predatory, but that of Cornwallis swept like a tempest through the commonwealth, already much weakened by her untiring exertions to sustain the army of Greene in the Carolinas, and to defend the many points of her territory, assailable by the attacks of the enemy's naval power.[1]

Mount Vernon was a prime target for Cornwallis, and vulnerable because the Potomac was navigable by warships. The Custis property in and near Williamsburg and on the Eastern Shore lay in the path of British troops advancing from the coast from Norfolk and North Carolina. Wash's account does not include the information that across the southern colonies hostilities had erupted in many places into a kind of free-for-all, with fighting between different factions that had scores to settle among themselves. There were many Loyalists in the South, who had suffered terribly at the hands of roving armed rebels and were taking their revenge now that the British had gained a foothold. In addition, the many widely scattered ethnic groups settled in the South—Germans, Irish, and Scots, as well as Native Americans, had scores to settle and often disliked and distrusted each other. Added to that were the roaming bands of slaves who had gone over to the British side. Martha's family members at Eltham and Pamocra were in the midst of a potentially explosive situation.

Loyalties were fluctuating. The Americans, the English, and the French all suffered desertions; those deserters who were caught were usually hanged or shot promptly to discourage others. Many Continental brigades were on the point of mutiny. Some were resolved by negotiation before they erupted, and others by hanging or shooting, and occasionally decapitating, the ringleaders. In England the *Norfolk Chronicle* contained an article on February 17, 1781, recording a mutiny among the American troops in New Jersey, the disastrous state of American finances, and, at the same time, the flavor of what was rapidly becoming a deadlock for England:

> The following is the most particular account that has yet been produced of the late revolt of the greater and more respectable part of the Congress' army, under the command of Mr. Washington. . . . The impatience of the rebel troops, and being long deprived of their pay in real money, and wholesome provisions, had determined many of the soldiers to a peremptory demand, that their arrears should be produced to them in solid money. . . . many perceiving the bankrupt condition of the Congress' finances . . . took occasion on Monday last (when the times of the enlistment of several hundred expired) boldly to require their pay in present cash and hard money: finding no revenue but the long expired paper currency produced to supply their demands, the malcontents frankly offered to give up their pay with all arrears, and return home . . . as they were determined to a man no longer to remain in the Continental service. . . . A cessation [mutiny] immediately ensued, consisting of the whole Pennsylvania line. . . .
>
> They presently secured four hundred head of live cattle; all the live horses of the neighboring country as they passed were surrendered to them; upwards of one hundred rifle-men had been detached [by the Continental army] to hang on and annoy their rear, but . . . rather than molest them, they [the riflemen] left their Officers and preferred to join their quondam fellow soldiers, in pursuit of the same object. . . . Thus reinforced, the total number of revolters

now amounts to two thousand two hundred men, and are daily increasing. . . . The only Continental troops now in Jersey, in the Congress' service, are that solitary brigade of Gen. Dayton, lately commanded by Brigadier Maxwell, who sometime since bootless quitted their service . . . total number seven hundred.

On Thursday last accounts of an action were received from the rebel country, which affords us hopes of important advantages newly obtained by royal arms in the Carolina's. . . .

North America, says a correspondent, continues to be the grave of Englishmen, the repository of English money, the source of Great Britain's troubles, and . . . Thro' her means, three powerful nations have now risen up against us [France and Spain had joined in the war on the side of America]. . . .

The revolt, or mutiny, of a part of Washington's army which has just reached our ears has this disagreeable circumstance attending it, that whatever discontents, quarrels and animosities prevail among the people of America, whatever hardships, distresses, and even misery they undergo, they show no hearty inclination to a reconciliation with the mother country! . . . An invincible obstinacy in the minds of the people overcomes all—Independence is still the cry.

Virginia currency was virtually worthless, as were the currencies of other colonies, and that issued by Congress was now equally so. To destabilize the colonial economy even further, the British pumped a huge quantity of counterfeit money into it. According to Wash Custis, it was a time when Virginia had "neither a coin in her treasury nor credit to obtain one." It was a state of affairs that hindered the already beleaguered Generals Greene and Lafayette in the South, because people in the South were hiding horses and provisions to avoid having to sell them to the Continental army for worthless currency. One British officer taken prisoner at Saratoga in 1777 and on parole in Virginia wrote: "At the present rate five hundred paper dollars [can be exchanged] for one guinea. The depreciation arises from the vast quantity of counterfeit, which any person who hazards the risk may have gratis at New York to circulate through the province . . . there are many persons now in actual possession of plantations which they purchased with the counterfeit money they brought from New York."[2]

In April George wrote, "We are at the end of our tether . . . now or never our deliverance must come." His only hope of deliverance lay with the French, and French commitment to the American cause was waning. By late spring 1781, the French were persuaded the Americans had come to the end of their resources and were unwilling to commit more men and resources to maintain an expensive campaign on their own in the American colonies much longer.

At headquarters, private family concerns added to the pressure of military ones for Martha and George. Jacky continued to make ill-advised land transactions, partly because he ignored George's warnings about the adverse impact of runaway inflation. His imprudence was dissipating the Custis assets. Meanwhile, Eleanor was expecting another baby in the spring, another source of worry, considering her health.

And in January news came from Virginia that Betty Washington Lewis's husband, Fielding Lewis, had died. Fielding Lewis had put his fortune into making arms and ammunition for the American army and had impoverished himself in the process, leaving Betty with six children and a large mortgage on their home Kenwood, outside Fredericksburg. If Betty could not pay the mortgage, the property would have to be sold—if the British did not burn it first. Alternatively, as the home of a prominent supporter of the American cause, Kenwood could easily have become one of the "plantations purchased with counterfeit money" referred to in the article above.

Martha and George were close to Betty and Fielding, and indebted to her for looking after Mary Washington, who had refused to move to Kenwood but lived within walking distance. Martha felt for her sister-in-law and invited Betty and the children to stay at Mount Vernon, but within a few months Betty had devised her own plan, to turn Kenwood into a girls' school.

That winter George's feckless brother Samuel Washington also died, leaving three impoverished orphan children for someone to look after.

In April the Washingtons learned Mount Vernon had come within a hairbreadth of being burned down. The British had come north from North Carolina, where Colonel Banastre Tarleton, the brutal commander of an irregular force, the British Legion, had unleashed a campaign of terror, raping women, brutally murdering civilians suspected of rebel sympathies as well as surrendering rebel soldiers and other prisoners of war, burning rebel homes, stealing slaves to resell in the Caribbean, and stealing any jewelry they could find, as well as livestock. When the British sailed up the Potomac to Mount Vernon in April, a frightened Lund Washington complied with their demand that he reprovision their ships, hoping that by doing so he could prevent them from destroying the estate. George was furious when he learned what had happened and wrote to Lund:

> I am sorry to hear . . . you should go on board the enemys Vessels, and furnish them with refreshments. It would have been a less painful circumstance to me, to have heard, that in consequence of your non-compliance with their request, they had burnt my House and laid the Plantation in ruins. You ought to have considered yourself as my representative, and should have reflected on the bad example of communicating with the enemy, and making a voluntary offer of refreshments to them with a view to prevent a conflagration.[3]

In fact, George was fuming at the loss of face and having been held up to ridicule by British officers who had reduced the commander in chief's manager to groveling. Though the British did not burn or pillage Mount

Vernon, or commandeer food and animals, they took one of the Mount Vernon boats, sixteen of George's slaves, and a number of Lund's slaves.

But however they irritated George, Lund's actions may have preserved the Washingtons' home. Anticipating she would soon be there, in May Martha wrote to Lund asking whether her house slave Betty had been spinning thread all winter as Martha had ordered, and whether the slave "Charlot," who was a sort of housekeeper, had done the work that Martha had left for her. This letter and several others were intercepted by the British. One of the discoveries the British made from them was that Martha's departure for Virginia was delayed until the end of June because she was extremely ill. She had suffered a violent monthlong bout of jaundice, possibly as a result of gallstones. Late in May George had written of her condition to Lund Washington, but that letter was one of those intercepted. On June 17 George had described Martha as being "extremely unwell. She continues low and weak."

Martha's misery was compounded when she learned that George had denied her the benefit of a present sent to her under a flag of truce, from Mrs. Martha Mortier, the widow of a British army paymaster:

> Mrs. Mortier presents her Compliments to Mrs Washington has been Informed that some Intercepted letters mention her being Indisposed and that she finds a difficulty in procuring some Necessary Articles for her recovery. Mrs M. has taken the liberty to send her such as this place affords, by means of a flag of truce, which she has procured for that purpose & begs leave to offer Mrs W. any other Assistance her situation may require.
>
> New York 15th June 1781[4]

Mrs. Mortier had sent an assortment of refreshing delicacies unobtainable in the Continental camp—boxes of lemons, limes, and oranges, tamarinds, pineapples, sweets, medicinal syrup, and tea—where they were lucky to eat salt meat and potatoes. Nauseous and bedridden, Martha could not have had a more enticing treat, but George refused to be drawn in by this gift from the enemy, aware of its propaganda potential, and promptly sent it back with a note to Mrs. Mortier:

> Headquarters June 21st 1781
> General Washington presents his compliments to Mrs. Mortier and thanks her for her very polite attention to Mrs. Washington, who has so perfectly recovered as to be able to set out for Virginia in a day or two. This being the case, General Washington hopes Mrs. Mortier will excuse his retuning the several articles which she in so kind a manner sent up by the Flag, assuring her at the same time, that he shall ever entertain a grateful sense of this mark of her benevolence.[5]

To confirm the truth of George's words, Martha left camp for Mount Vernon nine days later, still poorly, to make the long dusty journey in the summer heat. Lord Cornwallis, who had occupied Williamsburg, was in the process of removing a few miles southeast to Yorktown, which his troops and as many slaves as he could assemble were fortifying with stockades and trenches to serve as a naval station for the British fleet.

At Mount Vernon Martha found her new grandchild of four months, George Washington Parke Custis. Eleanor, as always, had had a hard time with the birth and was still not well, but she had survived. The baby, who would be known as "Mr. Tub" or "Wash," for short, had also been quite ill, possibly because Eleanor could not feed him properly, although a letter from George to Jacky suggests the baby may have contracted one of the many fevers endemic to the region. Wash was being looked after by Nelly's old wet nurse, Mrs. Anderson.

In September there was a sudden flurry of activity at Mount Vernon when George arrived home unexpectedly on the ninth. It was the first time he had been at Mount Vernon in six years, and now he was marching his troops south as fast as possible to the Virginia coast, where Lafayette and a gathering body of French and American troops had Cornwallis's army trapped at Yorktown. The British fleet had finally sailed north to New York, where the British commander in chief Henry Clinton anticipated an attack by the French fleet. In fact, the French fleet had arrived from the Caribbean and was massing in the Chesapeake near Yorktown.

On September 10, George was joined by two French officers, the Compte de Rochambeau and the Marquis de Chastellux, his own aides, and the French staff. George and his party stayed for only four days. Martha rose to the occasion, and for a brief interval it was like old times at Mount Vernon, with a house full of bustle and company, which now included Jacky, Eleanor, and the four children. After the straitened conditions and privations of camp life, the short stay at Mount Vernon, even in its rundown and shabby condition, was a splendid interlude for one of George's young aides, Jonathan Trumbull, son of the Connecticut governor. Trumbull wrote of his stay: "A numerous family [George's term for his staff officers] now present. All accommodated. An elegant seat and situation, great appearance of opulence and real exhibition of hospitality and princely entertainment."

Suddenly the house was full of military uniforms, messengers, dash, and authority. As soon as he heard of George's unexpected arrival, proud family man Jacky had brought Eleanor and the children at once in the carriage from Abingdon. Having never shown the least inclination for military life, he was suddenly overwhelmed by a sense of military glamor and seized with a desire to be part of things. Martha was too familiar with the conditions of military camps and the realities of war to think it a good plan, and Eleanor, still fragile, did not want her husband to go off to a dangerous situation, much less to be left with four children under the age of five. From George's point of view his inexperienced, impressionable stepson was more likely to be a hindrance than a help. Jacky, as ever, had his way. He was made an "aide-de-camp" to George and fitted out by Martha with a uniform of sorts, including an aide-de-camp's sash. In high spirits at being included in such an exciting entourage, Jacky rode off with the generals toward York-town on September 12, visiting his grandmother and other relatives in New Kent on the way.

Jacky wrote to Martha a month later, just as the Americans and the French had begun a fierce bombardment of Cornwallis's army, entrenched in Yorktown. Writing from "Camp Before York, October 12th, 1791," Jacky delivered the news he knew would interest his mother most. He told her he was well, that George was in "constant Fatigue," that he had visited his rel-atives in New Kent, and that his grandmother Frances, now living with Bartholomew, was well, but showing her age and wanting to see her great-granddaughters. He said that Bartholomew "suffered very much by the Enemy" and that Martha's sister Elizabeth, widowed in 1779, was living with a second husband, Leonard Henley. Jacky continued with news of some of the slaves who had left Mount Vernon:

> Please to inform Mr. Washington [Lund] that I have made every possible Enquiry after his Negroes, but have not seen any belonging to him, the Gen-eral or myself. I have heard that Ned [one of the slaves taken by the British in April] is in York a pioneer, old Joe Rachier is in the Neighborhood . . . I fear that most who left Us are not existing, the mortality that has taken place among the Wretches is really incredible. I have seen numbers lying dead in the Woods, and many so exhausted that they cannot walk.[6]

Jacky's reference to the numbers of dead slaves he had seen sheds light on one of the little-known tragedies of the Revolution, the fate of the slaves who had fled their masters to join the British. Aside from a few who made their way to Loyalist strongholds in Canada, the vast majority of these slaves met a wretched fate, as the British often reneged on their promise of free-dom in exchange for bearing arms. More commonly, the slaves were as badly used by the British as they had been used by their American masters, per-forming hard labor or working as servants to British soldiers and officers as a sort of army privilege.

Many slaves who looked forward to obtaining their freedom by serving the British were later sold by the British to the slave markets of the Caribbean. Many more died—wounded, starving, sick, exhausted, or simply abandoned because the British did not have sufficient provisions to continue feeding them. In a more sinister development, some slaves were deliberately infected with smallpox and sent into American lines in a macabre form of eighteenth-century biological warfare. Jacky's picture of the woods being full of dead slaves, putrefying unburied in the autumn heat, is a grisly image indeed.

It was hot, and there was as an unhealthy, fetid atmosphere both inside Yorktown and in the American and French camp. The Americans and the French kept up a steady bombardment, gradually destroying the town. The governor of Virginia, Thomas Nelson, who had a fine home in Yorktown, was asked by an artillery officer to point it out so they could direct their fire away from it. Nelson replied that as his was the finest house in town, it was where the British command would have holed up, and he told the Americans to fire away and destroy it. On the streets of Yorktown among the shattered buildings lay dead bodies without arms, legs, or heads. Starving horses were killed when they could no longer stand. Many of the British troops were ill with fever, and the rations inside the town reduced to putrid meat and worm-eaten biscuits. Those slaves still inside Yorktown were expelled, with no consideration for the probable consequences at the hands of their vengeful former masters.

Finally on October 17 the British sent a drummer boy and an officer waving a white handkerchief on a stick flag to meet Washington to discuss terms for British surrender of Yorktown. Two days later the Americans and British negotiators had hammered out an agreement and on October 19, the formal Articles of Capitulation were signed. Lord Cornwallis had surrendered.

The ceremony of surrender, a momentous event after six terrible years of much suffering on both sides, was affecting. The smartly uniformed French stood in one line under their white flags with gold fleurs-de-lis, and the Americans, save for a few in uniforms provided by France, looked like shabby scarecrows in filthy, tattered clothing. The British troops marched out to music, popularly believed to be the song entitled "The World Turned Upside Down," and laid down their arms, some in tears. Lord Cornwallis refused to attend, sulking in his tent and pleading illness, sending his second-in-command, Brigadier General Charles O'Hara, to surrender his sword. In a futile insulting gesture, General O'Hara first presented Cornwallis's sword to General Rochambeau, who refused to accept it, saying, "We are subordinates to the Americans. General Washington will give you your orders." General O'Hara was then forced to present his sword to George, but as O'Hara was Cornwallis's second-in-command, George made a gesture of his own, directing O'Hara to surrender to the American second-in-command, General Benjamin Lincoln.

Before the ceremony, George had ridden up and down his lines, warning his men not to exult at British expense, saying, "History will huzzah for us." A British officer later wrote that the Americans had behaved with admirable restraint and that the French, once the ceremony of surrender was over, had expressed their sympathy.

Jacky, who had been taken ill, was feverish and growing worse, but had stayed in camp to witness the ceremony. Though it was obviously an important victory for the Americans, no one yet appreciated its full significance. Yorktown would shortly prove to be the decisive battle of the Revolution, and Cornwallis's surrender in fact signaled British capitulation.

Lafayette presciently remarked, "The play, sir, is over."

While the American camp rejoiced in the aftermath, Jacky's condition deteriorated swiftly. He was diagnosed with "camp fever," a condition brought on by the combined effects of camp conditions, the poor food, polluted water, heat, fevers, the proximity of dead men and animals, and poor sanitation, all of which had a greater impact on someone like Jacky who had never before been exposed to them. Jacky was taken the thirty miles to Eltham, and from camp George dispatched Dr. Craik, a friend and companion from the days of the French and Indian Wars, to look after him.

It was six weeks after George and Jacky and their entourage had left for Yorktown that a messenger arrived at Mount Vernon with news of the British defeat. Martha had lived closely enough to developments throughout the war to grasp the significance of so important a victory, but any sense of elation was cut short by the arrival of another messenger shortly afterwards summoning Martha and Eleanor urgently to Eltham, where Jacky's condition was now critical. Martha, Eleanor and Betsy made as quick a journey as was possible, but even so the distance could not be covered in less than two days.

Betsy Custis, the only one of the children to accompany her mother and grandmother to Eltham, recollected the event many years later. Apart from the notation in George's diary, it is the only firsthand account of Jacky's death. It made a painful and lasting impression:

> I was their companion—& was grieved to see the late blooming face of my beloved father so changed that I should not have known him, but for his voice—all was done that medical skill and fond affection could perform to save him—my Mother never left him, seated on his Bed, his eyes were fastened on her—his Love had known no change. It was hard to die so young—he was not more than 27 years old when the cruel Spoiler came, & tore him from a World which he adorned—when told my father was no more, I insisted on seeing him, my nurse was going with me to the room—but we were stopt.[7]

Martha, Eleanor, and Betsy arrived before George, who was hurriedly summoned from Yorktown on November 5. He arrived at Eltham just as Jacky died. Martha and Eleanor were devastated, and George sincerely grieved for his stepson. The next day George wrote to Jonathan Trumbull: "I came here in time to see Mr. Custis breathe his last. About Eight o'clock yesterday evening he expired. The deep and solemn distress of the Mother, and affliction of the Wife of this amiable young Man, requires every comfort in my power to afford them. The last rights of the deceased I must also see performed; these will take me three or four days; when I shall proceed with Mrs. Washington and Mrs. Custis to Mount Vernon."[8]

It must have been a gloomy trip back home in the carriage for five-year-old Betsey, who recalled, "I well recollect the grief of my Mother, & Grandmother—& travelling up the Country again all clad in Black."

The sad party left Eltham on November 11 or 12, and stopped briefly at Fredericksburg. Mary Washington was away from home, but widowed Betty Lewis was there, tending the girls' school she had made in her home. By November 13 they were back at Mount Vernon, and George and Martha were planning to leave shortly for Philadelphia. Despite the fact that the end of the war seemed in sight, it was not yet entirely clear whether there was a need for a winter campaign. Martha had a only a few days to prepare for leaving, during which the Marquis de Chastellux stayed briefly at Mount Vernon. He left this affectionate, sympathetic account:

> I had the pleasure of passing a day or two with Mrs. Washington, at the General's house in Virginia, where she appeared to me one of the best women in the world, and beloved by all about her. She has no family by the general, but was surrounded by her grandchildren and Mrs. Custis, her son's widow. The family were then in mourning for Mr. Custis, whose premature death was a subject of public and private regret.[9]

Reading between the lines, we can believe that Martha was supported in her grief by the presence of her grandchildren, as well as the need to look after Eleanor, who had still not fully recovered from Wash's birth and was finding it difficult to cope with her sudden widowhood. Since it was clear that Eleanor was in no state to look after four young children, and to comfort Martha, George undertook to adopt the two youngest, Nelly and Wash, or, more accurately, to foster them, because there was never any legal adoption. After the blow of Jacky's death, nothing could have renewed Martha's sense of purpose in life so much as the prospect of looking after the "little folks," as George called them.

CHAPTER 16

A Long Time Going Home

In the aftermath of Jacky's death there was little time for Martha to give way to grief as she had done when Patcy died. As when Daniel died, Martha faced demands on all sides from people who needed her—from George, who was in a hurry now to go north and wanted Martha with him, to her small grandchildren and her distraught daughter-in-law. There was an uncanny parallel in Eleanor's being left a Custis widow with four young children after seven years of marriage at twenty-three, just as Martha had been left, twenty-four years earlier, a Custis widow with two young children after seven years of marriage at age twenty-five. Widowhood had left both women responsible for large plantation homes, Martha at White House and now Eleanor at Abingdon, and the vast Custis estate. Just as Martha had done years before, Eleanor needed a male guardian to safeguard the children's Custis inheritance.

Martha had only a few days to try to resolve the conflicting claims on her attention and make the best arrangements she could, because George planned to leave for Philadelphia as soon as possible. But decisions had to be made quickly about the best plan for the children. Eleanor was in no condition physically or mentally to look after all four small children, and once back at Abingdon she would have a great deal to do coping with estate business and many new responsibilities. Judging by Eleanor's comments on the arrangements many years later, George's offer to "adopt" Nelly and Wash may have sounded more like an order she was afraid to disobey, but George probably did what he was accustomed to doing in taking control of a difficult situation, while Martha and Eleanor were too grief-stricken immediately after Jacky's death to decide what to do.

According to family tradition as conveyed by Wash Custis, he and his sister were adopted at Jacky's deathbed, but George may have offered only to look after Eleanor's two youngest for as long as she wanted. Several other factors suggest that at the time George thought it a more temporary arrangement, possibly to distract and comfort Martha.

First of all, the adoption of the two children was never legally formalized by the Washingtons, though over time all of the family accepted the arrangement as an adoption. At that time it was not considered unusual for children to be brought up in the homes of relatives, even when both parents were living. Since the two elder girls were closer to their mother, having lived with Eleanor at Abingdon since their birth, it made sense not to separate them from her at this time. Nelly, however, had spent much of her first two years being looked after at Mount Vernon by Mrs. Anderson and Lund Washington's wife, and Wash, at six months, was being nursed by Mrs. Anderson. It made sense to relieve the overburdened Eleanor of the two youngest and keep Nelly and Wash at Mount Vernon.

The issue of who was to be the children's legal guardian was still open months later. In the spring of 1782, George wrote to Bartholomew Dandridge on the topic of having the same guardian for all four children, explaining that he personally was too occupied with army matters, and anticipated being so for some time, to undertake the duties of acting as legal guardian and trustee for the four children. He suggested that Bartholomew, now a judge, either undertake the guardianship himself or have legal guardians appointed as a matter of urgency. George had an incentive to avoid being drawn into taking on the financial affairs of Jacky's children. Having spent a great deal of time in managing the estates and keeping accounts of his stepchildren, he knew how onerous and time-consuming the job was. Jacky's estate would eventually be apportioned among the four children, and whoever became their guardian and trustee would have to administer four separate estates and keep four separate sets of accounts, twice the burden George had assumed.

Though Eleanor later wrote that she regretted having given in to the Washingtons' offer to look after Nelly and Wash, which she hinted had been forcefully made at a time when she was vulnerable, in fact there was never any suggestion Nelly and Wash were caught up in a "tug of love" situation between their mother and Martha and George. They remained on close and affectionate terms with Eleanor all their lives, and there was constant visiting back and forth between Mount Vernon and Abingdon, with members of one household always being welcome at the other, and Martha nursing Eleanor through several illnesses. The Washingtons taught Nelly and Wash to look upon Eleanor as their mother, while Martha and George were "Grandmamma" and "Grandpapa."

Martha's grandchildren were not the only ones for whom plans had to be made. She was still in no position to fulfill her promise to Anna Maria to look after Fanny Bassett at Mount Vernon. Too old to be left in the care of nurses, Fanny was going on thirteen, an age when a girl needed maternal attention and guidance from a mother figure, which was best provided in the homes of other relatives. Then there was the matter of Samuel Washington's three orphaned children, two boys and the youngest, a five-year-old daughter named Harriot Washington. For the time being, all George could do was apply the proceeds of the sale of one of his late brother's slaves to Harriot's upkeep, while he sent her older brothers to board at school.

Besides packing and making hasty arrangements for children who could not fend for themselves, Martha was concerned about her surviving sister Elizabeth. Since marrying in 1773, Elizabeth Dandridge Aylett had had a difficult time. She had been widowed in 1776 after less than three years of marriage. The notation in the family Bible reads "On the 7th Feb'y departed this life my dear Mr Aylett in the 29th year of his age." Elizabeth had given birth to two sons, one ten days after his father's death. That baby died seven months later in August, followed shortly by the death of her first son at age three. Both children may have been victims of the fevers, which took a toll on children each year during the muggy summer months. The notation of their deaths in the Bible is followed by a verse that testifies to the overwhelming grief of many a colonial mother:

Stay my dear children! Take thy dear mother, too,
Nor leave her here, a spectacle of woe!

In 1779, Elizabeth had married Leonard Henley and given birth to a daughter, Frances, who, like her cousin Anna Maria's daughter Frances, would also be known as Fanny. Just as she had been close to her younger sisters, Martha would always be particularly concerned for the welfare of their daughters, and both Fanny Bassett and Fanny Henley would, in turn, become surrogate daughters to Martha to take Patcy's place. In the normal course of events Martha would have enjoyed taking an active interest in Elizabeth's baby, visiting Elizabeth in New Kent, where Leonard Henley was employed as a Custis overseer and living with Elizabeth at White House, and would have had Elizabeth to stay at Mount Vernon. However, the pressures on George allowed her no time to see her sister. This was particularly worrying as there were disturbing signs that Elizabeth's new husband was an alcoholic, and possibly abusive.

There was also a new generation of mixed-race children at Mount Vernon. The fact that these children had last names marked a subtle change in status, giving them full named identities. There was Martha's year-old nephew, Ann Dandridge's son William, for one.

And, at about the time William was born, Martha's seamstress Betty, also known as "Mulatto Betty," had the second of two children who, like William, were children of a white man. In 1772 George had bought the contract of an indentured servant, an Irishman named Andrew Judge, who was probably a carpenter. Andrew Judge was contracted to work at Mount Vernon for seven years, and during that time he formed a relationship with Betty, who had come to Mount Vernon as a very young girl, as one of Martha's Custis dower slaves. Betty had borne Andrew Judge at least two daughters. The first was Ona, or Oney Judge, who was a little older than Nelly Custis. Martha was quite fond of Ona. Then, in about 1780, she had a girl named Philadelphia, or Delphy Judge. Andrew Judge left Mount Vernon when his term of indenture expired in 1779, and there is no evidence he maintained contact with Betty, Ona, or Philadelphia, but the girls kept his last name.

By this time it had become George's practice at Mount Vernon not to split up slave families or to sell any slave away from the estate without that slave's consent. Mulatto slaves were in general preferred as house servants, and so Betty ranked high in the house slave hierarchy. In the normal course of events Martha would have begun training Betty's children for particular household tasks from an early age. Now that would have to wait.

Despite Cornwallis's defeat, the war was not officially over. The British were still in the South and in possession of New York. Nevertheless, there was a general mood of euphoria and a general feeling that the end was close. The journey north was bittersweet for Martha as, reflecting the mood of optimism that had followed the Yorktown victory, the Washingtons' appearance en route was greeted with rapturous enthusiasm. Philadelphia was in the throes of celebrating when Martha and George arrived there on November 28, three weeks after Jacky's death.

Shortly after Martha and George reached Philadelphia, George's old friend and patron Lord Fairfax died on December 9 at Greenway Court, marking the end of an era for the Fairfaxes. He had remained staunchly Loyalist throughout the war, but had continued to reside at Greenway Court, undisturbed by any rebels or American militias, probably on George's orders. It was rumored he died of shock upon learning of Cornwallis's defeat, and called on his slave Joe to put him to bed to die. A popular verse of the time reflects the disbelief felt by all American Loyalists:

> Then up rose Joe, all at the word,
> And took his master's arm,
> And to his bed he softly led
> The lord of Greenway farm.
> Then thrice he called on Britain's name,
> And thrice he wept full sore,
> Then sighed—"O Lord thy will be done!"
> And word spake never more.

In Philadelphia Martha and George stayed at the home of Benjamin Chew, spending Christmas Day with their close friends Robert Morris and his wife, Mary. Robert Morris was a wealthy man who had acted as financier to the Revolution. As time passed, it gradually became clear that active hostilities were indeed over, and it was a matter of waiting for the mechanics of the peace treaty to be hammered out in Paris. Still facing George was the matter of disbanding the army, which could not take place as long as the British occupied New York. As a result Martha did not know how soon she could expect to go home, where so many people needed her attention. Instead, the Washingtons left Philadelphia in late March 1782 for Newburgh, New York, where the army was camped. George would have another eighteen months of camp life in front of him.

In Newburgh the Washingtons lived at headquarters set up in the Hasbrouck House. It was a one-story building with a view of the Hudson and the Fishkill Hills, with only seven rooms, and very cramped. The Washingtons entertained, as they always did, but there were limitations. The main room, which was entered directly from outdoors, was a large, square, low-ceilinged room with one window and seven doors. Martha had the use of the parlor, but it was the only thing approaching "spare" space in the house, and occasionally she had to vacate it so it could serve as a bedroom for an important visitor, such as the Marquis de Chastellux, who spent a night there. Lucy and Henry Knox were also living in Newburgh, and Lucy Knox held soirées.

In May news arrived of the birth of the dauphin of France, the king's son. The Washingtons and their guests traveled down the Hudson in barges to West Point for a huge celebration, including parades, gun salutes, fireworks, toasts, a grand dinner for five hundred people, and a ball, which George opened with Lucy Knox.

In July Martha finally returned to Mount Vernon, half expecting George would be able to join her. By now Lady Washington had become a famous figure in her own right. When she traveled through Philadelphia that summer on her way to Virginia, the Pennsylvania Assembly presented her with a coach that had belonged to William Penn. In Williamsburg she was presented with gold medals and the freedom of the city.

In October George wrote to Martha that he was not yet able to return even for a visit and asked her to come back north, as she had done during the war. Martha was finding the journey more and more onerous and exhausting, yet she prepared to go once more. A short note from George to Martha exists from that October. Martha never received it, because it was a letter of introduction written by George and carried by the young man, James Brown, who was to deliver it to her. In fact, James Brown never went as far south as Mount Vernon on that occasion and the note was undelivered, but it survives as the third known letter written by George to Martha.

While the note does no more than identify the bearer as the "son to a Gentleman . . . from whom I have received civilities," it is noteworthy for its salutation: "My dearest."[1]

By November Martha had returned to camp at Newburgh. Negotiations over the peace treaty were dragging on, and the British were slowly withdrawing their troops from the South. Rumors circulated that George wanted to be king of America.

The rumors were symptomatic of growing unrest among the troops, who had yet to be either paid or disbanded, as well as a general mood of political uncertainty. Throwing off the yoke of British rule had created a vacuum, and no one was clear about the way forward for the colonies. February 1783 marked the fifth anniversary of the alliance with France, which had proved so crucial. To celebrate the occasion in a way that would reduce the discontented muttering of the soldiers, George declared a pardon for all military prisoners.

There is an account of the occasion in a letter Martha supposedly wrote to her sister Anna Maria on February 7, 1783. That, however, is impossible because Anna Maria died in 1777. The actual letter is not known to exist but was quoted in Benson Lossing's *Mary and Martha, the Mother and Wife of Washington*. It does not quite sound like Martha, but something similar to what was described probably took place:

> [Newburgh February 7, 1783]
>
> Yesterday there was an interesting scene at Headquarters. Over fifty soldiers thinly clad, and with pale but happy faces, whom the General had pardoned in the morning for various crimes, came to express their gratitude for his mercy and kindness to them
>
> They had come in a body. One of them was spokesman for the rest. My heart was touched and my eyes were filled with tears. I gave the speaker some money to divide among them all, and bade them "go, and sin no more." The poor fellows kissed my hand and said "God bless Lady Washington". Poor fellows.[2]

The letter may be a fabrication, but the prisoners would indeed have been poorly dressed and thin, and some undoubtedly relieved that they would not be tried and hung for their offenses. What is significant is that Martha features in it. On all the evidence, Martha was extremely popular with the troops, whose general attitude toward her was expressed in their frequent accolade "God bless Lady Washington." She was even known to be a "gallant trooper." She was never known to complain, even in the worst of times, and she had the common touch. Martha boasted she had heard the opening and closing shot of each year's campaign, and while not strictly true, it hit the right note with the troops. It is no exaggeration to say the men adored

Martha, and if George wanted to improve relations with his troops, having Martha by his side when he pardoned the military prisoners was the cleverest possible stroke of public relations.

Because there was no longer any need for Martha to involve herself in war relief work, she passed the time in camp entertaining and doing handiwork, such as making hair nets, two of which she sent to Henry Knox. She also planted a garden on a slope in front of headquarters, with the help of a Dutch gardener. In the summer of 1783 Martha did not return to Mount Vernon but remained in Newburgh, where she was taken very ill with a fever. In late August she had recovered and went with George to stay in Princeton at Rocky Hill.

Back in Virginia, Eleanor often came to stay with her children at Mount Vernon during the Washingtons' absence, probably to keep an eye on the house. During one of these visits she met the Washingtons' friend Dr. David Stuart, a rather staid man with no money of his own and a modest estate at Hope Park. Soon Eleanor was being courted, and it was obvious to Martha she was thinking of marrying again. Arthur Lee, one of the Washingtons' friends, described Eleanor at that time as "a most tempting widow, independent of the jointure land." According to the sour recollection of Eleanor's daughter Betsy, later called Eliza:

> my Mother was 25, of a Gay turn high Spirits, which had been nurtured by a life of unchanging prosperity—eer a very long time she acquired resignation to her loss, & began to mingle with a world which always admired her—still the full bloom of Beauty, with an ample fortune she was sought by all who wished to secure *happiness* or fortune—She attracted Admiration whenever she appear'd, mounted on an elegant horse, which she rode well, she was certainly a most captivating object—I mourned for my father, and wonder'd she could forget him, & well convinced am I, that had I been so beloved by so charming a husband, I should have follw'd him to the grave—but 'tis most fortunate for her that she is different from me.[3]

It was hardly surprising that Eleanor was blooming. Since the age of sixteen Eleanor had spent most of her married life either pregnant or recovering from childbirth, and ill. The two-year period after Jacky's death was the first time she had fully recovered her health in years. However, Eleanor faced the same problems Martha had faced as Daniel's widow. Jacky had inherited not only his third share of his father's estate, but when Patcy died, he automatically inherited half of her third share as well. Jacky's four children would share the huge Custis fortune between them, and as time passed, the need for a guardian for Betsy, Patty, Nelly, and Wash and for someone to shoulder the responsibilities of managing the estate became more pressing. Eleanor was not capable of managing the estate herself. According to Betsy:

Two years after my father's departure, my Mother gave her hand to Dr. Stuart—she chose the man she believed would make the best Guardian for her children—Dr S was not then the gloomy Mortal he has been since—he had just returned from Europe—where he received every advantage of Education & was one of the most learned men of his day—he was a Man of respectable family, & a character free from reproach . . . he had little fortune and my Mother's friends disapproved of the choice she made but she independent of them, and finding herself incapable of managing her own or her children's property, determined to marry Dr S—he became her husband and the guardian of her children's fortune.[4]

If her mother's remarriage caused Betsy a pang, it had Martha and George's entire approbation. Martha could sympathize with Eleanor's wish to remarry, and they were both practical women who knew how important it was for the children to have a stepfather and guardian and for someone to take the Custis property in hand.

It is interesting that Eleanor took as her second husband a serious, sober, well-educated man, a complete contrast to the lively, devil-may-care Jacky. Her choice may have been dictated more by the need for a capable and sensible manager for the Custis property than by romantic considerations. Jacky had squandered a significant portion of the Custis assets on ill-advised land transactions, selling good land to purchase poor unproductive plots and compounding the loss by accepting payment in rapidly devaluing Virginia paper money. Even Betsy conceded Jacky had been "too little attentive to pecuniary concerns—he had never been brought up with any knowledge of business he made bad bargains & had greatly injured his Estate."

Betsy did not make these observations until nine years after George's death and obviously was unaware of just how futile all George's efforts had been to drum some business sense into her father. Had Jacky lived, he would undoubtedly have frittered away the remainder of the estate.

Martha returned to Mount Vernon in November 1783, ahead of George, who had to take leave of his officers and troops. The peace treaty had finally been signed, and the British were leaving New York. On December 19 George made a speech in Annapolis resigning his commission, hoping it would quash the rumors that he wanted to be a king or, as some people had feared, that he intended to stay on as a kind of military dictator. Nothing could have been further from the truth. George wanted only to get back to Mount Vernon and resume civilian life. Throughout the war he had written rather wistfully to Lund Washington, asking how renovations to the house were progressing, and about the welfare of his cherished fruit trees. Martha traveled from Mount Vernon to Annapolis to hear the speech.

Leaving Annapolis for Mount Vernon ahead of George, Martha was escorted part of the way by his former staff officers. George himself arrived home on Christmas Eve. In addition to Nelly and Wash and their nurse, the house swiftly filled up with company as people flocked to pay their respects and wish the Washingtons "the compliments of the season."

One young girl from Fredericksburg who had arrived with relatives and stayed at Mount Vernon wrote this account to a friend:

> I must tell you what a charming day I spent at Mount Vernon with Mama and Sally. The General and Madame came home on Christmas Eve, and such a racket the servants made, for they were glad of their coming. Three handsome young officers came with them. All Christmas afternoon people came to pay their Respects and Duty. Among them were stately Dames and gay young Women. The Gen'l seemed very happy and Mistress Washington was from Daybreak making everything as agreeable as possible for Everybody.

At last, they were home again for good, with a house full of company. Martha was in her element.

CHAPTER 17

"Under Their Own Vine and Fig Tree"

For several years after they arrived home, George wrote to friends of the joys of being once more "under their own vine and fig tree." While the words conjured up a tranquil, bucolic image, for both Washingtons, the return to Mount Vernon was far from restful.

The Washingtons' joy at being home and resuming their lives at Mount Vernon was tempered by the effect on their health of eight years of constant strain, uncertainty, anxiety, difficult living conditions, and poor food. Both were physically exhausted. George was growing deaf, and he had very few teeth left. By his own account, months after coming home he continued to wake each morning with an adrenaline rush, prepared to deal with wartime emergencies, and he found it required time to readjust to civilian life. Martha, less physically robust than her husband, felt the cumulative effects of the years of strain, camp conditions, and the long trips to and from camp even more than George, but both were worn-out. In January 1784 she wrote a friend in New Jersey, Hannah Boudinot, that she very much hoped the Boudinots would pay them a visit at Mount Vernon because her "frequent long Journeys have not only left me without inclination to undertake another, but almost disqualified me from doing it, as I find the fatiegue is too much for me to bear."

Peacetime life for the Washingtons at Mount Vernon soon became almost as "fatieguing" as the war had been. From the moment of their arrival home, both Washingtons had been promptly absorbed by the demands of their extended families, the condition of the estate, visitors, slaves, and the "little folks," as George called Nelly and Wash. There was no time for either of them to rest. The "little folks" began the new year by throwing the household into alarm when they both had measles in January. At Abingdon Eleanor Calvert Custis Stuart was pregnant, and Martha needed to keep an eye on her and the girls there. After George's eight-year absence, the neglected Mount Vernon finances were a muddle, and the estate showed the effects of lax management.

When Congress had elected George to command the Continental army in 1775, it was partly on the strength of his status as a Virginia squire, a man of vast property and independent fortune. In reality, Congress had an inflated idea of his wealth. With an estate which had grown to eight thousand acres in Virginia and twenty thousand more in the Ohio Valley, George was land-rich but cash-poor, a concept the Congress did not grasp easily. Martha's share of the Custis fortune had long been spent, but George had, nevertheless, refused to accept pay for his military service and claimed only his expenses, a proud but costly gesture.

No one appreciated this better than Martha. For the first fifteen years of their marriage George's close attention to every aspect of Mount Vernon, from mundane tasks such as fencing repairs to the breeding of livestock and experiments with new crops, had been the stuff of their daily conversations. Finances were now a source of worry for both of them.

George's financial position was complicated by inflation and the devaluation of Virginia currency. He summed up the cumulation of problems in a letter to George William Fairfax:

> My Accounts stand as I left them near ten years ago; those who owed me money, a very few instances excepted, availed themselves of what are called the tender laws, and paid me off with a shilling and sixpence in the pound. Those to whom I owed, I now have to pay under heavy taxes with specie, or its equivalent value.... I allotted this Winter ... to overhaul and adjust all my papers (which are in sad disorder, from the frequent hasty removals of them from the reach of our trans-atlantic foes, when their Ships appeared): but I reckoned without my host; Company and a continual reference of old military matters.[1]

The winter of 1784, their first full winter back home, was particularly cold and snowy, and occasionally Mount Vernon was cut off from the outside world. The Washingtons were grateful for these periods of enforced isolation because Mount Vernon had quickly filled with too many people for comfort. The world was soon beating a path to the door of the Revolution's greatest hero. In addition to the huge network of Washington and Dandridge relatives and friends, a steady stream of statesmen, old soldiers, merchants, clergymen, diplomats, and painters and sculptors who wanted to paint or model the hero, found their way to Mount Vernon.

Keeping up the standards of the house and its hospitality was expensive, time-consuming, and exhausting. The main burden fell on Martha, who, in addition to managing the house, tried to ensure that George could work undisturbed when he was trying to concentrate on their neglected business affairs in his study. She was very strict with Nelly and Wash, other visiting children, and the slaves to maintain quiet in the house if George was working.

Eleanor and her husband, Doctor Stuart, and Martha's granddaughters Betsy and Patty were often at Mount Vernon, as were George's many Washington and Lewis nephews, some of whom were acting as his aides. He had a number of aides who were not paid but remunerated only with room and board at Mount Vernon. Fanny Bassett arrived in January 1784, accompanied by her brothers and her father, Burwell Bassett, and when they left, she stayed behind. Widowed Betty Lewis came with her children.

George tried to keep hospitality at Mount Vernon simple, saying there was always "a glass of wine and a bit of mutton" for those who would be content with his simple fare, but the strain of coping with visitors began to tell on Martha. Visitors praised the method, economy, and punctuality that regulated domestic life at Mount Vernon, but a degree of almost military precision was required in order to cope with running a full-time open house. Anything else would have meant chaos. George finally wrote to his old steward Sam Fraunces in New York to ask if he could recommend a housekeeper to "relieve Mrs. Washington of the drudgery of seeing the table properly covered and things economically used."

With so much to do and the absolute necessity of keeping to a strict daily timetable, the Washingtons kept the hours they had before the war. As before the war, George rose about 4 A.M., and Martha soon after. Breakfast was, as before, at 8 in winter, and 7 in summer. Dinner was promptly at 3 P.M. except on Sundays, when it was served at 2. This, according to Nelly Custis, was to give the house slaves an afternoon off.

The house was too small for such a volume of people, and it, like the estate, was sadly dilapidated after nine years of neglect. In the spring of 1784, George shut his eyes to financial constraints, as he had done in 1757, and began a program of repairs and major improvements to extend the house. The roof was raised, two wings were added, and a piazza the length of the house was built on the riverfront side. Extra bedrooms were added to the attic level. Hordes of workmen in the house and the surrounding area raised clouds of plaster dust and created a constant din of hammering and sawing. Martha eventually had a new kitchen, washhouse, dairy, and spinning house, along with a new walled kitchen garden and a new "dry well," literally a waterless deep hole in the earth for storing meat, vegetables, and dairy produce in the summer heat. On top of the dry well was a pretty summer house. There was also now a newfangled building called an icehouse.

The grounds underwent a major landscaping program, with the addition of a lawn and a circular carriage drive in front of the western entrance;

"West Front of the Mansion," by Edward Savage 1792. Courtesy of the Mount Vernon Ladies' Association.

many new trees were planted, and a conservatory for exotic plants was constructed beyond Martha's walled kitchen garden. With two small lively children to keep out of mischief, and visitors to look after from morning till night, the building mess, noise, workmen, and confusion were wearisome.

The slaves, as always, did most of the physical labor, but managing this particular workforce was still its own uphill battle. In 1786, two years after the Washingtons' return, an inventory of slaves working in the Mansion House and its immediate environs showed forty-one slaves doing a variety of jobs. George's valet Will Lee, who had accompanied George through the Revolution, headed the list of the main household slaves. Will Lee's predecessor, Bishop, lived on one of the outlying farms with his daughter Sarah.

Among the others there was the butler Frank; a waiter named Austin, who was also the coachman; two cooks named Nathan and Hercules, whom the family called "Uncle Harkless" probably because the children could not pronounce "Hercules"; an elderly woman named Doll; three seamstresses, Betty, Lame Alice, and Charlotte; two housemaids, Sall and Caroline; two

"Eleanor Parke Custis," 'Nelly,' by Robert Edge Pine. Courtesy of the Mount Vernon Ladies' Association.

laundresses, Dolly and Sall Brass; and spinners Alice, Myrtilla, and Kitty, and an old and nearly blind spinner named Winny. There were also four carpenters, seven general laborers, a lame man who was a knitter, and Bristol, the gardener.

What is missing from the list is an indication of who Martha's personal maid was or who looked after Nelly and Wash. Caroline, the housemaid, probably served Martha, and Betty would have been fully occupied with the household sewing, which included the Washingtons' clothing, family mending, sheets, bedding, and slave clothes. Between Martha and her mother Betty, Oney Judge learned to sew, as Oney was trained for the job of waiting on Martha and looking after her clothes. Other young slave girls about the house included fourteen-year-old Sinah, Kitty's daughter, and thirteen-year-old Anna, Alice's daughter; both were old enough to work and may have had the job of looking after Nelly and Wash.

Martha continued to oversee production of cloth, and kept Alice, Myrtilla, and Kitty busy spinning and weaving wool, cotton, and linen, to pro-

"Martha Parke Custis," "Patty," by Robert Edge Pine. Courtesy of the Mount Vernon Ladies' Association.

"George Washington Parke Custis," "Wash," by Robert Edge Pine, copy by Adrian Lamb 1981. Courtesy of the Mount Vernon Ladies' Association.

vide all the material the estate needed for slave clothing. Martha personally knitted the stockings for Nelly and Wash from Mount Vernon wool. In early summer 1784 Martha sent to her sister-in-law Hannah Bushrod Washington asking if she could spare some of her own stock of cotton thread to make cloth, because her spinners had spun all the wool available and were sitting idle.

Her request coincided with an invitation from Hannah to Martha and George to visit her and George's brother John Augustine, known as Jack, at Bushfield Plantation, about eighty miles from Mount Vernon. Hannah and Jack had had a tragedy in February, when their youngest son, seventeen-year-old William Augustine, was killed at school in a shooting accident. Hannah had been devastated. Martha was fond of Hannah and would have enjoyed the trip, but it depended on George. She wrote to Hannah in June 1784: "It would give me much pleasure to come to Bushfield to visit you and will when it is convenient to the General to leve home on a visit; he has so much business of his one and the publicks to gather that I fear he will never find lazure to goe see his friends."

"Elizabeth Parke Custis," "Eliza," by Robert Edge Pine, copy by Adrian Lamb 1981. Courtesy of the Mount Vernon Ladies' Association.

George was already planning a trip, an extended visit in September 1784, to the land he owned west of the Appalachians, to investigate ways of making it produce some income. As it was rich farmland, he had an idea of advertising for tenant farmers to rent it. He was also involved in a scheme to open up the isolated western territory by means of navigation. It appears from Martha's letter that George did not visit Bushfield between the time of his return and June, and that he was too busy to escort Martha on a visit there at the time she was writing.

Whether George may have been at Bushfield alone earlier in the year or whether he did in fact take Martha for a visit is relevant to an issue raised by the descendants of a female slave at Bushfield as to whether George had a liaison with her, which produced a son. Venus Ford was a mulatto household slave at Bushfield, the same age as George's nephew Bushrod Washington. Venus gave birth to a son named West Ford either in 1784 or 1785. As a boy and a young man, West received special and preferential treatment from the Washingtons, as did Venus's own parents, suggesting West was closely connected to the Washington family by blood. He was educated, vaccinated against smallpox, eventually freed by Hannah, and given a substantial piece of property at Gum Springs. He married and raised a family and died at Mount Vernon, something of a celebrity, having been for many years the custodian of the Washington tomb.

It is generally accepted that West's father was probably a member of the Washington family, and there are a number of possibilities within the family. At Bushfield, George's favorite brother Jack, Jack and Hannah's son's Bushrod, a second son Corbin, or William Augustine, who died at seventeen, all could have fathered West. However, since the 1920s a rumor has persisted that West's father actually was George Washington, who may have had a relationship with Venus either at Bushfield or during a visit to Mount Vernon by Hannah, accompanied by Venus. Among West Ford's descendants, two different families have an oral tradition as to who the baby's father was. One story goes that when Hannah asked Venus about the baby's father, she answered, "It be the old general, missis." Family tradition should not be discounted, but there is as of yet no scientific proof. What is curious is that the story has survived for two hundred years. If not George's son, West Ford was likely to have been his great-nephew and is yet another example of the blood ties between Martha's family and their slaves.

What is certain is that whoever in the Washington family knew who was West's father, he or she kept quiet about it. Typically the "veil of silence" descended within the family, and if Martha learned about West or heard any rumors suggesting George was his father, there is no record of it.

Some insight into how Martha viewed the issue of white men preying on slave girls comes from a story recounted by Wash Custis. It involved a young aide to George, Colonel Smith, who was living at Mount Vernon as George's secretary, and Bishop's pretty daughter Sarah. In the course of an evening walk Colonel Smith happened on Bishop's house and saw Sarah, milking nearby. According to Smith, he saw that the pail of milk was too heavy and approached Sarah, offering to carry it. Sarah's response seems disproportionate to a simple offer of help, because according to Wash, Sarah dropped the pail of milk and ran screaming for help to her father. Smith went after her, only to be confronted by an enraged Bishop who threatened, as Wash recorded it, to "carry the matter up to his honor, aye, and to the madam, too. At the mention of the latter personage the unfortunate colonel felt something like an ague chill pass over his frame."

Smith tried to pacify Bishop with apologies, but it made matters worse. Bishop announced George would not permit Sarah to be insulted and "as to the madam, why the madam as good as brought up my girl."

Smith was worried enough about Martha's reaction to consult Will Lee. Will Lee didn't like Bishop, because Bishop, proud of his service with the British in the French and Indian Wars, made no secret of his view that mere Revolutionary veterans were "half soldiers." Lee was annoyed that Bishop would think of complaining about Smith, but thought Smith could probably explain himself to George. However, both men faltered at the thought that Martha might then hear about it. Smith persuaded Will Lee to intercept and attempt to explain to Bishop that Smith had meant no harm. Will Lee duly waylaid a still angry Bishop, who had changed into his old uniform and was on his way to the Mansion House. Will Lee disarmed Bishop by saying Bishop had no business having such a pretty daughter, making excuses for Smith that "young fellows will be young fellows" and urging, "It was not to be thought of that any such matter should reach the madam's ears." Bishop was eventually persuaded, for which Smith gave Will Lee a handsome tip.

Wash's telling of the story is cloaked in flowery language, but the underlying point, that it was immediately evident to Bishop, Smith, and Will Lee that Martha would not tolerate slave women and girls being attacked by their guests, comes through.

In addition to Nelly and Wash, the Washingtons had added another surrogate child to the household—pretty, sweet-tempered, sixteen-year-old

"Fanny Bassett," by Robert Edge Pine, 1785. Courtesy of the Mount Vernon Ladies' Association.

Fanny Bassett. Fanny was rapidly becoming indispensable to Martha, as her constant companion, assistant hostess, and right hand, amidst the visitors and builders' confusion and the demands of Nelly and Wash. In turn, Fanny, who had been farmed out to a series of relatives since her mother's death in 1777, enjoyed her aunt's attention. When Fanny finally left Mount Vernon to spend some time with her father and relatives in New Kent, Martha missed her terribly, as Martha wrote to her: "My dear Fanny . . . Tho' have never been alone since you left this,—yet I cannot say but I have missed your company very much."[2]

In New Kent, Fanny was probably missing more than just Martha's company at Mount Vernon. George had a nephew, George Augustine Washington, who had been one of General Lafayette's aides and who was also living at Mount Vernon. Like many others who were the worse for living in military camps for years, George Augustine was not in the best of health. He had a cough and occasional fevers. George had sent him to the West Indies to recover. George Augustine had returned somewhat better, and he and Fanny, much in each other's company, were falling in love.

Along with constant company to take up Martha's time, the house was inundated with gifts arriving from admirers, well-wishers, friends, and total strangers. The Washingtons never knew what the day might bring, but George and his aides were kept busy sending "grateful acknowledgements," and a place had to be found for everything. Among the gifts were a handsome Italian marble fireplace sent from an admirer in London, a set of andirons from Lafayette, plants, books, a fine set of Sevres china for Martha, and a pair of Chinese pheasants. Lafayette and the king of Spain each sent George a jackass to breed mules for work on the plantation.

In the autumn of 1784 the Marquis de Lafayette visited Mount Vernon. Though the Washingtons had warmly invited his wife to accompany him, she did not feel able to undertake a transatlantic crossing. Martha showed off her new outbuildings, and Lafayette planted a magnolia tree in Martha's garden. Lafayette was a most charming man and devoted to George, almost like a son to him. Both Washingtons were fond of him and truly happy to see him, but later, another well-meant gift of his to George drove Martha to distraction and an outburst of temper.

Knowing how fond George was of hunting, Lafayette followed his visit by sending George a pack of French hounds. The hounds were large, very strong, and completely undisciplined. Because of their fierce temperament, they were supposed to be kept penned up, but they were constantly escaping from their kennels and causing havoc among the farm animals and in the house. Martha detested them and Wash Custis recorded this anecdote:

Of the French hounds there was one named Vulcan, and we bear him the better in reminiscence from having often bestrid his back in the days of our juvenility. It happened that upon a large company sitting down to dinner at Mount Vernon one day, the lady of the mansion (my grandmother) discovered that the ham, the pride of every Virginia housewife's table, was missing from its accustomed post of honor. Upon questioning Frank, the butler, this portly, and at the same time most polite and accomplished of all butlers, observed that a ham, yes, a very fine ham had been prepared agreeably to the Madam's orders, but lo and behold! who should come into the kitchen, while the savory ham was smoking in its dish, but old Vulcan, the hound, and without more ado fastened his fangs into it; and although they of the kitchen had stood to such arms as they could get, and had fought the old spoiler desperately, yet Vulcan had finally triumphed, and bore off the prize, ay "cleanly, under the keeper's nose." The lady by no means relished the loss of a dish which formed the pride of her table, and uttered some remarks by no means favourable to dogs in general, while the chief, having heard the story, communicated it to his guests, and with them, laughed heartily.[3]

It was the end of the hounds. Nelly Custis recalled her grandmother's way of making her point with George: if Martha believed George was ignoring her, she would reach up and grasp him firmly by the lapels and say "General!" sharply until George looked down from his great height and she had his attention. She would then state her point, and George would laugh and do whatever Martha wanted.

Martha must have issued an ultimatum, because within a few months of this incident, George gave away his hounds and broke up his kennel, giving the excuse that he was too old and too busy to keep up his hunting, which had once been his great passion and which he had in fact resumed after the war. Instead, he undertook another grandiose project, which would have been incompatible with hounds, installing a herd of deer in an enclosed park between the house and the river. The governor of Maryland sent him some deer, and George wrote to George William Fairfax in England to ask for an additional pair of deer from England to breed with those from the governor.

Homecoming had many bittersweet moments for the Washingtons. They found the neighborhood much changed, and only a few of their old friends from the first fifteen years of their marriage were still living there. They had tried to maintain contact with the Fairfaxes during the war, though George had not wanted it to be generally known that he was writing to England. In England George William and Sally, suspected of spying for the Americans, had been kept under surveillance by royal authorities. The letters from George and the Fairfaxes were nearly all intercepted, and most never reached their intended destinations during the war.

Now back in regular contact, George wrote to the Fairfaxes that Martha's two grandchildren—"both promising children"—lived at Mount Vernon and that he was seeking a tutor for them. In return he learned that George William had had smallpox and that he and Sally had had to move from Toulston Manor in Yorkshire and were living quietly in Bath. George hoped the Fairfaxes would return to their old neighborhood and rebuild Belvoir.

In February 1785 George wrote again to the Fairfaxes, a letter often cited as proof of the fact George was still in love with Sally nearly forty years later. In fact, the tone of the letter is such that it is easier to believe any rivalry between Martha and Sally Cary Fairfax was long over, and probably had been since the early days of the Washingtons' marriage. George's letter unquestionably reflects the warmth of a longtime friendship, on both his and, as he writes, Martha's part. Whether it reflects more is a matter of nuance read into the terms he uses, but all the parties were now in their fifties, almost elderly by the standards of the day, who had suffered bereavements, thwarted ambition, political upheavals, and financial setbacks. At this time of life most people look back to their youth with nostalgia. George painted a sad picture of a ruined Belvoir:

> Mount Vernon, February 27, 1785
> My Dr. Sir,
>
> I cannot at this moment recur to the contents of those letters of mine to you which I suspect have miscarried; further than that they were all expressive of an earnest wish to see you and Mrs. Fairfax once more fixed in this country; and to beg that you would consider Mount Vernon as your home until you could build with convenience, in which request Mrs. Washington joins very sincerely. I never look towards Belvoir, without having this uppermost in my mind. But alas, Belvoir is no more! I took a ride there the other day to visit the ruins, and ruins indeed they are. The dwelling house and the two brick buildings in front, underwent the ravages of the fire; the walls of which are very much injured; the other Houses are sinking under the depredation of time and inattention, and I believe are now scarcely worth repairing. In a word, the whole are, or very soon will be, a heap of ruin. When I viewed them, when I considered that the happiest moments of my life had been spent there, when I could not trace a room (now all rubbish) that did not bring to my mind the recollection of pleasing scenes, I was obliged to fly from them; and came home with painful sensations, and sorrowing for the contrast.[4]

Likely much to George's disappointment, the Fairfaxes wrote they had no thoughts of returning and were content with their small house in Wridlington, where they passed the days working in their garden.

Distressing news came on Sunday, April 24, 1785, when an express arrived at Mount Vernon with the news that Martha's mother and her brother Bartholomew had died at Pamocra within days of each other.

Soon thereafter, Martha and George expanded the family circle again to take in Harriot Washington, the unruly little daughter of George's dead brother Samuel. George assumed responsibility for her support, because Harriot had inherited nothing. Taking her in was not an easy proposition, for Harriot seems to have been a very difficult child—noisy, boisterous, and so much in the habit of carelessly ruining her clothes that even George remonstrated and told her to be more careful, as he could not afford to keep buying her new things. Even Martha's legendary way with children did not prevent Harriot from being a trial.

In the summer of 1785 a distinguished English historian, Catherine Macaulay Graham, and her husband visited Mount Vernon, through an introduction from Mercy Otis Warren. Martha wrote Mercy a letter to thank her for sending them such an interesting visitor, but Mrs. Macaulay Graham seems to have passed her time at Mount Vernon mostly talking politics and arguing incessantly with George. Reading between the lines of Martha's letter to Mercy, there is the sense that Martha found such a bluestocking an exhausting sort of guest.

The love affair between Fanny Bassett and George Augustine Washington had reached the point where they wanted to marry. That Fanny's father was not entirely pleased by the match was evidenced by a letter from George to Burwell Bassett saying he made it a practice never to interfere when two people wanted to marry—suggesting that was exactly what Burwell Bassett had asked him to do—and if they did want to marry, as Fanny and his nephew insisted, George thought the sooner the better. Fanny's father may have been concerned both by the state of her intended groom's health and his lack of prospects.

Nonetheless, in the autumn of 1785 Fanny Bassett and George Augustine Washington had their way and were married at Mount Vernon one evening "just after the candles were lighted." Burwell Bassett was unable to attend at the last minute because of an attack of gout. The Fairfaxes sent a wedding present. After the marriage, George appointed George Augustine as manager at Mount Vernon in place of Lund Washington, so the couple had something to live on. At the time of the wedding Martha was, according to George, having a long spell of "indifferent" health. George himself was overwhelmed by correspondence and his business affairs, and resolved to find someone who could double as a tutor for the children and a private secretary to himself.

His old military colleague General Benjamin Lincoln recommended a young Harvard graduate named Tobias Lear from Portsmouth, New Hampshire. To distinguish the tutor from any hint of indentured servitude and clarify his position at Mount Vernon, George had written that the new tutor/secretary would "sit at my table, will live as I live, will mix with the company who resort to the house, will be treated in every respect with civility and proper attention. He will have his washing done in the family, and may have his socks darned by the maids."

Tobias Lear was a pleasant and intelligent young man who fit the bill perfectly. He arrived in 1786 and was an immediate success with Martha, George, and the children, soon becoming a permanent addition to the Washington household. It was soothing to have someone around to assist with, rather than to add to, the family burdens and worries.

Family burdens extended beyond the environs of Mount Vernon. As during her marriage to Jacky, Eleanor Calvert Custis Stuart continued to be regularly pregnant and ill, and as Doctor Stuart took over management of Jacky's estate, it was gradually becoming clearer and clearer that Jacky might have lost a considerable portion of the Custis money before his death. Meanwhile Eleanor was so occupied with her younger children that she had less time for her two elder daughters. Martha made an effort to have Betsy and Patty with her to give them some extra attention.

In January 1787 George noted in his diary that his "beloved brother John Augustine Washington" had died at Bushfield. George was saddened by death of his favorite brother, but Jack's death posed the immediate problem of what to do about their increasingly infirm mother. Mary Washington, still living alone in her little house in Fredericksburg, was unwell and complaining of poverty. Because Mary's widowed daughter Betty had her hands full with her own children and her school and her own financial problems, Jack and George had decided the best plan was for Mary to move to Bushfield.

Jack's death raised the alarming possibility that Martha's mother-in-law might now come to live at Mount Vernon. The state of the Washingtons' troubled finances and their hectic home life is reflected in a harassed letter George wrote to his mother early in 1787, giving every reason he could think of for her not to move in with him and Martha. Mary had complained she was short of money and hinted for an invitation to live at Mount Vernon. For George it would have been the last straw. George wrote:

> Mount Vernon February 15, 1787
> Hond. Madam
>   In consequence of your communication . . . of your want of money I . . . send you 15 Guineas, which believe me is all have, and which indeed ought to have been paid many days ago to another, agreeable to my own assurances. I have now demands upon me for more than £500, three hundred and forty odd of which is due for the tax of 1786; and I now not where or when, I shall receive one shilling to pay it. In the last two years I made no crops . . . my wheat is so bad, I cannot eat it myself or sell it to others, and Tobacco I make none. . . . my expences, not from any extravagance or any inclination on my part to live splendidly, but for the absolute support of my family and the visitors who are constantly here, are exceedingly high. . . .
>   My house is at your service, and [I] would press you most sincerely and most devoutly to accept it, but I am sure, and candor requires me to say, it will

never answer your purposes . . . for in truth it may be compared to a well resorted tavern, as scarcely any strangers who are going from north to south, or from south to north, do not spend a day or two at it. This would, were you to be an inhabitant of it, oblige you to do one of 3 things: 1ˢᵗ, to be always dressing to appear in company; 2ⁿᵈ, to come into [the room] in a dishabille, or 3ʳᵈ, to be as it were a prisoner in your own chamber. The first you'ld not like . . . it would be too fatiguing, The 2ⁿᵈ, I should not like, because those who resort here are . . . strangers and people of the first distinction. And the 3ʳᵈ . . . would not be pleasing to either of us. Nor indeed could you be retired in any room in my house; for what with the sitting up of company, the noise and bustle of servants, and many other things, you would not be able to enjoy . . . calmness and serenity of mind.[5]

Although written to Mary, who in the end did not insist on coming to Mount Vernon, the letter also casts some light on another demand on Martha, namely that she had to look presentable for company "of the first distinction" every waking minute, even while managing a huge household. Relying on her maids, and their laundering, mending, starching, and ironing skills to keep her clothes in perfect order, Martha had perfected the art of the swift, perfect early-morning toilette and could famously wear the same white morning dress for a week without getting it soiled as she went about her household tasks. While George could always take refuge in his study, widely known to be off-limits to everyone, Martha's uninterrupted hour after breakfast with her Bible and her prayers was her only calm moment of the day.

It was a hectic life, and Martha began to look back to her days with the army with a kind of nostalgia. Perhaps things seemed simpler in camp. A London merchant who visited Mount Vernon during this period recorded in his diary that he found Martha a most agreeable hostess, but noted:

It is astonishing with what raptures she spoke about the discipline of the army, the excellent order they were in, superior to any troops on the face of the earth towards the close of the war; even the English she said acknowledged it. What a pleasure she took in the sound of the fifes and drums, preferring it to any music that was ever heard; and then to see them reviewed a week or two before the men were disbanded, when they were all well clothed was she said a most heavenly sight. Almost every soldier shed tears at parting with the General. Mrs. Washington said it was a most melancholy sight.[6]

An enjoyable aspect of Martha's life was that Nelly at six was old enough to begin learning the basics of domestic management, cookery, sewing, and the treatment of sick slaves. Martha also taught Nelly some music. Tobias Lear gave the children their other lessons, and Nelly soon proved to be a better pupil than Wash.

As Nelly and Wash settled into the routine of their lessons, by the spring of 1787 Martha had a new cause for anxiety. By the end of 1786 Fanny was already pregnant and her husband George Augustine showed signs of tuberculosis. In April of 1787 Fanny gave birth to her first child, a son, at Mount Vernon. The baby lived for two weeks and died.

In May George left the chaos of Mount Vernon behind him to go to Philadelphia as a delegate to a Constitutional Convention to be held there in the coming months. He was elected president of the Convention and spent four hot summer months in Philadelphia as the Convention hammered out the terms of a document that would become the U.S. Constitution. Once drafted, it had to be adopted by each state, a process that would take many months.

In Philadelphia George was treated as a hero and was much in demand when the day's business at the Convention was finished. He stayed with his wealthy friend Robert Morris and visited, dined, and took tea with prominent members of Philadelphia society and sat for his portrait by Charles Willson Peale.

When he returned in the fall to Mount Vernon, George received a letter with the news that George William Fairfax had died in England. A letter to her sister-in-law in Virginia indicates Sally Cary Fairfax mourned her husband sincerely: "Weeping has deprived me of sight. I am ashamed to see my candlelight work, but if you can make out my meaning I am satisfied. I think before I wrote you that your dear Brother was as widely esteemed as any man in England. As proof of it, I now send you on the other side of this sheet of paper, what appeared in the London paper at the time of his decease. Myself nor any friends known by whom put in."[7]

If George's letter to George William Fairfax, recalling the "happiest moments of his life" is considered as evidence he was still in love with Sally Cary Fairfax, Sally's own letter suggests why Martha was able to be on good terms with Sally when they were near neighbors many years earlier.

In November some of George's Philadelphia friends and colleagues visited Mount Vernon. Among them was Elizabeth "Eliza" Willing Powel, an heiress who had married one of Philadelphia's wealthiest men. Eliza had a connection in Virginia, as her sister Mary Willing had married William Byrd III at Westover Plantation. William Byrd III had gone so deeply into debt that he committed suicide, leaving Mary to bring up her family alone in straitened circumstances.

A thoughtful, clever woman, Eliza wrote after her visit to praise Martha's hospitality, sent some items of finery, collars and sashes for the girls that Martha had requested from Philadelphia, and some child-sized books to "our little Favorite Master Custis." She also praised Nelly and Wash's "sweet conciliating manner," and took an interest in the health of Fanny, who had a bad cough and was pregnant again. She also offered to do errands for Martha in Philadelphia. She evidently found Martha sympathetic, because in writing to Martha, she felt able to unburden herself of many of her worries about her sister.

Martha's reply in January 1788 was drafted either by George or Tobias Lear. Obviously they thought Martha's grammar, spelling, and punctuation needed help, and that the letter called for certain phrases that characterized formal letters but that Martha never used herself, such as "I flatter myself with the hopes of seeing you" instead of "We hope to see you," or "I flatter myself that will be agreeable." Martha was a prolific letter writer to her family and close friends, but she dashed off what she had to say, ignored punctuation, asked about everyone's health, sent her love, and that was it. By copying his superiors in everything, as a young man George had acquired a gentleman's style of writing and a rather elaborately courteous way of expressing himself. Martha, like most women she knew, had little time for such refinements and flowery turns of phrase. It is interesting that as soon as Martha was in correspondence with the sort of people whom George did not want to have seeing his mother in a state of dishabille, he was so anxious for her to sound correct that he or Tobias drafted some of her letters. Much of Martha's surviving correspondence sounds stilted as a result.

Fanny's next baby was due in March 1788, and she planned to go to Eltham for her delivery. She left in January and Martha was dismayed that it would probably be May before she saw Fanny again—if everything went well. "Fanny," wrote Martha "is a child to me, and I am very lonesome when she is absent. Her ill luck with her first child is the only reason of her wishing to change the place of her lying inn this time. If her child lives, it will be sometime in May before she can come up—the distance is too farr for me to goe down to see her." Fanny might have found it more comfortable to stay at Mount Vernon and be nursed by Martha, but it was a popular belief at the time that "a change of air" was a tonic in itself. Given childbirth mortality rates, Martha was justifiably concerned.

At the same time Martha's nephew John, Bartholomew's son and executor, was struggling with his late father's will, gathering the assets of the estate in order to pay his father's debts. He wrote of his plans to sell the slaves, of whom a great many were women and children, to raise cash to buy an annuity for his mother and sister. John wanted to sell at least half of them, a typical way of raising capital, but a plan that conjures up the chilling image of slaves at Pamocra waiting to be picked out by the slave dealer for sale.

Around the fireplace in the parlor at Mount Vernon that winter the talk was inevitably of which states had or had not ratified the Constitution. Martha wrote to Fanny in February that "we have not a single article of news but politick which I do not concern myself about." She was more anxious about her family's health. She wrote that

My Dear little children have all been very well, till today my pretty little dear Boy complains of a pain in his stomach. I hope it proceeds from cold as he is much better than he was some months agoe . . . I cannot say but it makes me miserable if ever he complains let the cause be ever so trifleling—I hope the almighty will sparc him to me—. . . The General . . . got a bad cold . . . as to myself I am as usal—neither sick or well . . . if you should want any thing that I have I can assure my Dear Fanny that it would give me great pleasure to send her anything that would add to her pleasure or happyness.[8]

In March Fanny had a daughter whom she named Anna Maria, after her mother. The child and Fanny lived, and both returned to Mount Vernon in due course. The little girl was called Maria and soon became a great favorite with Martha. The number of children at Mount Vernon was increased in July, when John's younger sister Patty Dandridge was invited for an extended stay, no doubt to help out her widowed mother.

Martha was busy but continued to be in her element, this time surrounded by children to look after, girls to teach, young people to liven up the house, and her dear Fanny back home. There is a sense that for Martha by 1788 life at Mount Vernon was firmly back on a happy and even keel.

CHAPTER 18

"The General Is Gone to New York"

The house had been enlarged, and the chaos from rebuilding had dissipated. George was gradually rectifying the problems caused by Lund's lax management of Mount Vernon in his absence, but the Washingtons' financial problems remained so pressing that George was thinking of seeking an annuity from the Custis estate. He did have new moneymaking schemes, both at Mount Vernon and elsewhere, including the Potomac Navigation Company, a budding enterprise to link the Chesapeake via the Potomac to inland rivers to provide access to the western territories. This proposed undertaking dovetailed with George's plans to settle tenant farmers on his land in the Ohio Valley.

In the spring of 1788 the Washingtons received a letter from their friend the Marquis de Chastellux, who had visited Mount Vernon on several occasions. The marquis, a man described by Benson Lossing as "the life of every company into which he was introduced, while in this country . . . left a very pleasant impression at Mount Vernon," wrote to say he had married "a very accomplished lady, a relative of the Duke of Orleans."

George was delighted, and his letter of congratulation provides an insight into his own marriage to Martha:

> Mount Vernon, April 25,[-May 1] 1788
> My dear Marquis:
>   I was . . . not less delighted than surprised to come across that plain American word "my wife." A wife! well my dear Marquis, I can hardly refrain from smiling to find you are caught at last. I saw, by the eulogium you often made on the happiness of domestic life in America, that you had swallowed the bait and that you would as surely be taken (one day or another) as you was a Phi-

losopher and a Soldier. So your day has, at length, come. I am glad of it with all my heart and soul. It is quite good enough for you. Now you are well served for coming to fight in favor of the American Rebels, all the way across the Atlantic Ocean, by catching that terrible Contagion, domestic felicity, which time like the small pox or the plague, a man can have only once in his life: because it commonly lasts him (at least with us in America, I don't know how you manage these matters in France) for his whole life time.[1]

The Mansion House continued to serve as a hotel for countless visitors, but Martha had established a rigid domestic order behind the scenes, which enabled her to appear a serene hostess as well as to look after members of her extended family who were often in residence. Betsy and Patty Custis often came to stay with Nelly and Wash, and Bartholomew's daughter Patty Dandridge was practically living at Mount Vernon, along with Harriot, Fanny, and Maria.

Always happiest with one or more surrogate daughters around her, Martha was surrounded by girls—like Patcy would have been had she lived—who needed her. Martha taught them needlework and cookery and housekeeping, counseled them in deportment, and took them to church. In doing all this, Martha was undoubtedly reliving her own girlhood, passing on the same lessons she had learned from Frances many years ago at Chestnut Grove.

Martha had a rare knack for dealing with young people. She was an immensely thoughtful person, forever finding small presents for her friends and relatives, pleased for the girls to have pretty clothes, like the collar and other things she had ordered from her friend Eliza Powel in Philadelphia. Martha worried over their health and manners and posture, but having a sociable disposition herself, Martha always believed the girls should have as good a time and as much social life as the neighborhood afforded. The girls had music lessons, and once again there were dancing classes held at Mount Vernon for the young people in the neighborhood. By all accounts the girls were devoted to Martha.

The period of domestic tranquility that allowed Martha to devote so much time and attention to her surrogate daughters was about to be rudely interrupted. Once all the states had ratified the Constitution, the next order of business for the new federal Congress was to elect a president. Martha thought George was too old for the job and that he had already sacrificed enough of his time and effort to the American cause for further public service. He had rheumatism, had become slightly deaf, and had endured years of trouble with his teeth, including some painful dental experiments involving tooth implants, probably with teeth purchased from his slaves. Like Martha, he needed spectacles. Though he kept up the same punishing schedule of rising at 4 A.M. each morning and riding out to inspect the estate each day, dealing with a mountain of paperwork in the early hours and last thing before bed, at fifty-eight George was almost an old man. Martha had been hoping against hope that George would not be drawn into political life. She was sick of politics, and it was obvious how much they were both needed at Mount Vernon.

Yet, paradoxically, she may have been the one to signal that George might be persuaded to do so. She had seen how the trip to the Constitutional Congress had affected him. There is an anecdote that it was Martha herself who dropped the hint to a congressional visitor to Mount Vernon that George would not be averse to a greater degree of political involvement. It must have been an inadvertent comment, however, because when it transpired, she was appalled. With a majority of states having ratified the Constitution, Congress met in January 1789 to set in motion the procedure for electing a president. On April 6 the votes of the electoral college were counted, and the unanimous choice was George Washington as the first president of the United States.

This result had been a foregone conclusion, so much so that George had already written to Lafayette and others about his reservations about undertaking the office. George was torn between his inclination to stay home, now that he was finally beginning to get his affairs in order and Mount Vernon running productively, and his sense of duty. An overriding consideration was that he appreciated the need for a charismatic figure to head the new republican government, and he sensed that he was the only candidate for the office with the skill and authority to force the disparate factions of the new republic to work together. In a way, it was a natural outgrowth of his experiences commanding the army. George feared that without strong leadership from the outset, the fragile unity of what were in effect thirteen sovereign entities, would simply dissolve. He could not bear to think that the sacrifices of the Revolution had been for nothing. Because he could not afford to pay his outstanding debts, and anticipating his election, George borrowed £600 from an Alexandria merchant to settle his outstanding accounts before accepting the office.

On Tuesday, April 14, a congressional representative, Secretary Charles Thompson, arrived at Mount Vernon in the morning between ten and eleven. Martha was obliged to entertain him until George's return from his customary daily tour of the farms. Although normally George never returned before quarter to three, in time to change and powder his hair for dinner, on the fourteenth he returned at quarter to one. The two men disappeared into George's study, emerging in time for dinner. The atmosphere at dinner must have been pregnant with politics as well as anxiety on Martha's part. After dinner George rose and went upstairs to write the following letter to the president of the Congress, John Langdon:

Mount Vernon 14th April 1789
Sir:

 I had the honor to receive your official communication, by the hand of Mr. Secretary Thompson, about one o' clock this day. Having concluded to obey the important and flattering call of my country, and having been impressed with the idea of the expediency of my being with Congress at as early a period as possible, I propose to commence my journey on Thursday morning, which will be the day after tomorrow.[2]

That same evening George left Mount Vernon with Will Lee to pay a farewell visit to his mother in Fredericksburg. Mary Washington had never moved from her small house within walking distance of Kenwood, and she was suffering from breast cancer. It was the last time the two saw each other.

George spent the night at his mother's and returned to Mount Vernon on the evening of April 15. There appears to have been little opportunity to discuss his decision with Martha after the arrival of Secretary Thompson and before writing to Congress to accept. To have left any discussion with Martha until his return late on the fifteenth, hours before he was due to leave for New York, would have made no sense. Either the Washingtons had discussed the possibility before the fourteenth, and Martha knew he was going to accept, or George presented Martha with the kind of fait accompli that would have made any wife grit her teeth.

George left with Will Lee, his aide David Humphreys, and his secretary Tobias Lear for New York at ten in the morning on the sixteenth. Since they were taking the coach, George had asked Mary Washington to loan Martha her own coach until his could return to pick up Martha in a few weeks time and bring her to New York. The fact that Martha did not go with him suggests that she had not had enough time to make arrangements for her departure and even that the decision may have taken her by surprise. Judging by a letter Martha wrote to her nephew John Dandridge four days after George's precipitate departure, Martha was struggling to overcome her feelings of fury and dismay at the turn of events. Certainly her reluctance is clear. The tone of the letter also suggests that the news would come as a surprise to the rest of the family:

My Dear John   Mount Vernon. April the 20th 1789
 I am truly sorry to tell that the General is gone to New York,—Mr Charles Thompson came express to him, on the 14th—when or wheather he will ever come home again god only knows,—I think it was much too late for him to go in to publick life again, but it was not to be avoided, our family will be deranged as I must soon follow him

 I am greved at parting, and sorry to part with your sister, [Martha's niece Patty Dandridge, who had been at Mount Vernon since the previous July]—I expect to set out in the middle of may and have it not in my power to send Patty home; . . . I wish you could make it convenient to come up for Patty—as it is out of my power to send her down—the same horses that carred the General is to return for me to carry me to New York.[3]

George's progress to New York, the first capital of the American republic, was marked by celebration and an exuberant, but sometimes embarrassing, outpouring of public emotion at each stop on the way. The route was lined with throngs of cheering people. Already regarded as a hero in his own right, the president-to-be now assumed a greater significance as the living symbol of American republicanism. George Washington's larger-than-life public persona had been years in the making, but for Martha, George's triumphal progress north signaled a new role.

He got no further than the few miles to Alexandria when he was obliged to stop and participate in a festive public dinner in his honor, which included an oration from the mayor. Invited to respond, George, who was anxious to press on and avoid being the object of more adulation and sentimental addresses, replied, "Words fail me. Unutterable sensations must then be left to more expressive silence."

Public enthusiasm swelled. Crowds cheered, church bells rang, and guns were fired. George was greeted with ceremony at Georgetown and entertained at a large public supper at Baltimore. Trying to slip unobtrusively out of the city at 5:30 the next morning to avoid further manifestations of public feeling, George and his party found themselves saluted by cannon even at that hour and a mounted cavalcade of gentlemen ready to escort them.

At the Pennsylvania line the party was met by a body of troops to escort George to Philadelphia. Ever conscious of his image, George left the carriage and rode into Philadelphia on a superb white horse. He rode under a specially constructed triumphal arch covered in evergreens at Gray's Ferry on the Schuylkill River. Perched on the top was Angelica Peale, Charles Willson Peale's young daughter, who, as George passed below, let down a "handsomely ornamented civic crown of laurel" onto George's head. The inevitable dinner, with speeches and toasts and cheers, followed.

When George's party reached Trenton in New Jersey after a heavy storm, the sun burst through the clouds. As he entered the city, there were the usual throngs of people, cannons booming, and celebratory musket fire. The patriotic feelings of the local matrons, however, had reached fever pitch and found their own outlet. When George crossed the bridge over the Delaware, he rode under another triumphal arch, twenty feet high and supported by evergreen-covered pillars. Over the arch floated a banner that read, "THE DEFENDER OF THE MOTHERS WILL BE THE PROTECTOR OF THE DAUGHTERS."

As George approached the arch, local women and their daughters all dressed in white appeared on cue from behind the pillars, and young girls with wreaths and baskets of flowers danced out to scatter petals in his path and sing an ode written especially for the occasion.

At Elizabethtown Point, where George was to cross the river to New York, there was a magnificent barge to transport him, manned by thirteen pilots in white uniforms. The harbor was packed with ships and pleasure boats, all decked with flags in George's honor, with one exception: a Spanish man-of-war was conspicuously undecorated, prompting criticism from everyone.

When the barge carrying George pulled even with the man-of-war, the Spanish ship suddenly raised on every part of her rigging every known signal and flag of every nation, and fired a thirteen-gun salute, a display that delighted the cheering crowds.

In New York George was ceremonially escorted to the presidential mansion, a house at 10 Cherry Street (now an empty plot of land beneath the Brooklyn Bridge). He was inaugurated on April 30, wearing a dark brown suit and white silk stockings, all of American manufacture, with silver buckles on his shoes and his hair powdered. When he took the oath on the Bible presented to him, George added the words "So help me God," which have been used by presidents at their inaugurations ever since. The crowd burst into cheers of "Long live George Washington, president of the United States."

Martha was not present at the inauguration. She was not able to leave Mount Vernon until May 16. In any event the advance party from Mount Vernon—George, Tobias Lear, and David Humphreys—had preparations to make before Martha could easily assume her new role. Primarily there were arrangements to be made in the presidential mansion. Congress had rented one of the handsomest houses in New York. While it was mostly furnished with handsome new furniture, the ever-practical Martha had sent Tobias Lear a lengthy shopping list of practical and indispensable domestic articles the men would not have thought of. Included was kitchen equipment, which would be needed for an establishment that would be simultaneously the presidential offices, a family home, and accommodation for the presidential aides and the official presidential residence for social and diplomatic entertaining.

Another issue to be resolved was the proper protocol for the new republic: what George and Martha would be called in their official capacity, whether ladies would curtsy and men bow to either or both, whether they would shake hands, and what Martha's role as official hostess would be and what form her duties would take, who would assist her, and so on. The new government had no precedent to guide them in matters relating to etiquette, protocol, behavior, or formal titles. It is no exaggeration to say they quite literally had to "make it up as they went along."

The first order of business for George and his advisors, including his vice president John Adams, who had spent several years in England and France during the negotiations for the peace treaty that ended the Revolution and afterwards, wanted a title that would clearly indicate the president was on a par with "Royal George," and he favored the grander options such as "His Highness" or "His Serene Highness." George himself preferred the somewhat daft-sounding "His High Mightiness," because it was what the Elector of Holland was called. Since official business was on hold until the question was resolved, George finally lost patience and announced that he and Martha would be President and Mrs. Washington. Also among themselves they decided that Martha would preside at her own official "Drawing Room" on Friday evenings, when she would receive ladies and their husbands, fathers, or other male escorts.

While issues of etiquette and protocol were being hammered out in New York, Martha had a great deal to do supervising, packing, and drawing up detailed instructions for Fanny, who was going to be left in charge. A less organized woman and a less experienced housekeeper than her efficient aunt, Fanny had become a rather preoccupied twenty-one-year-old matron who would now have to manage a sick husband, Maria, Harriot, the house, and the household slaves who remained. Robert Lewis, Betty's son who had come to escort Martha, Nelly, and Wash, described an emotional leave-taking and departure from Mount Vernon: "After an early dinner and making all necessary arrangements in which we were greatly retarded it brought us to three o'clock in the afternoon when we left Mount Vernon. The servants of the house and a number of the field negroes made their appearance to take leave of their mistress—numbers of these poor wretches seemed most affected, my aunt equally so. We travelled together as far as Alexandria, and left my aunt at her request to proceed to Doct Stuarts."

Robert Lewis spent the night elsewhere but returned to Abingdon to collect Martha, Nelly, and Wash. He described the leave-taking at the Stuarts next morning as such as he "never again wishes to be witness to—leaving the family in tears—the children a-bawling—everything in the most lamentable situation."[4]

He noted that at Hammond's Ferry crossing over into Baltimore, the water was running very high and Martha was worried about whether it was safe to cross. Once on the other side, her new status as wife of the president was brought home to her when she was met by an escort of gentlemen from Baltimore who accompanied her to the home of her friends the Carrolls. According to Robert Lewis:

> Mrs. Carroll . . . had made a considerable preparation, as we found a large bowl of salubrious ice punch with fruits, etc., which had been plucked from the trees in a green house, lying on the tables in great abundance;—these after riding

twenty five or thirty miles without eating or drinking was no unwelcome luxuries, however, Mrs. Carroll could not complain that we had not done her punch honor, for in the course of one quarter of an hour . . . the bowl which held upwards of two gallons was entirely consumed to no little satisfaction of us all.

Robert Lewis also noted that in the evening Martha was engaged to drink tea at the home of another lady, a Mrs. MacHenry, followed by a reception with fireworks, which a number of prominent ladies attended to pay their respects to Martha. The party left the next morning at five. At Chester, Pennsylvania, Martha was met by a guard of honor from the First Troop of the Philadelphia Cavalry, many of whose members had known Martha personally from camp. Seven miles outside Philadelphia "this truly respectable personage," as Martha was described in the newspaper account, and her entourage were joined by a party of ladies who had driven out in their carriages to provide a female escort of honor.

Everyone proceeded to Grays Ferry, where a cold collation had been set out at an inn. Mary Morris, an old friend, arrived in her carriage, and she and Wash exchanged places in the carriages and the entourage went on to the Morris house amidst cheers and gun salutes. In the only recorded instance of Martha making any kind of speech, Martha stood in her carriage and thanked the troops and ladies who had escorted her.

Martha reached the Morris home on a Friday, where she and her party stayed two days. It was considered inappropriate to travel on Sunday, and they needed a rest. It had been a tiring and emotional journey for both Martha and the children. Nelly and Wash, who had spent all their short lives in the country, were almost overwhelmed by the days of excitement, cheering crowds, gun salutes, military escorts, and festive dinners, and by the time they reached Philadelphia Nelly was feeling sick in the carriage.

When they left on Monday Mrs. Morris and her daughter joined the procession to New York. Like George weeks earlier, Martha was cheered through New Jersey, as she had been elsewhere. Church bells rang as her carriage approached. At Trenton Martha was entertained by Governor Livingston at his home, Liberty Hall, where she spent the night. The next day, George, Robert Morris, and other gentlemen met Martha's party at Elizabethtown Point, to escort her into New York. With Martha patriotically—and probably symbolically—attired in a homespun gown, they were all taken across the river in the presidential barge, rowed by thirteen sailors in white, and met with a thirteen-gun salute from Battery Point.

The New York they entered was a small town on the tip of Manhattan, not nearly so glamorous or cosmopolitan as Philadelphia. Although Martha's new home at 10 Cherry Street was one of the best houses in the city—in fact it was known as "the Palace"—what greeted Martha was a modest three-story brick house with low ceilings, into which a great many people had to fit.

Martha began receiving in an official capacity at once. The day after she arrived in New York, visitors began thronging to the Cherry Street house to pay their respects. That evening the Washingtons held a "family" dinner, which included Governor Clinton, the French and Spanish ministers, and Vice President John Adams.

Abigail Adams, now wife of the vice president, was not yet in New York, but when she arrived—soon after Martha in June—she called at 10 Cherry Street without delay, and wrote an account of her favorable impression to her sister: "I took the earliest opportunity (the morning after my arrival) to go and pay my respects to Mrs. Washington. . . . She received me with great ease and politeness. She is plain in her dress but that plainness is the best of every article. She is in mourning. Her Hair is white, her Teeth beautifull, her person rather short than otherwise. . . . Her manners are modest and unassuming, dignified and feminine, not the Tincture of ha'ture about her."[5]

On the Friday two days after her arrival, Martha presided at her first official Friday Drawing Room. In fact, Martha's Drawing Room was the first official entertaining at the presidential mansion, where Martha and George hoped to strike a balance between dignified hospitality and extravagant excess. Martha's first Drawing Room was in some fashion an experiment to see if they had got the balance right.

Fortunately, Martha had spent so much of her life entertaining large gatherings of people that she managed easily. Abigail Adams, who would usually sit next to Martha when she attended, described an August Drawing Room to her sister: "I attended upon the last . . . I found it quite a crowded Room. The form of Reception is this, the servants announce & Col. Humphreys or Mr. Lear, receives every lady at the door, & Hands her up to Mrs. Washington to whom she makes a most respectfull courtesy and then is seated without noticing any of the rest of the company. The President then comes up and speaks to the Lady . . . The company are entertained with Ice creams and Lemonade and retire at their leasure performing the same ceremony when they quit the Room."[6]

Everyone at the Drawing Room was in full dress. George was dressed formally but without the ceremonial sword or hat he held under his arm when dressed to meet gentlemen in his official capacity. The lack of sword and hat signified he was a guest at his wife's evening. In addition to ice cream and lemonade, which were served in summer, refreshments included tea, coffee, and plum cake.

At one early Drawing Room a young lady nearly met with disaster. Wash Custis recorded the mortifying incident, which must have tested Martha's composure and seemed irresistibly funny to the children: "An incident occurred which might have been attended by serious consequences. Owing to the lowness of the ceiling in the drawing-room, the ostrich feathers on the head-dress of Miss McIvers, a belle of New York, took fire from the chandelier, to the no small alarm of the company. Major Jackson, an aide de camp to the president, with great presence of mind, and equal gallantry, flew to the rescue of the lady, and by clapping the burning plumes between his hands, extinguished the flame and the drawing room went on as usual."[7]

It was over a week before Martha had a chance to write to Fanny, who was to be her most frequent and intimate correspondent. Unlike the official letters increasingly drafted and written for her by Tobias Lear, Martha could pour out her true feelings to Fanny about the new position in which she found herself.

Martha's first letter was almost breathless:

> My dear Fanny   June 8 1789
>   I have been so much engaged since I came hear that I have never opened your Box or directions but shall soon have time as most visits are at an end— I have not had one half hour to myself since the day of my arrival,—my first care was to get the children to a good school, . . . My Hair is set and dressed every day—and I have put on white muslin Habits for the summer—you would I fear think me a good deal in the fashion if you could but see me.

Martha put a good face on things for Fanny. She had not wanted to go back into public life, and as the wife of the president, she was finding she had to be conscious of her every move. She would soon come to hate living in New York, but in the early days she was doing her best to accommodate herself to the new situation. She told Fanny she had had an "agreable" journey north and wrote that the house on Cherry Street was "a good one and handsomely furnished all new." She asked Fanny to send a black lace apron and handkerchief she had forgotten in the rush of leaving. Martha had no sooner arrived in New York than she began sending pretty presents to her female relatives back in Virginia. It was a pattern she kept up throughout George's time in office. Martha had been in New York only a few days with no time to herself, yet she told Fanny she had already had sent for a staymaker to order stays to Fanny's measurements and obtained some fashionable shoes, a pair with low heels for Fanny, and high heels for Eleanor, plus a pair each for "the dear little girls," Betsy and Patty Custis.

In June, shortly after Martha's arrival, George became desperately ill with a malignant carbuncle, a form of cancer, on his thigh. He was in agony and had to have surgery to remove the carbuncle. For a time it was thought he might not live, and people flocked to Cherry Street for news of his condition. Martha had the street outside blocked to carriages and straw laid on the pavement to dull the city's noise. George recovered slowly and by August was well enough to drive out in the carriage.

Martha sent Fanny, Harriot, Betsy, and Patty each a new prayer book and was grateful for Fanny's letters, which kept her abreast of things at

Mount Vernon. Many of the Mount Vernon slaves were ill that summer, and one slave had died. Patty Dandridge had been sent to stay with Fanny's sister-in-law. Martha wrote Fanny that the illness and death among the slaves was very sad, but that her housekeeper and seamstress "Charlot" was probably malingering. "Charlot will lay herself up for as little as anyone."

In September Mary Washington died. In her will Mary left George a tract of land in Stafford County, her slave boy George, her best bed, bedstead, and Virginia cloth curtains, a blue and white quilt, and her best dressing glass. She left her daughter-in-law Hannah Washington her purple cloak lined with shag, but not even a memento to Martha. George ordered the presidential household to observe what he called "republican mourning," which was simply black armbands.

By October George had regained his health and was well enough to set out on a monthlong tour of New England. Martha and the children stayed in New York, but by that time life at the presidential mansion had developed a routine that accommodated both the private lives and public business of the inhabitants.

The house was packed with people. In addition to the Washingtons, the children, chief secretary Tobias Lear, aide-de-camp William Jackson, and some of the slaves from Mount Vernon, there were three more of George's secretaries, including Robert Lewis. These last three were obliged to share a room. One of the secretaries, Colonel Humphreys, was a poet and, according to Wash, "would rise from his bed at any hour, and with stentorian voice, recite his verses . . . murdering the sleep" of the other two. Wash noted the two disturbed secretaries hated poetry the rest of their lives.

Martha was under constant public scrutiny, with no precedent to guide her. In general, people were well disposed toward the president's lady, but had Martha put a foot wrong, George's critics and political opponents would surely have pounced on her. In fact, most people who met Martha agreed with Abigail Adams and found her pleasant and unassuming with an elegant style of dressing, which suited her years. Martha knew instinctively how clothes conveyed a message, and the image she projected was carefully calculated to be simultaneously republican and elegant. Martha could finally put aside the homespun but wisely made no attempt to compete with the fashionable women and society beauties of New York and Philadelphia. After the restrictions of the war years they went for extremes of dress and accessories, with much jewelry and extravagant plumed headdresses, such as the one worn by the unfortunate Miss McIvers.

As Abigail Adams shrewdly observed, Martha dressed plainly, but in the finest fabrics. At her Drawing Rooms she wore a gray or black silk or black damask or black velvet gown, and a black lace kerchief. For driving in the carriage Martha usually wore a mulberry velvet cloak. Though a hairdresser called each morning to dress her hair, Martha then hid it under a cap. She was particularly vain about her caps, which were a miracle of fine pleats, lace, and starching, and had to be looked after specially by her young maid Oney Judge. The only area where she lapsed may have been in the size of her caps. Martha preferred them to be made quite high and elaborate, in the vain hope they would make her look taller. She wore little jewelry other than a locket. Her handkerchiefs and shoes were immaculate, and she was very fond of gloves.

To add to the image, the Washingtons had a splendid new coach ordered from England. It was painted cream, with red trim—the Washington colors—and had four panels painted by the Italian artist Cipriani depicting the four seasons. Venetian blinds could be pulled against the sun, and black leather curtains offered shelter from rain. The postilions were dressed in white livery with scarlet waistcoats, and the horses' harnesses were silver-plated and engraved with the Washington crest. Martha used the coach to visit her friends, for shopping expeditions, when she was often escorted by Tobias Lear, for family expeditions and to attend church services. On Saturdays the Washingtons and the children usually went for a drive around Manhattan in the coach, and on Sunday they all attended church at either St. Paul's or Trinity Church.

It may sound rather grand, but prominent New York families like the Van Rensselaers, the Jays, the Beekmans, and the Livingstons were not impressed with the Washingtons' style, which they felt was too restrained for the president, too "down-home." Congressman Thomas Rodney sneered: "After passing the ferry met Mrs. Washington in a coach, preceded by a Servant ½ mile ahead, and two gentlemen on horseback This was her suite. In old countries a lady of her rank would not be seen without a retinue of twenty persons. The Motions of the President and His Lady is the public Talk of all Ranks at & near New York."

For her part Martha was not concerned with New York's society, or their opinion of her, and she spent much of her time with the children or sewing when she was not officially engaged. She did not attend public balls. She occasionally attended the Thursday Assembly, but never danced, and went home early. Her friends included Abigail Adams, Betsy Schuyler Hamilton, wife of Secretary of the Treasury Alexander Hamilton, and Lucy Knox. When there were no formal official engagements, Martha and these ladies called on each other or their families and the Washingtons shared family dinners.

Congressman Rodney was one of the few people to voice any criticism of Martha herself, and it was for not behaving grandly enough. Here some Virginia snobbery surfaced. To Martha, who had known royal governors and was still called Lady Washington by many people, anyone who thought her rank depended on a retinue of twenty persons could safely be dismissed as vulgar. If this was the worst anyone could say about Martha, it suggests

Martha, with some help from Tobias Lear, had successfully calculated her appearance and behavior to reflect positively on George in the early days of his administration, and it was far from being an irrelevant consideration. It is a syndrome wearily familiar to political wives today: get as little as a hemline wrong or have a "bad hair day" and it diminishes her husband's political credibility.

Indeed, almost as soon as the cheering died down after the inauguration, Washington's presidential style was caught between two poles of criticism. Some, like Congressman Rodney, dismissed the Washingtons as too plain, while the "democrat" faction thought the Washingtons were aping royalty and veering dangerously close to a monarchical style. This, the "democrats" concluded, could mean only one thing, that George intended to exercise an alarmingly "kingly," or despotic, form of power. An aspect of the administration that became a focus of this public debate, because it had such a visible profile, was the pattern of official entertaining adopted at the presidential mansion. As time passed, Martha's role took on a subtle but increased significance.

CHAPTER 19

"A State Prisoner"

It soon became clear that Martha's Friday Drawing Rooms, a kind of open house that did not require an invitation and was open to ladies of any family prominent enough to attend, would not meet all the needs for official entertaining. People thronged to Cherry Street wanting to see George at all hours of the day and night, and George was faced with either having to cause offense by refusing to see anyone or having his time consumed by callers. It was decided that it would be most efficient to fix a time when men could call on the president each week. Tuesday afternoons between three and four were set aside for George's "Levee"; any respectably dressed gentleman might attend.

His hair powdered and gathered in a silk bag, George wore a black velvet coat and breeches, yellow gloves, and a ceremonial sword, and carried a cockaded hat under his arm to receive attendees, who were introduced individually by Tobias Lear or Major Jackson. George and the gentlemen did not shake hands but exchanged bows. George circulated, speaking to each man for a moment or two. On the stroke of four, the gentlemen were ushered out. George was criticized by some for not shaking hands, which he privately thought beneath the dignity of the president, as well as for the stiffness of his bows, which irritated him immensely.

Thursdays there were official dinners, attended by visiting dignitaries, congressmen and their wives in rotation, various members of the cabinet, and people from other parts of the country. The invitation was for four o'clock promptly. George allowed a five-minute period of grace to allow for watches keeping different time, but then dinner was served at precisely five minutes past four.

If the dinner guests were only gentlemen, Martha sat at the head of the table and George sat halfway down on her left. The most junior secretary sat at the foot and saw that everyone was attended to. When there was mixed company, Martha and George sat opposite each other, while another secretary took Martha's place at the end of the table. The ladies were seated on either side of their hostess, and the men were ranged on either side of their host. Sam Fraunces presided from the sidelines. All the dishes were placed on the table, and the secretaries helped everyone to food.

The dinners were said to be very good, rather like those at Mount Vernon, consisting of a variety of main courses, such as roast meat and poultry, and side dishes of vegetables for the first course and a huge selection of desserts and fruits for the second. There was wine, and at the end of the meal George went around the table toasting each guest individually, "Your health Sir, your health Madam." According to one senator, William Maclay, the grandness of the dinner conflicted with his republican sentiments, but he conceded that the food and wine had been excellent and that George had gratifyingly toasted him first. Maclay also recalled that the dinners were eaten in total silence, perhaps indicating a strained atmosphere.

After the toasts the ladies retired, and George sat with the men over wine or port, cracking nuts if they were available, for fifteen minutes. Then he excused himself and joined Martha and the ladies. The male guests who wanted to stay longer at the table drinking wine or port were kept company by the secretaries. These dinners usually lasted around two hours and were over by six. Sam Fraunces, George's steward, supervised the shopping and oversaw the running of the household and the work of the staff, which comprised fourteen hired white servants and house slaves from Mount Vernon: Hercules the cook, the maids Oney and Molly, and Austin Giles, Will, Paris, and Christopher Lee, George's valet. At official entertainments the servants wore livery.

The style of entertaining soon became the focus of adverse comment by George's detractors. The most notable opposition came from the democrats who opposed the Federalist view espoused by George and most of his cabinet, who believed that a strong federal political and economic system, including such measures as a federal bank, trade agreements, and a system of taxation to address the debts incurred during the war, was the only way the republic could survive. The democrats were bitterly opposed to any movement toward centralization, believing it to be inconsistent with the principles of liberty that had underpinned the revolution. The democrats viewed this centralization of governmental functions with alarm, believing it was the first step to reinstituting a monarchy.

The growing gulf between the ideals of the Revolution and the Federalist style was graphically highlighted by the government's treatment of war veterans, now a highly visible and disaffected element of American society. Congress had reneged on a promise to pay Revolutionary veterans, many of whom had only been small farmers or tradesmen, and were now disabled and impoverished, and disaffected. George was deeply ashamed by Congress's about-face on the issue, but there was a huge burden of American debt and he was battling to get measures passed to deal with it. As a result, the disaffected veterans were something of a loose cannon, and there were a great many of them. Their plight contrasted sharply with the style of entertaining at the presidential mansion.

These ragged veterans, however, were not suitably dressed to join the gentlemen at the president's Tuesday levees, nor were they invited to the Thursday official dinners. Their long-suffering wives would have been out of place at the Friday Drawing Rooms. However, many men who had fought with George, staying on in the army out of stubborn loyalty when supplies were low and the situation hopeless, felt sure that if they simply called on their old commander he was in a position to put everything right and see that they were paid. Others thought the general had gotten above himself and no longer cared. Both views could be manipulated by the opposition, because a great many veterans called at Cherry Street, only to be denied an audience with George. The effect was to antagonize the first group and confirm the pessimistic views of the second. While the Federalist press represented the Washingtons' entertainments at the presidential mansion as the height of society, the democratic press wrote scathingly of the plight of the veterans and lampooned Martha's "Queenly Drawing Rooms" and George's "Court like Levees." George's opposition might have made more damaging capital out of the situation had it not been for Martha, who turned out to be an invaluable political asset.

Wash Custis recalled how many old soldiers visited the presidential mansion almost every day, both in New York and later in Philadelphia. They called it "headquarters" and came to ask after the health of "His Excellency." George was always busy, so they often asked for "Lady Washington." Whatever George may have done to distance himself from the troops, Martha's popularity remained undimmed. She had been very well liked in the army, for her war relief efforts, her nursing, her cheerfulness, and her habit of interceding with George for offenders, and "Lady Washington" was still a great favorite. Martha often came to the door herself, and the soldiers reminisced with her about old times. She would then invite them to go to the steward's room for refreshments, and she would give each one a small gift of money and her personal good wishes "for the health and happiness of an old soldier."

Her kind treatment of the veterans conveys a sense that from her new perspective as wife of the president Martha looked back nostalgically to camp life. She once referred to her time as the president's wife as her "lost days," a term she never used for the more grueling experiences of the war. Compared to life at Mount Vernon or in camp, Martha's life in New York struck her as superficial.

At Mount Vernon Fanny had had another baby in the summer of 1790, a boy, named George Fayette, who lived. George Augustine, her husband, however, was getting worse. Martha continued sending presents home, including some calico for a frock for "dear Maria," a watch and chain for Fanny "such as Mrs. Adams the vice Presidents Lady and those in polite circles wares," and because Maria had been ill, "two little handkerchiefs to wipe her nose."

Between the lines of a letter to Marcy Otis Warren clearly drafted by Tobias Lear, Martha's dislike of her situation struggled to surface:

> I sometimes think the arrangement is not quite as it ought to have been, that I who had much rather be at home should occupy a place with which a great many younger and gayer women would be prodigiously pleased.—As my grand children and domestic connections made a great portion of the felicity which I looked for in this world—I shall hardly be able to find any substitute that would indemnify me for the Loss of such endearing society. I do not say this because I feel dissatisfied with my present station . . . for everybody and everything conspire to make me as contented as possible in it: yet I have too much of the vanity of human affairs to expect felicity from the splendid scenes of public life—I am still determined to be cheerful and to be happy in whatever situation I may be, for I have also learnt from experiance that the greater part of our happiness or misary depends upon our dispositions, and not our circumstances; we carry the seeds of the one, or the other about with us, in our minds, wherever we go.[1]

A less restrained letter to Fanny was more explicit: "I live a very dull life here and know nothing that passes in the town—I never goe to the publick place—indeed I think I am more like a state prisoner than anything else, there is certain bounds set for me which I must not depart from—and as I cannot doe as I like I am obstinate and stay at home a great deal."[2]

Taken together, these letters are extremely revealing. The letter to Fanny was written in late October 1789. Martha's dissatisfaction must have been growing more and more evident and may have become the subject of adverse comment by the time Tobias Lear drafted the letter to Mercy Otis Warren in December. The very fact that the latter alludes to possible reasons Martha would find herself discontented in her new position suggests that she felt discontent before adopting a positive attitude to overcome those feelings. The letter sends a clear message: the government appreciated that any hint that the president's wife was not happy was damaging to George. For Tobias Lear, George's image was a priority, and Martha was an increasingly important aspect of that image.

Aside from George, the most important thing for Martha was her grandchildren. She concentrated on Nelly and Wash, who were both entranced by the bustle and excitement of the city. Martha wrote to Fanny that Nelly was "a little wild creature and spends her time at the window looking at carriages &c passing by which is new to her and very common for children to do."

Lear no longer had time to teach Nelly and Wash their lessons, as George needed his secretarial assistance full-time. Wash did not go to school at first but had a tutor, a Mr. Murdoch, who soon discovered Wash had not learned much from Tobias Lear. Nelly, a sweet and lively girl of ten, had music and painting lessons at home and was enrolled as a day pupil at Mrs. Graham's school in Maiden Lane. The prospectus promised to teach girls "Reading, English, Spelling and Grammar, Plainwork, Embroidery, Cloathwork and various works of fancy Writing, Arithmetic, Geography, Drawing, painting, japanning, Philigree, Music, Dancing and the French language."

Back at Abingdon, Nelly's eldest sister Betsy fumed at her own restricted education. Envy had set in earlier, as Betsy and Patty's life with their continually pregnant mother, a dour stepfather, and a growing family of half siblings contrasted less and less favorably with that of Nelly and Wash at Mount Vernon, and now in New York, where they were clearly doted upon by the Washingtons and their fascinating guests.

Betsy carried her resentment at what she saw as her lack of advantages into middle age:

> My father in law [stepfather Dr Stuart] willed to give us every advantage, & procured an Instructor to teach us Music and other branches of Education— the first day he gave me the dedication of the Spectator to read it. I heard Dr S tell him "that was an extraordinary child & would if a boy make a Brilliant figure I told them to teach me what they pleased, and observed to them I thought it hard they would not teach me Greek & Latin because I was a girl— they laughed & said women ought not to know those things, & mending, writing, Arithmetic & Music was all I could be permitted to acquire.[3]

The good times Nelly appeared to be having in New York added fuel to the flame. By the winter of 1789, Nelly was being allowed to attend Martha's teas and was given the job of passing the cream and sugar. Everyone admired her; Martha was intensely proud of her granddaughter and believed it was never too early for girls to learn how to behave in company. It harked back to the lessons of Martha's own childhood, when girls learned from an early age how to play hostess to their parents' company. Eleanor fretted that Nelly would be spoiled by too much admiration and indulgence at a young age, but in fact Nelly's recollection that Martha was very strict with her and much more indulgent with Wash was confirmed by Wash in his later years.

When time allowed, the Washingtons took the children to the theater in a barnlike building on John Street where a resident theater troupe performed. They all loved plays, and a particular favorite was Sheridan's *The*

School for Scandal. George would take a box and invite friends to join them. The band would play the "President's March," and the audience would applaud as the Washingtons and their party made their appearance, and give three cheers before the performance could begin. They also attended the circus.

The first presidential year of 1789 closed on a note of unseasonably warm weather. The air was so balmy that for a New Year's Day reception the windows were thrown open as people crowded into the president's house. This New Year's Day was the first time Martha and her friend Abigail Adams had encountered what was traditionally a festive occasion in New York. Abigail wrote this account to her sister:

> There is a kind of cake in fashion upon this day call'd New Year's Cooky. This & Cherry Bounce as it is called in the old Dutch custom of treating their Friends upon the return of every New Year. The common people, who are ever ready to abuse Liberty on this day are apt to take rather too freely of the good things of this Life, and finding two of my servants not altogether qualified for Business, I remonstrated to them, but they excused it by saying it was New Year, & every body was joyous then. . . .
>
> In the Evening I attended the Drawing Room, it being Mrs. W's publick day. It was as much crowded as a Birth Night at St. James, and with Company as brilliantly drest, diamonds and great hoops excepted. My station is always at the right hand of Mrs. W's; through want of knowing what is right I find it sometimes occupied, but on such occasions the President never fails of seeing that it is relinquished for me, and having removed ladies several times they have now learnt to rise and give it to me.[4]

By the early months of 1790, Martha was growing resigned. She felt her time was consumed with pointless activities, such as unnecessary hairdressing, which were galling to a woman accustomed to managing a large household. She wrote to Mercy Otis Warren in June 1790 that "though I may not have a great deal of business of consequence to do; yet I have a great many avocations of one kind or another which imperceptibly consume my time."

One of these activities was keeping an eye on supplies needed in the house, many of which were unavailable in New York and had to be ordered from Philadelphia. Martha sent various orders to the president's factor in Philadelphia, Colonel Clement Biddle, such as an order for knives, forks, wine, "ginn," and liquors, and another order for orange flower water, pickled walnuts, clothes baskets, scrubbing brushes, mops, "perfumes for cooking," probably vanilla, lavender, or rosewater, and schoolbooks for the children.

In the spring of 1790 Tobias Lear married his childhood sweetheart Polly Long, and Polly joined Tobias as a part of the president's household.

Polly soon became a de facto social secretary to Martha, helping her with official functions, and Martha soon grew extremely fond of Polly. Despite the democratic opposition, Martha's Drawing Rooms continued to be a great success. George noted with satisfaction the "large numbers of respectable people" who crowded into them each week. It was obvious that Martha's vivacious personality was a useful counterpoint to George's formal gravity.

George's desire to behave correctly and project a dignified image commensurate with his office made him appear forbiddingly stiff and formal, an impression accentuated by his height, his commanding presence, his reputation as a war hero, and now his aura of political power. On being presented to him, many people were awed into tongue-tied reverence. Martha, by contrast, had the ability to take a kindly interest in whoever she was talking to without seeming vulgar or familiar, and she had a knack for making people feel comfortable. She genuinely enjoyed being sociable. Her reputation for her war work and her way with veterans added a dimension that increased her general popularity and reflected well on George.

Given that Martha never liked living in New York and that she was constantly worried about how Fanny was managing at Mount Vernon, where she knew Harriot ran rings around Fanny, and worried as they all were about George Augustine's deteriorating health, it is surprising Martha did not consider going back for a visit on her own. She had gone back and forth from Mount Vernon to military headquarters many times during the war, and though tired by the experience, she had had a military escort and had managed perfectly well. She could easily have made the trip back with Robert Lewis or another aide to escort her and the children.

Two reasons, probably, prevented her. First, it was politically expedient for George to have her with him, and second, Martha was probably concerned about the society women who simply adored her husband.

The presence of Martha and the children was politically advantageous. It cast George in the light of family man, which rounded out his public image nicely. Of course, George was a family man in a broader sense, part of a network of interrelated families across Virginia, with endless and intricate links of cousins, nieces, nephews, and so on, but this complicated pattern of family relationships, instinctively understood by most southerners then and now, did not translate easily into a public image conveying family values. Modern-day politicians know the value of such a family image and will go to any lengths to emphasize their own. In George's time the last thing the new republic needed was a figurehead with a reputation for loose living, or a man who was involved in sexual scandals or even vulnerable to rumors.

While the American Revolution was in a sense "rationalist," in that political support for and against it did not correspond with allegiance to a particular religion or church, America had a strong Christian religious orientation all the same that idealized the family. Just as today allegations of private sexual misconduct can impact disastrously on a politician's career, the same was true in Washington's time, though probably to a lesser extent. Had George been caught in extramarital affairs, at best it would have provided embarrassing fuel for a hostile opposition, but at worst it might have involved the president in a duel.

The portrait of the Washington family, by Edward Savage, is literally, a "picture perfect" First Family unit—George, Martha, Nelly, and Wash gathered around a table at Mount Vernon with a slave just visible in the background. That is not to say George was not genuinely devoted to Nelly and Wash—they and a great many other relatives' children benefited from his strong paternal instincts all his life—but a wife and children in the presidential mansion were undeniably a political asset.

The second consideration that may have kept Martha in New York was that her presence deflected the undercurrent of scandal, real or imagined, that permeated much of George's public life. At the very least it must have been trying for Martha. The fact that the rumors survive today is proof of rumors, not of their truth. Whatever their validity, they are a useful reminder that for all his status as America's foremost hero, George, and Martha too, were real people who spent much of their lives trying to fit a public role

"The Washington Family" by Edward Savage. Courtesy of the National Portrait Gallery, Smithsonian Institution.

thrust upon them. Both had been brought up in an atmosphere of sexual double standards, and many of the women Martha knew, including her own mother, somehow adapted, or turned a blind eye, to the fact that their husbands often had a slave mistress or a number of mulatto children. Martha may have chosen the same tactic.

For most of his life, George had a magnetic attraction for women. One twentieth-century journalist has compared him to Elvis Presley, and as odd and irreverent as the comparison sounds, it is a good analogy. George did have charisma. For men it was a charisma of command: his officers and troops would have followed him into the jaws of hell, where, in fact, he had very nearly led them. For women, he exerted a powerful, rugged sexual appeal combined with rather formal courtly manners. At one ball in Annapolis to mark the end of the war and the signing of the final peace treaty, he had been careful to dance with each of the women present, so that they "might all have a touch of him." Abigail Adams, though happily married to portly little John, found George deeply attractive. Many women couched their response to George's sexual attraction in terms of patriotic fervor.

That sophisticated Sally Cary Fairfax had been drawn to George even when he was a boisterous sixteen-year-old two years her junior is well known. The rumor that George was the father of General Thomas Posey persists to this day. Supposedly it was the British who, to undermine George's authority during the war, were responsible for allegations that George had a mistress in New Jersey and that he was rowed across the Hudson to visit her, that he kept a corporal's wife as his mistress in camp, and that he had a slave mistress in Virginia. On closer examination it seems curious the British would adopt this means of attack. The British were hardly prudes, and Generals Howe and Burgoyne and other officers were openly and notoriously involved with their mistresses without undermining morale in their armies or providing a propaganda boon to the Americans. It suggests that sexual misbehavior on anyone else's part would have had to be extremely blatant before the British would have considered it noteworthy. In fact, the smears may have come from George's detractors within the American ranks.

In a new twist, Owen Wister in *The Seven Ages of Washington*, published in 1907, not only refutes the rumors but also attributes them to a clergyman, and not the British. "It has been said—quite falsely—that Washington made his wife unhappy. A number of these scandals have a clergyman as their source; the various tales have been tracked down to the nothing they started from, even the apparently solid one of the Virginia tombstone bearing a name and the words 'The natural son of Washington'. There is no such tombstone and never was."[5]

However, even Wister must have known that Thomas Posey, one of George's rumored sons, had been governor general of the Indiana territory and is buried in Indiana and honored as one of its leading citizens. So the allegation of "a tombstone in Virginia" could not have meant Posey's. It suggests there were rumors of another "natural son of Washington." The issue of the paternity of the Bushfield slave, Venus Ford's son West, did not become widely known until recently, and given that it would have been unlikely a man of mixed race would have had "natural son of Washington" inscribed on his tomb in the nineteenth century—or even rumored to be inscribed on his tomb—Wister seems to be refuting claims of a third illegitimate son.

Nathaniel Hawthorne, writing to General Cass in 1854, made an oblique reference to Martha's response to women who threw themselves at George during his presidency. The English artist James Sharples, a well-known society painter, painted portraits of George and Martha in their latter years. Hawthorne wrote: "At Sharples' death his wife carried to England numerous outline and unfinished canvasses of lovely women, most of whom he met at Mount Vernon, at balls in Philadelphia. . . . Mean censorious scandal-mongers have hinted at their frequent presence as the reverse of agreeable to Martha, but beauty often times outlives envy . . . some display great loveliness, and all evidence that infinitude of womanly beauty and force of character marking the dames most in vogue at the Court of Mount Vernon."[6]

So no matter how much Martha hated New York, there was a powerful incentive to remain in public view by George's side, just as he had an interest in her doing so, though arguably she felt more confined than she ever had in the winter camps. But Nelly and Wash also enjoyed educational advantages in the schools in New York, and Abigail Adams and her daughter, also named Abigail, were a support. Widowed Kitty Greene visited New York, and in February the increasingly cramped conditions at 10 Cherry Street prompted a move to the Macomb house, a large mansion recently vacated by the French minister at 39–41 Broadway, between Trinity Church and Bowling Green. It was a much nicer house, with six stories and a lawn down to the Hudson. Across the river was a view of the forests in New Jersey.

The move was only temporary, however, as by February 1790 there were plans afoot to build a new capital city as the seat of government. The site of the new federal city was a subject of debate, negotiation, and horse trading. Meanwhile Congress decided to move the seat of government from New York to Philadelphia.

Since being elected president, George had suffered a succession of minor illnesses, far more, he joked, than he had suffered in eight years in the field and probably the result of his sedentary lifestyle. In May George caught a cold. Within days it had turned into pneumonia, and he deteriorated so quickly that four doctors called to attend him believed he would die. Word that the president was dying spread through New York. Martha had too great an acquaintance with sudden death not to believe the doctors or the evidence before her eyes. By the morning of May 15 the mansion was hushed and anxious. George was fighting for breath, and the end seemed near. Then suddenly in late afternoon his fever suddenly went down, and he began to sweat. Miraculously he began getting better. By May 20 the doctors pronounced him on the road to recovery, but George was convalescing for many weeks.

By June, with that crisis fresh in her mind and anxious for them all to have a holiday, Martha was hoping Congress would take a summer recess to allow them all to return to Mount Vernon for a few months.

Congress did break for the summer, and at the end of August the Washingtons left for Virginia. The presidential coach was preceded by an outrider who went ahead to warn of bad patches in the road. Martha, George, and the children went in the coach, and the secretaries rode on either side as an escort. Behind the coach was an open carriage with the maids, a carriage with the baggage, and mounted slaves leading extra horses. They went to Abingdon to pick up the Stuarts before going on to Mount Vernon.

At Abingdon Betsy Custis was in a fever of anticipation to see the Washingtons. Her self-dramatizing account of events from her childhood offers a foretaste of the difficult woman she became in later life, but it is probably true that she felt shunted aside by her own mother, owing to the demands of the younger Stuarts. Attentive as always to girls, Martha was concerned for the way her two eldest granddaughters were being brought up. Betsy seems to have been a pushy, needy child and, at fourteen, clearly in need of more attention than she was getting. Martha and, later, Nelly were models of discretion in never hinting how irritating Betsy must have been, but Martha realized that she would have to arrange for Betsy and Patty to spend more time with her.

Betsy left a typically dramatic account of how she had collapsed with a fever in grief when Martha left for New York in May 1789, and an equally dramatic account of their return in 1790:

> The Gen' was so ill that his life was despair'd of, & we felt much distress till assured of his safety—the Guardian Angel of America was near & preserved her God-like hero—the period approached when we were again to see those most dear to us—at length Austin my grandmothers footman, came on a day before to tell us they were near—my Mother was then confined with her third child—& Patty & I were half crazy for joy—when the Carriage stop'd, I could scarcely stand, I wept for joy, My Grandmother & the children embraced me first, then my Dear old Nurse [a Custis slave, probably Molly, who had nursed Betsy and to Betsy's dismay gone to New York to look after Nelly and Wash]— all wondered at my growth & improvement, & I was proud to be admired by them—Mrs Wn came some hours before the Presdt at length he rode up with two Gentlemen his Secretary.

Betsy and Patty went on to Mount Vernon with the Washingons, leaving Eleanor at Abingdon "pale & feeble" from childbirth. Eleanor joined the family there when she was better.

By September 5 the Washingtons were back home, and George wrote Tobias Lear in Philadelphia that Martha had been unwell since they arrived. Martha was temporarily released from her official role, but official business and a flood of dispatches followed the Washingtons to Mount Vernon. Abroad, the political crisis in France, in which the Washingtons' friend the Marquis de Lafayette was leading the influential Fayetteist faction, impacted on American policy vis-à-vis France, England, and Spain. In the fall of 1790 it seemed possible the tide of republicanism sweeping France would spread and topple the monarchies of the rest of Europe. In Haiti there was an uprising of Free Blacks in Port-au-Prince.

George was lobbying behind the scenes to ensure the site of the new federal city was virtually on Mount Vernon's doorstep, and he made a number of trips with Dr. David Stuart, a fellow commissioner overseeing its development, to the future District of Columbia, where he owned land. George also resumed his old habit of riding out on a circuit of daily inspection over a section of his eight thousand acres.

Martha dealt with the family and the usual influx of visitors. A visitor, Thomas Lee Shippen, noted that Martha's happiness in being home was "in exact proportion to the number of objects upon which she can dispense her benefits." He also said that Martha's first task each day was to go to the kitchen to see that the bread put out to rise the night before had risen properly.

Martha and George were naturally preoccupied with family affairs. By now George Augustine clearly had tuberculosis, and Fanny had a cough and an intermittent fever. Another family problem involved the Custis property. Nine years after Jacky's death, the Custis fortune inherited by his four children was in a tangled mess. The practice of girls' inheriting a financial interest in the estate still obtained, with the land generally going to the boys. Thus Wash stood to inherit the Custis lands Jacky had owned in the Tidewater, and the girls had an interest in the capital.

However, there was a complication with Abingdon. Jacky and Eleanor had lived there and spent money fixing it up to suit them, but Jacky had never completed the purchase and had still been negotiating the terms from the owner when he died suddenly at Yorktown. The value of the estate and the terms on which Jacky should agree to buy it had been a frequent subject of George's letters to Jacky during the war years. By 1790 a decision had to be taken either to buy Abingdon as agreed or abandon it altogether because the owner was threatening a lawsuit that would eat up the assets of the estate. Matters had dragged on in part because Martha's brother Bartholomew had been the executor of Jacky's estate, but Bartholomew had died in 1785, and Dr. Stuart had stepped in. The issues of intestacy, tangled affairs involving inherited Custis property, and the prospect of lawsuits had a painfully familiar ring to Martha, who could remember the trouble and expense of the Dunbar Suit.

The compromise worked out was that Eleanor would pay the owner rent for the time her family had lived at Abingdon, but to avoid dissipating more Custis money on what George advised was a bad bargain, Eleanor and David Stuart decided to move to a smaller property Stuart had bought, a two-thousand-acre estate called Hope Park.

Eleanor was anxious to conserve what was left of her daughters' fortune, but Betsy and Patty were horrified at the thought of moving. Betsy was fourteen and Patty thirteen, just at an age when they were old enough for dancing classes and parties. Betsy wrote that Eleanor had resolved to "bury herself in solitude" and them too. "The place [Hope Park] had nothing to recommend it. It was twenty Miles [from Alexandria]."

When the Washingtons left with Nelly and Wash for a new presidential residence in glittering Philadelphia on November 22, Betsy and Patty went gloomily to Hope Park. The Washingtons had a tedious five-day journey on roads that had turned to quagmires in heavy autumnal rain. The entourage made slow progress, and the coachman was drunk. When George could bear it no longer, he had the coachman drive one of the baggage wagons, which the inebriated man overturned in the mud.

After this trying journey, the Washington party found their presidential quarters not yet ready when they arrived in Philadelphia at the end of November.

Polly and Tobias Lear, who would have their quarters in the president's house, had spent the summer in Philadelphia overseeing the alterations on the house. Polly was pregnant, and they and the baby would live with the president's family. Lucy Knox and Abigail Adams had also arrived and were battling with furniture lost and trunks damaged by water in transit from New York.

Abigail took a dim view of the government's move to Philadelphia. She had had a house she liked at Richmond Hill in New York and was installed in one she disliked in Philadelphia. She regretted the move, observing tartly in a letter to her sister: "The grand and sublime at Richmond Hill, the Schuylkill being no more like the Hudson than I to Hercules. Mrs. Lear was in to see me yesterday, and assure me I am better off than Mrs. Washington will be when she arrives."

CHAPTER 20

Philadelphia

The move to Philadelphia marked a change in the presidential style, reflecting the influence of a bigger, more fashionable and cosmopolitan city than New York, as well as one more noted for its dissipated ways. It was curious that it should be so, because the city had Quaker roots, as did many of the wealthiest and most prominent Philadelphia families, but for years Philadelphia had capitalized on its advantageous location on the Schuylkill River, which was deep enough to allow rapid economic expansion as an inland trading port. After a year's residence in Philadelphia, Abigail Adams described it as "one continued scene of Parties upon parties, balls and entertainment equal to any European city." For many of the more straitlaced members of Congress, Philadelphia, with its theaters, gambling, and high society, was a den of iniquity. It was also an expensive place to live. Not only were prices high in the shops, but affordable housing was scarce and rents exorbitant, a situation that soon had the senators complaining bitterly that the town ran on money.

The new Washington home was a brick house rented from their close friend Robert Morris at 190 High Street, now 190 Market Street. George had declined the gift of a large house in a fashionable district, because he could not afford to furnish it. The house he rented was not in the best neighborhood, but it had big stables, a garden for the children, and room to extend the house to hold official functions. It was also near the Morrises. Throughout the fall, George had sent from Mount Vernon to Tobias Lear minutely detailed instructions for the improvements and alterations needed to accommodate the family and provide facilities for entertaining and housing slaves and servants.

It was the still unfinished building work and the resultant upheaval that the tired Washingtons encountered when they arrived at the end of November. When the workmen finally left, there were two large public rooms on the ground floor, plus a kind of butler's pantry for the house servants. The second floor had two drawing rooms, a smaller yellow one for the family and intimate entertaining, and a larger, grander "green room" where Martha could hold her receptions. The back part of the house was partitioned off for the Washingtons' private use, where the family and the maids had their rooms, and also housed a small private study and a dressing room for George. George had taken his usual interest in all the details: the decoration, furniture, hangings, carpets, ornaments, china, and silver with which the house was furnished. Typically, Martha was interested only in the practical side of housekeeping while George was the expert in giving a house the grand touch. This image had important political overtones, particularly in elegant Philadelphia.

The third floor housed Tobias and Polly Lear in a "good lodging room," an office, and two rooms for the secretaries. The attic had four rooms, one for the Hydes, the housekeeper and her husband the steward, one for George's valet, and two other servants' rooms. Over the stables, which held "only" twelve horses, was a room for the coachman and postilions. In addition, there were a smokehouse, converted into servants' quarters; a good washhouse; and a large carriage house for the family coach, the light carriage, and the chariot.

As before, a number of house slaves had been brought from Mount Vernon. Will Lee, who was too old and now crippled from a bad fall, was left behind at Mount Vernon. George's new valet was a young dower slave named Christopher Sheets. James and Fidas were the footmen, and George brought their wives, as well, to keep them happy. Austin the coachman and Hercules the cook, along with Hercules' son Richmond and Martha's maid Oney Judge, also made the journey. Possibly Molly, Nelly and Wash's nurse, came as well.

Nelly was enrolled in Mr. Wigden's school. Wash, nearly ten, and spoiled and fussed over by Martha, had made too little progress in his lessons to begin school. A tutor came to the house an hour before breakfast each morning, and then stayed to breakfast with the Washingtons and the Lears, before resuming his coaching of Wash. George continued to get up at four each morning to work in his study and pay a visit to his stables before breakfast. Martha kept to her habit of rising early too. A painter once engaged to paint a portrait of Martha was invited to come to the presidential mansion at the unthinkable hour of 8 A.M. Thinking they could not really have meant him to appear so early, the painter arrived slightly later. He found to his astonishment that Martha had been up for hours, had had breakfast, performed her devotions, given Nelly a music lesson, and read the paper.

Martha saw that George's favorite breakfast of Indian cakes, or cornmeal pancakes with honey, was always on the table, but otherwise breakfast at the house in Philadelphia was a meager affair compared with lavish plantation breakfasts. One visitor recalled there was only toast, bread and butter, and sliced tongue and that Martha served the tea and coffee. The visitor was shocked not to find any broiled fish, which was standard breakfast fare in Philadelphia.

By the time Martha held her first Drawing Room early in December, the work on the house had been pushed to a finish. As a new season of official entertaining got under way at the presidential mansion, the homespun image of the Washington presidency took on a more sophisticated cast. The way women dressed for the Philadelphia Drawing Rooms was one barometer of the new direction. Having dressed with impeccable circumspection in New York, Martha could not only afford to indulge her taste for finery, but she risked looking a bumpkin amidst the wealthy, fashion-conscious society beauties if she dressed down too much. Now the ongoing pressure to get the image right for political reasons was directed toward securing the administration's much-needed support of the wealthy and influential Philadelphia establishment.

Martha's attire at her Philadelphia Drawing Rooms was restrained by the standards of the city, but one eyewitness account of her ensemble at her first Philadelphia Drawing Room reflects how Martha's image changed in keeping with the overall presidential style. Martha greeted her guests from a sofa in front of the fire in the Green Room, wearing a gown of blue velvet over white satin, lace-flounced petticoats. Martha would also have been wearing high-heeled slippers, of satin, silk, or kid, and a fine cap. It had not been her practice to exchange curtsies in New York, but she now did so occasionally.

To put Martha's attire in a broader context, there is an account left by a Miss Charlotte Chambers of New York, which paints a picture of one of the Drawing Rooms. Miss Chambers, daughter of one of George's old acquaintances who was visiting Philadelphia one winter during George's presidency, was thrilled to receive an invitation to a Drawing Room. Anxious to get it right for this important occasion, Miss Chambers obviously spent much time dressing:

> Next morning I received an invitation by my father, from Mrs. Washington, to visit her, and Colonel Hartley politely offered to accompany me to the drawing room levee.
>
> On this evening my dress was white brocade silk, trimmed with silver, and white silk, high heeled shoes, embroidered with silver, and a light blue sash, with silver cord and tassel tied to the left side. My watch was suspended at the right and my hair was in its natural curls. Surmounting all was a small white hat and white ostrich feather, confined by brilliant band and buckle. Punctual to the moment, Colonel Hartley in his chariot arrived. . . .

The hall, stairs and drawing room of the President's house were well lighted by lamps and chandeliers. Mrs. Washington with Mrs. Knox sat near the fireplace. On our approach Mrs. Washington arose and made a courtesy—the gentlemen bowed most profoundly—and I calculated my declension to her own with critical exactness.

The President, soon after . . . advanced and I arose to receive and return his compliments with the respect and love my heart dictated.[1]

Likewise in this account, as at almost every other gathering, George was surrounded by similarly well-dressed young lovelies as well as older beauties, overflowing with "respect and love."

Ladies attending were handed from their carriages by George's secretaries and escorted to the room where Martha was receiving. An exception was made when the widow of General Montgomery or the widowed Kitty Greene attended. George personally escorted these ladies to and from their carriages.

The refreshments—tea, coffee, and plum cake—were the same as had been served in New York. Early on there was a problem when a hiatus in cooks meant no one could make the plum cakes properly and inferior ones had to be brought in. Mrs. Hyde, who seems to have shared cooking duties with Hercules, found cake making for the throngs at the Drawing Rooms the hardest part of her work.

A look at the list of ingredients and their quantities suggests why. Plum cake is similar to modern fruitcake, and Martha's recipes for large, fruit-laden cakes were hard work to make. One recipe called for forty eggs, four pounds of butter, five pounds of flour, and five pounds of fruit. Another required seven pounds of picked-over dried currants, as much as a peck of flour, and in some cases a "posset" made of ale and cream, which was used as the liquid in the cake. By the time the ingredients were combined, there was a vat of sticky batter, heavy as cement, that had to be thoroughly mixed and wrestled into baking tins for a long slow cooking. The advantage of these cakes was that they could be cut into very thin slices without crumbling and also that leftover plum cake would keep for months, so none of it went to waste.

The Philadelphia Drawing Rooms began at eight, instead of seven as in New York, and finished at ten. Usually a band played during the reception. It was Martha's habit to draw the evening to a close by rising and saying, "The General retires at 10 and I always precede him."

The president's Levees kept the same form as in New York, but the official Thursday dinners became grander and livelier occasions. According to Wash Custis, they were in "a very handsome style." As in New York, George expected his guests to be punctual and waited dinner for no one. Everyone assembled in the drawing room fifteen or twenty minutes before the dinner hour at four, and George spoke to each guest personally.

In the dining room the middle of the large oval dining table was decorated with oval silver "waiters," a kind of semicircular table ornament, in the center of which were placed small alabaster figures from classical mythology. Evidently these were fully dressed figures, because Wash hastened to add, "none of them such as to offend, in the smallest degree, against delicacy."

At each place a small roll of bread lay wrapped in a dinner napkin. One guest who dined in Philadelphia with the president, Martha, and a number of senators recalled that the dinner consisted of "roast beef, veal, turkeys, ducks, fowls, hams, etc: puddings, jellies, oranges, apples, nuts, almonds, figs, raisins and a variety of wines and punch. We took our leave at six, more than an hour after the candles were introduced . . . we were waited on by four or five men servants dressed in livery."

Because George felt compelled to entertain a wide variety of guests, the dinner parties each Thursday were important occasions. Normally Martha presided as hostess even when no other ladies were present, but her presence distinguished the official dinners from the men-only Levees. Many of the guests were quite colorful. John Adams wrote to Abigail: "Yesterday I dined with the President in company with John Walls, the King of the Cherokees, with a large number of his chiefs and their wives; among the rest, the widow and children of Hanging Man, a famous friend of ours, who was basely murdered by some White people. The president dined four sets of Indians on four several days last week."

When there were no official engagements, the Washingtons took the children to the South Street Theater, where they saw performances by the Old American Company. The Washington party would be met by the manager at the door and ushered into their box with some ceremony and two candles. They also went to the circus, or whatever amusements were available. On Saturdays they went for a drive in the presidential coach, and on Sundays they attended Christ Church on Second and Market Street. Other entertainments included dancing assemblies and concerts, and there were large balls held on the occasions of George's birthday, February 22, and on July 4. A dancing master was engaged to come to the house on Mondays, Wednesdays, and Fridays at five o'clock. Abigail Adams's granddaughter was invited to join Nelly and Wash in the dancing classes. Martha took Nelly shopping at Whitesides' Dry Goods Shop and bought her a spangled dress for dancing. Nelly and Wash so loved plays that they and some of their friends formed their own theater troupe in the attic and put on amateur productions, calling themselves the Young American Company.

To Martha Philadelphia represented a change for the better, and in any case she knew that they would not be there for long, because they were halfway through George's term as president; in another two years there was the happy prospect of going home. Martha had more old friends, such as Mrs. Morris, the Powels, the Logans, and the Chews, many of whom had country estates outside the city that reminded Martha of the kind of plantation life that had revolved around Williamsburg in her youth. She began to enjoy paying calls. The ladies always paid calls in the morning—that is, before the formal dinner hour of three or four o'clock. When ladies called on Martha, she stuck rigidly to the rule of repaying the visit on the third day afterwards.

When Martha went to call, a footman would knock on the door to the drawing room and announce "Mrs. Washington." Martha would enter escorted by Tobias Lear. She paid her calls in a grand new chariot, cream-colored and decorated with gilt medallions on the doors. Some grumbled that it was too grand for a republican president's wife.

The presence of pretty, sociable Polly Lear in the house contributed much to Martha's enjoyment of life in Philadelphia. With a more active social life, having Polly on hand as a social secretary and personal assistant to help plan official social functions relieved Martha from much of the burden of overseeing the arrangements for them. Beyond that, Martha enjoyed having a younger woman around, and because Polly was expecting a baby, Martha was able to fuss over her. In March 1791 Polly gave birth at the presidential mansion to a boy they named Benjamin Lincoln Lear. He soon became a great favorite with the Washingtons and the pet of the whole house.

As a matter of course, the smooth running of so large an establishment and the success of official entertaining depended on having an efficient, well-trained household staff. It was George, rather than Martha, who primarily dealt with staff matters, but he never hired anyone without Martha's approval. Behind the scenes for most of his presidency, George, who relied on a combination of slaves from Mount Vernon and hired white servants, wrestled with "the servant problem." It was a complicated one, for a number of reasons.

First, there was a shortage of white servants, let alone competent ones. After a few months' residence in New York Abigail Adams was writing to her sister about the difficulty of finding servants who were not drunks or criminals. "The chief of the servants here who are good for anything are negroes who are slaves. The white ones are all Foreigners and chiefly vagabonds." By November 1789 Abigail had "a pretty good Housekeeper, a tolerable footman, a middling cook, an indifferent steward and a vixen of a housemaid."

The situation was far worse in Philadelphia, and hiring staff for the presidential mansion involved the kinds of difficulties described by Abigail in a letter to her sister in January 1791:

> When I come to this place again I am determined to bring a *decent woman* who understands plain cooking with me. Such a vile low tribe you never was tormented with . . . I brought all my servants from N York, cook excepted, and

thought I could not have been worse off than I had been . . . in the whole Number, not a virtuous woman among them . . . I recruited with a new one last Monday, who brought written recommendations with her . . . [who] on Thursday got so drunk that she was carried to Bed, and so indecent, that footman, coachman and all were driven out of the house. Consequently she has turned herself out of doors.

Second, there was friction between the Mount Vernon slaves and the hired white servants. The white servants were reluctant to work when there were slaves onto whom their work could be unloaded. The slaves resented this and retaliated by undermining and sabotaging the work of the white servants. Each side complained about the other to George. The slaves and servants were also increasingly insolent; they felt the Washington household was a public and not a private one, and they could say what they liked. Animosity among the servants meant chaos for the Washingtons.

At one point George, on a trip to Mount Vernon, wrote to Tobias Lear in Philadelphia: "It might not be improper to hint to the servants who are with you (before they are joined by those with me) that it will be very idle and foolish in them to enter into any combinations for the purpose of supplanting those now in authority . . . these characters are indispensably necessary to take the trouble off the hands of Mrs. Washington and myself . . . any attempts therefore to counteract them in their line of duty . . . will be the strongest evidence of their own unworthiness and dispositions to be lazy if not dishonest."

Third, the staff, servants, and slaves alike increased the household expenses, already swollen by the bills for entertaining, by entertaining their friends in the kitchen, helping themselves to food and household items, and siphoning off wine from the casks George ordered to supply the official dinners. George estimated that for every glass of wine drunk upstairs, two were consumed downstairs. Kitchen accounts were scrutinized by Tobias Lear for discrepancies and fiddling: the "riot act" was read regularly to the household staff, but it had little effect. It was impossible to monitor or control consumption by the servants and slaves, and their friends.

When the Washingtons lived in New York and Sam Fraunces had been employed as the steward, even he was not above reproach. Fraunces had employed a cook named Mrs. Read and according to Marie Kimball who edited the 1940 edition of the *Martha Washington Cook Book,* "Between them they seem to have kept open house below stairs." George dismissed both Fraunces and Mrs. Read, but was plagued with difficulties in finding their replacements. While George advertised for a cook, one of the kitchen maids, Rachel Lewis stepped in to fill the breach. Rachel's area of expertise was not cooking, however, as she was a washerwoman, and in addition she proved to be too slovenly and unpleasant for the cooking to be left to her. A

French cook named Lamuir followed but lasted for only a month, to be replaced by a chef named John McVicar hired from Baltimore. However, McVicar had no skill at making cakes, and during his brief tenure the cakes for Martha's receptions and dinner parties had to be brought in. Eventually a Mr. Hyde was hired as Sam Fraunces' replacement and his wife was employed for the taxing job of cake making, while Mount Vernon slave Hercules acted as chief cook to the household.

Fourth, because of a new law passed in Pennsylvania in regard to slaves, a delicate problem with the Mount Vernon slaves arose. Any slave brought into Pennsylvania was deemed to be free after six months' residence there. Although George Washington is often held up as a model of the enlightened slave owner who freed his slaves on his death, the truth is more complex and less comfortable. His response to the new Pennsylvania law shows one side of his ambivalent attitude about slavery. Martha was less ambivalent than her husband and never seems to have questioned the system. Aside from the fact that the Washingtons regarded their slaves as their property and depended on them to make the presidential establishment run smoothly, most of the slaves from Mount Vernon were dower slaves, in whom Martha's Custis descendants had a financial interest. Had they been freed under the terms of the Pennsylvania law, George would have had to compensate the Custis estate for their value.

It was an issue that concerned George and Martha when George set out on a tour of the southern states in March 1791, because the slaves brought to Philadelphia in November were approaching the six-month limit. George asked Tobias Lear to have a quiet word with the attorney general, who had had a similar problem and been obliged to free his slaves. George cautioned that he mentioned the matter in strictest confidence, not to go beyond Tobias Lear or Martha, probably indicating an awareness that he was politically vulnerable to attacks from the growing abolitionist movement. While George was happy to go on using slaves, he now had to be careful about how this was perceived by the public. The following letter written to Tobias Lear in April shows an unpleasant side of both the Washingtons:

> The Attorney-General's case and mine I conceive, from a conversation I had with him regarding our slaves, is somewhat different. He in order to qualify himself for practice in the Courts of Pennsylvania, was obliged to take the Oath of Citizenship to that State, whilst my residence is incidental as an Officer of the Government only, but whether among people who are in the practice of enticing slaves even when there is no color of law for it, this distinction will avail I know not, and therefore beg you to take the best advise you can . . . in case I shall be found that any of my Slaves may, or any of them shall attempt their freedom at the expiration of six months, it is my wish and desire that you would send the whole, or such part of them as Mrs. Washington may not chuse

to keep home—for although I do not think they may be benefited by the change, yet the idea of freedom might be too great a temptation for them to resist. At any rate it might, if they conceived they had a right to it make them insolent in a State of Slavery. As all except Hercules and Paris are dower Negroes, it behoves me to prevent the emancipation of them, otherwise I shall not only lose the use of them, but may have them to pay for. If . . . it is found expedient to take them back to Virginia I wish to have it accomplished under pretext that I may deceive both them and the Public:—and none I think would so effectually do this, as Mrs. Washington coming to Virginia next month (towards the middle or end of it as she seemed to have a wish to do) if she can accomplish it by any agreeable and effective means . . . This would naturally bring her maid [Oney Judge] and Austin—and Hercules under the idea of coming home to cook. . . . I request these Sentiments and this advise may be known to none but yourself and Mrs. Washington.[2]

Martha did not go home herself—first she was ill and then none of the secretaries were free to escort her—but she participated in the deception and concocted pretexts to send the slaves back to Mount Vernon. On April 19 she sent a letter to Fanny by Austin, "who is come home to see his friends." The previous week Martha had sent some muslin borders for the seamstress Charlotte to hem, and for Austin to bring them back. "His stay will be short indeed I could but illy spare him at this time but to fulfil my promise to his wife." A few weeks later Martha sent Hercules home—with some ruffles for Wash's shirts to be hemmed by Charlotte, as poor little Wash's ruffles were "all in raggs."

At Mount Vernon Fanny was pregnant again, and Martha wrote they would plan their summer trip back to avoid disturbing her when the baby was due. The baby, a second boy, Charles Augustine, was born in June. Martha had one of her bad colds that spring and was too ill to think of traveling south to meet George on his return after several months on his southern tour. Martha was feeling low and complained, "so is all our family [well] except myself—only god knows wheather I shall ever be in tolerable health."

In August George Augustine, who had begun spitting up blood, took a trip "over the mountain" to Berkeley Springs to convalesce. Martha continued to send the slaves back with sewing for Charlotte and wrote Fanny that as they were planning to go down to Mount Vernon in September, she should hurry up Charlotte and Caroline in the annual task of making the slaves' winter clothing. A harrassed Fanny, who was having a harder and harder time coping with the demands of husband, small children, a new baby, and the household slaves, probably received these further instructions from her aunt with dismay. Wash's ruffles came back hemmed incorrectly by Charlotte. Martha was convinced Fanny did not pay enough attention to things, and wrote in exasperation:

My dear Fanny Philadelphia August the 29th 1791

Charlot [Charlotte] is so indolent that she will do nothing but what she is told she knows how work should be done—I cannot find how it is possible for her and Caroline [another house slave] to be altogether taken up in making the peoples [slaves'] cloths—if you suffer them to goe on so idele they will in a little time doe nothing but work for themselves . . . make Nathan [a cook] clean his kitchen and everything in it and about it very well—[3]

The Washingtons' domestic difficulties with their slaves need to be seen in wider context of what was happening between slaves and their owners elsewhere. In August 1791 the biggest slave revolt in the Western Hemisphere swept the island of Haiti, a French possession, where the idea of the rights of man, the idea that underpinned both the American and French Revolutions, had ignited a spark among the dissatisfied slaves, who lived under intolerably harsh conditions. They extracted a bloody revenge on their white owners. The long-standing paranoia in the southern states about slave rebellions was increased by a flood of refugees arriving from Haiti, all with horror stories about white planters and their families being butchered by their slaves. George wrote to the French minister, promising assistance to "quell the alarming insurrection of the Negros in Hispanola."

In the autumn of 1791 Martha's nephew John Dandridge wrote that he was still trying to untangle the affairs of Martha's brother Bartholomew. The settlement of Bartholomew Dandridge's estate had been delayed since his death in 1787, probably because a fire destroyed many of his records. Still outstanding was a loan of £600 Martha had made to Bartholomew many years earlier when she was the widow of Daniel Parke Custis and he was studying law. The bond for the outstanding debt was eventually allocated to the estate of Patsy Custis, and at her death Martha inherited it, so the bond automatically passed to George. With interest, by 1791 the debt exceeded £1,219, which Bartholomew's estate still owed George. George agreed to take title to all Bartholomew's slaves in lieu of payment.

During their holiday at Mount Vernon the contrast between Nelly's opportunities living in Philadelphia and those of her older sisters was more noticeable than ever as the girls grew older. There was an unmistakable confidence about Nelly, a bright child with a sunny disposition who was a favorite wherever she went. During the years when she had lived at Mount Vernon before George was elected president, George's secretary David Humphreys had taught her to recite verses from the Iliad. Now at twelve Nelly not only attended a good school, but she had painting lessons, music lessons, and dancing classes. She went to plays, was sent by carriage to play with her friends in the city, was an intimate of the grandest homes of socialites, members of the cabinet, and diplomats, and in addition to helping at Martha's receptions, was being allowed to accompany Martha to balls and parties.

To Betsy and Patty, she was the luckiest mortal alive. At Hope Park Dr. Stuart had hired a tutor the girls called "old Tracy." Betsy wrote, "I had no respect for my master, & treated him often with contempt, my sister joined me to torment him, he knew not how to make us respect him." As always, when the Washingtons were at Mount Vernon, the Stuarts came to stay, and Martha and the children—Nelly and Wash—and occasionally George, visited at Hope Park. Although Martha had always insisted the children refer to Eleanor as their mother and did everything she could to enable Eleanor to spend time with them, Nelly and Wash grew up having a distant, though affectionate, relationship with her.

Eleanor, continually pregnant or recovering, was hard-pressed to pay enough attention to any of her children. In the course of her life Eleanor was probably pregnant at least twenty times and had eleven children who lived. Concerned that Nelly was being spoiled by having too much too young, she may have feared Nelly might wind up married at the same tender age she had been. Eleanor wrote anxiously to Tobias Lear: "I am much alarm'd about My Dear Nelly. From her letters to her Sisters she appears too much engaged in dissipation. My Dear little artless child will I much fear soon be an affected, trifling Miss of the Town. She is too young to be admitted to Ball and Tea Parties. In a few months I suppose she will be taught to listen to every Fop. . . . Her Dear Grandmamma is too much pleased with the attentions paid to Nelly to judge of their impropriety."[4]

It was Wash, not Nelly, Eleanor should have worried about. Martha was as blindly doting and lenient with Wash as she had been with his father, Jacky. When at school, Wash proved to be a hopeless, undisciplined student, and Martha always blamed his teachers, never Wash. George saw history repeating itself and believed Martha's lenient attitude would lead to the same unfortunate consequences it had with Jacky. George did what he could to intervene with, as events would prove, mixed success.

In Philadelphia Nelly was the life and soul of the president's house. She made George laugh and Martha sigh that she was "half crasey." Martha wrote that when Nelly acquired more "gravatie" she would be a good girl. Visitors were charmed by the president's stepdaughter, her music, her exuberance, and the green parrot she was teaching to sing in French. Probably because Martha was far stricter than Eleanor believed, Nelly's head was not turned by the attention, and she was excessively devoted to her grandparents. Martha's constant companion since the age of four, Nelly had always been required to behave properly in her presence.

At twelve Nelly was far from being the "fine Miss" her mother feared. She was too interested in the many exciting things that absorbed her time— her lessons, her music, her books, her painting, her amateur theatrics, and her friends—to care much about her appearance. Nelly was going through a phase of complete indifference about her clothes, and at one point looked so disheveled that Eliza Powel asked her if she had put on her clothes with a pitchfork. Nelly recalled, "I was always too restless to take time & pains in dressing—If covered modestly, & clean, I cared for nothing else."

Other lessons Nelly learned from Martha concerned the wider responsibilities to the extended family and the obligation to dispense charity. It was always the custom at Mount Vernon to help out anyone in the neighborhood who might be in need. And of course the Washingtons were also involved in looking after a wide circle of their relatives' children who had been left orphans or fatherless. Nelly was aware of her grandmother's reputation for benevolence to those in need and saw how Martha behaved to the veterans who continued to visit the president's house. Martha's help was occasionally solicited by veterans' widows, and she was also the target of the occasional crank.

On February 22, 1792, a magnificent Birthday Ball was held in George's honor at the City Dancing Assembly, a variation in form on the Birthnight Balls held in the king's honor that George and Martha had attended many years ago in Williamsburg. The celebrations were accompanied by the usual panegyric to George, but as election year approached the political climate in Philadelphia was tense. He was the focus of constant criticism and caught between sparring members of his cabinet over issues such as assumption of national debt, excise taxes, and the mounting crisis in France. George was caught in the crossfire and so fed up with it that he would give way to embarrassing explosions of anger in cabinet meetings. By spring of 1792 George was drafting his speech of farewell for the following year, when his term expired, and Martha could look forward to going home. Both were eager to get back to Virginia.

Mount Vernon was once again going to rack and ruin in their absence. George Augustine was now too ill to manage the estate, and Fanny, never a competent manager, was finally overwhelmed. The slaves were unproductive without someone to keep them to their work, and showing an alarming degree of independence. George complained about their habits of pilfering, their dogs that worried the sheep and livestock, and the sparks that flew from carelessly carried torches as they went about at night. George wrote to his replacement manager Anthony Whiting to keep a closer eye on the slaves and decide which dogs were needed for work on the farm. All slaves' dogs not expressly sanctioned for that purpose were to be killed, and thereafter, if a slave was found with a dog without permission, the dog was to be hanged and the slave severely punished.

That spring Harriot Washington wrote asking George for money for a guitar. George sent the money and Harriot got her guitar, but by this time Harriot was running wild. Poor harassed Fanny did not have the authority to deal with a wayward teenager, so Harriot was sent to live with Betty Lewis in Fredericksburg, who, as head of a girls' school, was made of sterner stuff and better prepared to cope.

On July 1 Martha wrote Fanny they would leave for Mount Vernon on the twelfth and sent her usual detailed instructions in an exhaustive list of jobs to be done before their arrival, hinting these things would not be done otherwise: Fanny had to make sure the slaves cleaned the house from "the garret to the sellers," aired the beds, scalded the bedsteads, put up portable beds ready for the large numbers of company Martha routinely expected, wash and polish all china and glassware, see the table linen washed and ironed, the cupboards scrubbed, and "the gardener to have every thing in his garden that will be necessary to the House keeping way as vegetable is the best part of our living in the country."

When George Augustine returned from a trip to the spa at Berkeley Springs, he was so ill that he was bedridden for six weeks. In October he and Fanny left to spend the winter at Eltham, which was warmer than Mount Vernon. It was clear that he was dying and that Fanny herself was in the first stages of tuberculosis. In October George wrote from Mount Vernon to Tobias Lear that his nephew's "fate is unquestionably fixed & Fanny from prest. appearances, is very unpromisg. probably terminating in the same disorder."

When the Washingtons returned to Philadelphia with the presidential election looming, a reluctant George was under increasing pressure to stand for a second term as president. The thought of four more years' absence from home filled both Washingtons with despair. Finally their friend Eliza Powel made a finely calculated and persuasive appeal to George, playing on his sense of duty. There is no record of Martha's response to the news, but she, like George, was feeling her age and had had more than enough of public life. She also worried about the toll the strain of office was taking on him. The prospect of four more years must have seemed intolerable.

A deeply anxious Martha begged Fanny at Eltham to write regularly about how both she and her husband were. "I feared you were in a very delicate situation when I left you at Mount Vernon . . . tho' I know you are with your friends that is ready to give you every assistance and kindness—yet if there is any thing here that you cannot get whare you are that you may want—I beg you will let us know."

There was grim news everywhere. In January news came that Burwell Bassett had died in a fall from his horse. In France, where the Reign of Terror had begun, the Marquis de Lafayette was in prison in Austria for his part in trying to help the French royal family to escape. His wife had escaped and was in hiding. The Washingtons' friend Marquis de Chastellux had also been imprisoned and beheaded that year.

How to deal with the new regime in France was a delicate issue for George, as feelings in America remained strongly pro-French for their support during the Revolution. This popular view was undented by recent atrocities, and George and his administration were under political fire from all sides on that issue, at a sensitive time, given the forthcoming election. When George Augustine died at Eltham on February 5, there was no way for Martha to desert her post and go home to support Fanny. All Martha could do from a distance was to send love, a bonnet, and a cloak, counsel acceptance of God's will, and urge her to bear up for the children's sake.

George's sixty-first birthday was marked by church bells ringing and volleys of gunfire, but the family was in no mood for celebration and declined an invitation to a ball at the Powels, where Eliza Powel was celebrating her birthday on the same day as George. Two weeks later, on March 4 Martha and Betsy, Patty, Nelly, and Wash Custis all watched as Justice Cushing swore George in for a second term as president in Federal Hall. Later that day George marked the occasion by giving $150 for the relief of Philadelphia's poor.

CHAPTER 21

"Duty and Inclination"

Following the second inauguration both Martha and George were once again caught up in the exhausting battle to achieve a balance between the demands of their public lives in Philadelphia and their private family concerns in Virginia. George was too pressed with official business at the commencement of his second term to write to Fanny at once, but, even though it had been long expected, he and Martha were deeply shaken by George Augustine's death.

Martha wrote to Fanny on George's behalf, "while it pleases god to spare the President he will be a friend to you and to the children." George invited Fanny to bring the children to live at Mount Vernon, but if she did not want to do that, he offered as an alternative the use of a house he owned in Alexandria. Fanny chose Alexandria because she thought it would be easier to educate the children there. George sent workmen to carry out improvements to the house and decorate it for her. He made plans to go to Mount Vernon in April to see George Augustine's coffin buried in the family vault.

Fanny, who was disorganized and unassertive at the best of times, had made her home at Mount Vernon since the age of sixteen. Now she had to set up housekeeping in her own establishment for the first time, see to the children's education, and manage her property, slaves, and finances. Though she sensed Fanny was wilting under the pressure, from Philadelphia, Martha could do no more to help her niece than write encouraging letters, inviting her to take what she needed for the new house from Mount Vernon, give occasional advice about child rearing, and send shoes for the children. George, who was already educating Harriot's two orphaned brothers at his own expense, offered to take the eldest boy's education in hand.

Martha had to go on with her receptions, and she now allowed both thirteen-year-old Nelly and twelve-year-old Wash to attend. Betsy and Patty Custis, who had come for the inauguration, stayed in Philadelphia with their grandmother and also helped at the receptions. Tobias Lear noted that Betsy and Patty were "fine girls. I think it is much to be lamented that they . . . should be so much secluded from society." In Philadelphia Martha tried to make up for the dull time her granddaughters had at Hope Park, taking them about to tea, visiting, dinners, the assemblies, and Mr. Rickett's Circus. Martha and Eleanor both knew Betsy and Patty would benefit from some time spent in polished society and the opportunity to meet suitable young men. After several years in Philadelphia Martha had a wide circle of glamorous, wealthy and interesting friends, who, with their daughters were all disposed to pay every polite attention to Martha's granddaughters.

While Martha did her best to give the girls a good time in Philadelphia, Fanny wrote sadly that she looked forward to the comfort of seeing Martha at Mount Vernon that summer. In the meantime she proposed to take her children to visit their grandparents, George's brother Charles, who lived near Berkeley Springs. She planned to take Harriot Washington as well.

No date had been fixed for the Washingtons to leave Philadelphia for Mount Vernon that summer. One day in July Martha and Polly went shopping, and on their return, Polly felt ill. A few weeks later Martha wrote Fanny, "We have had a melloncholy time hear for about a fortnight past Mrs Lear was taken with a fever—the doctor was called in but to no purpose her illness increased until the eighth day she was taken from us—she never lost her senses till just before she expired—Mr Lear bares his loss like a philosiphor she is generally lamented by all that knew her." George was one of the pallbearers at Polly's funeral.[1]

Polly was probably one of the first victims of a yellow fever epidemic that was gradually taking hold in Philadelphia that summer. The fever had been brought to the city by refugees from the slave revolt in Haiti, and in Philadelphia the heat and humidity provided the ideal conditions for it to thrive. Within weeks of Polly's death Philadelphia was in the grip of a terrible disease, which turned people yellow and their vomit black, and could kill in half a day. It ravaged the city like a medieval plague.

By the end of August the death toll was rising. Up to fifty people a day were dying, and those who could were leaving the city. Even so, those fleeing the city were often turned away elsewhere by people who feared the refugees brought contagion with them. No one knew what caused the fever—one medical man attributed it to rotting coffee at the docks—and people went about the streets with camphor- or vinegar-soaked cloths held to their noses for protection. The treatment applied by many doctors was as much a killer as the disease, as doctors mercilessly purged and bled already weak sufferers to rid them of their "bad humors." Patients were as likely to die of dehydration or, because bleeding was an inexact remedy, from the simple loss of blood as from the fever. Blacks were believed to be immune to the disease, and they drove the death carts and collected the corpses.

The Powels had been invited to pay a visit to Mount Vernon at the end of the summer. With the outbreak of the epidemic, Eliza's husband, like George, decided it would set a bad example for the prominent citizens to leave, but thought Eliza should go with Martha and the children. Eliza wrote a note to Martha saying the decision had been left to her, and that "this has thrown me into a Dilemma the most painful. The Conflict between Duty and Inclination is a severe Trial of my Feelings; but as I believe it is always best to adhere to the line of Duty, I beg to decline the Pleasure I proposed to myself in accompanying you to Virginia at this time. The Possibility of his being ill during my Absence & thereby deprived of the Consolation and Aid he might derive from my Attention to him would be to me a lasting Source of Affliction."[2]

In this passage Eliza Powel elegantly summed up an outlook that Martha and many contemporary women shared. When confronted with a choice between duty and obligation, they would always choose to do their duty. Abiding by this principle was often difficult, and it did not necessarily guarantee happiness. The benefit derived from sticking to duty was one probably more comprehensible to eighteenth- and nineteenth-century women, like Martha, Eliza, and Martha's granddaughter Nelly, than it would be today, when, broadly speaking, women are encouraged to seek self-fulfilment. To a woman of these earlier generations, self was not the primary consideration. If the end result of opting for duty over inclination did not make a woman happy, it did confer the satisfaction of having observed a higher law or abiding by a higher moral standard. This philosophy had motivated Martha to join George in the military camps and kept her by his side in public life. Martha's life was circumscribed by obligations to other people, from family to the slaves, but she saw her wifely "Duty" as paramount, and it always dictated her choices. She understood Eliza perfectly and would have done the same thing without giving it a second thought.

Eliza went no further from Philadelphia that summer than a short trip to her brother's home outside the city in September. Her husband joined her there and was on his way back to the city when he was taken ill. He died within days, leaving Eliza sadly vindicated in her election of duty.

Betsy and Alexander Hamilton also caught the fever. Alexander Hamilton had grown up in the West Indies, had seen fevers before, and wisely called for one of the French doctors, who was familiar with West Indian fevers. Instead of bleeding and purging, to the horror of his American counterparts, the doctor treated his patients with cool baths, cool drinks, and rest. The opposing treatments took on political overtones of being "Federalist" or "Republican" [French] cures. Since France was in the grip of the Reign of Terror, many people eschewed French medical treatment as a gesture, but the Hamiltons survived. Martha, who was very fond of Betsy Schuyler Hamilton, sent them a note of congratulation, prayers, and good wishes for their recovery and six bottles of her best wine. Wine was believed to strengthen recovering invalids. Martha also begged them to send to her housekeeper Mrs. Emerson for more if they wanted it or anything else they needed.

Arrangements were made for Martha and the children to go to Mount Vernon on their own that autumn with an escort. George, in addition to trying to avoid being drawn into a military confrontation, which had arisen with Britain on trade issues, and conscious as ever of his image, thought it set the wrong example for the president to leave the city in a time of crisis. A firm adherent of Eliza Powel's view of duty but frantic about Nelly and Wash, as well as George contracting the fever, Martha resorted to blackmail and adamantly refused to leave without him. George was unwilling to expose her and the children to danger any longer, and capitulated. On September 10 the family left for Mount Vernon, where they stayed until cooler weather arrived in November and brought an end to the epidemic.

The Washingtons returned to a traumatized city. Many of their old friends were dead. The house was quieter than it had been without Polly, and little Benjamin Lincoln Lear had been taken to Tobias Lear's mother, Mary Lear, in Portsmouth, New Hampshire. Over time Mary Lear became a great friend of the Washingtons, and they exchanged letters about Benjamin's progress. Slowly the life of the capital resumed, but in January 1794, when Martha wrote to Fanny, the city was still not back to normal: "They have suffered so much that it can not be got over soon by those that was in the city—almost every family has lost some of thair friends—and black seems to be the general dress of the city—the players are not allowed to come hear nor has there been any assembly."[3]

Illness also plagued several of Martha's relations in New Kent, including Fanny's brothers and Martha's niece Patty Dandridge. Things were also not going well for Martha's youngest sister Elizabeth, and her alcoholic, abusive wastrel of a husband, Leonard Henley. Martha was especially concerned for her sister, as Elizabeth had a large family of young children, and Martha asked Fanny to let her know how Elizabeth was.

As the months of the second term passed, official engagements began to take up more and more of Martha's time. Martha's daily schedule now included an hour between eleven and twelve each morning set aside to receive lady visitors in more informal circumstances than her official receptions.

Wash had been tutored sufficiently to be accepted by a boys' academy at Germantown, but once there, his academic progress was predictably sluggish. While Wash whiled away his time unproductively at the academy, Nelly shouldered a formidable load of subjects—French, Italian, English, Geography, mathematics, history, drawing, painting, singing, and music. Nelly thought nothing of getting up at quarter to five to prepare her Italian lesson. Nelly and Wash both attended Robardet's dancing classes. George, who loved listening to Nelly sing and play, bought her a magnificent harpsichord from England. Martha, who loved music and regretted she had not had an instrument or good instruction when she was Nelly's age, was determined Nelly would make the most of her golden opportunity. She obliged a reluctant Nelly to practice for hours every day. Wash recalled, "The poor girl would play and cry, and cry and play, for long hours under the immediate eye of her grandmother, a rigid disciplinarian in all things." The end result was that Nelly played beautifully and found music to be one of her greatest pleasures all her life.

In February Martha wrote to Fanny that Philadelphia was very cold and the river was frozen and that Philadelphia was dull. The fever had closed most of the entertainments for which Philadelphia was famous, and many people were still in mourning. Everyone wanted the assemblies to begin again, for a new theater to open and the players to return. In the kind of statement that distinguishes Martha's shrewd insights from the high-flown sentiments written on her behalf by Tobias Lear, Martha homed in on the superficial side of Philadelphia: "Something of that sort seems to be necessary as a great number of people in this town is very much at a loss how to spend their time agreably The gay are always fond of some new seens let it be what it may—I dare say a very little time will ware of the gloom if gay amusements are permitted hear."[4]

A few weeks later things were going badly for Elizabeth, whom Martha now called her "porre sister." Her entire family had been ill, and another of Elizabeth's sons had died. Martha wrote to Fanny, "They seem to me to be always sick. I shall be much obliged to you if you will make some inquire into her wants if you can do it in a delicate way as I know she is very unwilling to let me hear that she is in want of any trifle, as I shall be glad to give her any thing that I can or do anything that would contribute to her happyness."

In the early spring Martha again had Betsy and Patty Custis with her for an extended stay. The girls were brought up from Hope Park by Mrs. Robert Peter, the wife of a prominent Georgetown merchant. They arrived with bad colds but soon rallied, enjoying their status as the president's stepgranddaughters, which meant everyone noticed them, and they went with Nelly on an excursion to New York. Back at Hope Park Eleanor gave birth to another son.

There was excitement in the air that spring: it was soon obvious that sixteen-year-old Patty was being courted by Thomas Peter. Soon afterwards Martha wrote to Fanny, "Patty and Mr. Peter is to make a match . . . in the last letter I had from Mrs Stuart . . . Patty has given him leve to visit her as a lover . . . if it is so I shall be very happy to see her settled with a prospect of being happy—I really believe she is a very deserving girl—I am told he is clever."

After five weeks with her grandmother, Patty returned home to be courted some more and plan her wedding, while Betsy, who wished to stay longer, remained in Philadelphia.

In her later years, Martha had begun to lose her teeth. Aside from the discomfort, it must have been a blow to her vanity. In the eighteenth century a full set of good teeth was rare enough to count as an attractive feature, and Martha had always had such pretty teeth that people commented on them. There is no mention of her suffering the agonies George did with his teeth, nor did she attempt the experimental dental surgery of the day to implant bought teeth in her gums. George paid some of his slaves for their teeth for this purpose, but the surgery was unsuccessful. But Martha had been using dentures for some time, because in the spring of 1794 she wrote to a dentist named Mr. Whitlock asking for some new dentures as her old ones were nearly worn out.

As spring wore on, George was so busy that Martha despaired of getting back to Mount Vernon for their summer holiday. She longed to be there to help Fanny set up housekeeping in Alexandria, where the alterations on the house George had provided for her and the children were being finished. Martha again begged Fanny to choose what she needed from Mount Vernon, telling her she would need more to set up housekeeping than she expected. As far as Martha could judge from a distance, Fanny seemed incapable of making such simple decisions or managing her children properly. She was so anxious to see Fanny and help her get organized that she considered coming back alone for a quick visit but reluctantly decided against it, as "I am always so much fatigued after I get home for several days—that I could not think of setting out again for some time." Since she asked Fanny to send her medicinal supplies of rosewater and mint water up to Philadelphia, Martha may have been suffering again from "cholic," indigestion, or her "bilious complaints."

Fanny's tendency to spoil her children occasionally alarmed Martha on their behalf. Fanny evidently wrote to Martha that Maria had been ill, prompting this exasperated advice from her aunt and shedding light on the kinds of childhood ailments with which mothers of the period had to cope: "I hope [Maria] has got quite well before this—I have not a doubt but that worms is the principle cause of her complaints Children that eat everything they like and feed as heartily as yours does must be full of worms—indeed my dear Fanny I never saw children stuffed as yours as when I went down and reather wondered that they were able to be tolerable with such lodes as they used to put into their little stomachs."[5]

In June George paid a flying visit to Mount Vernon and nearly suffered a bad fall when his horse slipped on some rocks above the Potomac. In his effort to stay in the saddle George wrenched his back quite badly. Until she knew he was not seriously injured, Martha was frantic with worry. Normally unable to travel without a gentleman to escort her, her carriage, and postilions, she was prepared to take the next public stage or hire horses to get to George as quickly as possible. She sent an urgent letter to Fanny: "I have been so unhappy about the Presidt that I did not know what to do . . . if he is not getting better my dear Fanny don't let me be deceived . . . I besech you to let me now how he is as soon as you can." She was persuaded it was not a serious injury, and George returned to Philadelphia, somewhat the worse for wear.

As they were not returning to Mount Vernon for their holiday, George rented a house at Germantown, a resort a few miles northwest of Philadelphia, where the family went at the end of July. George had treatment for a spot on his face that was sore, which Martha feared might be cancerous.

Betsy Custis, home again at Hope Park, watched, undoubtedly with frustration, how Patty's wedding, planned for early winter 1795, absorbed the little time Eleanor had to spend with her two eldest daughters. She had felt much happier with the Washingtons, where as *Miss Custis* she had received the attention that was her due as the eldest and an heiress in her own right. Until her marriage, the eldest daughter in a family had the distinction of being *the* Miss of her family, and her younger sisters were known by their Christian names. Patty was thus Miss Martha Custis, and Nelly was Miss Eleanor Custis. Back at gloomy Hope Park it made little difference what she was called; it was galling to have a younger sister marry first, and little consolation to remain "Miss Custis" in those circumstances.

Betsy was quite likely dissatisfied and longing to be in love, because to unburden her feelings of teenage yearning and angst at being the unmarried sister, she wrote the Washingtons a letter about her feelings of distress and her longing to fall in love and marry. The letter does not survive, though George's answer to it does. George's letter is particularly interesting because it reveals even more about his attitude toward marriage in general, and by implication, it reflects on his own:

> My dear Betsy
>
> Do not then in your contemplation of the marriage state, look for perfect felicity before you consent to wed. Nor conceive, from the fine tales the Poets & lovers of old have told us, of the transports of mutual love, that heaven has taken its abode on earth: nor deceive yourself in supposing, that the only means by which these are to be obtained, is to drink deep of the cup, & revel in an ocean of love. Love is a mighty pretty thing; but like all other delicious things, it is cloying; and when the first transports of the passion subside, which it assuredly will do, and yield—oftentimes too late—to more sober reflections, it serves to convince, that love is too dainty a food to live upon *alone,* and ought

not to be considered farther than as a necessary ingredient for that matrimonial happiness which results from a combination of causes; none of which are of greater importance, than that the object on whom it is placed, should possess good sense—good dispositions—and the means of supporting you in the way you have been brought up. Such qualifications cannot fail to attract (after marriage) your esteem & regard, into wch or into disgust, sooner or later, love naturally resolves itself . . . there is no truth more certain, that all our enjoyments fall short of our expectations; and to none does it apply with more force than to the gratification of the passions.[6]

Historians have speculated to what extent George drew on his feelings for Sally in giving this advice, but it seems clear that he knew what matrimonial happiness was and valued it enough to give Betsy sound advice that transports of passion were not a reliable foundation for it.

Having received a letter from Fanny saying she was "depresd" and had learned "not to look for happiness in this world," Martha came close to losing her patience. She wrote Fanny a bracing letter telling her it was high time Fanny stopped moaning, counted her blessings and pulled herself together. It may have crossed Martha's mind by this time that had she been on the spot, Fanny would have lapsed even further into passive, helpless dependency and that it was just as well they were too far away for that to happen. Martha was sympathetic but practical, telling Fanny that if she lived among her friends and relatives she could not be forever depending on them to manage her affairs. "I very sincearly wish you would exert yourself without depending upon others as that is the only way to be happy . . . I would rouse myself and not trouble any mortal—your concerns are not so large but that you might with proper attention have them always kept in good order . . . you have enough if you will manage it right."

In September the Washingtons returned to a city free of fever but stricken with an outbreak of diphtheria that carried off many children. Martha fretted about Wash's poor academic performance, which she felt sure could not be his fault: "He [Wash] does not learn as much as he might if the Master took proper care to make the children attentive to thair books." George knew better than to remonstrate.[7]

Tobias Lear returned from a trip to Europe, where he had gone partly on official business and partly for the purpose of finding industrious German immigrants to lease the twenty thousand acres of land George still owned near the Ohio River, which had never been developed or cultivated. In order to do some errands for George, Tobias paid a visit to Mount Vernon before going to Philadelphia. Fanny was there at the same time. At the end of September Fanny wrote to say Tobias had proposed to her. Fanny urgently sought Martha's advice.

Martha, ever a friend of matrimony, replied:

My dear Fanny, I wish I could give you unerring advise. . . . you must be gov-
ernd by your own judgement . . . it is a matter more interesting to yourself than
any other . . . —as to the President, he never has nor never will, as you have
often hear him say, inter meddle in matrimonial concerns, he joins with me
however in wishing you every happyness this world can give . . . he [Tobias]
always appeared very attentive to his wife and child . . . is I belive, a man of
strict honor and probity; and one with whom you would have as good a
prospect of happyness as with any one I know.[8]

Two weeks later Fanny wrote that she had decided to accept.

Martha's patience was sorely tried with Fanny simultaneously on two
other matters. The wife and daughter of Senator Ralph Izard were to be in
the Mount Vernon neighborhood, and as the daughter, Miss Izard, was a
particular friend of Nelly's, Martha asked Fanny to look after them. To
Martha's embarrassment Fanny was unaccountably absent, and the Izards
stayed only one night at Mount Vernon, looked after by Frank the butler.
The second matter was the fact Fanny had made free with George's stocks
of wine at Mount Vernon, handing it out to anyone who came merely out of
curiosity to see the president's home. Martha was again exasperated with
her niece: "The President seemed a good deal surprised—at the quantity of
wine that you have given out. . . . I beg you will not give out another Bottle
out of the vault."

As the new school year began for the children, Martha's "dear Little
Washington" had had to change schools. He was now at the College of Pennsylvania, later to become the University of Pennsylvania, where he "is doing
not half so well as I could wish." This time Martha blamed Wash's poor academic performance on the poor quality of the Philadelphia schools.

The ongoing divergence of political opinions about the boundaries of
federal versus state powers made itself felt in the Washington family, with
the Democrat press continuing to jibe at Martha's Drawing Rooms as "tending to give her a super-eminency and as introductory to the paraphernalia
of courts." Martha was always careful to steer well clear of political issues
and could never be drawn into any expression of her views. But she did
express herself in private. A note in Wash's *Memoirs and Recollections of
Washington* recalls:

With what feelings the excellent woman regarded these democrats is shown
by an anecdote of the same period. She was a severe disciplinarian, and Nelly
Custis was not often permitted by her to be idle or follow her own caprices.
The young girl was compelled to practice at the harpsichord four or five hours
every day, and one morning when she should have been playing, her grandmother entered the room, remarking she had not heard the music, and that

she had observed some person going out, whose name she would very much like to know. Nelly was silent, and suddenly her attention was arrested by a blemish on the wall, which had been newly painted a delicate cream color. "Ah! it was no federalist," she exclaimed, looking at the spot just above the settee; "none but a filthy democrat would mark a place with his good for nothing head in that manner!"[9]

If Nelly was embarrassingly quick to pick up unladylike expressions such as "filthy democrat" overheard at home, she was an equally apt pupil in absorbing Martha's devotional practices. Nelly's schoolmate and lifelong friend, Elizabeth Bordley Gibson, described a more serious side of Nelly. She had spent the afternoon with Nelly, and when there was no company and no official reception, Martha kept an early bedtime:

> One evening my father's carriage was later in coming for me and my dear young friend invited me to accompany her to her grandmama's room. There, after some little chat, Mrs. Washington apologized to me for pursuing her usual preparations for the night, and Nelly entered upon her accustomed duty by reading a chapter and a psalm from the old family Bible, after which all knelt in evening prayer; Mrs. Washington's faithful maid then sang a verse of some soothing hymn, and leaning down, [Nelly] received the parting blessing for the night, with some emphatic remarks on her duties, improvements, etc. The effect of these habits and teachings appeared in the granddaughter's character through life.[10]

Even when Nelly entertained friends of her own, it was always her habit to leave them and accompany Martha for this nighttime ritual.

Nelly was a bridesmaid at Patty's wedding in Alexandria in January. Martha, who was unable to attend, undoubtedly lectured Nelly at length about the ladylike deportment required of the sister of the bride beforehand. For the occasion Nelly wore a fine new dress and Martha's watch, and officially was almost "grown up."

Though girls no longer married at quite such a young age as they had done in Martha's youth, Patty was not quite eighteen at the time of her wedding. For Nelly at fourteen, marriage within a few years was a distinct possibility. Martha was concerned that Nelly was almost grown up and becoming perhaps too distant from her mother—Nelly herself may have let drop some remarks, or Eleanor may have expressed a wish to spend more time with her daughter—and decided that though she hated to part with her favorite granddaughter Nelly should spend the next winter at Hope Park. Nelly had to steel herself to the idea, because she always hated being parted from Martha, but curiously for such a bright and lively girl, she rarely disputed Martha's judgment.

On February 22, 1795, there was a fabulous Birthday Ball for George in glamorous Philadelphia style. Miss Chambers was there and recorded being met at the door by a master of ceremonies who conducted her and her party to Martha. Again, Martha half-rose to receive them. Miss Chambers noted Martha was dressed in fine silk but with no jewels or other ornaments, in contrast to the wives of foreign dignitaries seated around her who were "glittering from the floor to the summit of their headdress . . . such superabundance of ornament struck me as injudicious. We look too much at the gold and pearls to do justice to the lady [wearing them]."

In New Kent, after a brief spell of good behavior, Elizabeth Henley's husband was drinking heavily again and making her life miserable. Martha wrote: "I am very much greved to hear that my pore sister is in such a wreched situation it is impossible that things can go one tolerably if Mr Henley is always drinking brandy—everything he has must suffer—be sides the strain it must give to his family—I fear he has but little affection for them . . . pore Dear Betsy has had a hard lot in this world I hope her children will be a comfort to her. . . . —I often think of her with the greatest concern."

Martha hoped Elizabeth would come to stay at Mount Vernon with her that summer: "I should be very glad if it could so happen that she would come up to see me when I go home—she is in such distress that I fear she will never have resolution to leve her children to come so long a journey . . . if she can come your brother B[urwell Bassett Jr.] promised to let her have a manservant to bring her up."[11]

Betsy Custis, even more bored at Hope Park now that Patty was gone, begged Martha to allow her to come stay in Philadelphia that spring. Martha obtained permission from Eleanor, but once Betsy arrived, she irritated Martha by moping around the house, staying home from church and the dancing assembly, and not returning visits paid expressly for the polite purpose of waiting on Miss Custis. Martha sighed that "the girls have lived so long in solatude that they do not know how to get the better of it." Betsy was obliged to attend the wedding of one of Robert Morris's daughters, which did nothing to lift her spirits. A month later Betsy was still moping, and it seemed to be catching. She and Nelly had taken to spending all their time looking out the window, watching the world go by.

By the end of May Martha was sending Fanny her usual detailed instructions to prepare for their arrival and company to follow, by having the house cleaned from attics to cellars, gooseberries bottled and cherries dried, and the cellars, meat store, and dairy inspected. She also wanted Fanny to keep a closer eye on the house slaves, because from a distance Martha could do nothing to control them. In the Washingtons' absence the slaves seized the limited opportunities at their disposal to improve their lot and grew vegetables, raised poultry, caught fish, and made off with newborn lambs and any food left in the smokehouse, not only for their own use but to sell in the market in Alexandria. Martha suspected Kitty, the slave who looked after supplies kept in cellars, meat stores, and dairy, was doing precisely this. From time to time both George and Martha fumed that things had come to such a pass that it was as if the slaves were working only for themselves!

When Fanny wrote that one of her slave children had died, Martha wrote back:"Black children are liable to so many accidents and complaints that one is hardly sure of keeping them I hope you will not find him much loss the Blacks are so bad in their nature that they have not the least gratatude for the kindness that may be shewed to them."

At the end of the summer of 1795, George Washington Lafayette, who was close to Nelly's age, escaped from France and arrived in America with his tutor. His father was still in prison, and relations between France and the United States remained tense. To his great regret and intense embarrassment, George felt unable, for political reasons, to invite his namesake to live at the presidential mansion. He did make arrangements for him to stay with a friend in Boston. George Washington Lafayette was not the only French person to be ignored for reasons of political expediency. In a gesture that must have hurt her pride terribly, the widow of the Marquis de Chastellux, the "accomplished lady and relative of the Duke of Orleans," was in such straits she wrote a letter appealing to George personally for financial assistance in recognition of the services her late husband had rendered the Americans. Her letter was never answered. Martha knew of the political situation between France and the United States but found it agonizing not to be able to help old friends.

In August it was clear Patty Custis Peter was pregnant with her first child, and Fanny Bassett Washington married Tobias Lear. Martha had sent her some new silk gowns for her trousseau.

At Mount Vernon in September, the appointed day came and went for a visit from Elizabeth Henley, but Elizabeth never arrived. Martha had been looking forward to her visit, but at the last minute something prevented her from coming, possibly an illness or the effects of abuse—from the tenor of Martha's letters, we can speculate that Elizabeth may have been afraid in the end of leaving her children at the mercy of Leonard Henley and his drunken rages. Elizabeth may also have been ashamed of the contrast between her miserable situation and that of her prominent eldest sister. Martha was bitterly disappointed but wrote, "I dare say Betty you have good reasons for not coming . . . as it is probable that we shall never meet again in this world You have my prayers for this worlds blessing . . . farewell my dear Betty."

CHAPTER 22

Transitions

All her life Martha was haunted by Patcy's death and gravitated toward young girls, looking for some reflection of her lost daughter. In Nelly, Martha's "Dear Child," Martha found a most devoted, intelligent, and sweet-natured replacement to comfort her, but her motherly beneficence extended to many others, and the bonds she formed with them were an important focus of her life. Ironically, had her daughter lived, it is likely Patcy's epilepsy would have kept Martha at Mount Vernon and prevented her from joining George in the army camps or in the capital. Nor would Martha have been able to devote so much of her time to the many young women in whom she took an interest.

Parting with Nelly was a trial, but Martha knew that it was her duty to see that Nelly spent an extended period of time with Eleanor. On October 13, 1795, she deposited an anguished Nelly at Hope Park; Martha planned to come down to Mount Vernon early in the spring to bring Nelly back. Nelly did not mind leaving the amusements of Philadelphia but had been dreading saying goodbye to Martha, who was returning to Philadelphia. After three days at Hope Park, Nelly wrote Elizabeth Bordley: "I have gone through the greatest trial, I have ever experienced—parting with my beloved Grandmama. This is the first separation for any time since I was two years old. Since my fathers death she has been ever more than a Mother to me, and the President the most affectionate of Fathers. I love them more than any one. You can guess then how severely I must feel this parting, even for a short time. I have been so long from My Mama that Grandmama thought it proper & necessary for me to spend this winter with her."[1]

What is particularly interesting about this passage is that Nelly had already absorbed Martha's philosophy on the need to regulate conduct by the guiding principle of duty in general, and duty to the family in particular. Since early childhood Nelly had observed Martha's involvement in family matters and the way she kept in touch with, and assisted, her female relatives, even when she was obliged to live at a distance from them. As a young woman, Nelly was doing her best to emulate Martha, and Nelly's outlook on life, as set out in her letters to Elizabeth Bordley, became increasingly a mirror image of Martha's.

In Philadelphia the official entertaining continued, but Martha found the house noticeably quieter that fall. Tobias Lear, married to Fanny, and with four children between them, had resigned to start his own company in Washington, D.C., and with Nelly away, there were no hours of harpsichord practice or girlish voices singing duets as Nelly and her friends were fond of doing, and there was no Nelly to entertain company after dinner with her lively chatter and music. Nelly had once turned down an invitation to a friend's party because a large number of congressmen were coming to dinner, and she had to stay in to entertain them, as she understood they liked to hear music, though, Nelly added, she thought they could not tell one note from another.

When Nelly was not at school or with her friends, she and Martha habitually spent hours in each other's company, sewing, embroidering, doing beadwork, performing their devotions, visiting, shopping, and attending church. Martha missed her adoring shadow, chief acolyte, assistant hostess, and constant companion. Knowing this, Nelly suffered too at Hope Park. As a measure of how far Martha was prepared to go to make Nelly happy, besides her pet parrot she allowed Nelly a dog, and the dog, named Frisk, kept Martha company in his owner's absence.

Martha was devoted to Wash, but he was not company for his grandmother in the same way a young woman could be. When Wash was in the house, it was usually because he was passing through in a rush. As a young man of sixteen he was beyond Martha's influence, though showing the effects of her overindulgence when he was younger. Martha, still with the same blind spot with Wash she had had with Jacky, never allowed George to exercise any restraint or discipline over her "Dear pretty Boy." Although his education and guidance had been turned over to George, it was too late. Though genuinely fond of his step-grandson, George saw history repeating itself with no progress having been made. Wash was still as lazy and inattentive at school as his feckless, charming, and indolent father had been, promising to amount to the same kind of rich ne'er-do-well. George battled on, trying a change of tack by sending Wash to Princeton College, with much good advice about working hard and the best ways to make friends. George wrote a cautiously hopeful note to Tobias Lear: "Washington Custis has got settled at Princeton College, and I think under favourable auspices, but the change from his former habits is so great and sudden, and his hours for study so much increased beyond what he as been accustomed to, that though he promises to be attentive, it is easy to perceive he is not at all reconciled to it yet."

Martha and George spent Christmas 1795 at home and held a reception on New Year's Day. As the year began without Nelly, Martha did what she always did when separated from a member of her family. She exchanged lengthy letters with Nelly, giving her the news of their Philadelphia friends and expressing her usual interest in everyone's health, especially that of Eleanor and her Stuart children, all of whom had been ill that winter. At Nelly's request Martha was having a picture drawn of herself. Martha sent Nelly advice about picking up her clothes, keeping her feet dry, and cleaning her teeth, reinforced by presents of some toothbrushes and tooth powder, a "prity" book, the "pretiest gold chain I could find," and pocket handkerchiefs.

In return Nelly wrote sympathizing with Betsy's disgruntled view of life at Hope Park. Nelly described it as being "in the windings of a forest obscured" where "we seldom see a living creature except the family." Nelly found more entertainment at the end of January 1796, when she went to stay with the Peters and their new baby in Washington. Patty's baby was a girl named Martha Elizabeth Eleanor Peter, after Patty, her mother, grandmother, and mother-in-law. Nelly was thrilled to be an aunt, writing to Elizabeth that she had grown inches taller on the strength of it. She called the baby a fat, handsome, good-tempered clever toad. Nelly, a credit to her grandmother's training, crowed proudly to Elizabeth Bordley that when Eleanor and Betsy had left to go back to Hope Park, they left her in charge of the household, as a "housekeeper, Nurse—(and a long train of Etcetra's)."

While visiting her sister, Nelly called on Fanny and Tobias Lear in Alexandria. Fanny was ill and had sent for Nelly. It was a sobering visit, the first time Nelly was confronted with mortality. Fanny was in the terminal stages of tuberculosis.

During her Washington stay, Nelly wrote to let Elizabeth Bordley in on a family secret. Betsy Custis, who henceforth insisted upon being called "Eliza," was engaged to an older man, Thomas Law of Washington. This, wrote Nelly exuberantly, meant she would be promoted to the honor of being Miss Custis. Martha and George were not happy about Eliza's choice. Thomas Law was a thirty-nine-year-old Englishman, a nephew of the Bishop of Carlisle and a brother to Lord Ellenborough. He had spent time in India, where he had married, and he had three grown "Indian" sons. He claimed to be a widower, but a faint question seems to have hung over his actual marital status. He had made a fortune in England and had begun speculating in land in Washington. Described by a contemporary as being "an eccentric man of great nervous excitability and quick impulse," he may have seen a commercial advantage in marrying the step-granddaughter of the president. Accustomed as the Washingtons and the Stuarts were to a society with a wide network of family relationships from New York to South Carolina, the Washingtons were concerned that Eliza intended to marry someone of whom they could not say, in the broadest sense, "We know his people."

That said, Martha could not depend on George or Dr. Stuart advising Eliza. George always stuck to a policy of not interfering with people who intended to marry and had already written to Eliza all the advice he was going to give her on the subject of marriage. Dour Dr. Stuart was even less likely to influence headstrong Eliza, now determined to get married.

Nelly stayed for two months with the Peters, but it was not all house-keeping and nursing. "I have been to two balls—& my Sisters wedding. The balls were very agreeable and I danced a good deal. Dancing you know has always been my delight—& I prefer balls to any other amusement," she wrote Elizabeth Bordley. When Nelly had returned to Hope Park for Eliza's wedding, Thomas Law drove her in his chariot. At Eliza's request the wedding was a very quiet and private affair. Nelly did not share Martha's misgivings about Eliza's groom, and wrote Elizabeth Bordley—and probably in a similar vein to Martha and George, who did not attend—that "Sister Eliza was married the twenty first—and left us on Thursday. She has every chance for happiness—a good hearted affectionate husband—one most sincerely attached to her—& She is the same to him."

George and Martha sent a note of congratulation to the happy couple instead of attending the wedding. George also wrote to Nelly, responding to comments she had made on the balls, marriage, and young men, declaring herself unimpressed with the young men of the day and her "determination never to give herself a moments uneasiness on account of any of them." George doted on Nelly, and aware she was of an age to need it, he wrote her a letter of advice on the subject of beaux, flirtation, and marriage, similar to that given to Eliza a year earlier. Beginning with arch congratulations on the happy fact of having an equal number of men and women and therefore no shortage of dancing partners, he continued in a more serious vein:

> A hint here; men and women feel the same inclination towards each other *now* that they have always done.... And *you,* as others have done, may find, perhaps, that the passions of your sex are easier roused than allayed. Do not therefore boast too soon of your insensibility. In the composition of the human frame there is a good deal of inflammable matter ... when the torch is put to it, that which is within you may bursts into blaze....
>
> love may and therefore ought to be under the guidance of reason ... whilst you remain Eleanor [Parke] Custis Spinster ... when the fire is beginning to kindle and your heart growing warm, propound these questions to it. Who s the invader? Have I competent knowledge of him? Is he a man of good character? A man of sense? For be assured a sensible woman can never be happy

with a fool What has been his walk in life? Is he a gambler? a spendthrift, a drunkard? Is his fortune sufficient to maintain me in the manner I have been accustomed to live, and my sisters do live? and is he one to whom my friends can have no reasonable objection?[2]

After cautioning Nelly against flirting and warning her that "a thorough paced coquette dies in celibacy as a punishment for her attempts to mislead others by encouraging looks, words or actions, given for no purpose but to draw men on to make overtures that they may be rejected." George concludes by wishing Nelly "a good husband, when you want and deserve one."

Nelly would take this advice to heart, but there is a heartfelt tone in these lines, which echoes the passion in George's letter to Sally Cary Fairfax, shortly before he married Martha.

Almost simultaneously with Eliza's wedding, the Washingtons were living in hourly dread of sad news from Tobias Lear, who had written on March 21 and 23 that Fanny was sinking fast.

On March 25 Lear wrote: "The Partner of my life is no more! and I am too much distressed at this moment to add more."

Martha felt the loss of the young woman she had described as "a daughter to me" and a link with her sister Anna Maria. Martha struggled with her duty to bow to the will of Providence but could not help giving way to grief. "Your former letter prepared us for the stroke, which that of the 25th instant announced; but it has fallen heavily notwithstanding."

Tobias wrote to his mother in Portsmouth that he could not manage the four young children on his own, so she prepared to make the trip south to Washington to collect them. Martha told Mary Stillson Lear that they were unable to help with the children, but George wrote to the head of the Moravian School in Bethlehem, Pennsylvania, a boarding school for girls, to see if they could take eight-year-old Maria.

Then from Fredericksburg came unexpected news of another young woman relative. Sixteen-year-old Harriot Washington had acquired a suitor, named Mr. Parks, about whom George knew nothing. Harriot had been too nervous to write to George herself. The first George knew of it was when Mr. Parks wrote to him in March, enclosing a letter from Betty Lewis, by way of introduction, to ask for Harriot's hand. Betty had made inquiries about Mr. Parks and assured George he was "very much respected by all his acquaintance, sober, sedate and attentive to business." As Harriot was penniless, she was bound to have a hard time finding a husband, and Betty's view was that if Mr. Parks was as respectable as he seemed, Harriot was lucky. George had believed the best they could do for her was take her in at Mount Vernon when he retired, and he had hoped in this way to give Harriot a chance to meet some decent men. Now faced with a suitor for Harriot, George was concerned, as he had been with Eliza's suitor Mr. Law, that the family knew nothing of Mr. Parks's family or whether he could afford to support Harriot and any children they might have. Along with concern for Harriot, there was an element of self-interest. If Harriot was abandoned or widowed, the first person she would turn to for help for herself and any children would be George. Betty was already on Harriot's side, so George undertook to make further inquiries. Evidently he found the Parks family to be as respectable as Betty had said, and also that Harriot's intended could afford to support her. Harriot and her Mr. Parks were married the following year.

In May while Nelly was waiting for her "Beloved Grandmama" to come to Hope Park to collect her, another young woman who had spent her life at Martha's side was quietly making plans to disappear from the presidential mansion. As Martha prepared to go home for the summer, her maid, twenty-two-year-old Oney Judge, was packing her own belongings and smuggling them gradually out of the house to friends, before finally slipping out of the house unnoticed one evening while the family was at dinner. Oney disappeared from sight into a network of Free Blacks and servants who hid her until she could be smuggled aboard a ship leaving Philadelphia. Martha was stunned by Oney's defection—hurt, furious, and inconvenienced beyond measure. She had been fond of Oney since childhood and personally had a hand in Oney's upbringing. Oney had graduated to the position of Martha's personal maid, and she was a skilled seamstress. For all these reasons, Oney had been a particular favorite of Martha's, a surrogate daughter among the slaves.

Oney's mother Betty had a long-standing relationship with Martha, a responsible position in the house, and superior status in the slave hierarchy. She received preferential treatment, as did her daughters Oney and Delphy. Oney was as much a child of Mount Vernon as Nelly and, being an intelligent and independent-minded young woman, may have compared her prospects to Nelly's privileged life and found them wanting. The unfair discrepancies in their situations may have been accented by the fact that in terms of coloring, there was little difference between dark-haired Nelly and fair-skinned Oney, the child of a mixed-race mother and a white father.

Trained from childhood by Martha herself, Oney was, in George's words, "Mistress of her needle," and as Martha's chief maid, she had charge of Martha's clothing and the washing, starching, and laundering of Martha's extravagant caps. She helped Martha dress in the morning, undress for bed each night, and was part of Martha's nightly ritual of prayer and hymn singing. Like a lady in waiting, Oney attended Martha on her visits to other ladies and made friends with other servants and slaves while she waited— such good friends, in fact, that she not only learned about the Pennsylvania legislation that freed slaves after six months' residence, but she was quick to work out why the slaves at the president's house were periodically sent back to Mount Vernon on flimsy excuses.

Martha was still in turmoil over Oney's defection when she picked up Nelly at Hope Park. To add insult to injury, George had refused to advertise for his runaway slave. Martha fulminated about Oney's ingratitude despite the kindness Martha had shown her, and Nelly absorbed another lesson about the relationship between mistresses and their slaves; no matter how kind the former were, the latter were at heart ungrateful wretches.

At Mount Vernon, Oney's defection was a bittersweet event in the slave quarters. Aside from the eleven slaves Lund Washington had sold to pay the taxes during the Revolution, George had adopted a policy of not selling a slave away from the plantation without that slave's consent. He also recognized slave "marriages" and family relationships. It was less a matter of philanthropy or that contradiction in terms "enlightened slave owning" than a pragmatic realization that slaves worked better and were less likely to run away if they were not separated from their families. The result was that many of George's Washington slaves and Martha's Custis dower slaves had intermarried. Oney was part of an extended slave family, and the people she had known since she was born were likely never to see her again.

First among them were Oney's mother Betty and her sixteen-year-old sister Delphy. They knew that if Oney were not captured and returned they would never see her again either. But if she was captured they also realized that Oney would be severely punished, possibly by being sold South to the brutal conditions of the rice or indigo plantations in Carolina. George might then purchase another young slave woman for Martha to replace Oney. George was a stern enough disciplinarian to make all the slaves hope Oney was not apprehended.

A deceptively gentle account of the "white" response to Oney's defection was written during Oney's lifetime by Mrs. C. M. Kirkland, based on an interview with a Virginia woman, a Miss Langdon, who spoke to the runaway Oney:

> When Mrs. Washington's favorite maid Oney, the woman who had long been her personal attendant, done her fine sewing and prepared her caps—a nice matter of home clear starching, quilling and frilling in those days—when this Oney ran away, and Mrs. Washington, missing her every moment, and not knowing where to look for a substitute, descried the General to advertise, offering a reward for her, he wholly declined, with a laugh . . . saying it would appear finely for *him* to be advertising for runaway slaves.
>
> The woman, Oney, went to one of the Eastern states and called on a young lady who was intimate with general Washington's family, who had seen her a thousand times at her mistress' side, and who was of course, exceedingly surprised to see her so far from home, knowing she was indispensable to Mrs. Washington.

"Why Oney," said Miss L [Langdon] "where in the world have you come from?"

"Come from New York, missis", said Oney

"But why did you come away—how can Mrs. Washington do without you?"

Oney hung her head at this, but after a moment replied—

"Run away missis."

"Run away! And from such an excellent place—Why, what could induce you? You had a room to yourself and only nice, light work to do, and every indulgence—"

"Yes I know but I wanted to be free missis; wanted to learn to read and write—"

This was Oney's only motive; and she remained in Maine, married and settled there, and was her own mistress ever after, although very probably harder work and poorer far than had been her lot at the president's.

This anecdote I had from the lips of the lady herself [Miss Langdon] now living in the city of New York.[3]

It was not exactly the case that George laughed, declined to advertise for Oney, and did nothing else. What he did was bide his time. Martha was emphatic that she could not manage without Oney and wanted her back very badly—a slave was a slave—Oney was also a dower slave, and as dower property, belonged to Martha's heirs after her death. George was entitled to the use only of the dower slaves. If he sold or freed any, he had to reimburse the Custis estate for their worth, and he did not want to have to "buy" Oney's freedom. Finally, if Oney, a privileged house slave, ran away, it set a particularly bad example for the other slaves. That summer at Mount Vernon, Oney's absence was felt and noted in the slave quarters, and there was an extra element of tension between the Washingtons and the slaves as the issue of Oney's eventual fate hung in the air while George considered the next step.

None of this affected Nelly's enjoyment of life that summer. Restored to her grandparents and with her mother, sisters, and new niece visiting often, Nelly was in high spirits: "I ride sometimes on Horseback, walk, read, write French—work, play & sing & always think the weeks go off too fast." Nelly had a fall from her horse when a low-hanging branch knocked her off. Martha was "very much frightened" and forbade her to ride again, until Nelly convinced her her "neck was not to be broken yet awhile."

That summer Mount Vernon was, as ever, full of company, including George Washington Lafayette, whom George and Martha could no longer bear to exclude from their home, and his tutor, Felix Frestel. Another Frenchman, architect Benjamin Latrobe, arrived at Mount Vernon with a letter of introduction from George's nephew Bushrod Washington. Latrobe admired the orderly appearance of the plantation with its "good fences, clean grounds and extensive cultivation" but in general found Virginia plantation houses shabbier than the houses of the gentry in England. Latrobe stayed to dinner and was charmed by his host and hostess. He noted George treated George Washington Lafayette like a son and was entranced by sixteen-year-old Nelly with her dark hair and wearing a fashionable French dress. Nelly's days of putting her clothes on "with a pitchfork" were over and she was beginning to take an interest in her appearance. Dinner was leisurely and afterwards, at about six, the family took coffee on the veranda with its sweeping views over the Potomac. Latrobe was startled to find the whole family went to bed at an early hour without supper.

The Washingtons' mood at Mount Vernon that summer of 1796 was buoyant. The last summer of George's presidency, the Washingtons could finally look forward to the prospect of coming home for good. George's second term would officially end in March 1797, but he had already been drafting his farewell address for some time.

Between traveling back and forth to Philadelphia on government business, drafting his farewell speech, and graciously entertaining a wide range of company, in September 1796 George had also begun trying to recover Oney, by fair means or foul, without drawing attention to the fact. George had his secretary of the treasury, Oliver Wolcott Jr., make discreet inquiries.

Miss Langdon had done more than chat with Oney and remonstrate with her over leaving such a good place. She also informed the authorities of Oney's whereabouts. Thanks to Miss Langdon, Oney was traced to Portsmouth, New Hampshire, where a Portsmouth captain named John Bowles had transported her on his ship, *The Nancy*, probably suspecting she was a runaway slave but asking no questions. At the time anyone convicted of aiding and abetting a runaway slave could be fined heavily or even sentenced to death.

Wolcott contacted Joseph Whipple, the customs inspector at Portsmouth, to alert him to the situation, and George wrote ordering him to "seize her and put her on board a Vessel bound immediately to this place [Mount Vernon] or to Alexandria."

At first Whipple followed his instructions and discovered where Oney was living in Portsmouth. But because antislavery sentiment was running high in much of New England, Whipple did not think it politic to rouse it in pursuit of the president's slave. He secretly booked a passage on a ship due to sail to Virginia and planned to apprehend Oney quietly and avoid a public fuss. Whipple sent a message to the place Oney was living to offer her a job working in his family. Oney, who needed work, duly went to Whipple's house for an interview. However, in the course of the false job interview, Whipple found himself impressed by Oney, despite himself, and resolved to see if he could deal with the situation differently. He wrote to George's intermediary in the matter, Oliver Wolcott Jr.:

After a cautious examination it appeared to me that she had not been decoyed away as had been apprehended, but . . . a wish for complete freedom, . . . had been her only motive for absconding. It gave me great satisfaction to find that when uninfluenced by fear she . . . great affection for her Master & Mistress and without hesitation declared her willingness to return & to serve with fidelity during the lives of the President and his Lady if she could be freed on their decease . . . she would rather suffer death than return to slavery and liable to be sold or given to other [unintelligible] . . . it would be a pleasing circumstance both to the President & his Lady should she go back without compunction I prevailed on her to confide in my obtaining the freedom she so earnestly wishes for. She made cheerful preparations to go on board the Vessel which was to have sailed in a few hours and of her own accord proposed concealing her intention from her acquaintances lest they should discourage her from he purpose . . . I am extremely sorry to add as I can see the girl is a valuable servant to her Mistress that the vessel being detained by a contrary wind her intention was discovered next day by her acquaintances who dissuaded her from returning and vessel sailed without her.[4]

George and Martha were outraged by Oney's attempt to blackmail them into giving her her freedom, and more pressure was put on a reluctant Whipple to find a discreet way of recovering Martha's slave. This played out against what had become a stormy second term for George, one dogged by accusations by an increasingly vitriolic Democrat press of political and financial corruption. In 1795 anti-Washington sentiment was spiked by Tom Paine, author of "Common Sense," the manifesto of the American Revolution. Paine had believed that after the American Revolution Washington's administration would reward him with a government post. When it failed to do so, he went to France, where he had become involved in politics, then been imprisoned by the Jacobins. In prison Paine appealed desperately but in vain to his old friend George Washington for help. Nearly dead from fever, he was accidentally passed over for execution when his cell door was marked on the wrong side with the chalk cross indicating that the inmate was marked for the guillotine the next day.

Paine was understandably bitter about what he saw as a personal betrayal, and after his release in 1794, he wrote George several letters full of invective, caviling at George's refusal to respond to his anguished appeals from prison and George's political betrayal of the aims of the Revolution in trying to make himself a figurehead. He was particularly scathing about what he perceived to be the cult of Washington, and the way the Washingtons were becoming the American equivalent of royalty. He accused George of treachery.

To Paine's horror the Americans were also negotiating a trade treaty with England and dissociating themselves from revolutionary developments in

France. Paine was beside himself and in 1795 wrote a poem, which was soon circulated "to the Sculptor who should make the statue of Washington":

> Take from the mine the coldest hardest stone,
> It needs no fashion it is Washington;
> But if you chisel, let your strokes be rude;
> And on his breast engrave INGRATITUDE

It was fuel for the anti-Federalists and immensely damaging for George personally. Paine followed up with more invective in 1796: "treacherous in friendship . . . and a hypocrite in public life . . . the world will be puzzled to decide if you are an apostate or an impostor; whether you have abandoned good principles or if you ever had any."[5]

What is forgotten today is that at the time enough people viewed the Washington cult of personality with alarm for this to strike a responsive chord: the issues surrounding George's personality cult/monarchical style were part and parcel of the wider debate about centralized power versus the rights of individual states. With political opinion divided along these lines, the issue of slavery was coming to the fore as another issue that was inconsistent with Revolutionary ideals—and the fact George was a slave owner was fuel to that particular fire. There was growing pressure for the abolition of slavery, which was aimed at the South and slave owners. Support for abolition, however, did not divide neatly between the Federalist and Democrat poles of thought, though most of the southern Democrats were, predictably, opposed. Under the circumstances, for George to pursue a young runaway slave woman risked a backlash of adverse propaganda. In the matter of Oney, George decided to bide his time.

The farewell address was published on September 19 in the *American Daily Advertiser*. It was a giant step on the road home, and Martha was torn between relief at seeing George's resignation set in stone and anxiety that something would happen to draw her worn-out husband back into the fray of public life.

Her anxiety was nearly fulfilled for reasons partly involving George, who, as anxious to go home as she was, had invested so much of his life in the new republic that at the last moment he was almost reluctant to relinquish his involvement, and partly with the difficulty of finding his successor. People who observed George closely sensed an undercurrent of ambition, and his detractors in the anti-Federalist camp and the press had long denounced him as a power-hungry, would-be King George I of America. Many politicians refused to join the contest, and the two emerging rivals, George's vice president, John Adams, a Federalist, and Thomas Jefferson, former secretary of state and an ardent Republican, now retired at Monticello, both affected reluctance to succeed George. In the end it was a close vote, with Adams winning by three votes in the Electoral College. Jefferson, as runner-up, succeeded to the title of vice president. Martha breathed more easily.

Returning to Philadelphia, the Washingtons found the last months of George's term telescoped into a whirlwind of activity. Martha continued to divide her attention between political life and family matters. In Portsmouth, New Hampshire, Tobias Lear's mother was finding four young children a handful. Eight-year-old Maria was distressed and bewildered, first by her mother's move to Washington with her new stepfather, then by Fanny's death, and was being particularly difficult. George's application to enter her as a boarder in the Moravian School at Bethlehem, Pennsylvania, had come to nothing because the school was full. George promised to have a word with the head of the school. When Mary Lear indicated she simply could not manage, Martha dealt with the crisis as well as she could from a distance, writing to Mary Lear:

> Mr Lear I think would do well to send her [Maria] to her uncle [Burwell Bassett Jr.] till something better could be done for her—we cannot take the child in hear our family is large— . . . I was extremely sorry to be told after Maria went from Mr Laws—how ill she had behaved to you had I known it I would have reprimanded her very seriously—she has always been a spoiled child— . . . I loved the childs mother and I love her it gives me pain to think that a child as circumstansed as she is should not have a disposition to make herself friends—her youth will plead for her.[6]

George personally contacted the principal of the school in Bethlehem, who agreed to admit Maria, but a few months later, in January 1797, George wrote that Maria would not be taking up her place there after all: "Maria Washington . . . is in very declining health (in short that she is in a consumption) and therefore adjudged by her Aunt with whom she lives, to be unfit for the change."

Oney Judge remained in Portsmouth. She planned to marry a "Black Jack," or a black sailor, named Jack Staines. In December, when she had the banns posted for her marriage as required by law, Joseph Whipple made a halfhearted attempt to get the certificate for the banns delayed, and wrote a discreet letter to George telling him that he would do what he could, but he did not think it worth inflaming public opinion. By that time George and Martha had resigned themselves to Oney's departure and seemed to have given up the attempts to recover her. Oney married Jack Staines in January 1797.

Judging by her frequent use of remedies such as distilled peppermint water and a calming, medicinal brandy flavored with fruit kernels called "Noyau" from Martinique, the stress of the final days of George's term took a toll on Martha's health. During this period Martha suffered almost constantly from "cholic." It was a blanket term that covered a wide variety of complaints, from indigestion to gallstones. Possibly it was exacerbated by all the last-minute entertaining she had to do.

There was a round of official farewell dinners. At dinner on March 3, George happily toasted the company for the last time in his capacity as president. That evening, Martha held her last Drawing Room. The atmosphere at both was emotional.

On February 22 George's sixty-fifth birthday was celebrated all day. Well-wishers jammed the house on Market Street to pay their respects between noon and three. That night up to twelve hundred people attended a huge ball at Rickett's amphitheater. Henrietta Liston, the wife of the British ambassador and a friend of the Washingtons, noted that the American ladies danced beautifully, and that "it was the only advantage they seemed to have derived from their intercourse with French." George danced, and as was customary, Martha did not. One account describes her wearing "orange satin trimmed with flowers over a lemon silk petticoat decorated with wreaths of roses and silver braid, orange plumes in her hair and black lace mittens." If the account is correct, it was a departure from her habitual restrained style, but Martha was feeling jubilant that her days in the public eye were numbered. When the time came for supper at eleven, the brilliant assembly made such a rush for the food that several people were nearly trampled underfoot.

On March 4 George attended the inauguration of John Adams. Martha was not present, but Nelly was there, visibly agitated by the emotion of the event, which soon gripped the whole assemblage. George, tall and commanding in black velvet despite his age, stood towering over the new president as short, rotund John Adams took the oath and made his inaugural address to a weeping audience whose eyes were fixed on his predecessor.

That night at a public banquet, "Washington's March" was played over and over, and in a foretaste of the excess of public adulation to come, Charles Willson Peale unveiled a transparency, depicting George on a horse accompanied by a female figure wearing the cap of Liberty and an altar with the words PUBLIC GRATITUDE written large.

Tobias Lear came from Washington to help pack up the Washingtons' effects and supervise the removal of some to Mount Vernon and the sale of others. On the afternoon of March 6, the new president, John Adams, and the vice president, Thomas Jefferson, came for a farewell dinner with the Washingtons. The last-minute chaos of packing, deciding what was to go and what was to be left for the Adams, and farewells were exacerbated by the disappearance of Hercules the cook. Unable to face returning to Mount Vernon, Hercules had run away.

Early on the morning of March 9, the Washingtons and their party set out for Mount Vernon in an entourage consisting of George, Martha, Nelly, George Washington Lafayette, Felix Frestel, and the slaves, save for Hercules and Oney. The journey was enlivened by Nelly's pets. George wrote, "On the one hand I am called upon to remember the parrot, on the other to remember the dog. For my own part I should not mind if both were forgot."

As the Washington entourage left Philadelphia behind, no one paused to consider that this marked Martha's retirement from public life as well as George's. It was not until a hundred years later that a late-nineteenth-century biography of Martha provided this perceptive acknowledgment of her role in the first two terms of the American presidency:

> That the two persons who were destined to give form and balance to the political and social function of the republic should have come from the most aristocratic of the Colonies, and from its most refined and exclusive circle, must be looked upon as something more than a happy accident, unless we count birth, breeding, early surroundings, and all the circumstances that go to form character, simply accidents. An executive mansion presided over by a man and woman who combined with the most ardent patriotism a dignity, elegance and moderation that would have graced the court of any Old World sovereign, saved the social functions of the new nation from the crudeness and bald simplicity of extreme republicanism, as well as from the luxury and excess that often mark the sudden elevation to power and place of those who have spent their early years in obscurity.[7]

CHAPTER 23

"Once More, Under Our Own Vine and Fig Tree"

Georgia would not be allowed to slip quietly into private life. The trip south, always a challenge given the uncertain state of the roads, was slowed even further by people wishing to pay a final tribute to the retired president, turning the trip home into a triumphal journey. Military escorts, gunfire salutes, and people cheering accompanied them all the way home. Nelly wrote that the Light Horse of Delaware and Maryland escorted them to Baltimore, where the entire population turned out to welcome George to the city in carriages, on horseback, or on foot. Some Georgetown gentlemen rowed the party across to the federal city, where the party called at the Laws' house to find Eliza, Patty, and their babies. Eliza had recently given birth to a daughter also named Eliza, and Patty a second daughter named Columbia. Nelly wrote that both her sisters looked terrible, and that Eliza had been very ill. She found the babies adorable, though, and Patty's daughter Eleanor, her "sweet toad," now the "fattest, most saucy, charming, entertaining mischevious little monkey."

In April word came that Betty Lewis had died. At Hope Park, Eleanor Stuart, who had had another baby, had been poorly for six months, and was too ill to come to Mount Vernon immediately to see Nelly. Martha was laid low with a bad cold and cough, combined with the aftereffects of exhaustion from the journey. For a month Nelly refused to budge from Mount Vernon until Martha was better, and then set out to see Eleanor for the first time since her return from Philadelphia. She noted her mother looked as ill from the aftereffects of childbirth as her sisters did. From there Nelly went back to Washington to pay Patty and Eliza a visit.

Nelly was now seventeen, and although she herself lightheartedly voiced her determination to remain "E.P. Custis Spinster for Life," and professed herself perfectly happy at Mount Vernon with her grandparents, Martha knew the inevitable next step was for Nelly to get married and have a home of her own. She worried that now that they no longer lived in Philadelphia, Nelly risked being buried in the country. A girl had to be out in society in order to meet eligible men, and at every opportunity Martha waved Nelly off to stay with her sisters in Washington, to enjoy herself. Nelly did thoroughly enjoy herself—attending race meetings, balls, and parties, dancing until all hours—but, as of yet, she had been unimpressed with any of the young men she met. She was always happy to return home to her grandparents.

When Martha was finally up and about after weeks prostrated with her cold and exhaustion, the chaos in the house nearly drove her back to her bed. As during the war years, the house and estate had become seriously dilapidated over the past eight years, despite the Washingtons' occasional visits home. The floor in the grand new dining room addition was collapsing, marble mantels were falling off of walls, and new doors and wainscoting were needed, as well as fresh paint. Within weeks of returning, George had tackled the repairs with enthusiasm, writing to a friend that "I am surrounded by joiners, masons, painters, etc etc,. I have scarcely a room to put a friend into or to set in myself, without the music of hammers, or the odiferous smell of paint." To Wash at Princeton he wrote: "We are all in the midst of litter and dirt, occasioned by joiners, masons, painters, and upholsterers, working in the house, all parts of which, as well as the outbuildings, are much out of repair." Everyone was relieved when the household goods, sent by water from Philadelphia, arrived undamaged. The Washingtons had taken the precaution of bringing their silver back with them in the carriage.

George, who often repeated what he wrote to one person in letters to others, wrote contentedly to his friends that he and Martha were thrilled to be home at last, once more "under our own vine and fig tree." April was, wrote Nelly, the loveliest time of the year at Mount Vernon, and Martha could remember that the first time she had seen her new home as Mrs. Washington had been in April thirty-eight years earlier. Now it was a different kind of homecoming for an elderly couple whose hearts still lifted at the sight of home as they looked forward to reestablishing their interrupted country life.

As before, the "vine and fig tree" meant a return to long, active days and hard work. Martha and George kept up their habit of rising early. George divided his time between his study and the fields. The estate was badly rundown, and the financial position as precarious as ever. In addition to getting the estate up and running and productive again, which meant monitoring experiments with new seeds and crops, George was now involved in property and building in Washington, the Potomac Navigation Company, and disposing of his tracts of land in the west. George faced a huge volume of correspondence and paperwork, as the world began to beat a path to the door of the ex-president. He had also begun a project to organize his official letters and papers for publication. It was a huge task, with many documents needing to be copied by hand. To relieve himself of some of the work, George hired a secretary named Albin Rawlins, who came to live at Mount Vernon.

No longer swallowed up in official social duties, Martha's time was now overtaken by the demands of housekeeping, entertaining company, the household slaves, and Nelly, Nelly's friends and her great-grandchildren. Eliza Law, Patty Peter, and their daughters, Eleanor Stuart and all her children, regularly came to stay, in addition to Nelly, Wash occasionally, George Washington Lafayette, and Felix Frestel. Other visitors swelled the numbers.

According to Wash Custis, in an attempt to fit more time into the day the family breakfast hour was moved back to seven, by which time George had done three hours of paperwork in his study. George then went off on horseback to inspect work in progress until quarter to three. Dinner was laid each day before a throng of family and friends, and often tourists who had just "dropped in." After dinner George and Martha sat with their company, on the terrace in summer and by the fire in the Prussian blue sitting room in winter. George, chafing inside to get back to the mountain of paperwork in his study, occasionally read aloud or the company would talk, and Martha would sew. Occasionally Nelly played the harpsichord and sang. By now Martha and George were in their mid-sixties, and tired more easily, so much so that, uncharacteristically, George was willing to let some things, like paperwork and unanswered correspondence, slide from one day to the next. In July there was an occurrence so rare that George wrote of it to a friend "unless someone pops in unexpectedly, Mrs. Washington and I will do what I believe has not been within the last twenty years by us, that is to sit down to dinner by ourselves."

Eliza Powel, who had purchased a writing desk from the Washingtons before they left Philadelphia, wrote to George to say that on opening up the desk, she had found a large packet of letters from Martha to George, tied up and labeled. Eliza twitted her friend about their being love letters, but assured George—and asked him to assure Martha,—that she had not looked at them and sent them back sealed up under her late husband's seal.

George's reply is one of his few direct comments on his relationship to Martha:

My dear Madam . . .
  Had it not been for one circumstance, which bye the bye is a pretty material one—viz—that I had no love letters to lose the introductory without the

explanatory part of your letter would have caused a serious alarm; and might have tried how far my nerves were able to sustain having betray the confidence of a lady. But although I have nothing to apprehend on that score, I am not less surprised at my having left those of Mrs. Washington' in my writing desk; when as I supposed I had emptied all the drawers; mistaken in this I have to thank you for the delicacy with which they have been treated. But admitting that they had fallen into more inquisitive hands, the correspondence would, I am persuaded, have been found to be more fraught with expressions of friendship than of *enamoured* love, and consequently, if the ideas of the possessor of them, with respect to the latter passion, should have been of the *Romantic* order to have given them the warmth, which was not inherent, they might have been consigned to the flames.[1]

Historians have often read this statement as a reflection of the loveless nature of the Washington marriage, but aside from the fact that romantic letter writing was never Martha's style—the closest she came was calling George "my Dearest"—how many sixty-five-year-old men, confronted with a packet of correspondence from a wife of forty years, no matter how happily married, would not be able to point to the mundane nature of their content?

That August rumors circulated in Philadelphia to the effect that George Washington Lafayette stayed so long at Mount Vernon because he and Nelly intended to marry. As inherently suitable the thought of such a match between George's namesake and the son of his great admirer and his adored step-granddaughter might have been, it came to nothing. Nelly persisted in regarding George Washington Lafayette as her young adopted brother, despite the fact that her grandfather's namesake had an intelligence, a quickness of mind, and an attractive, sympathetic character that complemented her own very well. Moreover, he came from a family as devoted to Nelly's grandparents as even Nelly could wish. From the perspective of two hundred years later, there is an inescapable sense that these two would have been a perfect match. But Nelly was probably subconsciously looking for someone like George, which automatically excluded younger men, and, less subconsciously, Nelly would never have taken any step that might take her away from Mount Vernon. She was the last person in the world to consider marrying a man whose home was on foreign soil. Nelly wrote to Elizabeth, begging her to scotch the rumors: *"being in love with him* is entirely out of the question. Therefore I *shall certainly never be engaged or married to him*—as *whoever* is my Husband I must *first* love Him *with all my Heart*— that is *not romantically*, but *esteem* & *prefer him before all others, that Man* I am *not yet* acquainted with."[2]

Nelly had obviously taken George's advice on marriage to heart, but the subject of men, marriage, and possible husbands was one on which Martha would also have given Nelly the benefit of her own experience. She told

Nelly, as she told Wash, the story of her own courting by George following
a chance meeting at the Chamberlaynes so many years ago. Martha intended
the account to be instructive, but it had been a very quick engagement.
Nelly, in forming her ideas on love and marriage, took George's advice on
marriage to heart, but emulating Martha in all things, she concluded that,
provided George's strictures were observed, true love would come in a
George-like form, and if her adored grandmother was right, a quick engagement should follow and that her marriage would be very much like that of
her grandparents.

While these opinions were taking hold in Nelly's mind, in August George
wrote to one of his Lewis nephews, Betty's son Lawrence Lewis, inviting him
to come to Mount Vernon. On top of a crisis in the kitchen due to Hercules'
defection, George and Martha were finding that entertaining the great volume of company was wearing them out, even with Nelly's help. A thirty-year-
old widower, whose first wife had died in childbirth after a year of marriage,
Lawrence was at loose ends. He was a steady type who had previously served
as an aide to George. George wrote that the position he was offering
Lawrence carried only room and board at Mount Vernon, but no pay:

> As both your Aunt and I are in the decline of life, and regular in our habits,
> especially in our hours of rising and going to bed; I require some person (fit
> and proper) to ease me of the trouble of entertaining company; particularly of
> Nights, as it is my inclination to retire (and unless prevented by very particu-
> lar company, always do retire) either to bed, or to my study, soon after candle
> light. In taking these duties . . . off my hands, it would render me a very accept-
> able service, and for a little time *only,* to come an hour in the day . . . devoted
> to the recording of some Papers.

In August, to Martha's delight, there was another addition to the household, when her teenage niece Fanny Henley came to stay, brought up from
New Kent by her father Leonard Henley as far as Bushfield. Martha wrote
to her sister Elizabeth that "our dear Fanny came safe to mount vernon."
There were, she wrote, the usual summer "fluxes" at Mount Vernon. Nelly
had been ill, and she and the General were in "tolerable" health. In this letter in which Martha also complained of being run off her feet by the housekeeping and having no cook, she concluded in a rush that "I hope the time
will come when it may be conveniat for you to make a trip to see us as it is
the first wish of my heart to see you often."

Nelly and Fanny soon went to Washington to stay with the Peters and
the Laws. They were there four weeks, but led a quiet life, spending most
of their time playing with the babies—"sweet Toads." Martha was thankful
that Nelly discovered a maternal streak that was inconsistent with "E.P.
Custis, Spinster for Life."

Tobias Lear, living in Washington, wrote that he planned to return to Mount Vernon. When Tobias had married Fanny Bassett Washington in 1795, George had granted him and Fanny a rent-free lease on a piece of land called Walnut Tree Farm. Tobias now intended to bring his son, Benjamin Lincoln Lear and Fanny's two boys, George Fayette and Charles Augustine, all of whom were nearly the same age, to Walnut Tree Farm to live and to personally oversee their education.

As time went by, Martha found it more and more difficult to cope in the absence of Hercules, and there was no adequate replacement to be found among the slaves. The disappearance of Hercules and Oney had inconvenienced Martha dreadfully and interrupted the smooth running of the household. She made the point forcefully to George. The loss of Oney and Hercules, which coincided with a period of economic decline for many of the big estates in Virginia, helped crystallize George's thinking on the issue of slavery generally.

George had always reckoned his worth in terms of land and slaves and never expressed qualms about the institution of slavery until late in life, when he began to appreciate just how uneconomical slavery was at Mount Vernon and elsewhere. Retired from the presidency and turning his attention once more to Mount Vernon's profitability, he found he had more slaves on the estate than the estate could support. This reflected a pattern in much of Virginia, where huge areas of land had been depleted by years of growing tobacco. There had been a long cycle of bad weather that had affected the crops. An English traveler in 1796 had noted the "worn out" appearance of land in Virginia. Although slaves were fed, housed, and clothed as cheaply as possible, they often cost more to maintain than they contributed. This made disposing of the slaves an attractive proposition. There was a growing market for slaves further south in the rice fields and indigo plantations of the Carolinas, and further south and west, in Louisiana and Mississippi, where cotton growing was catching on.

However, working conditions further south and west were harsh and the climate fiercely hot and unhealthy. Many of the larger planters were reluctant to sell their slaves south, except as a last resort. Also, because a number of the larger Virginia planters had kept slave families on their estates more or less intact over several generations, the slaves had begun to marry and establish families on plantations where they lived or with a slave on a neighboring one. Thus, Virginia at the end of the eighteenth century was crisscrossed with a network of slave family relationships, which mirrored those of the white families in the previous century. There was also a well-developed hierarchy within slave ranks, as several generations had bred light-skinned mulattos, who were preferred as house servants and received special treatment and privileges, Oney and Delphy Judge being perfect examples. As ladies' maids, with nice clothes, household food, light work, and the same training in needlework at Martha's hands as that given to Nelly, they were a world removed from the women who spread dung, dug fence posts, and sweated in the fields.

The mood among large planters in Virginia was not "abolitionist" in the sense that the term was understood by the growing movement in the northern states, but given that the economic picture had altered on the plantation, there was a fuzzy realization that there was a "slave problem" and that something needed to be done about it. George spoke for many when he said he wished to be free of "this species of property." By the time of his retirement, George had decided that he would "never become the master of another slave by purchase," acknowledging that as long as slaves were held in unwilling bondage they would run away, and that "I wish from my soul that the legislature of this state could see the policy of a gradual abolition of slavery."

To people living in the twenty-first century, the obvious answer was for George—and other like-minded planters—to free the slaves immediately. At the time however this option was hedged with complications which made it less straightforward a solution than it seems today. Although the law requiring freed slaves to leave the state within six months had been repealed (temporarily, it was reinstated several years later), a freed slave was at considerable risk of being captured by slave traders and sold south. The onus of proving emancipation fell on the slave, who even if able to produce the "deed of emancipation," was likely to find the slave traders uninterested in a piece of paper. Second, it was one thing to free an elderly slave too old to cause trouble—and probably with no means of supporting him or herself—but the prospect of Free Blacks in large numbers made whites uneasy. The bloody slave rebellion in Haiti was fresh in everyone's collective memory. Added to this was the fact that life was extremely difficult for Free Blacks, who were often used to having food, clothing, and shelter provided, and now had to make their way hiring out their labor, applying such skills as they had acquired. Many former slaves found the going so hard they looked back nostalgically to their days on the plantation.

In the last year of his presidency George had written to Dr. David Stuart in strictest confidence about his own plan to disengage himself from his slaves. It was not dictated by benevolence. He had a plan to advertise in Europe for industrious tenant farmers to rent out the farms which made up Mount Vernon, to whom he proposed to rent out his slaves. This, at one stroke, would free him from having to superintend the estate and make it profitable, as well as from the battle to make the slaves productive. All George would have to do was collect the rent for both.

George wanted to keep the proposal quiet until he could actually put it into effect, because renting his slaves out would put them at the disposal of other masters. Families would be split up according to the wishes and needs of the renters, and he knew the slaves would be deeply distressed at the breakup of their families. George admitted to Dr Stuart he knew this: "If I can succeed so far as to be enabled to give up the Dower Negroes at all and at terms below what are impartial to me, & shall say their hire is worth, it will amount to the full extent of my expectation, and this I would wish to accomplish before the other part of my plan [the tenant farmers] is attempted:—and quite enough it will be, when it is considered how much the Dower negroes and my own are intermarried and the former with the neighboring negroes, to part with whom will be an affecting and trying affair, happen when it will."

However, the greater slave issue aside, by the summer of 1797 it was the lack of a cook that preoccupied the Washingtons, particularly as the company was as abundant as ever. The Washingtons wrote to Eliza Powel to see if she could recommend a cook to hire for wages in Philadelphia, though as Abigail Adams found, there was a shortage of competent, reasonably sober, noncriminal candidates there to serve as servants of any kind. In May Martha painted a picture of the household staff at her disposal then sent Eliza a job description, writing that the cook would not have to perform any of the kitchen drudgery, but would have to "superintend boath and make others perform the duties allotted them is all that would be asked . . . There are always two persons, a man and a woman, in the Kitchen; and servants enough in the house for all needful purposes—These require Instructions in some cases, and looking after in all.—To be trust worthy . . . sober and attentive, are essential requisits in any large family, but more so among blacks-many of whom will impose when they can do it."

After some trouble, Eliza wrote back recommending a particular Frenchman, but Martha turned him down because his wages were too high and he was "unacquainted with blacks." In August Martha wrote to her sister Elizabeth Henley: "I should have written to you last week but companey prevented—I am obliged to be my one Housekeeper which takes up the greatest part of my time,—our cook Hercules went away so that I am as much at a loss for a cook as for a housekeeper.-altogether I am sadly plaiged."[3]

In November, still unable to hire a cook, George relaxed his intention never to buy another slave, and wrote to his nephew Major George Lewis:

> The running off of my cook, has been a most inconvenient thing to this family; and what renders it more disagreeable is, that I had resolved never to become the master of another slave by purchase, but this resolution I fear I must break.
>
> I have endeavored to hire, black or white, but am not yet supplied.—A few days ago having occasion to write to Mr. Bushrod Washington. . . . I asked if one was to be found in Richmond. [he] confirmed that the late Gov Brooke had a good cook whose only problem was a "fondness for liquor due to be sold in Fredericksburg."

George asked Major Lewis to see the man, and see if he had a wife and children. If the cook seemed suitable, Major Lewis was to buy him under his own name for George.[4]

In October George Washington Lafayette received word that there had been a change of government in France and that his father had been released from prison. He and Felix Frestel left Mount Vernon at once to find a passage home. En route they stopped at Princeton to see Wash and give him $100 he had asked George to send him.

Since coming to Princeton in November 1796 Wash had made steady demands for money but sent good reports of his own application to his studies. Wash's glowing reports of his progress were contradicted by his sudden expulsion in October 1797. There had been mounting complaints by the president of Princeton, Samuel Stanhope Smith, to George about Wash's "conduct," probably involving girls. George, who had told Smith on a previous occasion that "from his infancy I have discovered an almost unconquerable disposition to indolence in everything he did that did not tend to his amusements" replied in October "as an expression of my regret, at the conduct and behavior of young Custis would avail nothing I shall not trouble you by the attempt."

Fed up with his charge, George packed Wash off to Hope Park and Dr. Stuart, asking the Stuarts to find out what it was Wash wanted to do next. After talking it over with Wash, Dr. Stuart replied that Wash "found his habits of indolence and inattention so unconquerable, that he did not expect to derive any benefit form the plans pursued [in a college]." Dr. Stuart proposed to come to Mount Vernon to discuss Wash's future with George. The two men decided leaving Wash at loose ends was a more dangerous prospect than sending him to yet another college, unwilling though he was to go. Wash was accordingly enrolled at St. John's College in Annapolis, with a good deal of advice from George, which Wash proceeded to ignore.

As one young man left Mount Vernon, another arrived. In November Lawrence Lewis accepted his uncle's offer. Among the visitors to Mount Vernon that autumn were the Listons, the British minister to the United States and his attractive wife, Henrietta. Henrietta Liston invited Nelly to come back with her for an extended visit to Philadelphia, but though she was fond of Mrs. Liston and would have enjoyed seeing her many Philadelphia friends, Nelly declined. "I could not leave my Beloved Grandmama so lonesome & to go so far from her to a place where I have so long been accustomed to stay with her entirely."

At an age when marriage was the next step, and longing to be a mother of some "sweet toads" of her own, the strength of Nelly's attachment to Mount Vernon and her grandparents was beginning to worry Martha. Martha rejoiced in her granddaughter's company but was concerned that this attitude on Nelly's part would grow ever more fixed. She had never intended for her close relationship with Nelly to lead to this degree of dependence on Nelly's part. She was strongly of the view that young women ought to get married and aware that she and George would not be there forever. Nelly was a popular belle at the balls, parties, and race meetings she attended, yet she continued to keep young men at arms' length.

In November Martha had sent Fanny home reluctantly at her parents' insistence. Fanny Henley had begun to engage Martha's affections just as her cousin Fanny Bassett had done fifteen years earlier. Martha wrote to Elizabeth, "My Dear sister we hardly know how to part with my dear Fanny but the commands of Parents must be obayed I hope she will get home so well you will be enduced to let her come again to stay with us—pore Nelly is all most broken hearted at parting with her cousin."

From Philadelphia there was news that the city had experienced another terrible bout of yellow fever the previous summer and that the Washingtons' old friends the Morrises were disgraced. Wealthy Robert Morris had overstretched himself in land speculation and had been duped by some of his business associates. Unable to meet the payments on loans taken out to fund his land purchases, he had been declared bankrupt and was in a debtor's prison in Philadelphia. He put a gallant face on it, but his wife Mary, a close friend of Martha, and his daughter were devastated and humiliated. The Washingtons grieved for their friends the older Morrises, and Nelly was sad for their daughter, her good friend Maria Morris, to whom she wrote repeatedly without any response from Maria. Eliza Powel wrote that Mrs. Morris's state was "truly deplorable."

On George's birthday in February 1798, the Washingtons attended a ball at Alexandria with Nelly, who danced until two in the morning. Shortly afterwards Nelly went to her two sisters for a giddy season in Washington, attending tea parties, the theater, cotillions and balls, dancing until the small hours and up again for breakfast soon afterwards to begin another round. Many of the balls and dances were held specifically in Nelly's honor. The unspoken object on the part of everyone from Nelly's sisters to her hostesses to her grandmother was to allow Nelly to meet a suitable husband. As usual Nelly poked fun at the beaux and cheerfully went back to Martha at Mount Vernon, saying she had nearly "lamed herself dancing."

In a rare hark back to earlier days, there were Fairfaxes visiting Mount Vernon once again. Bryan Fairfax and his wife Jane were frequent callers at Mount Vernon from their nearby home at Mount Eagle. Bryan had been ordained in England as an Episcopal minister, and the Fairfaxes planned another trip to England. The previous Lord Fairfax having recently died, the purpose of Bryan Fairfax's trip was to have his title as eighth Baron Fairfax confirmed by the House of Lords. Sally Cary Fairfax now lived in near poverty in Bath, and the contrast in their circumstances was a poignant one. The Washingtons both wrote to Sally so Bryan could take their letters when he saw her. George dictated one letter, which Martha copied out and signed.

My Dear Mrs Fairfax   Mount Vernon May the 17ᵗʰ 1798
    although many years have elapsed since I have either received or written
one [letter] to you . . . my affection and regard for you, have undergone no
diminuation, and that it is among my greatest regrets now I am again fixed (I
hope for life) at this place not having you as a neighbor and companion.

This letter gave Sally news of the neighborhood, that nearly all their old
friends who were constantly at Belvoir and Mount Vernon had died, and that
everyone Sally had known in Alexandria was no longer living. They balanced
this sad account with news of the new generation of Fairfaxes, and Martha's
family and granddaughters, their husbands and children, Nelly and Wash.
    Martha closed with "I am Dear Madam with great esteem and regard
your affectionate Friend M Washington"[5]
    George wrote another:

My dear Madam: Mount Vernon May 16ᵗʰ 1798
    Five and twenty years, nearly, have passed away . . . since I have considered
myself . . . in a situation to endulge myself in a familiar intercourse with my
friends, by letter. . . . During this period so many important events have
occurred . . . as the compass of a letter would give you but an inadequate idea
of. . . . None of these events, however, nor all of them together, have been able
to eradicate from my mind, the recollection of those happy moments, the happiest in my life, which I have enjoyed in your company.
    Worn out in a manner by the toils of my past labour, I am again seated under
my Vine and Fig tree . . . it is a matter of sore regret, when I cast my eyes
towards Belvoir, which I often do, to reflect that the former Inhabitants of it,
with whom we lived in such harmony and friendship, no longer reside there;
and that the ruins can only be viewed as the memento of former pleasures.[6]

George did not often give way to nostalgia or sentiment, but a heartfelt
emotion underscores his contemplation of departed friends, the blackened
shell of a once-great house, and a woman he had loved deeply. It is not
known whether he showed Martha this letter, or whether Sally kept it as she
kept the love letter George had written to her from the frontier in September 1758, months before his wedding to Martha. The earlier love letter was
found in an old trunk of Sally's effects discovered in the 1870s. The original
of George's letter of 1798 may have been there too, because the version
above comes not from the original but from George's letterpress, the book
in which he took a copy of his letters by "pressing" them.
    That summer a Polish poet and refugee, Julian Ursyn Niemcewicz,
recently released from a Russian prison, came to visit and spent two weeks
at Mount Vernon. He was introduced to the Washingtons at the home of
Patty and Thomas Peter. Revolutionary to revolutionary, Niemcewicz and

George discussed crops, until interrupted by Eliza Law's small daughter, to whom George gave a piece of peach cheese (similar to peach leather, made from dried and pressed fruit). Niemcewicz's first impression of Martha was that she was the same age as George, and he could not help noticing her cap. Martha was "small, with lively eyes, a gay air and extremely kind. She had on a gown, with an even hem, of stiff white cotton, fitting very tightly, or rather attached from all sides with pins. A bonnet of white gauze, ribbons of the same color, encircling her head tightly, leaving the forehead completely uncovered and hiding only half of her white hair, which in back was done up in a little pigtail. She was at one time one of the most beautiful women in America and today there remains something extremely agreeable and attractive about her."

Niemcewicz was charmed by George and the family, especially Eliza, Patty, and Nelly "all three the most beautiful women that one could see," and later went on to visit at Mount Vernon where he was charmed by the house, the Sevres china, his fellow guests, Martha's kitchen garden with its well-cultivated "Corrents, Rasberys, Strawberys an Gusberys" plus cherries and peaches, and the fishing. They sat on the terrace where Martha served punch. Dinner for twenty was held in the great hall with the doors open to the cross-breeze. Nelly played some music for them, and after dinner everyone repaired to the terrace for the breeze and the view.

He noted many of the portraits hanging in the house were badly damaged, including the one painted of Martha by John Wollaston when she was twenty-six. George took him to see his prize bull, his sheep, his jackasses, the distillery, and his mill. Niemcewicz also wanted to see the slave quarters. He had been appalled by the slaves he saw by the roadside, hoeing and dressed in rags. He was informed by a slave-owning Quaker that "the condition of the slaves in Virginia is very miserable. . . . The masters usually sleep with the negresses, and the children they have by him are slaves and are handed down as such to their children; in a way that one brother is the slave to another brother."[7]

A visit to the slave quarters behind the mansion house left him shocked by the contrast between the gracious estate and the lives of the family with their carriages, Sevres, and pretty privileged children:

> Blacks. We entered one of the huts of the Blacks, for one can not call them by the name of houses. They are more miserable than the most miserable of the cottages of our peasants. The husband and wife sleep on a mean pallet, the children on the ground; a very bad fireplace, some utensils for cooking, but in the middle of this poverty some cups and a teapot. A boy of 15 was lying on the ground, sick and in terrible convulsions. The Gl. had sent to Alexandria to fetch a doctor. A very small garden planted with vegetables was close by, with 5 or 6 hens, each one leading ten to fifteen chickens. It is the only comfort that

is permitted them; for they may not keep either ducks, geese or pigs. They sell the poultry in Alexandria and procure for themselves a few amenities. They allot them each *one pack* [peck], one gallon [*sic*] of maize per week; this makes one quart a day, an half as much for the children, with 20 herrings each per month. At harvest time those that work in the fields have salt meat; in addition a jacket and a pair of homespun breeches per year. Not counting women and children the Gl. has 300 negroes of whom a large number belong to Mrs. Washington.[8]

There was more trouble with Wash that summer. Wash had neglected to write home from Annapolis regularly as he had promised to do, but rumors reached Mount Vernon and Hope Park that he had become seriously involved with a young lady in Annapolis. Eleanor believed he had gotten engaged, George and Martha suspected that he had gotten the girl pregnant. An exasperated George, who believed Wash was idiotic to risk becoming the prey of a fortune hunter in this way, wrote:

Dear Washington,　　　　　　　　　　　　　　　Mount Vernon 13th 1798
   It is now four weeks since any person of this family has heard *from* you, although you were requested to write to someone in it, once a fortnight, knowing (as you must do) how apt your grandmamma is to suspect that you are sick, or some accident has happened to you, when you omit this?
   I have said, that none of us have heard from you, but it behooves me to add, that from persons in Alexandria, lately from Annapolis, we have, with much surprise, been informed of your devoting much time, to paying particular attentions to, a certain young lady of that place! . . . sure I am it is not time for you to think of forming a serious attachment of this kind, and *particular* attentions without this would be [dishonourable] and might involve a [consequence] of wch you are not aware. In forming a connection, which is to be binding for life, many considerations, besides the mere gratification of the passions, and of more durability, are essential to happiness.[9]

Wash's response was that he was *not* engaged—that because the girl did not want to wait until he was old enough to seek the Washingtons' consent to get engaged, they had parted amicably. His mother and grandparents breathed a sigh of relief.
   That summer, to Martha's alarm, George very nearly went back into active military service as ongoing hostilities between the Unites States and revolutionary France escalated. George was actually recommissioned commander in chief in July. The prospect of George going off again and back into military life was not something she wished to contemplate. Then, equally alarmingly, in August George suffered a serious attack of malaria. After three days of his usual "let it go as it came" policy when ill, his condition deteriorated. George

finally took to his bed in a very bad way and sent for his friend Dr. Craik to dose him with "jesuits' bark," or quinine. He was extremely ill for a month.

To aggravate this crisis Wash Custis decided to end his academic career, and he came home on August 5. George once again sent him to the Stuarts, saying Wash seemed to him either to be "moped or stupid, says nothing and is always in some hole or corner excluded from company." This time Dr. Stuart and George decided that there was no point forcing Wash back to college, and that Tobias Lear could teach him at home, which was tantamount to saying Wash would never have to pick up another book.

In November Martha watched George go off to Philadelphia for a long stay to consult with the government over the establishment of a standing army and to get new teeth, as his old ones had turned black. To keep Martha from becoming lonely in his absence, the Peters, the Laws, the Stuarts, and their associated children descended upon Mount Vernon by turns and occasionally all together. The presence of her three small great-grandchildren were a lively distraction for Martha. Fanny Henley came back to visit, and then went to Washington to stay with the Peters, where Patty was pregnant with her third child. Martha asked Fanny to find some books for her in Washington, a set of volumes called "Children of the Abbey" by Regina Maria Roche, which Fanny did and which Nelly probably read to her in the evenings after dinner. In the Mount Vernon library today is a copy containing volumes 3 and 4 of the set. There is an inscription inside written by Nelly dated February 2, 1799, "I EP Custis value his old Novel because my revered and loved grandmother Mrs M Washington read and liked it. 1840."

Lawrence Lewis who had lived at Mount Vernon for the past year had not been as much help entertaining the company as George envisaged. The last person to entertain anyone, he was a staid man, not very lively, and the exact opposite of Nelly, so much so that George was stunned on his return from Philadelphia to find that Nelly and Lawrence were engaged. He had had no inkling there was any attraction between the two. Nelly wrote playfully to Elizabeth Bordley that: "Cupid, a small micheivous Urchin who has been trying some time to humble my pride, took me by surprise ... in the *very moment* that I had ... made the sage and prudent resolve of passing through my life, as a *prim starched Spinster* ... & thought my Heart impenetrable he slyly called in Lawrence Lewis to his aid, & transfixed me with a Dart, before I knew where I was."

George, stuck to his habit of not interfering with people who wanted to marry, but was not convinced it was an ideal match for Nelly. However, he could not put a finger on what was wrong. Nelly was a strong-minded, intelligent young woman and in fixing on Lawrence Lewis no one could accuse her of having made a giddy, romantic choice. In fact, she had followed his advice to the letter and, like her grandmother, decided on a quick engagement. If George was concerned at what seemed to him to be a sudden mismatch, Martha took

"Eleanor Parke Custis Lewis," by James Sharples, about the time of her marriage to Lawrence Lewis in 1799. Courtesy of Woodlawn Plantation.

a different view. Worried for quite a time that Nelly was locking herself into spinsterhood, she was relieved Nelly had finally fixed on someone.

Nelly herself seems to have found the fact that Lawrence was George's nephew a powerful attraction, and marrying within the family ensured she would not have to go far from her grandparents. Both she and Lawrence liked the idea of settling nearby. Certainly Lawrence was nothing like the foppish young men she danced with and made fun of in her letters to her friends. As a wedding present George gave Nelly and Lawrence a two-thousand-acre tract of land at Mount Vernon on which to build a home. The couple would live at Mount Vernon until it was finished, and Nelly would not have to vacate her blue bedroom with its corner fireplace.

Martha and Nelly planned the wedding to take place at Mount Vernon on George's sixty-seventh birthday, February 22, 1799. Nelly would be the first American bride to wear a veil with her wedding dress. She decided on it after Lawrence saw her behind a lace curtain one day during their courtship and told her she looked very pretty. Nelly wanted George to give her away wearing a fine new uniform he had ordered from Philadelphia, but the tailor was held up by a shortage of the gold thread he needed to finish the uniform and it did not arrive in time. In place of it George wore his old Continental army uniform. There was company to dinner, including Reverend Thomas Davis, an Episcopal minister. Afterwards George and Nelly went to change for the marriage ceremony. Nelly came down the grand staircase at Mount Vernon on George's arm, and at the foot of the stairs in the wide hallway, she and Lawrence were married "just after the candles were lighted."

The festivities continued for over a week in the best tradition of plantation weddings, and threw the house into an uproar. George wrote to one correspondent that he could do nothing until the prolonged wedding festivities had finished. The journal of Agnes Lee, *Growing Up in the 1850's* records the eyewitness account of an elderly Mount Vernon slave woman, known only as old Mammy: "What tales she [Mammy] could tell of those 'good old times', of Mrs. Washington's beauty and good management.... And when my beautiful Aunt Lewis was married 'how ole Mistis let all the servants come in to see it & gave them such good things to eat' 'how Ole Mistis was dressed so splendid, in a light flowered satin ... Aunt Lewis all in something white, beautiful too.'"

Seven weeks after the wedding in May Nelly and Lawrence departed on the traditional round of bridal visits to relatives and friends, starting with Hope Park before going on elsewhere to be made a fuss of. Nelly enjoyed herself and wrote how kind everyone was to them, but "I left my Beloved & reverend Grandmama with sincere regret, & it was some time before I could feel reconciled to travelling without her." The Lewises went south to New Kent particularly to visit White House, which Nelly was anxious to see. On his honeymoon, Lawrence contracted an eye infection and had to lie in a darkened bedroom for four weeks, which threw the program of visits off schedule; and Nelly herself contracted influenza and very soon she was pregnant.

Martha had had one of her bouts of illness in Nelly's absence, suffering from a recurring fever and "ague," as well as a cold. No one wrote to Nelly of it because they knew Nelly would have cut short her honeymoon to come home to look after Martha.

A strange story based on a letter supposedly written by Martha to "a kinswoman in New Kent" about this time comes from Benson Lossing, author of *Mary and Martha, the Mother and Wife of Washington.* Lossing claimed to have seen it at Arlington, the home Wash Custis built outside Washington, and copied it in the following form. The language, spelling, and punctuation are not typical of Martha, but it is true she was recovering from her illness at the time of the letter, and the letter, if written by her, must have been heavily edited by someone. Whatever its source, the letter has featured in the Martha Washington story ever since:

September 18th 1799
At midsummer the General had a dream so deeply impressed on his mind that he could not shake it off for several days. He dreamed that he and I were sitting in the summer house, conversing upon the happy life we had spent, and

looking forward to a great many more years on earth, when suddenly there was a great light all around us, and then an almost invisible figure of a sweet angel stood by my side, and whispered in my ear. I suddenly turned pale and then began to vanish from his sight and he was left alone. I had just risen from the bed when he awoke and told me his dream, saying "you know a contrary result indicated by dreams may be expected. I may soon leave you." I tried to drive from his mind the sadness that had taken possession of it, by laughing at the absurdity of being disturbed by an idle dream, which at the worst indicated I would not be taken from him; but I could not, and it was not until after dinner that he recovered any cheerfulness. I found in the library, a few days afterwards, some scraps of paper which showed he had been writing a Will, and had copied it. When I was so very sick lately, I thought of this dream and concluded my time had come, and that I should be taken first.[10]

It is true that Martha was so ill in early September 1799 that George called Dr. Craik to see her on September 1 and 6. Dr. Craik prescribed the "bark," indicating Martha may have had a form of malaria. It is also true that George signed a new will subsequent to the one he had made in June 1775 and written to Martha about on the eve of his leaving Philadelphia for Cambridge to assume command of the Continental army on 9th July 1799. Martha was ill nearly until Nelly returned in late October, and may well have thought that during this protracted bout of illness she was on her deathbed.

Martha was better by the time Nelly returned, and they were both soon busy preparing for the baby, "trappings for the sweet stranger," as Nelly put it. Nelly was delighted at the prospect of becoming a mother and happy with her husband. "I am united to one who is in every respect calculated to ensure my happiness." Martha and Nelly fell back into their old habits of spending time together at their needlework and their devotions.

On November 20 a midwife arrived, probably because Nelly was going into labor. On the twenty-first Eleanor and her two eldest Stuart daughters arrived. Despite the impending childbirth, guests continued to arrive for dinner and to stay throughout the next seven days, among them Drs. Craik and Stuart. Dr. Craik was present when Nelly finally gave birth the morning of November 27 to a daughter she named Frances Parke Lewis, always known as "Parke." Martha had given Nelly a handsome walnut cradle and she and Eleanor gave advice and fussed over the new mother and made her and the baby comfortable in Nelly's bedroom. Nelly never suffered in her pregnancies as much as Eleanor did, but she was not very well after the birth and labor, which may have lasted a week. She was forbidden to leave her bed, but was well looked after by her favorite person—her grandmother.

CHAPTER 24

"No More Trials to Pass Through"

By December 3 Eleanor could see that six days after the birth, Nelly was not as badly off as she herself normally was after giving birth, and she felt confident enough to return to Hope Park, where her own small children needed her presence. But when the doctors told Nelly she was not to leave her bed until she was fully recovered—for at least several weeks—no one was inclined to shrug off their advice. Lawrence's first wife Susan had died in childbirth within a year of her marriage. Martha did not want Nelly to suffer the same fate.

There was nothing Lawrence could do but leave Nelly in her bed and Parke in her cradle to be looked after by Martha. On December 9 Lawrence and Wash left for a trip to Wash's estates in New Kent. Having suffered yet another financial setback the previous growing season, when a cycle of drought and heavy rain brought a poor harvest, George was busy in his study working out a new crop rotation scheme he was planning in minute detail up to 1803. He was setting up another trip to his western holdings when the spring came.

There were people to dinner every day as usual, including Bryan Fairfax, now Lord Fairfax, back from England, and his family. On December 11 George noted in his diary there had been a large ring around the moon, a harbinger of bad weather. On the morning of the twelfth there was snow, followed by hail and a cold rain. The Washingtons and their guests took the usual early breakfast, and George rode out to the estate in his usual way. He came back wet but because he was, unusually, late for dinner, and he did not stop to change his clothes. He remained in his damp clothes till bedtime.

The next day George had a sore throat but went out to supervise the removal of some trees. By dinner he was hoarse, and Tobias Lear, now working at the mansion house to organize George's papers, suggested he take something for it. George never took anything for a cold; had he shown the slightest inclination to do anything other than his usual "let it go as it came," Martha would have produced poultices and home cold remedies galore.

After dinner on the thirteenth, Martha, George, and Tobias sat peacefully by the fire in the parlor, with Martha sewing and Tobias reading from the newspaper. Just before bedtime Martha put her sewing down and went up to check on Nelly and Parke. According to Wash Custis, George stayed late in his study that night before coming to bed. The fires died down in the fireplaces, and the sleeping house grew cold.

A few hours later, early on the morning of Saturday, December 14, George woke Martha, indicating his throat was very sore and he was having trouble breathing. Martha wanted to get up to summon help, but he refused to allow her to get out of bed. Without the fires the house was freezing, and he was afraid she would take a chill and get another one of her violent colds. The two old people huddled under the covers until dawn while George grew worse, his temperature soared, and his swollen throat constricted. When the slave came in to light the morning fire in the bedroom just before daybreak, Martha sent her running to fetch Tobias Lear.

Lear found George in an alarming state, burning with fever, almost unable to swallow, and fighting to breathe. Lear sent an urgent message to George's old friend Dr. Craik. At George's insistence Lear sent for one of the overseers, George Rawlins, to bleed him. An overseer was often the first person summoned in emergencies if it appeared bleeding was called for. Given the caliber of people who became overseers—even George famously complained that many of his were brutal alcoholics—being bled by an overseer does not appear a reassuring prospect. However, the thinking of the day was that illness was often connected to "bad humors" in the blood or digestive system. Bleeding and purging were logical ways to get them out of the system. Overseers often had to act as veterinarians when animals were sick, and had experience in bleeding animals.

While waiting for Rawlins, Martha hurried to prepare a home remedy of molasses, vinegar, and butter that she hoped would ease his throat. George nearly choked to death trying to swallow a little of it. Rawlins arrived and opened a vein, a traumatic process for all concerned. Rawlins made a gash in George's arm and they all watched while the blood collected in a bowl. George thought the cut in his arm was not deep enough and ordered Rawlins to cut wider and deeper. Martha begged both men to stop. According to research carried out for an article in the *New England Journal of Medicine,* Rawlins removed around twelve to fourteen ounces of blood, before the flow was staunched.[1]

Martha brought more home remedies: a piece of wet flannel to wrap around his throat and a footbath. George insist on getting up and dressing but then collapsed into a chair by the fire. Dr. Craik had not yet arrived, and Martha, increasingly alarmed, had Tobias Lear send for Dr. Robert Gustavus Brown, who had trained in medicine at Edinborough and was a respected colleague of Dr. Craik. Lear believed George had "quinsy," a violent sore throat that could be fatal. He had had it previously during the war and had been so ill everyone had expected him to die.

By nine that morning Dr. Craik had arrived. He bled George again and put a poultice on George's throat. Martha tried to get him to gargle with a mixture of sage tea and vinegar. Once again, George nearly choked. Dr. Craik sent off for a third doctor from Alexandria, Dr. Elisha Cullen Dick.

In the interim before Dick's arrival, George was given calomel as a purge. The purge simply added to George's torment without relieving his breathing. As his breathing was growing worse, by the time Dr. Dick arrived in midafternoon the doctors decided more blood should be let. By now it was the third or forth time George had been bled, and this was followed by another purge. Nothing had any effect on George's worsening condition. Late in the afternoon a third doctor arrived, Dr. Brown from Maryland.

When not fetching home remedies, Martha sat by George's bed, alternately knitting, reading her Bible, praying, or just waiting. It was not the first time she had kept a vigil at what everyone believed was George's deathbed. Tobias Lear's detailed account of the movements of everyone during the long day does not say anything about Martha, other than the fact she was present at George's side, but that is because Tobias Lear, who also saw himself as indispensable to George, emphasized his own role in the events of the day. As the day wore on, the sickroom became a hellish mess of blood-soaked linen, implements for cutting veins, bedpans, and grim-faced doctors surrounding their tortured patient. Almost eighty ounces of blood had been let in the course of the day.[2] Nelly, the one person who might have helped Martha, was still confined to her bed. In order for her to reach her grandparents' bedroom, which was accessible only by its own flight of stairs, she would have had to leave her own room, go down one flight of stairs and climb another. If Martha did not summon Nelly because this was too much exertion for her over two weeks after Parke's birth, it suggests that Nelly's condition continued to worry Martha.

At some point Martha was joined by her dower slaves Molly, an old woman who had nursed the children, her maid Caroline Branham, and Charlotte, her head household slave. George's valet Christopher Sheets stood by the door until George realized he had been standing in the same place all day and beckoned for him to sit down.

Late that afternoon George indicated to Martha she should go to his study and bring the two wills he kept there, the one he had written in 1775 in Philadelphia and a later one signed in July 1799. He instructed her to burn the older one. The doctors and Lear tried to lift and turn George to a more comfortable position, but nothing eased him for long. George asked for Lawrence Lewis and Wash, and Dr. Craik told him they would not return from New Kent for several more days. George believed he was dying and told his old friend Dr.Craik, "Doctor I die hard but I am not afraid to go. I believed from my first attack I should not survive it."

As afternoon wore on into evening George begged the doctors not to treat him any further and to let him die in peace. "I feel myself going" he said, "I thank you for you attentions, but I pray you to take no more trouble about me. Let me go off quietly; I cannot last long."

The room was silent save for George's croaked requests to know the time. By ten o'clock George was almost past speech. Finally he turned to Tobias Lear and making a monumental effort said, "I am just going. Have me decently buried and do not let my body be put into the vault in less than three days after I am dead." At the last minute he was terrified of being buried alive, a common fear at a time when a coma was sometimes indistinguishable from death. After asking if Lear understood, and getting Lear's agreement, George said " 'Tis well." He took his own pulse. By twenty minutes past ten he was dead.

Martha, sitting at the foot of the bed was the first to speak. In a flat voice she asked if he had gone. No one in the room had the heart to say anything. Tobias Lear lifted his hand in acknowledgment. That George should be dead confounded all of Martha's past experience—she had nursed him on many occasions that the doctors and even George believed to be his deathbed, yet in the end he had always recovered. He had survived wars without a scratch and a catalogue of diseases that could have killed him many times over. Now her seemingly indestructible husband was dead eighteen hours after he had woken her to say he had been taken ill with a sore throat.

What seems missing from the account is any mention of a farewell or parting words to Martha, who had been his longtime companion and partner as well as his wife. Most of what is known about George's death comes from the account written—after the event—by Tobias Lear, though Dr. Craik left a briefer record. It seems unthinkable George would not have said something to Martha, but if he did, neither Tobias Lear nor Dr. Craik mentioned it in their accounts of George's death, nor does any family tradition involving his last words to Martha appear in Wash Custis's *Memoirs*. Either George did not say anything to Martha before dying, or everyone conspired to allow his last words to her to remain private. At his death, as throughout their married lives, they were surrounded by people.

" 'Tis well," said Martha finally in an unemotional voice. "All is now over. I shall soon follow him. I have no more trials to pass through." Tobias Lear noted Martha sounded firm and collected, and showed no sign of grief, but eventually she had to be helped out of the room.

Later that night George's body was taken downstairs and laid out on the dining room table in the green dining hall. After that night, Martha never again entered the bedroom she had shared with George, with its dressing room at the back where George had dressed quietly each morning to avoid waking her, the six-foot-square bed in which he had died, the fine furnishings and bed curtains that he had chosen. Some people believed she was following an old Virginia custom of abandoning a room where someone had recently died when Martha removed herself to a small, inconvenient, and uncomfortable room in the attic floor above. It was up a narrow wooden staircase, the kind that gives back a hollow echo of ascending footsteps. From the window Martha had a view of the crumbling family vault at Mount Vernon.

She left Tobias Lear to make all the necessary arrangements. When it was finally clear to him that George was actually dying, Lear had written hasty notes summoning the Laws and the Peters, and by the next day, December 15 the household was in shock, awaiting their arrival. Thomas Law arrived around 10 A.M. A dry-eyed Martha refused to come downstairs but sent for Lear and told him to order a coffin from Alexandria. He wrote more notes notifying the family and friends. That morning the Peters also arrived, and then Eliza Law later that afternoon, with their friend Dr. William Thornton, an architect and a doctor. Dr. Craik stayed on, to discuss the best date for the funeral with Thomas Peter and Thomas Law and whether it should be postponed until the following weekend to allow all the family time to reach Mount Vernon. It was decided that as George had died of an "inflammatory" disease, it would not be advisable to wait so long that the body might decompose distressingly. Wednesday, December 18, was fixed as the date for the funeral. Meanwhile, in a foretaste of some of the horrors that awaited everyone in the aftermath of George's death, Dr Thornton had arrived with a bizarre plan to resuscitate the late president:

> When that great and excellent man died, Thomas Law . . . and his lady . . . called on me to visit the Genl. as a friend and physician, for he was dying of croup. I departed in the fullest confidence of being able to relieve him, by tracheotomy. When we arrived to my unspeakable grief, we found him laid out a stiffened copse. . . . The weather was very cold, and he remained in a frozen state, for several days. I proposed to attempt his restoration, in the following manner. First to thaw him in cold water, then to lay him in blankets, and by degrees and by friction to give him warmth, and to put into activity the minute blood vessels, at the same time to open a passage to his lungs by the trachea, and to inflate them with air, to produce an artificial respiration, and to transfuse blood into him from a lamb.[3]

The idea must have stunned and horrified those gathering at Mount Vernon, and since it was the last thing Martha needed to hear, everyone probably agreed it should be kept from her. Thornton went on to note, unsurprisingly, "I was not seconded in this proposal."

Martha sent word for Tobias Lear to come upstairs to discuss funeral arrangements, and he found Martha's composure was "more distressing than a flood of tears."

On December 16 Eleanor Stuart and her daughters arrived in the afternoon. The vault was opened and cleaned. Martha ordered a new door to be made for the vault, as opposed to bricking it back up, saying the vault would have to be opened again before long for her. A mahogany lead-lined coffin was being made as quickly as possible in Alexandria. Mr. Anderson, the Mount Vernon farm manager, went to Alexandria to get things needed for the funeral, including dark cloth for mourning for the house slaves and overseers.

Tobias Lear was told that the Alexandria Masons Militia and others would attend on Wednesday, and since Martha would go no further than her own and Nelly's rooms, he assumed control and gave orders to the household slaves to prepare refreshments. Mr. Robert Hamilton sent word that a schooner would moor off the Mount Vernon dock and fire a salute as the body was being carried down the hill to the vault.

That night Tobias wrote to his mother, Martha's friend Mary Stillson Lear, that Martha still seemed unable to take in what had happened: "She has preserved the same pious fortitude. It afflicts me to see her. The world now appears no longer desirable to her—and yet she yields not to grief."

Martha asked for a number of people to be notified, including the Mason family at Gunston Hall, and Charles Willson Peale and his family. The Reverend Mr. Davis, who had married Nelly and Lawrence less than a year before, was asked to read the burial service.

On Tuesday the seventeenth the coffin arrived and George's body was put into it. The coffin was then sealed in a lead-lined case.

On Wednesday the funeral, scheduled to begin at noon, was delayed by three hours. Neither Nelly nor Martha attended, but both probably watched from the upstairs windows. The funeral procession finally formed up at three. It consisted of troops on horses and on foot, a military band playing a dirge, members of the clergy, George's riderless horse with his saddle, holster, and pistols led by house slaves Cyrus and Wilson, dressed in black. The coffin was carried by Freemasons and officers. The principal mourners were Eleanor Stuart and Eliza Law, the two eldest Stuart daughters, Bryan Fairfax's daughter and her cousin, Thomas Law, Thomas Peter, Tobias Lear, Dr. Craik, Lord Fairfax and his son. In the house Martha and Nelly could hear the boom of the guns from the river and the mournful sound of the military band as the cortege made its way slowly from the house down the hill to the vault.

Mr. Davis read the funeral service, the Masons performed their ceremonies, and the body was placed in the vault. After the service everyone went back to the house for refreshments and most of the mourners then left. The leftover refreshments were distributed to the slaves. Dr. Craik, Dr.

Thornton, and Thomas Peter stayed the night. Martha did not appear to speak to anyone and stayed upstairs. Tobias Lear, who had been going on sheer willpower since the night George died, went exhausted to his room and wept.

On December 23 Congress passed a resolution to ask all Americans to wear a crepe mourning band on their arm for thirty days, as well as a resolution to write to Mrs. Washington with condolences, and a request that Washington's remains might be interred in a specially built sarcophagus in the Capitol building.

For the next week a shattered and emotional Tobias tried to deal with George's papers in the study, to get them into some kind of order. Martha kept out of sight. As well as abandoning the bedroom she had shared with George, she never again entered George's study. It had always been exclusively his own room, the one place in the house no one entered without an invitation. Christmas Day brought a plumber from Alexandria to solder the top onto the coffin, and Bushrod Washington, George's nephew and heir arrived. Bushrod did not wish to view his uncle's remains, so Tobias accompanied the plumber to the vault for a last farewell. "I attended the closing of the coffin—and beheld for the last time that face wh.shall be seen no more here; *but wh. I hope to meet in Heaven.*" The new wooden door to the vault was nailed shut.

Letters of condolence began to pour in from friends, family, political connections, and a host of strangers. Each one had to be acknowledged, but Martha was unequal to dealing with the task. Nelly, now out of bed but numb with grief, and Tobias Lear wrote most of them for her. As the days passed, Martha began to unnerve everyone with her stoic calm and dry eyes. It is probable that she was in shock, but she did not give way to grief until President John Adams called in person at Mount Vernon at the end of December to deliver personal letters of condolence from himself and Abigail and a formal copy of Congress's resolution.

The resolution was a masterpiece of male insensitivity. The only prospect, albeit a melancholy one, left to Martha in the aftermath of George's death was her expectation of being buried next to him in the family vault to await the resurrection, which she, as a deeply religious woman, was sure would come. Not content with the sacrifices George and she had made in the cause of public service, an officious Congress now proposed to separate her from George in death.

The letter read:

Madam   Philadelphia, December 27.1799
    In conformity with the desire of Congress, I do myself the honor to inclose ... a copy of their resolutions, passed the twenty fourth instant occasioned by the decease of your late Consort, General George Washington, assuring you

of the profound respect Congress will ever bear, to your person and Character, and of their condolence on this afflicting dispensation of Providence. In pursuance of the same desire, I entreat your assent to the interment of the remains of the General under the marble monument to be erected in the capitol . . . to commemorate the great events of his military and political life.

> Madam your faithful and
> obedient Servant
> John Adams.

After receiving this letter and the Adams's short personal notes, Martha finally broke down. Abigail reported to her sister that, although the letters were short, it took Martha two hours to get through them. The reply Tobias Lear drafted to John Adams must have cost Martha what little was left of her strength to sign. It also invites the question as to how much pressure Martha was put under to sign. Certainly Lear would have been far more concerned about Washington's posthumous reputation, while Martha, now an elderly woman, was possibly too grief-stricken and vulnerable to oppose a scheme that immeasurably compounded her grief. Nelly may have been persuaded that it was what George would have wanted, and the combination of Nelly and Tobias probably wore down what little resistance Martha could put up. The answer prepared by Tobias Lear speaks volumes about the conflict between the Washingtons' personal and public lives:

> Sir   Mount Vernon December 31 1799
> While I feel with the keenest anguish the late Disposition of Divine Providence I cannot be insensible to the mournful tributes of respect and veneration which are paid to the memory of my dear deceased Husband—and as his best services and most anxious wishes were always devoted to the welfare and happiness of his country—to know they were truly appreciated and greatfully remembered affords no inconsiderable consolation. Taught by the great example which I have so long had before me never to oppose my private wishes to the public will—I must consent to the request made by congress—which you have had the goodness to transmit to me—and in doing this I need not—I cannot say what a sacrifice of individual feeling I make to a sense of public duty.[4]

Even as Martha was being reduced to further depths of misery at this final proof of the country's hold over George, in death as in life, George's nephew and heir Bushrod Washington was drafting a brisk letter of advice to Martha on practical matters. Two weeks after George's death he sent her a letter reminding her that as she was both one of George's executors as well as a beneficiary under the will with the use of Mount Vernon for life, there were practical matters that had to be attended to: the will had to be probated, commissioners appointed to value the estate, legatees informed of bequests, debts and legacies paid, various properties sold and rented, George's personal possessions either disposed or sold. Bushrod also included a list of things Martha would be advised to sell: "Should my Aunt pursue the plan I have recommended of getting clear of her negroes & of plantation cares and troubles, there will be horses, Mules, cattle, sheep, hogs & plantation utensils for sale to a considerable amount."

But this advice to "get clear of . . . plantation cares & troubles" however sensible, was like advising her to get clear of the life she had had with George, one that had centered on the plantation and its cares and troubles.

Wash Custis's "official version" of the way Martha adapted to widowhood was typically sentimental:

> Although the great sun of attraction had sunk in the west, still the radiance shed by his illustrious life and actions drew crowds of pilgrims to his tomb. The establishment of Mount Vernon was kept up to its former standard, and the lady presided with her wonted ease and dignity of manner, at her hospitable board. She relaxed not her attentions to her domestic concerns, performing the arduous duties of the mistress of so extensive an establishment, although in the sixty-ninth year of her age, and evidently suffering in her spirits from the heavy bereavement she had so lately sustained.

The reality was different and harsher. Martha spent more and more of her time in her garret chamber, furnished simply with a single bed, a carpet, three chairs, a table, a looking glass and a Franklin stove. Wash had a room opposite hers. In the corridor, which may have been a sort of sitting room, were an armchair, a leather couch, and two trunks. Two days after George's death, Martha told Thomas Law she would "never again quit this scene." Martha kept that promise. She never again left Mount Vernon after George's death, not even to attend church.

She continued to be inundated with correspondence, sermons, memorial addresses, testimonials, orations, and requests for locks of George's hair. People condoled with her on her "afflicting loss" and the "melancholy occasion." Meaning well, they reminded her, "It is our duty to bear up against our misfortune, & not repine at the will of the most High." Tobias and Nelly drafted her acknowledgments, often couched in the third person: "Mrs Washington begs Bishop Madison's acceptance of her most grateful acknowledgements for his excellent Discourse which he has been so good as to send her, and which she receives as a valuable Testimony of his sincere condolence in her late afflictive Loss." Within months Congress granted Martha franking privileges, saving her a fortune in postage for these acknowledgments.

An entire industry of funerary art sprang into being, with everything from urns and embroidered wall hangings to teapots covered in morbid images of graves and weeping females wearing sashes emblazoned with

"Liberty!" or bizarrely depicting George amidst the angels in clouds of glory as the Pater Patriae, with titles like "He in Glory, We in Tears." Martha ignored what she could and wore out a path walking between Washington's tomb and the river. In the words of one visitor, Martha seemed "much broke [in spirit] since I saw her last."

Wash was correct in recalling that there continued to be visitors at Mount Vernon. As had long been the tradition on Virginia plantations, visitors arrived no matter what the crisis: births, deathbeds, weddings, funerals, and illness. Mount Vernon had been famed for its hospitality ever since Martha had arrived as a bride forty-three years earlier, and even *in extremis* of grief, she continued to go through the motions and to rise to the occasion, even when she had no idea who the people were. Washington's reputation had for years been a magnet for friends and curious strangers, who abused the hospitality of the house, and they came in their hordes to gape at the general's tomb, house, and widow. Martha's friend Mrs. Charles Thornton wrote in her diary that when she and her husband arrived at Mount Vernon for a visit in August 1800 a young couple no one had seen before was present: "We got to Mrs Washington's about two O'clock. Found there a young man & woman, whom Mrs Washington had the civility to ask in, tho' they had no letter of introduction, and only sent in to ask leave to see the house&c Miss Eliza Tomkins from Phila[delphi]a & Mr Quarrier from Richmond—They staid to dinner &did not seem to be conscious of the impropriety of their conduct in taking such a liberty."

To her visitors Martha talked constantly on subjects related to George and began to focus on her anticipation of her own death. Henrietta Liston, the wife of the British ambassador and an old friend from the years of Washington's terms as president, visited Mount Vernon in 1800. Martha, wrote Mrs Liston, "received us with her usual kindness, and not without tears . . . our spirits were much dampened, and I listened with tender interest to a sorrow which she said was truly breaking her heart."

However, Mrs. Liston was clearly puzzled at the intensity of Martha's grief and made another interesting observation: "Washington was a more respectful than a tender husband certainly, yet we found this excellent Woman grieving incessantly. She repeatedly told me, during the few days we had it in our power to stay with her, that all comfort had fled with her Husband, and that she waited anxiously for her dissolution. And indeed it was evident that her health was fast declining and her heart breaking. We parted with much kindness on both sides, never Alas! To meet again."

Without George's close attention to the management of the estate and supervision of the slaves, the slaves did as little as possible and were often absent. Martha was unable to exercise any control. Mount Vernon grew increasingly shabby and dilapidated, lapsing rapidly from its former glory days. A researcher for the Mount Vernon Ladies' Association noted:

Visitors to Mount Vernon recorded disrepair and shabbiness, which reflected the loss of both George Washington's strong management ability and attention to detail, as well as Mrs. Washington's depression. One visitor noted about the stable that it had "nothing in its appearance very neat or remarkable" and told of seeing a barnyard, "which is not very clean", where he saw "several scrubby cows & oxen, whose lank sides bespoke the leanness of their pasture," a situation Washington would have abhorred. Of the furnishings in the mansion, this same individual remarked that "in general, it may be said of the furniture, chairs, carpet and hangings, &c. that they had seen their best days."[5]

Nelly Custis Lewis and her family who continued to live at Mount Vernon after her marriage provided the only bright spot in Martha's life. Nelly and Lawrence were slowly building their new home, Woodlawn, on the land George had given them as a wedding present, but Nelly could not contemplate leaving her grandmother alone. The Lewises stayed on at Mount Vernon, where Nelly battled to manage the house, which was slowly sliding into disrepair, help with the company, and keep her grandmother's spirits up as much as possible. After a lifetime spent revolving around domestic matters, visitors noted she continued to focus on "Domestic Cares" as far as she was able, and that she passed much of her time "Reading and Knitting." In 1801 Nelly's pregnancy and the birth of a second daughter distracted Martha temporarily. The new baby was named Martha Betty, after Martha and Lawrence's mother Betty Lewis. Martha was particularly fond of Parke, so much so that Nelly feared Parke was becoming spoiled by her great-grandmother's indulgence of Parke's every whim. Martha's other granddaughters, their children, and Eleanor Stuart continued to spend time at Mount Vernon.

It was clear to everyone at Mount Vernon that Martha Washington was failing, but that did not keep the visitors from coming to call. By the end of her life, Martha was clearly suffering from some form of mental stress or possibly dementia. A nineteenth-century biographer, Margaret C. Conkling, wrote delicately forty-eight years later that the Washingtons' doctor and longtime family friend Dr. James Craik, treating Martha in her final illness was aware of an "insidious mental foe that had but too surely undermined the strength of his patient."

Martha's mental condition may have been caused or exacerbated by a more sinister development. Rumors persisted that the Mount Vernon slaves were attempting to kill her, thanks to a well-intentioned provision in George Washington's will.

By the time of George's death there were over 300 slaves at Mount Vernon; 123 of these he owned outright and the remainder were dower slaves, which on Martha's death would revert to the Custis heirs—the children of Martha's son, Jacky, and their children. In the absence of legislation that would free slaves, Washington had taken the only course open to him and, in his will, obliged his executors to free all his own slaves—after Martha's death.

It may have been the best George could do legally, but it left Martha in a precarious position. Over one hundred slaves now found their freedom contingent on Martha's death, an event that would simultaneously render many of their family members property of Martha's Custis heirs. Unless he could compensate the Custis estate for their value, for which the will made no provision, Washington did not have legal power to manumit the Custis slaves, and giving effect to the provision to free his own slaves meant the inevitable breakup of the families, as some members would be free and some remain enslaved.

The rumor that the Mount Vernon slaves were attempting to hasten Martha's death spread beyond the family. Edward Everett Hale wrote, "I have been assured by gentlemen who lived in northern Virginia that the universal impression there was that the slaves of the Washington plantation hurried Martha Washington's death because their own liberty was secured by Washington's will after her death. I do not believe this bad statement can be authenticated, but there is no doubt, I believe, that Madison made a similar will liberating his slaves after Mrs. Madison's death and that he changed his will on account of this rumour."[6]

Abigail Adams, wife of President John Adams, visited Martha at Mount Vernon in 1800 and wrote "in the state in which they [the slaves] were left by the General, to be free at her death, she did not feel as tho her Life was safe in their Hands, many of whom would be told it was there interest to get rid of her—She therefore was advised to set them all free at the close of the year."

A year after Washington's death, Wash Custis, one of the executors, made this guarded allusion to the provision for the Washington slaves in the will: "The slaves were left to be emancipated at the death of Mrs. Washington; but it was found necessary (for *prudential* reasons) to give them their freedom in one year after the general's decease." In fact, the Washington slaves were freed a year after George's death on the advice of Bushrod Washington. There had been at least one alarming incident, when Judge Bushrod Washington was urgently called from the circuit court where he was presiding because there had been an attempt to set fire to Mount Vernon. It was widely believed some of the Mount Vernon slaves were implicated.

In October 1801 Martha had another bout of illness. Even anticipating her own death, she displayed her old fondness for clothes and a sense of the fitting image. She chose and set aside a white gown in readiness for the time when she followed her "departed Friend." She had made other careful preparations for death, including a will, which disposed of all her possessions and the contents of the house in detailed bequests to her grandchildren, extended family, and friends. When Bushrod Washington took possession, he found the mansion house stripped of everything save the portrait of Lawrence Washington.

According to family tradition, Martha was seen burning papers before her death, among them nearly all the private correspondence between her husband and herself. This may have been prompted by a wish to keep the details of their private relationship from prying eyes, but it has led to speculation the letters contained information Martha—and possibly Washington himself—did not wish to be generally known. All that was left were two letters written to her by Washington from Philadelphia in the summer of 1775, just after he had been appointed by Congress to command the newly formed Continental army, which she must have overlooked. These were later discovered in a writing desk bequeathed to Patty Peter.

A relative visiting Martha in the early spring 1802 noted Martha had been suffering from "a wretched cold" and "the poor old Lady looks badly . . . I fear she will not be long here." Another visitor noted,

> The pleasure which we had anticipated in this visit was greatly diminished by the illness of Lady Washington. She is confined to her bed & from the account given by Doctor Craik, the family physician, has not many days to survive. . . . The death of her husband affected her sensibly. She has not entered either his study or the apartment in which he died since the removal of his corpse. . . . She now promised Doctor Craik that should she recover from the present attack, she will consent to lodge in some other part of the house more airy & commodious; of this there is little probability as her health has been wasting for the last twelve months & yesterday a chilly fit deprived her, during the paroxysm, of the power of speech. He thinks another must deprive her of life.[7]

Martha had been, in her own words, "neither sick nor well" for years, and only a shadow of her former self since George died. Her final illness, a bilious fever, lasted for seventeen days. Her grandson George Washington Parke Custis recorded this pious, official account of Martha's death:

> The lady herself was perfectly aware that her hour was nigh; she assembled her grandchildren at her bedside, and discoursed to them on their respective duties through life, spoke of the happy influence of religion on the affairs of this world, of the consolation they had afforded her in many and trying afflictions, and of the hopes they held out of a blessed immortality; and then surrounded by her weeping relatives, friends and domestics, the venerable relict of Washington resigned her life into the hands of her Creator, in the seventy-first year of her age.

There were many obituaries, though most short and in the same vein. On June 5 a notice appeared in the *Alexandria Gazette* "Died at Mount Vernon on Sunday evening the 22nd of May, 1802 Mrs. Martha Washington, widow of the late illustrious General George Washington. To those amiable and Christian virtues which adorn the female character, she added dignity of manners, superiority of understanding, a mind intelligent and elevated. The silence of respectful grief is our best eulogy."

The *New England Pledium* carried another, fuller one which would have pleased Martha:

> Composure and resignation were uniformly displayed during seventeen days depredations of a severe fever. From the commencement she declared she was undergoing the last trial and had long been prepared for her dissolution. She took the sacrament from Mr. DAVIS, imparted her last advice and benedictions to her weeping relations, and sent for a white gown, which she had previously laid by for her last dress- thus in the closing scene, as in all preceding ones, nothing was omitted. The conjugal, maternal, and domestic duties had all been fulfilled in an exemplary manner. She was the worthy partner of the worthiest of men, and those who witnessed their conduct could not determine which excelled in their different characters, both were so well sustained on every occasion. They lived an honor and a pattern to their country, and are taken from us to receive the rewards—promised to the faithful and the just.

The family held a quiet funeral. Martha's grandson-in-law Thomas Law, holding the hand of his five year old daughter, was among the most afflicted. The wooden door was pried off the vault and Martha was buried in a lead coffin beside George.

The resolution of Congress to move his body came to nothing in the end, though Martha did not have the sad consolation of knowing she and George would stay side by side in death, as she had hoped. The Washingtons' remains were later removed to a new vault not far from the old one, at the bottom of a hill leading down from the house and overlooking the Potomac. They remain there today. Washington's coffin was placed inside a new marble sarcophagus with a sculptured lid, representing the American shield suspended over the flag of the Union. On the arch over the vault are the words WITHIN THIS ENCLOSURE REST THE REMAINS OF GENERAL GEORGE WASHINGTON. Martha's coffin was placed likewise in a new marble sarcophagus. Its surface has been left plain, testifying to silence and respectful grief.

Three months after Martha's death there was the kind of inquiry Martha herself would have felt was fitting and proper. It came from one lady, a distant family connection of Martha's, to another. Lucy Ludwell Paradise in London wrote to Portia Lee Hodgson in Virginia,

> My Dear Niece,   July 31st 1802:
>   I read in the newspaper of June 30 that Mrs. Martha Washington the wife of our great and good General and President Washington was dead. Let me know if it is true and tell me the month and her age and what was the illness

which was the cause of her death. I went directly into Mourning and I shall continue in Mourning 6 months.

Like her brother Wash, whose *Memoir* provided so many insights into his grandmother and her marriage, in later life Nelly drew on her own memories of the Washingtons and left this tribute to Martha:

I had the most perfect model of female excellence ever with me as my monitress, who acted the part of a tender an devoted parent, loving me as only a mother can love, and never extenuating or approving in me what she disapproved in others. She never omitted her private devotions, or her public duties; . . . she and her husband were so perfectly united and happy . . . after forty years of devoted affection and uninterrupted happiness, she resigned him without a murmur into the arms of his Savior and his God, with the assured hope of his eternal felicity.[8]

Epilogue

Martha was a central figure in the lives of many of her relatives and acquaintances. Here is what became of some of them.

The remainder of **Nelly Custis Lewis**'s life was a sad contrast to its bright beginnings. The night her adored Grandmother died, Nelly's one-year-old daughter Martha Betty contracted measles. Nelly, who was pregnant, and Parke caught them too, and all three became very ill. Parke survived, but Martha Betty died. A few months later Nelly gave birth to a son, Lawrence Fielding Lewis, who died immediately. Nelly and Lawrence had been slowly building their house, "Woodlawn," on the tract of land that had been George Washington's wedding present, but it was not yet finished when Martha died. However, Judge Bushrod Washington wished to move into Mount Vernon immediately after Martha's death so Nelly, Lawrence, and Parke were forced to move in with Betty Carter, Lawrence's married sister. Before Woodlawn was finished, Nelly had another baby, her fourth child in four years. Between 1802 and 1804 a bereaved and overwhelmed Nelly experienced some kind of breakdown.

Lawrence Lewis, whom Nelly had blindly imagined as cast in her grand-father's image, became even moreso the prim tedious hypochondriac, somewhat lacking in ambition, that he had been all along. Lacking George's drive and ambition, he was never particularly successful as a planter, and Nelly and Lawrence were desperately short of money for most of their lives. The large and beautiful house at Woodlawn was built using Nelly's share of the Custis fortune. Nelly struggled to do her duty by her husband, but the affection soon went out of the marriage. By the time of his death in 1839, Lawrence Lewis had taken to large regular doses of opium for his many ailments. As intensely maternal and attached to her home as her grandmother had been, Nelly lived to bury all but one of her eight children and to see Woodlawn sold. Her main consolations, other than her children, were needlework and religion—just as they had been for Martha.

Martha's niece **Fanny Henley,** daughter of Martha's youngest sister Elizabeth Henley, became the third wife of Tobias Lear a year after Martha's death. She died with no children of her own.

Tobias Lear eventually received several government appointments including that of consul general to the North African coast, where he and Fanny lived for nine years in Algiers. After 1812, he became a secretary in the War Department. He and Fanny and his son Benjamin Lincoln lived a few blocks from the White House. Despite a happy marriage and his government employment, Tobias suffered from severe headaches, and later, depression. He shot himself on October 11, 1816. He left no suicide note and died without having made a will.

Martha's daughter-in-law **Eleanor Calvert Custis Stuart** died at Hope Park in 1811, probably of tuberculosis and worn out by the effect of at least twenty pregnancies. She had given birth to eleven children who lived. Her sister-in-law, Rosalie Stier Calvert, believed Eleanor had raised her Stuart daughters with an exaggerated idea of their own importance: "None of our Stuart nieces are married nor ever will be I fear. Their mother paid scant heed to their education and bought them up as if they were to marry English Lords, and I don't believe they accept the offers made to them."

Maria Washington, Fanny Bassett Washington's daughter, did not develop tuberculosis as a child. Her disease went dormant for some time, and she married and gave birth to two children before her death at the age of twenty-seven.

Martha Parke Custis Peter and her husband Thomas Peter built a beautiful home at Tudor Place in Georgetown with her Custis inheritance. Five of their six children survived to adulthood, including their youngest daughter, Britiannia Wellington Peter, who lived until 1911.

Eliza Parke Custis Law and her husband Thomas Law ended their marriage. Rosalie Stier Calvert, who knew Eliza well, thought she was a strange woman, and described her as of 1805:

> Since childhood Mrs L demonstrated a violent and romantic disposition. Her father recognised that her singular personality would bring her unhappiness and he tried to correct it but he died while she was still very young. Her mother remarried and from a number of lovers made a very prudent choice for the welfare of her children . . . When Mrs. L entered society she was pretty, rich and quite intelligent. Her relations and connections were the most respectable. Consequently she was greatly admired and flattered. . . . After rejecting some brilliant offers, she married Mr. L whom you know well, against the wishes of all her relations. Never were two people less suited to life together, but during the life of her grandmother Mrs. Washington, to whom she was most attached, they restrained themselves in order to spare her pain. After [Mrs. Washington's] death, Mr. L went to England, and soon after his return they

decided to separate. Never was anything stranger because they only reproach each other about their manners and dispositions.[1]

Eliza and Thomas Law separated in 1804, and Eliza took the name Mrs. Custis. Thomas Law was granted custody of their one child, a girl also named Eliza. He undertook to pay her full maintenance and to pay his ex-wife fifteen hundred dollars a year. The Laws were officially divorced in 1810.

George Washington Parke Custis came into his huge Custis inheritance the year of Martha's death and built a grandiose mansion he named "Arlington" after the old Custis property on the Eastern Shore, where his great-grandfather, the irascible Colonel John Custis IV had been buried in 1749. Wash was became a curious nexus for the Custis family, their slaves, and the Dandridges. He married sixteen-year-old Mary Ann Fitzhugh in 1804, but he also probably had a number of liaisons with his slaves, and before his marriage freed several small slave children in circumstances that suggested they were his. After his marriage he had at least one more child by a house slave named Arianna Carter. Arianna was believed to have been a Custis dower slave but there has never been any trace of her found in any of the Custis slave records.

Arianna and Wash's child was Martha's great-granddaughter Maria Carter Custis, born about 1806. Family tradition says she and Wash's one surviving child of his marriage, a daughter named Mary Anna Randolph Custis, were raised and educated together at Arlington, and both were married in the drawing room there by the same Presbyterian minister.

Mary Anna Randolph Custis married Robert E. Lee, who later became the Confederate general. Maria Carter Custis married another slave named Charles Syphax. Wash freed Maria, and later her husband, Charles, and gave the couple seventeen acres of land at Arlington. During the Civil War the house and property at Arlington were occupied by Union forces, who buried some of their dead on the property. After the war the U.S. government confiscated the estate for unpaid taxes. The Lees tried to pay the taxes and recover it, but lost. At the same time Maria Carter Custis Syphax tried to reclaim the seventeen acres left her by her father Wash, but there was a problem because Wash had never transferred the land to Maria by the necessary deed. The land once given to Maria and Charles is today a part of Arlington National Cemetery.

Maria and Charles Syphax had a large family who were prominent in the Free Black community in Washington and who have many descendants today.

Martha's half sister **Ann Dandridge Costin** lived at Mount Vernon until Martha died, then went to live at Woodlawn with Nelly Custis Lewis. Though she is said to have married a Mount Vernon slave named Costin after her son William's birth, no male slave named Costin has been found in the inventories of slaves taken at Mount Vernon in 1786 and 1799. It is

Martha's great granddaughter "Maria Carter Custis Syphax," daughter of Arlington house slave Arianna Carter and George Washington Parke Custis. Courtesy of the Custis-Lee Mansion, Arlington,

perfectly possible that the man who married Martha Washington's half sister was quietly emancipated. Nothing more is known of Ann's husband. Ann died at Woodlawn. Her son William Costin married dower slave Philadelphia Judge, Oney's younger sister. After Martha's death, Philadelphia, or Delphy as she was known in the family, was allowed to buy her freedom for one dollar by Thomas Law, which suggests that Eliza Custis Law had inherited Delphy as part of the Custis slave property divided among Martha's heirs. William and Delphy lived in Washington, where William was prominent as a church leader and worked at the Bank of Washington as a messenger until his death in 1842. They had seven children, including a daughter, Louisa Parke Costin, who had her own well-known school for black girls in Washington, and sons who were prominent in the black churches. They also raised four orphan children.

Delphy was more fortunate than most of her fellow dower slaves at Mount Vernon. As George had feared families and children were indeed split up on Martha's death.

Oney Judge Staines had a difficult life. She was never apprehended and forced back to Virginia, but she probably never saw her mother or sister Delphy again. She learned to read and write, as she had wished to do, and was a regular church attendee. She and her husband Jack had three children, two daughters and a son. When Jack Staines died in 1803, Oney and the children had a hard time making ends meet. They boarded with a white family in New Hampshire in return for looking after the elderly father of the family. Her son went to sea and never returned. Oney's daughters died and Oney was supported in her old age by charity. She was interviewed for an abolitionist paper late in her life and asked if she regretted her escape. "No," she said, "I am free, and have, I trust, been made a child of God by the means."[2]

There was an attempt to steal George's body from the old family vault in about 1830. A new vault was built and all family members reinterred in 1831. Both Martha and George were reburied in the white marble sarcophagi, which can be seen just inside the gated vault today.

For years afterwards a manumitted mulatto slave named West Ford was custodian of the Washington burial vault. West Ford outlived Washington's heir and nephew Supreme Court Justice Bushrod Washington and was known to have had Washington blood. At the time it was commonly believed West Ford was the child of one of Bushrod Washington's brothers and a mulatto slave woman. In a curious twist of fate there has been much media coverage in recent years that, according to family tradition handed down to West Ford's descendants, their Washington ancestor was in fact *George* Washington. There has been as yet no scientific evidence to substantiate or disprove the claim.

George and Martha Washington would have been saddened by the continuing decline of their beloved home after Martha's death. **Mount Vernon** was inherited by Judge Bushrod Washington, but George had ensured there were no slaves left to work the estate, and it would have taken a massive infusion of capital either to buy and manage enough new slaves or to get in tenant farmers to make the estate productive. Bushrod was a lawyer, not a farmer. Since he and his wife Hannah had no children, the estate was passed to his nephew, his brother Corbin's son John Augustine Washington II. His son John Augustine III inherited it, but by that time it had gone to rack and ruin, with many of the outbuildings burnt down and the estate reduced to a quarter of its original size. It was beyond John III's ability to rescue it. Just before the Civil War Pamela Ann Cunningham and the Mount Vernon Ladies' Association rescued the property.

White House, the Custis plantation on the Pamunkey where Martha had gone as Daniel Parke Custis' eighteen-year-old bride, was still standing during the Civil War. Union troops were stationed there, at White House

Landing, and Wash's daughter, by then Mrs. Robert E. Lee, had left a note on the door begging any occupying forces to respect the first married home of Martha Washington. General McClellan gave orders that the house was not to be damaged, but as the troops were leaving there was an accidental fire, and it burned to the ground. Chestnut Grove, Martha's birthplace, was destroyed by fire in 1926.

A Culinary Lagniappe

Recipes from *Martha Washington's Booke of Cookery and Booke of Sweet-meats*
Transcribed by Karen Hess.

To Make a Great Cake

Take a peck of flower, 4 nutmeggs grated, halfe an ounce of cloves & mace, & as much cinnamon, & as much caraway seeds beaten, 3 quarters of A pound of sugar mingled with 7 pound of currans pickt clean & rubd clean with a cloth, A pinte of good ale barme, & almost A pinte of lukewarm water, 3 pound of butter melted. first strow in a little salt upon ye flowre, then mingle all ye spice together, & strow into ye flower, & strow in yr water, barme, & butter. when all is well mingled, kned it up & let it ly an houre by ye fire covrd close with a cloth. mingle ye currans &ye sugar with ye dow. 2 hours will bake it.

[Author's note: I have not tried this myself though I have tried similar ones. "Ale barme" is yeast proofed in ale. About two cakes of live yeast, proofed in the ale, would be about right for this amount of dry ingredients. A "pinte" here may mean the English pint of 20 fluid ounces, 2 and ½ cups instead of 16 fluid ounces in the American pint. Since this is a risen yeast cake, not plum cake, the end result would be similar to Italian pannetone, though spicier, fruitier, and, as it lacks eggs, more dense. My guess is that this cake would have been baked in a vast shaped mold so it could rise handsomely, in a medium oven, with the heat reduced to a very slow oven as soon as the cake had risen to take a firm shape. Too slow an oven at the outset means a tidal wave of yeasty dough all over the oven.]

To Make a Gooseberry or Apple Creame

Take gooseberries or apples & scald them very tender, then put them in a little hearb sive or cullender & bruise them with ye back of a spoon; & the pulp yt comes thorough A sive or Cullender, you must take & season with rosewater & sugar. yn mix some good cream with it and make of it what thicknes you please & soe serve it up.

To Make Oxford Kates Sausages

Take ye leane of a legg of porke, or veale, & 4 pound of beef suet, or butter, & shred ym together very fine.yn season ym with 3 quarter of an ounce of pepper & halfe as much of cloves & mace, a good handfull of sage, shread small, & what salt fits yr palate. mingle these together, yn take 10 eggs, all but 3 whites., & temper altogether with yr hands. & when you use ym, roule ym out about ye length an bigness of yr finger. you may roule ym up in flower, If you like it, but it is better without. When you fry ym, ye butter must boil in ye pan before you put ym in. when they are pretty browne, take ym up. theyr sauce is mustard.

To Dress a Dish of Mushrumps

Take yr firme mushumps & pill ye scin from them & scrape away all ye red yt grows on ye inside of them, & pill yr stalks likewise. If you finde them firm, throw them as you doe them into faire water & let them ly 3 or 4 hours, then take them out of ye water & set them on ye fire in a pan. theyr owne liquor will stew them. put in an ounion cut in halves and often shake them. as ye water rises, cast it away till you finde them allmoste dry. then take out the ounion & put in a little sweet cream yt is thick & shrod in some time & parseley, & put in some grated nutmeg, & a little grose pepper, & a little salt, & soe let them boyle, shakeing them sell together. & put in A piece of fresh butter, giving them another shake, & soe dish them up.

[Author's note: The soaking and peeling were probably necessary in Martha's day when the mushrooms were gathered wild from the fields to remove grit and animal manure. This would be an unnecessary step with modern cultivated mushrooms. However, as these have less taste than the sort of mushrooms Martha used, this dish would be improved by the addition of dried cepes or chanterelle mushrooms, soaked briefly as per the package instructions.]

To Candy Flowers in Theyr Naturall Culler

Take ye flowers with theyr stalks, & wash them in rose water, wherein gum arabeck is dissolved. then take fine searced sugar, & dust it over them. & set them A drying in a sive, set in an oven. & they will glister like sugar candy.

[Author's note: These sugared flowers would be pretty on a wedding cake.]

To Make Sweet Water to Perfume Cloaths in ye Foulding after
They Are Wash'd

Take a quart of damask rose water, & put it in a glass with a handful of lavender flowers, 2 ounces of orris, one dram of muske, ye weight of A pence in
ambergreece, & as much civit, 4 drops of oyle of cloves. stop this close &
set it in ye sun A fortnight. when you use this water, put A spoonful of it into
halfe a basone of spring water, & put it into a glass, and sprinkle yr cloathes
therewith in ye foulding. ye dreggs yt are left in the bottom of ye glass when
the water is spent, will make as much more If you kep them, & put fresh
rose water to them. & then put a spoonful or 2 of it in ye like premention'd
quantity of spring water.

Notes

Introduction

1. Ellet, Elizabeth F., *Women of the American Revolution* (Philadelphia: George W. Jacobs & Co, 1900), 17.

2. Desmond, Alice Curtis, *Martha Washington: Our First First Lady* (New York: Dodd Mead & Co., 1943).

3. Smith, Captain John, *The Generall Historie of Virginia, New England and the Summer Isles, Vol I* (Glascow: James Maclehoge and Sons, 1907).

4. Ibid.

5. Byrd, William II, *The Secret Diary of William Byrd of Westover 1709–1712*, edited by Louis B. Wright and Marion Tingling (Richmond: Dietz Press, 1941).

6. Morgan, Philip D., *Slave Counterpoint* (Chapel Hill: Published for the Omohundro Institute of Early American History and Culture by University of North Carolina Press, 1998), 15–16.

7. Hughes, Rupert, *George Washington 1732–1762: The Human Being and the Hero* (New York; William Morrow and Co., 1926).

Chapter One

1. Cook, Richard Pye, Letter of, to Mrs. John Stewart, July 16, 1887, Virginia Historical Society Mss 2C 7734a.

2. U.S. Congress *41st Congress. 2nd Session, House of Representatives Ex. Do. No. 315, "Special report of the Commissioner of Education on the Condition and Improvement of Public Schools in the District of Columbia" submitted to the Senate June 1868, and to the House, with Additions, June 13, 1870* (Washington, D.C.: Government Printing Office, 1871), 203–4.

3. Records of St. Peter's Parish, New Kent County.

4. Will of Francis Dandridge, February 21, 1763; proved November 19, 1765 "Virginia Gleanings in England," p. 217, *http://www.genealogy.com/cgi-bin/ifa_ load.cgi?img=/ifa/data/186/images/Virginia-20,* visited March 16, 2001.

5. Conkling, Margaret C., *Memoirs of the Mother and Wife of Washington* (New York: C. M. Saxton, Barker & Co., 1858).

6. Custis, George Washington Parke, *Recollections and Private Memoirs of Washington,* (New York: Derby & Jackson, 1860), 495.

7. Fithian, Philip Vickers, *Journal and Letters of Philip Vickers Fithian 1773–1774* (Williamsburg, Va.: Colonial Williamsburg Inc., 1965).

8. Cook, Richard Pye, to Mrs. John Stewart, July 16, 1887.

9. Byrd, William, *The Secret Diary of William Byrd of Westover, Vol. I.*

10. Fithian, *Journal and Letters of Philip Vickers Fithian,* 84.

11. Ibid, 38–39.

12. Mazyck, Walter, *George Washington and the Negro* (Washington, D.C.: Associated Publishers, Inc., 1932).

13. Ford, Worthington Chauncey, ed., *Letters of Jonathan Boucher to George Washington* (Brooklyn: Historical Printing Club, 1899), 6.

14. Custis, *Recollections and Private Memoirs of Washington,* 503.

Chapter Two

1. "Portrait of Martha Belle of New Kent," by Polly Longsworth, *Colonial Williamsburg Gazette* (Summer 1988), 6.

2. Custis, *Recollections and Private Memoirs of Washington,* 496.

3. "Self Portrait: Eliza Custis, 1808," Virginia Magazine of History and Biography, 90.

4. Wharton, Anne Hollingsworth, *Martha Washington* (London; John Murray, 1897).

5. Fields, Joseph E, ed. *Worthy Partner, the Papers of Martha Washington* (Westport, Conn.: Greenwood Press, 1994), 423.

6. Ibid., 438 n. 24.

7. Ibid., 424.

8. Morgan, Philip D., *Slave Counterpoint* (Chapel Hill: University of North Carolina Press, 1998), 98.

9. Fields, *Worthy Partner,* 430–33.

10. Custis, *Recollections and Private Memoirs of Washington,* 496.

Chapter Three

1. Fields, ed., *Worthy Partner, the Papers of Martha Washington,* Complete Inventory by Counties of the Estate of Daniel Parke Custis, 63–68.

2. *Martha Washington's Booke of Cookery and Booke of Sweetmeats,* transcribed by Karen Hess, New York: Columbia University Press, 1995.

3. *The Martha Washington Cookbook,* edited by Marie Kimball (New York: Coward McCann, 1940), 51.

4. *Worthy Partner,* 431.

5. Ibid., 433.

6. Heming, editor *The Statutes at Large,* Vol. 3, 86–88.

7. Noel-Hume, Ivor, *All the Best Rubbish: History in a Green Bottle* (New York: Harper and Row, 1974).

8. Custis, *Recollections and Private Memoirs of Washington,* 497.

9. *Worthy Partner, the Papers of Martha Washington,* 431.

Chapter Four

1. Robert Carter Nicholas to Martha Custis, August 7, 1757, *Recollections and Private Memoirs of Washington,* 497–98.

2. Martha Custis to John Hanbury and Co., August 20, 1757, *Worthy Partner, the Papers of Martha Washington,* 6.

3. Ibid., 74–75.

4. "Portrait of Martha Belle of New Kent," by Polly Longsworth, *Colonial Williamsburg Magazine* (Summer 1988), 10.

5. Daniel Parke Custis to John Mercer, January 4, 1758, *Worthy Partner, the Papers of Martha Washington,* 31.

6. Jon Mercer to Martha Custis January 4, 1758, Ibid., 29–30.

7. John Mercer to Martha Custis, April 24, 1758, Ibid., 39–40.

8. Custis, *Memoirs and Private Recollections of Washington,* 500–501.

Chapter Five

1. Rasmussen, William M. S., and Robert S. Tilton, editors, *George Washington, the Man Behind the Myths* (Charlottesville: University Press of Virginia, 1999), 5.

2. Will of Augustine Washington, April 1743, The George Washington Papers at the Library of Congress. *http://memory.loc.gov/cgi-binampage?collId=mgw4&fileName=gwpage029.*

3. *Recollections and Memoir of Washington,* 131.

4. Harrison, Maureen, and Steve Gilbert, *George Washington in His Own Words.* "Master George Washington's Rules of Civility and Decent Behavior in Company and Conversation," (New York: Barnes & Noble), 7, 12.

5. George Washington to John Augustine Washington, May 28, 1755. The George Washington Papers at the Library of Congress.

6. "The Fairfaxes and George Washington," *http://www.pbs.org/wgbh/pages/fontline/shows/secret/famous/washington/html.*

7. Ibid.

8. *Mount Vernon and Its Associations,* 45–46.

9. Rasmussen and Tilton, *George Washington, the Man behind the Myths,* 60.

10. Ibid., 60–61.

11. Harrison, Constance C., "A Little Centennial Lady," *Scribner's Monthly,* June 1876.

Chapter Six

1. *Worthy Partner, the Papers of Martha Washington,* 455.

2. *Recollections and Private Memoirs of Washington,* 501–502.

3. Walter, James, *Memorials of Washington and Mary his Mother and Martha his Wife From Letters and Papers of Robert Cary and James Sharples* (New York: Scribner's Sons, 1887), 34–35.

4. Fedric, Francis, *Slave Life in Virginia and Kentucky or Fifty Years of Slavery in the Southern States of America* (London: Wertheim, MacIntosh, and Hunt., 1863), 41–46.

5. Letters of George Washington.

6. *Recollections and Private Memoirs of Washington,* 153.

7. *George Washington, the Man behind the Myths,* 94.

Chapter Seven

1. Lossing, Benson J. *The Home of Washington, or Mount Vernon and Its Associations* (Hartford, Conn.: A. S. Hale & Company, 1871), 67.

2. *Recollections and Private Memoirs of Washington,* 166n.

3. Cresswell, Nicholas, *The Journal of Nicholas Cresswell* (Norwood Mass.: Dial Press, 1924), 270.

4. Ford, Paul Leicester, *The True George Washington* (Philadelphia: J. B. Lippincott Co., 1897), 177.

5. *Recollections and Private Memoirs of Washington,* 386.

6. George Washington to Francis Dandridge, 1763, in Sparks, Jared, ed., *The Writings of George Washington, vol. 2* (Boston: American Stationers' Company, John B. Russell, 1837), 342.

7. Ibid., 86–92.

8. *George Washington, the Man behind the Myths,* 88.

9. Ibid., 90.

10. Martha Washington to Anna Maria Bassett, June 1, 1760, *Worthy Partner, the Papers of Martha Washington,* 134.

11. Martha Washington to Margaret Green, September 29, 1760, Ibid., 135.

12. Martha Washington to Anna Maria Bassett, April 6, 1762, Ibid., 146.

13. Floyd, Nicholas Jackson, *Biographical Genealogies of the Virginia-Kentucky Floyd Families* with notes on some collateral branches (Baltimore: Williams and Wilkins, 1912), 33–34.

14. *Worthy Partner, the Papers of Martha Washington,* 105–08.

15. *The Home of Washington or Mount Vernon and Its Associations,* 73–75.

16. Martha Washington to Anna Maria Bassett, August 28, 1762, *Worthy Partner, the Papers of Martha Washington,* 147–48.

17. Martha Washington to Mrs. Shelbury, August 1764, Ibid., 148.

18. *Journal and letters of Philip Vickers Fithian 1773–1774,* 33–34.

19. Martha Washington to George Washington, March 30, 1767, *Worthy Partner, the Papers of Martha Washington,* 149.

Chapter Eight

1. Abbot, W. W., and Dorothy Twohig, eds., *The Papers of George Washington, Confederation Series,* vol.4, April 1786–January 1787 (Charlottesville: University Press of Virginia 1995), 310n. 10.

2. Cresswell, Nicholas, *The Journal of Nicholas Cresswell* (Norwood, Mass.: Dial Press, 1924), 21.

3. Ellis, Joseph J., *Founding Brothers: The Revolutionary Generation* (New York: Alfred A. Knopf, 2001), 65.

4. Meyer, Edith Patterson, *Petticoat Patriots of the American Revolution* (New York: Vanguard Press, 1976), 31.

5. Martha Washington to Mrs. S. Thorpe, July 15, 1772, *Worthy Partner, the Papers of Martha Washington*, 151.

6. Fitzpatrick, John C., ed. *The Diaries of George Washington, vol. 2* (Boston and New York: Houghton Mifflin Company, 50.

7. Ibid., 50.

8. Ford, Worthington Chauncy, ed., *Letters of Jonathan Boucher to George Washington* (Brooklyn, N.Y.: Historical Printing Club, 1899), 6.

9. Andrews, John, M.D., W. Meadows, and J. Clark, *Cases of the Epilepsy, Hysteric Fits and St. Vitus Dance with the Process of Cure* (Cornhill, 1746).

10. Lechtenberg, Richard, M.D., *Epilepsy and the Family* (Cambridge, Mass.: Harvard University Press, 1984), 3.

11. *Cases of the Epilepsy; Hysteric Fits and St. Vitus Dance.*

12. *Epilepsy and the Family.*

13. Sparks, Jared, *The Writings of George Washington*, vol. 2 (Boston: John B. Russell, 1837), 363.

Chapter Nine

1. Jonathan Boucher to George Washington, April 8, 1773, *http://memory.loc. gov/ammem/mgwquery.html*, The George Washington Papers at the Library of Congress 1741–1799, Series 4, General Correspondence, 1097–1799, Image 915.

2. George Washington to Benedict Calvert, April 3, 1773, Ibid., Image 95.

3. Benedict Calvert to George Washington, April 8, 1773, *Letters to Washington and Accompanying Papers*, Stanislaus Murray Hamilton, ed., Ibid., Image 917.

4. George Washington to Burwell Bassett, June 20, 1773, Ibid., *The Papers of George Washington, The Diaries of George Washington*, vol. 3, Donald Jackson, ed., and Dorothy Twohig, assoc. ed., 188.

5. John Murray, Earl of Dunmore, to George Washington, July 3, 1773, *Letters to Washington and Accompanying Papers*, Image 962.

6. John Parke Custis to Martha C. Washington, July 5, 1773, George Washington Papers at the Library of Congress, 1741–1799: Series 4, General Correspondence, 1697–1799, Image 970.

7. Ford, Paul Leicester, *The True George Washington* (Philadelphia: J. B. Lippincott Company, 1897).

8. George Washington to Myles Cooper, Dec. 15, 1773, *The Writings of George Washington from the Original Manuscript Sources, 1745–1799*, John C. Fitzpatrick, ed., vol. 3, George Washington papers at the Library of Congress.

9. *The Journal of Nicholas Cresswell*, 27–28.

10. Hughes, Rupert, *George Washington, the Rebel and the Patriot* (New York: William Morrow & Company, 1927), 222.

11. *The Journal of Nicholas Cresswell.*

12. Dixon and Hunter's *Virginia Gazette,* April 22, 1775.

Chapter Ten

1. *Purdie's Virginia Gazette,* Friday, April 21, 1775.

2. Custis, *Recollections and Private Memoirs of Washington,* 151–52.

3. Thane, Elswyth, *A Family Quarrel* (New York: Van Rees Press, 1959), 39.

4. Hughes, Rupert, *George Washington, the Rebel and the Patriot 1762–1777* (New York: William Morrow, 1927), 241.

5. Thane, *A Family Quarrel,* 161.

6. Lossing, *The Home of Washington,* 119.

7. Berlin, Ira, *Many Thousands Gone: The First Two Centuries of Slavery in North America* (Cambridge, Mass.: Harvard University Press, 1998), 258–59.

8. Desmond, Alice Curtis, *Martha Washington, Our First Lady* (New York: Dodd, Meade, 1943), 142.

9. Meyer, *Petticoat Patriots,* 43.

10. French, Allen, "The First George Washington Scandal," paper presented to the Massachusetts Historical Society, November 1935.

11. Ibid.

12. *Worthy Partner, the Papers of Martha Washington,* 163n.2.

13. George Washington to Lund Washington, November 26, 1775, *The Writings of George Washington from the Original Manuscript Sources, 1745–1799,* John C. Fitzpatrick, ed., Vol. 4, The George Washington Papers at the Library of Congress.

14. Desmond, *Martha Washington, Our First Lady,* 142.

Chapter Eleven

1. Hibbert, Christopher, *Redcoats and Rebels: The War for America 1770–1781* (London: Grafton Books, 1990), 70–71.

2. Martha Washington to Elizabeth Ramsay, December 30, 1775, *Worthy Partner, the Papers of Martha Washington,* 164.

3. Hibbert, *Redcoats and Rebels,* 36.

4. Ibid., 62.

5. Hoffman, Ronald, and Peter J. Albert, eds., *Women in the Age of the American Revolution* (Charlottesville: University Press of Virginia, 1989), 12.

6. Hughes, *George Washington, the Rebel and the Patriot 1762–1777,* 296.

7. Greene, George Washington, *The Life of Nathanael Greene, vol. 1* (New York: G. P. Putnam and Son, 1867), 143.

8. Ibid., 193.

9. Wharton, Anne Hollingsworth, *Martha Washington* (London: John Murray, 1897), 100.

10. Martha Washington to Mercy Otis Warren January 8, 1776, *Worthy Partner, the Papers of Martha Washington,* 166.

11. Martha Washington to Anna Maria Bassett, January 31, 1776, Ibid., 166–67.

12. John Parke Custis to Martha Washington, June 9, 1776, Ibid., 169.

13. Bryan, William Alfred, *George Washington in American Literature* (New York: Columbia University Press, 1952).

14. George Washington, July 24, 1776, General Orders, *The Writings of George Washington from the Original Manuscript Sources, 1745–1799,* John C. Fitzpatrick, ed.-Vol 5. The George Washington Papers at the Library of Congress.

15. John Parke Custis to George Washington, August 8, 1776, *Recollections and Private Memoirs of Washington,* 536.

16. John Parke Custis to Martha Washington, August 21, 1776, *Worthy Partner, the Papers of Martha Washington,* 170–71.

17. Hibbert, *Redcoats and Rebels,* 122.

18. Ibid., 172.

Chapter Twelve

1. Hervey, Nathaniel, *The Memory of Washington* (Boston: J. Munro, 1852), 87.

2. Greene, *The Life of Nathanael Greene,* 309.

3. Ibid., 356.

4. Hibbert, *Redcoats and Rebels,* 184.

5. Hoffman and Albert, *Women in the Age of the American Revolution,* 15.

6. Martha Washington to Anna Maria Bassett, November 18, 1777, *Worthy Partner, the Papers of Martha Washington,* 174.

7. Martha Washington to Burwell Bassett, December 22, 1777, Ibid., 175–76.

Chapter Thirteen

1. *The Diary of Joseph Plumb Martin,* Mid-December 1777, *http://mrbooth. com/edu/constit/dairies.html.*

2. *The Diary of Albigence Waldo,* December 14, 1777, Ibid.

3. George Washington to Governor George Clinton, February 16, 1778, *The Writings of George Washington from the Original Manuscript Sources, 1745–1799,* John C. Fitzpatrick, ed., vol. 10.

4. *Mary and Martha, the Mother and Wife of Washington,* 171–72.

5. Wharton, Anne Hollingsworth, *Martha Washington* (London: John Murray, 1897), 122–23.

6. Meyer, *Petticoat Patriots of the Revolution,* 101.

7. Ibid., 102.

8. Wharton, Anne Hollingsworth, *Through Colonial Doorways* (Philadelphia: J. B. Lippincott Company, 1893), 218.

9. Martha Washington to Mercy Otis Warren, March 7, 1778, *Worthy Partner, the Papers of Martha Washington,* 177–78.

10. *http://www.oneida-nation.net/facts/poly-cooper.html.*

Chapter Fourteen

1. Hibbert, *Redcoats and Rebels,* 209–10.

2. Martha Washington to Eleanor and John Parke Custis, March 19, 1778 [*sic*], *Recollections and Private Memoirs of Washington,* 547–48.

3. *Mary and Martha, Mother and Wife of Washington*, 85.

4. Custis, *Recollections and Private Memoirs of Washington*, 559–61.

5. Ibid.

6. Ibid., 563.

7. Ibid., 558.

8. George Washington to Diego Jose de Navarro, April 30, 1780, *The George Washington Papers at the Library of Congress 1741–1799 Series 3h*, the Varick Transcripts.

9. Martha Washington to Burwell Bassett, July 18, 1780, *Worthy Partner, the Papers of Martha Washington*, 183.

10. Hoyt, William, "Self Portrait: Eliza Custis, 1808," *Virginia Historical Magazine*, 93–94.

Chapter Fifteen

1. Custis, *Recollections and Private Memoirs of Washington*, 332.

2. Hibbert, *Redcoats and Rebels*, 258.

3. George Washington to Lund Washington, April 30, 1781, *The Writings of George Washington 1745–1799*, John C,. Fitzpatrick, editor.

4. Mrs. Martha Mortier to Martha Washington, June 15, 1781, *Worthy Partner, the Papers of Martha Washington*, 186.

5. George Washington to Mrs. Martha Mortier, June 21, 1781, Ibid., 187.

6. John Parke Custis to Martha Washington, October 12, 1781, Ibid., 187.

7. Hoyt, "Self-Portrait: Eliza Parke Custis 1808," 96.

8. George Washington to Jonathan Trumbull Jr., November 6, 1781, Donald Jackson, ed., and Dorothy Twohig, assoc. ed., *The Diaries of George Washington*, vol 3 and *The Papers of George Washington.* (Charlottesville, University Press of Virginia, 1978).

9. Ellet, *The Women of the American Revolution*, vol. 1: 24.

Chapter Sixteen

1. George Washington to Martha Washington, October 1, 1782, *Worthy Partner, The Papers of Martha Washington*, 188.

2. Ibid., 189.

3. "Self-Portrait: Eliza Custis 1808," 96.

4. Ibid.

Chapter Seventeen

1. George Washington to George William Fairfax, February 27th, 1785, *The George Washington papers at the Library of Congress 1741–1799: Series 2 Letterbooks.*

2. Martha Washington to Frances Bassett, August 7, 1784, *Worthy Partner, the Papers of Martha Washington*, 195.

3. Custis, *Recollections and Private Memoirs of Washington*, 388–89.

4. George Washington to George William Fairfax, February 27, 1785, *The Writings of George Washington from the Original Manuscript Sources*, John C. Fitzpatrick, ed., vol. 28.

5. George Washington to Mary Ball Washington, February 15, 1787, John C. Fitzpatrick, ed., vol. 29.

6. Niles, Blair, *Martha's Husband* (New York: McGraw Hill, 1951), 215.

7. Ibid., 221.

8. Martha Washington to Fanny Bassett Washington, February 25, 1788, *Worthy Partner, the Papers of Martha Washington*, 205–206.

Chapter Eighteen

1. George Washington to Francois Jean, Compte de Chastellux, April 25, 1788, *The Writings of George Washington*, John C. Fitzpatrick, ed., vol. 29.

2. *Mount Vernon and Its Associations*, 207–8.

3. Martha Washington to John Dandridge, April 20, 1789, *Worthy Partner, the Papers of Martha Washington*, 213.

4. Wharton, *Martha Washington*.

5. Abigail Adams to Mary Smith Cranch, June 28, 1789, *New Letters of Abigail Adams*, Stewart Mitchell, ed. (Boston: Houghton Mifflin Co. 1947).

6. Ibid.

7. Custis, *Recollections and Private Memoirs of Washington*, 396.

Chapter Nineteen

1. Martha Washington to Mercy Otis Warren, December 26, 1789, *Worthy Partner, the Papers of Martha Washington*, 223–24.

2. Martha Washington to Fanny Bassett Washington, October 23, 1789, Ibid., 220.

3. "Eliza Custis: Self Portrait 1808," p. 97.

4. New Letters of Abigail Adams.

5. Wister, Owen, *The Seven Ages of Washington* (New York: Macmillan Company, 1907), 127.

6. Nathaniel Hawthone to General Cass, 1854, in James Walter, *Memorials of Washington and Mary His Mother and Martha His Wife, From Letters and Papers of Robert Cary and James Sharples* (New York,: Scribner's Sons, 1887), 34–5.

Chapter Twenty

1. Wharton, *Martha Washington*, 228.

2. George Washington to Tobias Lear, April 12, 1791, *Letters from George Washington to Tobias Lear, Reprinted from the Originals in the Collection of Mr. William Bixley of St. Louis, Mo* (Rochester, N.Y.: William H. Sampson, 1905), 32.

3. Martha Washington to Fanny Bassett Washington, August 29, 1791, *Worthy Partner, the Papers of Martha Washington*, 233.

4. Eleanor Custis Stuart to Tobia Lear, April 18, 1790. *Nelly Custis Child of Mount Vernon*, by David L. Riblett, the Mount Vernon Ladies' Association, Mount Vernon, Virginia 1993, 20.

Chapter Twenty-one

1. Martha Washington to Fanny Bassett Washington, August 4, 1793. *Worthy Partner, the Papers of Martha Washington*, 250.

2. Elizabeth Willing Powel to Martha Washington, August 9, 1793. *Worthy Partner, the Papers of Martha Washington*, 251–252.

3. Martha Washington to Fanny Bassett Washington, January 14, 1794. *Worthy Partner, the Papers of Martha Washington*, 254–255.

4. Martha Washington to Fanny Bassett Washington, February 10, 1794. *Worthy Partner, the Papers of Martha Washington*, 256.

5. Martha Washington to Fanny Bassett Washington, June 15, 1794. *Worthy Partner, the Papers of Martha Washington*, 268–269.

6. George Washington to Elizabeth Parke Custis, September 14, 1794, *http://minerva.acc.virginia.edu/gwpaprs/marriage/bcustis1.html*.

7. Martha Washington to Fanny Bassett Washington, September 29, 1794. *Worthy Partner, the Papers of Martha Washington*, 276–277.

8. Martha Washington to Fanny Bassett Washington, September 29, 1794, *Worthy Partner, the Papers of Martha Washington*, 276–77.

9. Custis, *Recollections of Washington*, 408n.

10. Riblett, David L., *Nelly Custis, Child of Mount Vernon* (Mount Vernon, Va.: Mount Vernon Ladies' Association; 1993), 23.

11. Martha Washington to Fanny Bassett Washington, April 6, 1795, *Worthy Partner, the Papers of Martha Washington*, 284.

Chapter Twenty-two

1. Eleanor Parke Custis to Elizabeth Bordley, October 19, 1795, *George Washington's Beautiful Nelly: The Letters of Eleanor Parke Custis Lewis to Elizabeth Bordley Gibson 1794–1851*, edited by Patricia Brady (Columbia: University of South Carolina Press, 1991), 21–23.

2. George Washington to Eleanor Parke Custis, March 21, 1796. *Memoir and Private Recollections* of Washington, 41–44.

3. Kirkland, Mrs. C. M., *Memoirs of Washington* (New York: D. Appleton & Co, 1857), 468–70.

4. Joseph Whipple to Oliver Wolcott Jr., October 4, 1796, *George Washington Papers at the Library of Congress 1741–1799*, Series 4, General Correspondence.

5. *Tom Paine A Political Life*, by John Keane, 431.

6. Martha Washington to Mary Stillson Lear, November 4, 1796, *Worthy Partner, the Papers of Martha Washington,* 29.

7. Wharton, *Martha Washington,* 194.

Chapter Twenty-three

1. George Washington to Elizabeth Willing Powel, March 26, 1797, *Worthy Partner, the Papers of Martha Washington,* 464.

2. Eleanor Parke Custis to Elizabeth Bordley Gibson, August 20, 1797, *George Washington's Beautiful Nelly,* University of South Carolina Press, Columbia, 1991, 38–39.

3. Martha Washington to Elizabeth Dandridge Henley, August 20, 1797, *Worthy Partner,* 307.

4. George Washington to Major George Lewis, November 13, 1797, *Letters from George Washington to Tobias Lear with an Appendix.*

5. Martha Washington to Sally Cary Fairfax, May 17, 1798, *Worthy Partner, the Papers of Martha Washington,* 314–15.

6. George Washington to Sarah Cary Fairfax, May 16, 1798, *The Writings of George Washington,* John C. Fitzpatrick, editor, vol. 36.

7. Niemcewicz, Julian Ursyn, *Under their Vine and Fig Tree Travels Through America in 1797–1799.* Translated by J. E. Budka (Elizabeth, N.J.: Grassman Publishing Company, 1964), 91.

8. Ibid., 100–101.

9. George Washington to George Washington Parke Custis, June 13, 1798, *http://www.virginia.edu/gwpaprs/marriage/gwpcustis.html.*

10. Fields, ed., *Worthy Partner, the Papers of Martha Washington,* 321.

Chapter Twenty-four

1. "Death of a President," *New England Journal of Medicine,* Dec. 9, 1999, *www.nejm.org/content/1999/0341/0024/1845.*

2. Ibid.

3. Harris, C. M. ed. *The Papers of William Thornton.* (Charlottesville: University Press of Virginia, 1995), vol I, 528; also at *www.virginia.edu/gwpapers/ exhibits/ mourning/thornton.html.* "William Thornton Recalls the Death of Washington."

4. Martha Washington to President John Adams, December 31, 1799, Ibid. 332–333.

5. *To Follow her Departed Friend: The Last Years and Death of Martha Washington,* A Report for the Anniversaries Committee of the Mount Vernon Ladies' Association, by Mary V. Thompson, Research Specialist, April 25, 2000.

6. Decatur, Stephen, Jr., *The Private Affairs of George Washington.* (Boston: Houghton Mifflin, 1933).

7. Eliza Cope Harrison, ed., *Philadelphia Merchant: The Diasy of Thomas P. Cope 1800–1851* (South Bend, Indiana: Gateway Editions, 1978), 111–112, 113.

8. Conkling, *Mother and Wife of Washington,* 246.

Epilogue

1. Calcott, Margaret Law, editor, *Mistress of Riversdale The Plantation Letters of Rosalie Stier Calvert 1795–1821* (Baltimore: Johns Hopkins University Press, 1991), 111.

2. Evelyn Gerson, *Ona Judge Staines, A Thirst for Complete Freedom & Her Escape from President Washington, www.seacoastnh.com/blackhistory/ ona.html*.

Bibliography

Alden, John R. *George Washington, a Biography.* Baton Rouge: Louisiana State University Press, 1984.

Andree, John, *M.D. Cases of the Epilepsy, Hysteric Fits and St Vitus Dance with the Process of Cure.* Cornhill: W. Meadows and J. Clark, 1746.

Aptheker, Herbert. *A History of the American People in the Colonial Period.* New York: International Publishers, 1959.

———. *American Negro Slave Revolts.* New York: Columbia University Press, 1943.

Bourne, Miriam Anne. *First Family George Washington and His Intimate Relations.* New York: W. W. Norton & Company, 1982.

Brady, Patricia, editor. *George Washington's Beautiful Nelly: The Letters of Eleanor Parke Custis Lewis to Elizabeth Bordley Gibson, 1794–1851.* Columbia: University of South Carolina Press, 1991.

Brodie, Fawn M. *Thomas Jefferson: An Intimate History.* London: Eyre Methuen, 1974.

Bryan, William Alfred. *George Washington in American Literature 1775–1865.* New York: Columbia University Press, 1952.

Calcott, Margaret Law, editor. *Mistress of Riversdale: The Plantation Letters of Rosalie Stier Calvert, 1795–1821.* Baltimore: Johns Hopkins University Press, 1991.

Clark, Allan C. *Greenleaf and Law in the Federal City.* Washington, D.C.: Press of W. F. Roberts, 1901.

Conkling, Margaret C. *Memoirs of the Mother and Wife of Washington.* Auburn, N. Y., 1850.

Cook, Richard Pye. Letter to Mary Amanda Williamson Steward, July 16, 1887. Richmond: Virginia Historical Society.

Cooke, John Esten. *Virginia, a History of the People.* Boston: Houghton, Mifflin, 1897.

Craven, Avery, ed. *To Markie Lee—Letters of Robert E. Lee to Martha Custis Williams.* Cambridge: Harvard University Press, 1933.

Custis, George Washington Parke. *Recollections and Private Memoirs of Washington by His Adopted Son George Washington Parke Custis, with a Memoir of the Author by His Daughter; and Illustrative and Explanatory Notes, by Benson J. Lossing.* New York: Derby & Jackson, 1860.

Davidson, Philip. *Propaganda and the American Revolution.* New York: W. W. Norton & Company, Inc., 1941.

Decatur, Stephen, Jr. *The Private Affairs of George Washington.* Boston: Houghton Mifflin, 1933.

Desmond, Alice Curtis. *Martha Washington, Our First Lady.* New York: Dodd Mead & Company, 1943.

Earle, Alice Morse. *Costume of Colonial Times.* New York: Charles Scribner's Sons, 1894.

Ellet, Elizabeth F. *Women of the American Revolution.* George W. Jacobs & Co., 1900.

Ellis, Joseph J. *Founding Brothers.* New York: Alfred A. Knopf, 2001.

Fedric, Francis. *Slave Life in Virginia and Kentucky, or Fifty Years of Slavery in the Southern States of America.* London: Wertheim, MacIntosh and Hult, 1863.

Fields, Joseph E., ed. *Worthy Partner, the Papers of Martha Washington.* Greenwood Press, 1994.

Fithian Philip Vickers. *Journal and Letters of Philip Vickers Fithian 1743–1774.* Williamsburg, Va.: Colonial Williamsburg Inc., 1965.

Ford, Paul Leicester. *The True George Washington.* Philadelphia: J. B. Lippincott Company, 1897.

Franklin, John Hope, and Loren Schweninger. *Runaway Slaves: Rebels on the Plantation.* New York: Oxford University Press, 1999.

Greene, George Washington. *The Life of Nathanael Greene.* New York: G. P. Putnam and Son, 1867.

Griswold, Rufus Wilmot. *The Republican Court, or American Society in the Days of Washington.* New York: D. Appleton, 1854.

Hervey, Nathaniel. *The Memory of Washington.* Boston: J. Munroe, 1852.

Hess, Karen, transcriber. *Martha Washington's Booke of Cookery and Booke of Sweetmeets.* New York: Columbia University Press, 1995.

Hibbert, Christopher. *Redcoats and Rebels: The War for America 1770–1781.* London: Grafton Books, 1990.

Hoffman, Ronald, and Peter J. Albert, eds. *Women in the Age of the American Revolution.* Charlottesville: University Press of Virginia, 1989.

Hughes, Rupert. *George Washington, the Rebel and the Patriot.* New York: William Morrow, 1927.

———. *George Washington, the Human Being and the Hero.* New York: William Morrow & Company, 1926.

Hume, Ivor Noel. *All the Best Rubbish: History in a Green Bottle.* New York: Harper and Row, 1974.

Jackson, Donald, and Dorothy Twohig, eds. *The Diaries of George Washington.* Charlottesville: University Press of Virginia, 1976.

Ketchum, Richard M. *The World of George Washington.* New York: American Heritage Publishing Company Inc, 1974.

Kimball, Marie. *The Martha Washington Cookbook.* New York: Coward McCann, 1940.

Kirkland, Mrs. C. M. *Memoirs of Washington.* New York: D. Appleton & Co., 1857.

Kitman, Marvin. *The Making of the President 1789.* London: Weidenfield and Nicholson, 1989.

Lechtenberg, Richard, M.D. *Epilepsy and the Family.* Cambridge: Harvard University Press, 1984.

Lossing, Benson J. *The Home of Washington: Mount Vernon and Its Associations.* Hartford, Conn.: S. Hale & Company, 1871.

Mazyck, Walter H. *George Washington and the Negro.* Washington, D.C.: Associated Publishers, Inc., 1932.

Meyer, Edith Patterson. *Petticoat Patriots of the American Revolution.* New York: Vanguard Press, 1976.

Mitchell, Stuart, ed. *New Letters of Abigail Adams, 1788–1801.* Boston: Houghton Mifflin Company, 1947.

Mullen, Gerald W. *Slave Resistance in Eighteenth-Century Virginia.* New York: Oxford University Press, 1972.

Niemcewicz, Julian Ursyn. *Under Their Vine and Fig Tree, Travels Through America in 1797–1799,* translated and edited by J. E. Budka. Elizabeth, N.J.: Grassman Publishing Company, 1964.

Niles, Blair. *Martha's Husband.* New York: McGraw Hill, 1961.

Prussing, Eugene E. *The Estate of George Washington, Deceased.* Boston: Little, Brown and Company, 1927.

Rasmussen, William M. S., and Robert S. Tilton. *George Washington: The Man Behind the Myths.* Charlottesville: University Press of Virginia, 1999.

Ribblett, David L. *Nelly Custis, Child of Mount Vernon.* Mount Vernon Ladies' Association, Virginia, 1993.

Robinson Family Papers 1740–1887. Virginia Historical Society mss 1 R5685 b 1632.

Smith, Richard Norton. *Patriarch George Washington and the New American Nation.* Boston/New York: Houghton Mifflin Company, 1993.

Sparks, Jared, ed. *The Writings of George Washington, Vols 1–4* American Stationers' Company, John B. Russell, 1837.

Thane, Elswyth. *A Family Quarrel.* New York: Van Rees Press, 1959.

Threlfal, W., M.D. *Essay on Epilepsy.* London: Z. Stuart, Bookseller on Paternoster Row, 1772.

Walter, James. *Memorials of Washington and Mary His Mother and Martha His Wife.* New York: Charles Scribner's Sons, 1887.

Wharton, Anne Hollingsworth. *Martha Washington.* London: John Murray, 1897.

———. *Through Colonial Doorways.* Philadelphia: J. B. Lippincott Company, 1893.

Wister, Owen. *The Seven Ages of Washington.* New York: Macmillan Company, 1907.

Articles

"The First Washington Scandal," a paper presented to the November 1935 meeting of the Massachusetts Historical Society, *Proceedings of the Massachusetts Historical Society* October 1932–May 1936, Vol 65.

Gray, Arthur Powell. "The White House-Washington's Marriage Place." *The Virginia Magazine of History and Biography, Vol XLII- No. 3* July 1934, Virginia Historical Society.

Longsworth, Polly. "Portrait of Martha, Belle of New Kent." *Magazine of Colonial Williamsburg,* Summer 1988.

Robertson, John William, M.D. "On Land and Sea: A Pictorial review of the Eastern Shore of Virginia." Onancock, Va: Eastern Shore News Inc.

"Self Portrait by Eliza Custis," *Virginia Magazine of History and Biography* 53 (April 1945).

Thompson, Mary V. "The Private Life of George Washington's Slaves," *Virginia Cavalcade* 48, no. 4 (Autumn 1999); 178–90.

Westlake, James R. "Mount Vernon." *Sons of the American Revolution Magazine* (Spring 1999).

Zuppan, Zoe. "John Custis of Williamsburg." *Virginia Magazine of History and Biography,* vol. 90, 1992.

Miscellaneous

Another Secret Diary of William Byrd of Westover 1739–1741. Edited by Maude C. Woodfin, Richmond, Va.: Dietz Press Inc, 1942.

Cary, Wilson Miles. "The Dandridges of Virginia." from *Genealogies of Virginia Families.* Vol 2, *Virginia Magazine of History and Biography.*

Cary, Wilson Miles. "Descendants of Rev. Rowland Jones, First Rector of Bruton Parish, Va." *Genealogies of Virginia Families.* Vol III, *Virginia Magazine of History and Biography.*

Letters from George Washington to Tobias Lear with an Appendix, Reprinted from the originals in the Collection of Mr. William K. Bixby of St. Louis Mo. Rochester, New York 1905.

Letters of Jonathan Boucher to George Washington, edited by Worthingon Chauncy Ford, Brooklyn, New York: Historical Printing Club, 1899.

Old New Kent County Some Account of the Planters, Plantations and Places in Kent County, Vols 1 and 2, compiled and copyrighted 1977 by Malcolm Hart Harris, M.D., West Point, Virginia.

"Special report of the Commissioner of Education on the Condition and Improvement of Public Schools in the District of Columbia." Submitted to the Senate June 1868, and to the House with Additions June 1870 Ex. Doc. No. 315, 41st Congress, 2nd Session, Washington Government Printing Office, 1870.

The Secret Diary of William Byrd of Westover 1709–1712. Edited by Louis B. Wright and Marion Tingling. Richmond, Va.: Dietz Press, 1941.

Online Internet Resources

Chronology of the History of Slavery
   home.inreach.com/usm/slavechron.html
Excerpts from The Diary of Joseph Plumb Martin
   mrbooth.com/edu/constit/diaries/html
"Death of a President" from the *New England Journal of Medicine,* December 9th, 1999, Vol. 341, No. 24
   www.nejm/content/1999/0341/0024/1845.asp

From the Diary of Albigence Waldo, Surgeon at Valley Forge 1777
  odur.let.rug.nl/~usa/D/1776–1800/war/waldo.htm
George Washington Papers at the Library of Congress
  mmemory.loc.gov/ammem/gwhtml/gwseries.html
"Ona Judge Staines: Escape from Washington" by Evelyn Gerson
  www.seacoastnh.com/blackhistory/ona.html
" 'Sleep' William Thornton Recalls the Death of Washington"
  www.virginia.edu/gwpapers/exhibits/mourning/thornton.html

Index

Notes: GW throughout the index refers to George Washington; pages in italics refer to illustrations